FATIMA: THE SIGNS AND SECRETS

Dedicated to my beloved husband Tim

and all of our children-

Daniel, Brandon, Bernadette, Stephan,

Matthew and Michael-

and with love and gratitude

to Connie Korte & Catherine Christiansen,

for their generous help

and who share with me their devotion

to the Sacred and Immaculate Hearts.

To Jesus through Mary!

Fatima: The Signs and Secrets

Marianna Bartold

"In that same hour, he rejoiced in the Holy Ghost, and said: I confess to thee, O Father, Lord of heaven and earth, **because thou hast hidden these things from the wise and prudent, and hast revealed them to little ones.**"
-Lk. 10:21.

KIC (Keeping It Catholic) • Lapeer, MI 48446

Fatima: The Signs and Secrets
Copyright © 2014 Marianna Bartold

ISBN: 978-0-9862203-0-2

All Scriptural quotations were taken from the Holy Bible, Douay-Rheims translation, with revisions and footnotes (in the text in italics) by Bishop Richard Challoner, 1749-52. Taken from a hardcopy of the 1899 Edition by the John Murphy Company. IMPRIMATUR: James Cardinal Gibbons, Archbishop of Baltimore, September 1, 1899.

Please direct any correspondence to the publisher:

KIC
788 S. Main St.
Ste. 119, PMB 110
Lapeer, MI 48446

Printed and bound in the United States of America

Contents

SECTION I

SECTION II

SECTION III

SECTION IV

SECTION V

SECTION VI

PRAYERS AND PROMISES

CHAPTER 1

Fatima's Prophetic Mission:

St. Michael and the Great Battle in Heaven

"We would be mistaken to think that Fatima's *prophetic* mission is complete."[1] Those words, uttered by Pope Benedict XVI during his May 2010 homily at Fatima, gave the Church a stupendously thought-provoking insight. Only three years earlier, on the 90th anniversary of Fatima, the Pope had said something similar: "The apparitions of Our Lady of Fatima…are without doubt, the most *prophetic* of all modern apparitions."[2] Before him, Pope John Paul II acknowledged that his own predecessors gave Our Lady of Fatima special recognition, because her messages were more *prophetic* than any previous Marian apparitions which were approved by the Church as worthy of belief. He also said in his sermon of May 13, 1982 that "Fatima places an obligation on the Church." Certainly, Popes of the Roman Catholic Church do not say such things of mere private revelations, which impose on the Church no such duty.

Of Fatima, it can be truly said that no other Church-approved apparition has received such world-wide attention or has been the subject of such controversy within the Church herself. It is not that the Church doesn't recognize Fatima as worthy of belief, because the decision in favor of Fatima was made in 1930. Rather, the internal debate among the Church's members, high and low, center on two subjects: The Virgin's request that a reigning Pope and the world's bishops solemnly consecrate Russia to her Immaculate Heart and also on what is called "The Third Secret of Fatima."

In 1984, Pope Benedict XVI (then Cardinal Ratzinger, and now Bishop Emeritus of Rome) said that "the things contained in this 'Third Secret' correspond to what has been announced in Scripture and has been said again and again in many other Marian apparitions, beginning with the Fatima

---

[1] *Pope: we would be mistaken to think that Fatima's prophetic message is complete*, Asia News, May 13, 2010
[http://www.asianews.it/news-en/Pope:-we-would-be-mistaken-to-think-that-Fatima%C3%A2%E2%82%AC%E2%84%A2s-prophetic-mission-is-complete-18398.html]
[2] Pope Benedict XVI, *Sermon at Fatima*, May 13, 2007. [Emphasis added.]

apparitions in their *known* contents."[3] Since the Third Secret of Fatima corresponds to Scripture, it must be said that the Church knows all scriptural prophecies are fulfilled—*except those foretelling the "last days."*

However, as previously mentioned, in May 2010, Pope Benedict XVI purposely chose to use the descriptive term "prophetic" in defining Fatima's "mission." So let us look to the meaning of these words as the Church provides them:

"**Prophecy**: A definite prediction of a future event which depends on the free will of God or man, and therefore can be known only by divine revelation. Some prophecies are conditional...Others are unconditional; for example, Christ foretold His death and resurrection...Christ Himself often appealed to prophecies as proof of His divinity and divine *mission*."[4]

As for "**mission**," the root meaning of this word is "sending."[5] As it is used in ecclesiastical and theological writing, a "mission" (a *sending*) is usually accomplished in at least one of three distinct ways. As will be seen, all three of the following definitions of the word "mission" appear to apply to the Fatima revelations:

• First, a "mission" is a place to which missionaries are *sent* by the Church to establish the Faith "**where the majority are not yet converted or have fallen away from the Faith.**"[6] Missionary work "for the conversion of infidels has always been an important part of the Church's work, since Christ *sent* the Apostles to preach to all nations and to make all men His disciples."[7]

• Second, a "mission" is a "series of sermons and religious exercises conducted in a parish over a certain period of a number of days by priests *sent* into the parish to renew the religious fervor of the faithful. **To renew the Christian Faith and practice of Catholics**, the sermons and instructions of a mission usually deal with the fundamentals of the Christian life: the purpose of man; sin; redemption; the justice, mercy, love, and graces of God; death; hell; and heaven."[8]

• Third and most significant, **a "mission" is a direct action (a "divine sending") made by God Himself for the salvation of His people**. The Holy

---

[3] Ratzinger, Cardinal Joseph, as quoted by Vittorio Messori, "Here is Why the Faith is in Crisis," *Jesus* Magazine, November 11, 1984: p. 79.

[4] "My Catholic Encyclopedia." *The Family Rosary Edition of the Holy Bible* [Chicago, IL: The Catholic Press, Inc., 1952]: p. 211. [Emphasis added.]

[5] Ibid., p. 166.

[6] *The Concise Catholic Dictionary*. [Kansas, MO: The Angelus Press, 1992. Republished from the original 1943 edition, with Nihil Obstat and Imprimatur]: p. 223.

[7] "My Catholic Encyclopedia," loc.cit. [Emphasis in the original.]

[8] Ibid. [Emphasis in the original.]

Scriptures infallibly record that "the Son is *sent* into the world by the Father,[9] and that the Holy Ghost is *sent* by both the Father and the Son[10]—but in no place in the Scriptures do we read of the Father being *sent* into the world. Hence, theologians use the term divine *mission*, or 'sending,' to designate the procession of one Divine Person from another in the Holy Trinity with the connotation of some effect of the procession in creatures, through a new presence of the Divine Person in that creature."[11]

Who the Holy Trinity Sent to Fatima

At Fatima, the very first creature *sent* by the Holy Trinity was an angel who identified himself as "the Angel of Peace" and later as "the Angel Guardian" of Portugal.[12] The angel's three appearances to the young shepherd children were a prelude to the Virgin Mary's later visits. It can be stated with moral certainty that this angel is none other than St. Michael the Archangel, whose very presence at Fatima provides the initial and great insights into what Pope Benedict XVI called "Fatima's prophetic mission."

For almost one thousand years, St. Michael has been recognized by the Catholic nation of Portugal as its Angel Guardian and the Angel of Peace. Frère Michel de la Sainte Trinité, historian and expert on the Fatima apparitions, observed "that good Portuguese historians are inclined to recognize in him [Fatima's Angel of Peace] St. Michael the Archangel, their patron and protector, who had always been venerated as the Guardian Angel of their country...King Alfonso Henriques [1139-1185], founder of the nation and of the dynasty, having been baptized in a chapel dedicated to St. Michael, chose the Archangel as the special protector of his armies and his kingdom." In 1514, at the request of King Manuel I, Pope Leo X granted the Portuguese nation a special feast in honor of their Angel Guardian, traditionally recognized as St. Michael. In Portugal's national monastery at Batalha, "the monks chanted each day an antiphon and prayer in honor of St. Michael, the Guardian Angel of Portugal."

Frère Michel additionally notes, "Fr. Martins dos Reis [another Fatima historian/author] has observed that the other title by which the Angel of Fatima revealed himself—'I am the Angel of Peace'—also suggests his identification with St. Michael the Archangel. Indeed, in the Portuguese tradition, where he is

---

[9] Jn. 3: 17, 5:23; 6:39, 58; Gal. 4:4.
[10] Jn. 14:26; 15:26; 16:7.
[11] Apoc. 1:11.
[12] Sr.. Mary Lucia of the Immaculate Heart. *Fatima in Lucia's Own Words: Sr. Lucia's Memoirs.* [Fatima, Portugal: Postulation Centre, 1976]: pp. 62, 64. (Hereafter, Sr. Mary Lucia, *Memoirs*, 1976 edition.)

quite prominent, St. Michael is often called the Angel of Peace, especially in the liturgical office of St. Elizabeth of Portugal." Finally, Frère Michel concludes, "In addition, in the Roman Breviary as well as in the litanies, the Archangel is invoked under these titles: 'Auctor pacis' (Author of Peace) and 'Angelus pacis Michael' (Michael, the Angel of Peace).[13] It seems that it was this Angel of Peace–St. Michael the Archangel–who was *sent* to the little ones at Fatima "to fill them with a very elevated mystical grace, by which they felt themselves penetrated by the Divine Presence."[14]

St. Michael, from *Genesis* to *Apocalypse*

And so, we may ask –**who is St. Michael and why was he sent to the three Fatima children?** Like all angels, he is a pure spirit (without a body), created by God. Both St. Augustine and Pope St. Gregory the Great state that "*angel* is the name of an office," but the word *angel* "expresses neither their essential nature nor their essential function; viz.: that of attendants upon God's throne…"[15]

"Angel" means "messenger," and so an angel acts as a divine messenger *sent* by God. The Holy Scriptures reveal that God *sends* angels to announce His will, to correct, punish, teach, rebuke, or console.[16] Angels appear in the *Holy Bible* from beginning to end, from *Genesis* through the *Apocalypse*. The Scriptures further disclose that the angels are not all equal to each other.[17] It is commonly taught that there exists a hierarchy (an order) of the angels, known as the nine choirs. The nine choirs are divided into three "triads" (i.e., a group of three; a trio).

The highest triad consists of the seraphim, cherubim, and thrones; their specific concern or purpose is the contemplation of God. The middle triad is made of the dominions, virtues, and powers, who are appointed to concern themselves with the order of the universe but also other causes. Finally, the last (or "lowest") triad is of principalities, archangels and angels. Amongst the specific concerns of this last triad is the welfare of the people, and it is to this choir that St. Michael belongs.

---

[13] Frère Michel de la Sainte Trinité, *The Whole Truth about Fatima (TWTF), Science and the Facts,* Vol. I. [Buffalo, NY: Immaculate Heart Publications, 1989]: pp. 93-95. (Hereafter, Frère Michel, *TWTF* followed by Vol. I, II or III.)

[14] Ibid., p. 71.

[15] Pope, Hugh. "Angels." *The Catholic Encyclopedia.* Vol. 1. [New York: Robert Appleton Company, 1907] [http://www.newadvent.org/cathen/01476d.htm].

[16] Ps. 102:20; Matt. 4:11; 13:49; 26:53.

[17] Dan. 10:13; Apoc. 12:7.

What is an archangel? The meaning of this word, which comes from the Greek, is "prince-angel." Although he is in the last order of angels, St. Michael the Archangel became Prince of the Heavenly Host[18] because he was the first to rise up against Lucifer and the other angels who rebelled against God. It was St. Michael who cried out, "Who is like unto God?" and it was he and his angels who "smote the rebel Lucifer and his followers in the conflict of the heavenly host."[19] The fallen angels were cast from heaven and condemned to hell.[20]

Five times is the name of Michael the angel explicitly mentioned in the Holy Scriptures—three times by the prophet Daniel, once by St. Jude, and once by St. John in the *Apocalypse*. All of these passages provide further enlightenment about why the great St. Michael the Archangel was *sent* to the Fatima children:

• **In** *the Prophecy of Daniel*, Chapter 10, the Holy Scriptures give Michael's name for the first time. Daniel's chapters 7-12 are considered to be his four "apocalyptic" chapters because, like the later *Apocalypse*, they foretell things that were, things that are, and things that shall be. What is also made clear in these same four chapters is Daniel's reliance on heavenly creatures, *sent* to him by God, who **explain** the visions given to him.

Beginning with Chapters 7 and 8, Daniel wrote the first of his prophetic and apocalyptic visions. Explanations of these visions were given by the angel Gabriel, who appeared to him as a man.[21] In Chapter 10, it is recorded: "In the third year of Cyrus king of the Persians, a word was revealed to Daniel surnamed Baltassar, and a true word, and great strength: and he *understood* the word: for there is *need of understanding* in a vision."[22] Following this event, the prophet Daniel mourned and fasted for 21 days.

(These words from Holy Scripture provide insight into the Great Secret of Fatima, especially the Third Secret Vision which, like Daniel's vision, could be described in the same way: "a word was revealed to Lucia, surnamed dos Santos, and to Francisco and Jacinta, surnamed Marto; and a true word, and great strength; and they *understood* the word: for there is *need of understanding* in a vision." In other words, the children of Fatima, like the

---

[18] Jude 1:9.
[19] Butler, Alban. *Lives of the Saints.*(Forgotten Books): p. 372. Cited in "St. Michael (Roman Catholic)," *Wikipedia*.
[http://en.wikipedia.org/wiki/Saint_Michael_%28Roman_Catholic%29#cite_note-Alban_Butler_page_372-13]
[20] 2 Pet. 2:4.
[21] Dan. 8: 15-26; 9: 21-27.
[22] Dan. 10:1. [Emphasis added.]

prophet Daniel, heard words to explain the two visions within the "Great Secret" they were given by God. In a similar manner, they also would make personal sacrifices to God in reparation for sin.)

Then appeared a good angel (whose name is not given by Daniel, but who may have been Gabriel returning to the prophet), saying, "Daniel, thou man of desires, understand the words that I speak to thee, and stand upright: for I am **sent** now to thee."[23] After speaking of Daniel's prayers and sacrifices, the angel revealed, "I am come for thy words,"[24] and then declared, "But the prince of the kingdom of the Persians resisted me one and twenty days; and behold **Michael, one of the chief princes,** came to help me, and I remained there by the king of the Persians. But I am come to teach thee what things shall befall thy people in the latter days, for as yet the vision is for days."[25]

It must first be explained that "the prince of the kingdom of the Persians" was a fallen angel, a demon of great power who resisted the good angel for 21 days—i.e., a full three weeks. A mere human could not continue to resist one of God's angels for such a length of time, but a demon of great strength could. We know that many angels became corrupted, resisted the Holy Trinity, and eternally lost their places in Heaven. Although forever darkened, they retained their powers of intellect, strength, and hierarchical order. St. Paul tells us, "Put you on the armour of God, that you may be able to stand against the deceits of the devil. For our wrestling is not against flesh and blood; but against **principalities** and **powers**, against the **rulers of the world of this darkness**, against the **spirits of wickedness** in the **high places**."[26] The Bible's *Douay-Rheims* translation includes a note to this verse, which states: "*In the high places*: or heavenly places. That is to say, in the air, the lowest of the celestial regions; in which God permits these wicked spirits or fallen angels to wander."

Our Lord Himself, when rebuking the Pharisees for attributing His miracles to Satan, speaks of the differing degrees of wickedness among the demons: "And when an unclean spirit is gone out of a man he walketh through dry places seeking rest, and findeth none. Then he saith: I will return into my house from whence I came out. And coming he findeth it empty, swept, and garnished. Then he goeth, and taketh with him seven other spirits **more wicked than himself,** and they enter in and dwell there: and the last state of that man is made worse than the first. So shall it be also to this wicked generation."[27] Thus we understand that individuals, rulers, regions or countries which reject the

---

[23] Dan. 10:11. [Emphasis added.]
[24] Dan. 10: 12.
[25] Dan. 10:13-14.
[26] Eph. 6: 11-12. [Emphasis added.]
[27] Mt. 12: 43-45. [Emphasis added.]

Triune God and the one religion by which He wishes to be adored and glorified most certainly open themselves to demonic rule.

To return to the prophet Daniel, he had for 21 days fasted and prayed in reparation to the Lord, for he had seen a great and terrifying vision of what would befall his people. Although he understood the vision, he did not yet know that it was a vision "for days"–meaning far into the future, the end times. The 21 days were thrice the ancient custom of seven days' of fasting, which tell us that Daniel's 21 days of sacrifice displayed extreme sorrow and extraordinary penance. Unbeknownst to Daniel, the 21 days of his penance and reparation offered to God coincided with the angel's battle with a powerfully resistant devil, the "prince of the kingdom of the Persians." However, it becomes clear that Daniel's acts of reparation were accepted by God, for the angel spoke of Daniel's sacrifices and also told him, almost in a confiding manner, of his own struggle against the "prince" (meaning leader, one of a higher order) demon of the Persians. Since angels of Heaven do not engage in idle gossip or expect human sympathy, it is also certain that God wished Daniel to know what had transpired and that, due to his own prayers and penances, St. Michael was *sent* by God to assist the good but lesser angel.

At the end of the same chapter, the good angel declares: "But I will tell thee what is set down in the scripture of truth: and none is my helper in all these things, but **Michael your prince**."[28] Once again, Scripture attests that Michael is a prince. Even further, the angel states to Daniel that Michael is "*your* prince," meaning the prince of the elect, those who belong to God's kingdom on earth and follow His commandments. In the Old Testament, the chosen people were those of the earthly Israel, but this ancient nation was a living figure-type of the spiritual Israel (today known as the Roman Catholic Church) that would be established by the Messiah, Jesus Christ.

• Michael's name is mentioned a third time in *The Prophecy of Daniel*, when the good angel speaks of the last events of the end times (the *Novissimi*), the time when anti-Christ shall appear and persecute God's people: "But at that time shall **Michael** rise up, the great prince, who standeth for the children of thy people: and a time shall come such as never was from the time that nations began even until that time. (**Author's note**: One sentence from the 1973 message of Our Lady of Akita is remarkably similar to this Scriptural prophecy, as one will see elsewhere in this book.) And at that time shall thy people be saved, every one that shall be found written in the book. And many

---

[28] Dan.10:21.

of those that sleep in the dust of the earth, shall awake: some unto life everlasting, and others unto reproach, to see it always."[29]

• In the *Epistle of St. Jude (1:9)*: "When **Michael the archangel**, disputing with the devil, contended about the body of Moses, he durst not bring against him the judgment of railing speech, but said: *The Lord command thee.*"

First, this Scripture passage explicitly reveals that Michael belongs to the order of the archangels.

Second, the quotation helps us grasp the difference between the proper honor due to one of God's chosen creatures and the worship due to God Himself. According to Origen, St. Jude referred to an ancient Jewish tradition, made known by revelation, that St. Michael concealed the tomb of Moses at God's command, because Satan moved to incite the ancient Hebrews against honoring the body of Moses as a precious relic; rather, the devil planned to deceive them into worshiping Moses' body with the worship meant only for God.[30]

Third, it is implicitly understood that Michael was *sent* by God to give the devil a command that came from the Lord and not from himself.

• In the *Apocalypse of St. John (12:7)*: "And there was a great battle in heaven, **Michael** and his angels fought with the dragon, and the dragon fought and his angels: And they prevailed not, neither was their place found any more in heaven. And that great dragon was cast out, that old serpent, who is called the devil and Satan, who seduceth the whole world; and he was cast unto the earth, and his angels were thrown down with him. And I heard a loud voice in heaven, saying: Now is come salvation, and strength, and the kingdom of our God, and the power of his Christ: because the accuser of our brethren is cast forth, who accused them before our God day and night."

In writing of this epic war in heaven, St. John "speaks of the great conflict at the *end of time*, which reflects also the battle in heaven at the *beginning* of time."[31] This is known because, in apocalyptic symbolism, the word "heaven" means "the Church,"[32] God's kingdom on earth. In other words, there shall be a

---

[29] Dan. 12:1.

[30] Origen. *De Principiis* III. 2.2. Cited in Holweck, Frederick. "St. Michael the Archangel." *The Catholic Encyclopedia, Vol. 10.* [New York: Robert Appleton Company, 1911.] [http://www.newadvent.org/cathen/10275b.htm]

[31] Holweck, Frederick. "St. Michael the Archangel." *The Catholic Encyclopedia, Vol.10.* [New York: Robert Appleton Company, 1911] [http://www.newadvent.org/cathen/10275b.htm]

[32] Kramer, Rev. Herman Bernard. *The Book of Destiny.* [Rockford, IL: TAN Books & Publishers, 1975. Originally published in 1955 by Buechler Publishing Co., Belleville, IL. Reprinted in 1972 by Apostolate of Christian Action, Fresno, CA using entirely new type set

great battle *in the Church*, between Michael and his angels and the dragon and his angels—a last war so great that it mirrors the first, terrible combat between the good and fallen angels.

Another consideration is the Venerable Bede's interpretation, summarized in *The Book of Destiny*: "If 'heaven' is the Church on earth in the *Apocalypse*...[t]he angels who fight under the leadership of Michael are the loyal bishops and priests of the Church, while the angels of the dragon are the sinful priests and bishops."[33] In the final battle of the last days, states Butler's *Lives of the Saints*, "when Antichrist shall have set up his kingdom on earth, it is St. Michael who will unfurl once more the standard of the cross, sound the last trumpet, bind together the false prophet and the beast and hurl them for all eternity into the burning pool."[34]

Too, the Church Fathers believe that other parts of Holy Scripture allude to St. Michael's presence, although his name is not openly given. For example, the Fathers believe Michael "was the cherub who stood at the gate of paradise, 'to keep the way of the tree of life,'[35] the angel through whom God published the Decalogue to his chosen people, the angel who stood in the way against Balaam,[36] [and] the angel[37] who routed the army of Sennacherib."[38]

Through Scripture and Tradition, God has revealed to the universal Church that St. Michael is the prince and guardian of His people. Catholic Tradition also teaches that St. Michael fulfills the four following offices:

1) Michael, as God's first loyal defender, fights against Satan while this world lasts.

2) Michael is the rescuer of the souls of the faithful from the power of the enemy, especially at the hour of death.

3) Michael is the champion of God's people—"the Jews in the Old Dispensation, the Christians of the New; therefore he is the patron of the Church, and of the orders of knights during the Middle Ages."[39]

4) Michael is the Angel of Judgment, calling souls away from earth and bringing them to the Throne of God.

---

under the author's supervision, from which TAN's 1975 printing was made]: p. 200. (Hereafter, Kramer, Rev. H.B., *The Book of Destiny*)

[33] Ibid., pp. 288-289.
[34] Butler, loc. cit.
[35] Gen. 3:24.
[36] Num. 22:22.
[37] 2 Kings 19:35.
[38] Holweck, loc. cit.
[39] Ibid.

It is this same great archangel whom God *sent* to Fatima; Michael, Prince of the Heavenly Host, chosen to precede the "great sign" that would appear in heaven (the Church)–*the* "woman clothed with the sun."[40]

A Foreshadowing at Fatima

How did the Fatima apparitions begin? Lucia dos Santos, the seventh and youngest child of Antonio and Maria Rosa dos Santos, was seven years old when she became shepherdess to the family's flock. While together with three other neighboring shepherd children, Lucia and her friends thrice saw a mysterious figure in the air, like a statue made of snow. This figure is believed to be a presage of the angelic apparitions that Lucia would later behold with her younger cousins, Francisco and Jacinta Marto, both of whom are now *beati* (called "Blessed" by the Church). Lucia and her cousins would, in the spring and summer of 1916, receive three clear apparitions of the Angel, who literally identified himself as *"the Angel of Peace"* and *"Angel Guardian, the Angel of Portugal."*

Years later, Lucia (who became a nun) would under obedience to her bishop, Jose Alves Correira da Silva, write a series of memoirs, which were later published as a collection under the title, "Fatima in Lucia's Own Words." The Bishop of Leiria made this request when, in 1935, the body of her younger cousin, the child Jacinta, was exhumed from the grave and her face was found incorrupt. After the bishop sent a photograph of Jacinta's opened casket to Lucia in the convent, Lucia sent a letter of thanks that also humbly declared her own conviction of Jacinta's holiness.

According to Fr. Thomas McGlynn, O.P. who, under Lucia's direction, made a statue of Our Lady of Fatima, Lucia's thank-you letter "aroused the Bishop's curiosity–perhaps many graces given to the children had been hidden all these years. He, therefore, commanded Lucia to write her memoirs."[41] Each memoir led to a further order to write another, resulting in four memoirs, all written in a diary-like form but addressed to the bishop. These memoirs were written between 1936 and 1941 (Memoir I was written in 1936; Memoir II was written in 1937; Memoirs III and IV were both written in 1941).[42]

In these accounts, Lucia wrote about her cousins' lives, her own, the angelic portents of 1915 followed by angelic visitations in 1916, sacrifices her cousins offered to God, the apparitions of Our Lady in 1917, and a few later

---

[40] Apoc. 12:1.

[41] McGlynn, O.P., Thomas. *Vision of Fatima.* [Boston: Little Brown and Co., 1949]: pp. 28-29.

[42] Walsh, William Thomas. *Our Lady of Fatima.* [Image Book: New York, May 1990. First Image edition published 1954]: pp. 207-209.

appendices about apparitions and locutions she received as a nun. The memoirs are in addition to other correspondence to her superiors regarding the apparitions and the "Great Secret" of Fatima, in its three distinct parts. Recalling how the angel apparition began, she related:

"News that I was beginning my life as a shepherdess spread rapidly among the other shepherds; almost all of them came and offered to be my companions. I said 'Yes' to everybody, and arranged with each one to meet on the slopes of the serra. Next day, the serra was a solid mass of sheep with their shepherds, as though a cloud had descended upon it. But I felt ill at ease in the midst of such a hubbub.

"I therefore chose three companions from among the shepherds, and without saying a word to anyone, we arranged to pasture our sheep on the opposite slopes. These were the three I chose: Teresa Matias, her sister Maria Rosa and Maria Justino. On the following day, we set out in the direction of a hill known as the Cabego. We went up the northern slope. Valinhos, a place that Your Excellency already knows by name, is on the southern side of the same hill. On the eastern slope is the cave I have already spoken of, in my account of Jacinta. Together with our flocks, we climbed almost to the top of the hill. At our feet lay a wide expanse of trees—olives, oaks, pines, holmoaks, and so on, that stretched away down towards the level valley below.

"Around midday, we ate our lunch. After this, I invited my companions to pray the Rosary with me, to which they eagerly agreed. We had hardly begun when, there before our eyes, we saw a figure poised in the air above the trees; it looked like a statue made of snow, rendered almost transparent by the rays of the sun.

'What is that?' asked my companions, quite frightened.

'I don't know!'

"We went on praying, with our eyes fixed on the figure before us, and as we finished our prayer, the figure disappeared. As was usual with me, I resolved to say nothing; but my companions told their families what had happened the very moment they reached home. The news soon spread, and one day when I arrived home, my mother questioned me:

'Look here! They say you've seen I don't know what, up there. What was it you saw?'

'I don't know,' and as I could not explain it myself, I went on: 'It looked like a person wrapped up in a sheet!' As I meant to say that I couldn't discern its features, I added: 'You couldn't make out any eyes, or hands, on it.'

"My mother put an end to the whole matter with a gesture of disgust: 'Childish nonsense!'

"After some time, we returned with our flocks to the same place, and the very same thing happened again. My companions once more told the whole story. After a brief interval, the same thing was repeated. It was the third time that my mother heard all these things being talked about outside, without my having said a single word about them at home. She called me, therefore, quite displeased, and demanded:

'Now, let us see! What is it that you girls say you saw over there?'

'I don't know, Mother. I don't know what it is!'

"Some people started making fun of us. My sisters, recalling that for some time after my First Communion I had been quite abstracted, used to ask me rather scornfully:

'Do you see someone wrapped in a sheet?'

"I felt these contemptuous words and gestures very keenly, as up to now I had been used to nothing but caresses. But this was nothing, really. You see, I did not know what the good Lord had in store for me in the future."[43]

Three Cousins See the Angel, 1916

Lucia's memoirs also relate that a year later, sometime in the spring of 1916, "Francisco and Jacinta sought and obtained permission from their parents to start taking care of their own flock. So I left my good companions, and I joined my cousins, Francisco and Jacinta, instead. To avoid going to the serra with all the other shepherds, we arranged to pasture our flocks on properties belonging to my uncle and aunt and my parents.

"One fine day, we set out with our sheep for some land that my parents owned, which lay at the foot of the eastern slope of the hill that I have already mentioned. This property was called Chousa Velha. Soon after our arrival, about midmorning, a fine drizzle began to fall, so fine that it seemed like mist. We went up the hillside, followed by our flocks, looking for an overhanging boulder where we could take shelter. Thus it was for the first time that we entered this blessed hollow among the rocks. It stood in the middle of an olive grove belonging to my godfather Anastacio. From there, you could see the little village where I was born, my parents' home, and the hamlets of Casa Velha and Eira da Pedra. The olive grove, owned by several people, extended to within the confines of the hamlets themselves. We spent the day there among the rocks, in spite of the fact that the rain was over and the sun was shining bright and clear. We ate our lunch and said our Rosary. I'm not sure whether we said it that day in the way I have already described to Your Excellency,

---

[43] Sr. Mary Lucia of the Immaculate Heart. *Fatima in Lucia's Own Words: Sr. Lucia's Memoirs.* [Fatima, Portugal: Postulation Centre, 16th Edition, July 2007]: pp. 70-71. (Hereafter, Sr. Mary Lucia, *Memoirs*, 2007 edition.)

saying just the word *Hail Mary* and *Our Father* on each bead, so great was our eagerness to get to our play! Our prayer finished, we started to play 'pebbles'!"

"We had enjoyed the game for a few moments only, when a strong wind began to shake the trees. We looked up, startled, to see what was happening, for the day was unusually calm. Then we saw coming towards us, above the olive trees, the figure I have already spoken about. Jacinta and Francisco had never seen it before, nor had I ever mentioned it to them. As it drew closer, we were able to distinguish its features. It was a young man, about fourteen or fifteen years old, whiter than snow, transparent as crystal when the sun shines through it, and of great beauty. On reaching us, he said:

'Do not be afraid! I am the Angel of Peace. Pray with me.'

"Kneeling on the ground, he bowed down until his forehead touched the ground, and made us repeat these words three times:

'My God, I believe, I adore, I hope and I love Thee! I ask pardon of Thee for those who do not believe, do not adore, do not hope and do not love Thee.'

Then, rising, he said: **'Pray thus. The Hearts of Jesus and Mary are attentive to the voice of your supplications.'**

"His words engraved themselves so deeply on our minds that we could never forget them. From then on, we used to spend long periods of time, prostrate like the Angel, repeating his words, until sometimes we fell, exhausted. I warned my companions, right away, that this must be kept secret and, thank God, they did what I wanted.

"Some time passed, and summer came, when we had to go home for siesta. One day, we were playing on the stone slabs of the well down at the bottom of the garden belonging to my parents, which we called the Arneiro...Suddenly, we saw beside us the same figure, or rather Angel, as it seemed to me.

'What are you doing?' he asked. **'Pray, pray very much! The most holy Hearts of Jesus and Mary have designs of mercy on you. Offer prayers and sacrifices constantly to the Most High.'**

'How are we to make sacrifices?' I asked.

'Make of everything you can a sacrifice, and offer it to God as an act of reparation for the sins by which He is offended, and in supplication for the conversion of sinners. You will thus draw down peace upon your country. I am its Angel Guardian, the Angel of Portugal. Above all, accept and bear with submission, the suffering which the Lord will send you.'

"A considerable time had elapsed, when one day we went to pasture our sheep on a property belonging to my parents, which lay on the slope of the hill I have mentioned, a little higher up than Valinhos. It is an olive grove called Pregueira. After our lunch, we decided to go and pray in the hollow among the rocks on the opposite side of the hill. To get there, we went around the slope, and had to climb over some rocks above the Pregueira. The sheep could only scramble over these rocks with great difficulty.

"As soon as we arrived there, we knelt down, with our foreheads touching the ground, and began to repeat the prayer of the Angel: 'My God, I believe, I adore, I hope and I love Thee...' I don't know how many times we had repeated this prayer, when an extraordinary light shone upon us. We sprang up to see what was happening, and beheld the Angel. He was holding a chalice in his left hand, with the Host suspended above it, from which some drops of blood fell into the chalice.

"Leaving the chalice suspended in the air, the Angel knelt down beside us and made us repeat three times:

'O Most Holy Trinity, Father, Son and Holy Ghost, I adore Thee profoundly, and I offer Thee the Most Precious Body, Blood, Soul and Divinity of Jesus Christ, present in all the tabernacles of the world, in reparation for the outrages, sacrileges and indifferences with which He Himself is offended. And, through the infinite merits of His most Sacred Heart, and those of the Immaculate Heart of Mary, I beg of Thee the conversion of all poor sinners.'

"Then, rising, he took the chalice and the Host in his hands. He gave the Sacred Host to me, and shared the Blood from the chalice between Jacinta and Francisco, saying as he did so:

'Take and drink the Body and Blood of Jesus Christ, horribly outraged by ungrateful men! Make reparation for their crimes and console your God.'

"Once again, he prostrated on the ground and repeated with us, three times more, the same prayer '*Most Holy Trinity...*' and then disappeared.

"We remained a long time in this position, repeating the same words over and over again. When at last we stood up, we noticed that it was already dark, and therefore time to return home."

It was the last time the three children saw the Angel, but they did not tell anyone of him. Francisco would ask Lucia questions because, as she and Jacinta had discovered, he could see the angel but he could not hear his words. The same would also occur with the later apparitions of the Virgin Mary.

After the first visitation of the Angel, as Lucia said, "It did not occur to us to speak about this Apparition, nor did we think of recommending that it be kept secret; the very Apparition itself imposed secrecy. It was so intimate, that it was not easy to speak of it at all." She would also write, "The supernatural atmosphere which enveloped us was so intense, that we were for a long time scarcely aware of our own existence...The presence of God made itself felt so intimately and so intensely that we did not even venture to speak to one another. Next day, we were still immersed in this spiritual atmosphere."

As for the final vision of the Angel of Peace, Lucia would later confide in her memoirs, "Impelled by the power of the supernatural that enveloped us, we imitated all that the Angel had done, prostrating ourselves on the ground as he did and repeating the prayers that he said. The force of the presence of God was so intense that it absorbed and almost completely annihilated us. It seemed to deprive us even of the use of our bodily senses for a considerable length of time. During those days, we performed all our exterior actions as though guided by that same supernatural being who was impelling us thereto. The peace and happiness which we felt were great, but wholly interior, for our souls were completely immersed in God."[44]

---

[44] Ibid., p. 159.

CHAPTER 2

The Signs at Fatima,

May-September 1917

"I dwelt in the highest places and my throne is in a pillar of a cloud."
−Ecclesiasticus 24:7

When people think about the Fatima apparitions, most recall in their minds a particular image of Our Lady, dressed all in white, standing with her bare feet upon a white puff of cloud. Rarely, one may see a holy card or picture of Our Lady of Fatima, with a backdrop of a twilight sky scattered with stars. What is not generally known is that the delicate white mist of cloud under the Virgin's feet, the changed sky, and the stars are not artistic embellishments. People who came to the Fatima apparitions witnessed the unusual white cloud and other phenomena, all which hold a "highly symbolic and mystical significance."[45]

Our Lady's first visit to a small hamlet called Fatima, Portugal took place when the sun was directly overhead (called solar noon) on Sunday, May 13, 1917. Appearing in an open field known as the Cova da Iria (the Cove of Irene), "a Lady dressed all in white" stood lightly atop a *carrasqueira*, a young holmoak sapling that stood about three feet high and bore glossy, green leaves. On that day, the Lady appeared to three young children−Lucia dos Santos (age 10) and her two younger cousins, Francisco and Jacinta Marto (ages 9 and 7, respectively), and she asked them to return each month through October, "on the 13th day, at this same hour" (solar noon).[46] Promising to later give her name, she said only of herself, "I am of Heaven."[47]

In her memoirs, Lucia briefly related the first apparition:

"High up on the slope in the Cova da Iria, I was playing with Jacinta and Francisco at building a little stone wall around a clump of furze. Suddenly we saw what seemed to be a flash of lightning.

'We'd better go home,' I said to my cousins, 'that's lightning; we may have a thunderstorm.'

'Yes, indeed!' they answered.

"We began to go down the slope, hurrying the sheep along towards the road. We were more or less half-way down the slope, and almost level with a

---

[45] Frère Michel, *TWTF,* Vol. I, p. 238.
[46] Ibid., pp.112-113.
[47] Ibid, p.112.

large holmoak tree that stood there, when we saw another flash of lightning. We had only gone a few steps further when, there before us on a small holmoak, we beheld a Lady all dressed in white. She was more brilliant than the sun, and radiated a light more clear and intense than a crystal glass filled with sparkling water, when the rays of the burning sun shine through it.

"We stopped, astounded, before the Apparition. We were so close, just a few feet from her, that we were bathed in the light which surrounded her, or rather, which radiated from her. Then Our Lady spoke to us:

'*Do not be afraid. I will do you no harm.*'

'Where does your Grace come from?'

'*I am of Heaven.*'

'What does Your Grace want of me?'

'*I have come to ask you to come here for six months in succession, on the 13th day, at this same hour. Later on, I will tell you who I am and what I want. Afterwards, I will return here yet a seventh time.*'

'Shall I go to Heaven too?'

'*Yes, you will.*'

'And Jacinta?'

'*She will go also.*'

'And Francisco?'

'*He will go there too, but he must say many Rosaries.*'

"Then I remembered to ask about two girls who had died recently. They were friends of mine and used to come to my home to learn weaving with my eldest sister.

'Is Maria das Neves in Heaven?'

'*Yes, she is.*' (I think she was about 16 years old).

'And Amelia?'

'*She will be in Purgatory until the end of the world.*' (It seems to me that she was between 18 and 20 years of age).

'*Are you willing to offer yourselves to God and bear all the sufferings He wills to send you, as an act of reparation for the sins by which He is offended, and of supplication for the conversion of sinners?*'

'Yes, we are willing.'

'*Then you are going to have much to suffer, but the grace of God will be your comfort.*'

"As she pronounced these last words '...*the grace of God will be your comfort,*' Our Lady opened her hands for the first time, communicating to us a light so intense that, as it streamed from her hands, its rays penetrated our hearts and the innermost depths of our souls, making us see ourselves in God, Who was that light, more clearly than we see ourselves in the best of mirrors.

Then, moved by an interior impulse that was also communicated to us, we fell on our knees, repeating in our hearts:

'**O Most Holy Trinity, I adore Thee! My God, my God, I love Thee in the most Blessed Sacrament!**'

"After a few moments, Our Lady spoke again:

'*Pray the Rosary every day, in order to obtain peace for the world, and the end of the war.*'

"Then she began to rise serenely, going up towards the east, until she disappeared in the immensity of space. The light that surrounded her seemed to open up a path before her in the firmament, and for this reason we sometimes said that we saw Heaven opening."

Lucia went on to explain, "The Apparitions of Our Lady inspired neither fear nor fright, but rather surprise. When I was asked if I had experienced fear, and I said that we had, I was referring to the fear we felt when we saw the flashes of lightning and thought that a thunderstorm was at hand. It was from this that we wished to escape, as we were used to seeing lightning only when it thundered. Besides, the flashes of lightning were not really lightning, but the reflected rays of a light which was approaching. It was because we saw the light, that we sometimes said we saw Our Lady coming; but, properly speaking, we only perceived Our Lady in that light when she was already on the holmoak tree. The fact that we did not know how to explain this, and that we wished to avoid questions, caused us to say sometimes that we saw her coming, and other times that we did not. When we said we saw her coming, we were referring to the approach of the light, which after all was herself. And when we said we did not see her coming, we were referring to the fact that we really saw Our Lady only when she was on the holmoak."[48]

Another interesting detail became known years later. When assisting Fr. Thomas McGlynn, O.P., who sculpted the first statue of Our Lady of Fatima, Lucia told him, "She always had a star on her tunic" and "She always had a cord with a little ball of light."[49] As he asked for details of color, Lucia said, "The light of Our Lady was white, and the star was yellow…She was all of light. The light had various tones, yellow and white and various other colors. It was more intense and less intense. It was by the different tones and by the differences of intensity that one saw what was hand and what was mantle and what was face and what was tunic."[50]

---

[48] Sr. Mary Lucia, *Memoirs,* 2007 edition: p. 162.
[49] McGlynn,. *Vision of Fatima.*: p. 64.
[50] Ibid., pp. 68-69.

Questioned again at a later point, she thrice confirmed to Fr. McGlynn that the star and the cord were yellow, *not* the color of gold. Lucia, incidentally, described both the cord and the star as a **more intense** and **yellow** light.

The yellow star that shone between the knee and hem of the Fatima Virgin's tunic is known as the "Star of Esther," a symbolic reference to the Old Testament history of Queen Esther, the Jewish queen of pagan Persia, who saved her people from total annihilation on the 13th day of Adar. Church Doctors like St. Albert the Great (called "the Great" due for his surpassing knowledge and wisdom in science, philosophy, and theology, he is also known in Latin as St. Albertus Magnus) and St. Alphonsus de Liguori (Italian Catholic bishop, spiritual writer, scholastic philosopher and theologian) recognized Queen Esther as a historical figure-type of the Virgin Mary.

The Fatima apparitions reveal so much more of this typology that my study on Queen Esther and the date of 13 Adar (according to the ancient Hebrew calendar) and their varied links to Our Lady of Fatima resulted in my 2008 series of articles, initially published in *Catholic Family News* and then, with the copyright notice attributing the rights to me, on my own blog. The first article in the series (*"Hidden Revelations: The Star of Esther and the Secrets of Fatima"*) gained the most attention. Unfortunately, it has also been copied in full or in part to various pages on the Internet, often with neither proper credit nor my permission. That said, after the 2008 series was published, *"Hidden Revelations"* eventually became a subject of Internet discussions and debates on various Catholic boards.

By 2013, however, "Hidden Revelations," especially the sections on Esther's original Hebrew name and its meaning, as well as the significance of the 13th day of Adar to Fatima, became increasingly recognized as valid input. Imitation may be the sincerest form of flattery, because sections of the work (including its footnotes) were quoted *verbatim*, in sermons and articles both on and off the Internet, but again without any acknowledgement of the author. I ask the reader to kindly understand that, for the two following reasons, I only provide this brief mention of my study and my 2008 article(s) because: **1)** It is not difficult to foresee that there will be those who shall presume that I have utilized the work of another while neglecting the courtesy of mentioning the source. Giving credit where it is due is one thing for which I always strive in my writing, as I trust that both the number of this book's footnotes (over 1,000 in total) and the manuscript's mention of specific sources will prove, and **2)** most imperative, the typology of Queen Esther to the Virgin Mary of Fatima is so striking that the 2008 series, all of which is my original work, is later shared (and only slightly rearranged in order) as Chapters 10-13 of this book.

June: The First Signs

Except for the children, there were no other people present in May. Lucia had no intention of mentioning to anyone the Apparition. She asked her cousins to also saying nothing, to which they both agreed. However, little Jacinta could not contain her enthusiasm and immediately told her mother, Olympia Marto. While Olympia was incredulous, her husband Ti Marto did not hesitate to muse that it could be possible that the Virgin appeared to the three children, as she had done at Lourdes and LaSalette. He knew his children never lied and that they had not enough knowledge to make up such a detailed story. However, Jacinta's revelation led to severe repercussions for her cousin Lucia, whose mother for some reason believed her forthright and youngest child was lying.

As word of the Vision spread, however, a great number assumed that the "Lady dressed all in white" was the Holy Mother of God. Starting in June 1917, each month brought an increasing number of both pilgrims and scoffers alike. Each month, only the three children could see the Lady. Each month, the ever-growing crowd (who did not see the Apparition of the Lady) was permitted to witness seemingly inexplicable, external signs which attested to the presence of a heavenly being.

When the Virgin returned on Wednesday, June 13, 1917, the three children were waiting for her. So were at least 50 other people who came to see for themselves what was really happening in Fatima. June 13 was the Feast of St. Anthony of Padua, a very popular day among the Catholics of Portugal. Lucia's mother had hoped that the village festival in honor of St. Anthony would halt Lucia from going to the Cova, while the parents of Francisco and Jacinta allowed the little ones to decide where they would go that day.

• It was at this June apparition that onlookers first saw a little cloud over the holmoak tree. Maria Carreira, one of those who saw the mysterious vapor only as the Apparition ended, said "we saw nothing but a slight cloud, just a few inches away from the foliage, rising slowly toward the *east*." At another time, she said that "it was a little cloud...which went up gently in the direction of the *east*, until it finally disappeared completely."[51] It seems that Lucia and her cousins did not see this cloud resting on the holmoak tree because, in after years, Lucia would say, "The people spoke of a cloud but I saw none. Our Lady's feet rested lightly on the top of the leaves."[52]

• "During the vision," stated another witness, "the branches of the tree were bent down all around" as if someone was stepping upon them. Yet another witness remarked that "when Lucia announced that Our Lady was leaving in

---

[51] Frère Michel, *TWTF,* Vol. I, p.161.
[52] McGlynn, loc. cit.

the direction of the *east*, all the branches of the tree picked up and leaned in the same direction, as if Our Lady, as she left, had let her dress rest upon the boughs."[53]

• When the cloud was no longer in sight, others also noticed that the little holmoak tree's shoots, which had formerly been standing upright, were bent and inclined toward the *east*.[54]

• Moments earlier, during the Apparition, some of the fifty onlookers discerned an unintelligible murmur, "like the sound of a very faint voice, but we could not understand what it was saying; it was like the buzzing of a bee."[55] Heard only between Lucia's words to the invisible Lady, the mysterious sound appeared to be the Lady's responses to the child.

What the Children Saw

As the witnesses saw or heard these first signs in June, what did the children experience? It soon became apparent that all three children could see the Lady, but Francisco could not hear her. Lucia, the eldest cousin, was the only one who spoke to the heavenly visitor. Once more, we rely on Lucia's written testimony.

"As soon as Jacinta, Francisco and I had finished praying the Rosary, with a number of other people who were present, we saw once more the flash reflecting the light which was approaching (which we called lightning). The next moment, Our Lady was there on the holmoak, exactly the same as in May."

(However, in June, there was one slight difference which the child Lucia would not reveal until she was a nun and writing the memoirs. In the June 1917 apparition alone, the Lady showed the children her Immaculate Heart, encircled and pierced by thorns but displaying no swords through the Heart, as in usual artistic renditions of the Sorrowful and Immaculate Heart of Mary. When one considers this difference, it also makes sense, for the swords represent the Virgin's sorrows as the Mother of Christ, especially during His Passion and Crucifixion. The thorns, however, represent the sins of mankind. The children interiorly felt that they should not reveal this "secret," which they would in July learn is the true center of the Fatima message.)

'**What do you want of me?**' I asked.

---

[53] Frère Michel, Ibid., pp. 160-161. Also see John de Marchi, I.M.C, *The True Story of Fatima* [Constable, NY: The Fatima Center. Republished from the 1947 edition]: p. 23.
[54] Ibid.
[55] Ibid, p. 160.

'I wish you to come here on the 13th of next month, to pray the Rosary every day, and to learn to read. Later, I will tell you what I want.'

"I asked for the cure of a sick person.

'If he is converted, he will be cured during the year.'

'I would like to ask you to take us to Heaven.'

'Yes. I will take Jacinta and Francisco soon. But you are to stay here some time longer. Jesus wishes to make use of you to make me known and loved. He wants to establish in the world devotion to my Immaculate Heart. I promise salvation to those who embrace it, and those souls will be loved by God like flowers placed by me to adorn His throne.'

'Am I to stay here alone?' I asked, sadly.

'No, my daughter. Are you suffering a great deal? Don't lose heart. I will never forsake you. My Immaculate Heart will be your refuge, and the path that will lead you to God.'

"As Our Lady spoke these last words, she opened her hands and for the second time, she communicated to us the rays of that same immense light. We saw ourselves in this light, as it were, immersed in God. Jacinta and Francisco seemed to be in that part of the light which rose towards Heaven, and I in that which was poured out on the earth. In front of the palm of Our Lady's right hand was a heart encircled by thorns which pierced it. We understood that this was the Immaculate Heart of Mary, outraged by the sins of humanity, and seeking reparation."

Of the light, Lucia would later reveal, "I think that, on that day, the main purpose of this light was to infuse within us a special knowledge and love for the Immaculate Heart of Mary…From that day onwards, our hearts were filled with a more ardent love for the Immaculate Heart of Mary."[56]

"You know now, Your Excellency, what we referred to when we said that Our Lady had **revealed a secret to us in June.** At the time, Our Lady did not tell us to keep it secret, but we felt moved to do so by God."

The secret of June 1917 was the Immaculate Heart of Mary which, as the children immediately grasped, was "outraged by the sins of humanity, and seeking reparation." This manifestation in June, the month in which the Church honors the Sacred Heart of Jesus, also shows that it is God's will to make the Virgin Mary better known and loved, honoring her Heart beside the adoration of His own.

---

[56] Sr. Mary Lucia, *Memoirs,* 2007 edition: p. 222.

July: Six Signs Granted to the People
On July 13, the Lady promised the children, "In October, I will tell you who I am and what I want, and I will perform a miracle so that all may believe." Then the Virgin showed and told the children a secret—what is today known as the "Great Secret" of Fatima, which has three distinct parts called the First Secret, the Second Secret, and the Third Secret.[57] For the growing crowd of people [58] who came to see the child visionaries, many (but not all) would also see and hear the unexpected, as follows:

1. Most of the witnesses who were closest to the spot where the Lady appeared heard a far-away, indescribable sound, perceived only in response to Lucia's words.[59]

2. The atmosphere changed. As one witness stated, "The luminosity of the sky noticeably decreased, as during an eclipse, the whole time the ecstasy of the children lasted,"[60] and stars were seen in the midday sky.

3. At the height of a Portuguese summer, the very hot temperature suddenly dropped to a pleasant degree, accompanied by "a cool fresh breeze."[61]

4. The color of the atmosphere became yellow as gold.[62]

5. During the Vision, a cloud again appeared and rested on the holmoak tree—but this time it gently spilled down and extended *around* the children.[63]

6. A "large clap of thunder" was heard just seconds before the eldest child, Lucia, suddenly jumped up from her kneeling position, exclaiming, "There she goes! There she goes!" as the Lady departed. The thunder shook the ground, so that a small arch placed by the apparition site "trembled as if in an earthquake."[64]

In her memoirs to the bishop, Lucia described what she and her cousins witnessed during this central Fatima apparition, the one in which the children were given the "Great Secret" in its three distinct parts. One will note in the

---

[57] Sr. Mary Lucia, *Memoirs*, 1976 edition: p. 165.

[58] Estimates of the number of individuals who came to Fatima, Portugal on July 13, 1917 vary from 800 to 5,000. Clearly, such a disparity is revealing, depending on the veracity or the ulterior motives of witnesses. Be that as it may, the events of July 13—including the announcement of a "sign" that would be given in October—resulted in an estimated 70,000-100,000 people present at Fatima on October 13, 1917, the day of the Miracle of the Sun. See Frère Michel, *TWTF,* Vol. I, pp. 185, 214.

[59] Frère Michel, op. cit., p. 183.

[60] Ibid.

[61] Walsh, *Our Lady of Fatima,* p. 80.

[62] Frère Michel, loc.cit.

[63] Ibid.

[64] Ibid.

following memoirs the manner in which she records the Virgin's words, especially the sentence which Fatima scholars agree introduces the Third Secret: "In Portugal, the dogma of the faith will always be preserved, **etc.**"–the *et cetera* clearly denoting that there is more to follow.

"A few moments after arriving at the Cova da Iria, near the holmoak, where a large number of people were praying the Rosary, we saw the flash of light once more, and a moment later Our Lady appeared on the holmoak.

'**What do you want of me?**' I asked.

'*I want you to come here on the 13th of next month, to continue to pray the Rosary every day in honour of Our Lady of the Rosary, in order to obtain peace for the world and the end of the war, because only she can help you.*'

'I would like to ask you to tell us who you are, and to work a miracle so that everybody will believe that you are appearing to us.'

'*Continue to come here every month. In October, I will tell you who I am and what I want, and I will perform a miracle for all to see and believe.*'

"I then made some requests, but I cannot recall now just what they were. What I do remember is that Our Lady said it was necessary for such people to pray the Rosary in order to obtain these graces during the year. And she continued:

'*Sacrifice yourselves for sinners, and say many times, especially whenever you make some sacrifice:* **O my Jesus, it is for love of Thee, for the conversion of sinners, and in reparation for the sins committed against the Immaculate Heart of Mary.**'

"As Our Lady spoke these last words, she opened her hands once more, as she had done during the two previous months. The rays of light seemed to penetrate the earth, and we saw as it were a sea of fire. Plunged in this fire were demons and souls in human form, like transparent burning embers, all blackened or burnished bronze, floating about in the conflagration, now raised into the air by the flames that issued from within themselves together with great clouds of smoke now falling back on every side like sparks in huge fires, without weight or equilibrium, amid shrieks and groans of pain and despair, which horrified us and made us tremble with fear. (It must have been this sight which caused me to cry out, as people say they heard me). The demons could be distinguished by their terrifying and repellent likeness to frightful and unknown animals, black and transparent like burning coals.

"Terrified and as if to plead for succor, we looked up at Our Lady, who said to us, so kindly and so sadly:

'*You have seen hell where the souls of poor sinners go. To save them, God wishes to establish in the world devotion to my Immaculate Heart. If what I say to you is done, many souls will be saved and there will be peace. The war is going to end; but if people do not cease offending God, a worse one will break out during the reign of Pius XI. When you see a night illumined by an unknown light, know that this is the great sign given you by God that He is about to punish the world for its crimes, by means of war, famine, and persecutions of the Church and of the Holy Father.'*[65]

'To prevent this, I shall come to ask for the consecration of Russia to my Immaculate Heart, and the Communion of Reparation on the First Saturdays. If my requests are heeded, Russia will be converted, and there will be peace; if not, she will spread her errors throughout the world, causing wars and persecutions of the Church. The good will be martyred, the Holy Father will have much to suffer, various nations will be annihilated. In the end, my Immaculate Heart will triumph. The Holy Father will consecrate Russia to me, and she will be converted, and an era of peace will be granted to the world.'

'In Portugal, the dogma of the Faith will always be preserved; etc...Do *not tell this to anybody. Francisco, yes, you may tell him.'"*

(Again we are reminded that Francisco alone, who could see the Vision, could not hear the Virgin's words. The same phenomenon had occurred with the Angel's visits. Afterward, when the children were alone, Francisco would ask the two girls what the Angel or the Lady had told them.)

The Virgin's sentence about Portugal and the dogma of the Faith, as mentioned earlier, is considered by Fatima scholars as the opening text of the Third Secret. Reason alone conveys that the "et cetera" reveals that clarifying words follow, otherwise the prophecy about Portugal and the dogma of the Faith is incomplete. After all, it has been known for decades that the "Great Secret of Fatima", as also heretofore mentioned, is not three separate Secrets but one *whole* Secret with three distinct parts.

The Third Secret also contains a **Vision**, which clearly relates to the missing text of Our Lady's words: "In Portugal, the dogma of the Faith will always be preserved, *etc.*" It was not until June 26, 2000, that the Vatican finally released the description of what some prelates (but never any Pope) claim is the whole Third Secret (but which many logically conclude is only *a part* of the entire Third Secret). The following English translation is how it appears on the Vatican website:

---

[65] This was the aurora borealis on the night of January 25th to 26th, 1938, which Lucia considered to be the God-given sign of which the Virgin warned if her requests were not heeded. This unusual sign occurred shortly before Adolph Hitler illegally annexed Austria to Germany.

"After the two parts which I have already explained, at the left of Our Lady and a little above, we saw an Angel with a flaming sword in his left hand; flashing, it gave out flames that looked as though they would set the world on fire; but they died out in contact with the splendour that Our Lady radiated towards him from her right hand: pointing to the earth with his right hand, the Angel cried out in a loud voice: 'Penance, Penance, Penance!'

"And we saw in an immense light that is God: 'something similar to how people appear in a mirror when they pass in front of it;' a Bishop dressed in White 'we had the impression that it was the Holy Father.' Other Bishops, Priests, men and women Religious going up a steep mountain, at the top of which there was a big Cross of rough-hewn trunks as of a cork-tree with the bark; before reaching there the Holy Father passed through a big city half in ruins and half trembling with halting step, afflicted with pain and sorrow, he prayed for the souls of the corpses he met on his way; having reached the top of the mountain, on his knees at the foot of the big Cross he was killed by a group of soldiers who fired bullets and arrows at him, and in the same way there died one after another the other Bishops, Priests, men and women Religious, and various lay people of different ranks and positions. Beneath the two arms of the Cross there were two Angels each with a crystal aspersorium in his hand, in which they gathered up the blood of the Martyrs and with it sprinkled the souls that were making their way to God."[66]

After the Great Secret was revealed, Lucia related that the Virgin Mary then said:

"*'When you pray the Rosary, say after each mystery:* **O my Jesus, forgive us our sins, save us from the fires of hell. Lead all souls to Heaven, especially those with the greatest need of Thy mercy.**'

"After this, there was a moment of silence, and then I asked: 'Is there anything more that you want of me?'

'*No, I do not want anything more of you today.*'

"Then, as before Our Lady began to ascend towards the east, until she finally disappeared in the immense distance of the firmament."

The children were immediately surrounded by people with questions: "What did the Lady say to you? Why did you go so white? Why did you cry out in fear? What happened?"

Lucia could only answer, "It's a secret."

The crowds continued to close in, so that Ti Marto (as the father of Francisco and Jacinta was called in the village) lifted little Jacinta, covered her

---

[66] *The Message of Fatima.* (English edition). Congregation for the Doctrine of the Faith. [Vatican City: Liberia Editrice Vaticana, 2000]: p. 43.

face with his hat, and made his way through the throng. Two other men carried Lucia and Francisco, holding the children high in their arms. As she was being carried above shoulder-level, the exhausted Lucia announced to the crowd that the Lady promised a Miracle for October 13. One can imagine the effect of the stunning announcement on a crowd that had already witnessed such amazing signs. Due to those present at the July 1917 apparition, word of the promised Miracle quickly spread throughout Portugal.

August: The Lady's Invisible Presence and a Boom of Thunder

In the morning of August 13, the children were abducted by the Masonic mayor of their locality. They were, therefore, unable to meet the Lady at the appointed place and time. Certainly, Heaven knew that the children were not present at the Cova di Iria, where the Apparition appeared. But God deigned to grant certain signs to the throng of people, thus manifesting the Lady's unseen presence.

The sun shone brightly in the clear August sky, and those who came to Fatima eagerly awaited the arrival of the children and the noon hour. Then word came and spread throughout the crowd that the mayor had kidnapped the young visionaries. As the people began to talk among themselves, the hour of solar noon commenced—as did certain signs previously seen and heard in July:

• First came an extremely loud boom of thunder, which so badly frightened the people that many scattered and ran, thinking they would be killed. Maria Carreira, eyewitness to every Fatima apparition since June 1917, said, "Some thought the thunder came from the road; others thought it came from the holmoak; but it seemed to me that it came from a distance. It frightened us all..."[67]

• A flash of lightning, following the thunder, also garnered the attention of the now-silenced crowd. This "flash," seen only by the three children, served as the sign of the Virgin's approach.[68] In August, when the children were not present, it was the crowd who perceived it.[69]

• Immediately after the "flash," a little cloud, described as very delicate and very white, appeared and hovered over the little holmoak tree for a few minutes, "and then rose in the air and disappeared."

• Simultaneously, there was a change of atmosphere, in which people saw "all the colors of the rainbow, pink, red, blue...The trees seemed to be made not of leaves but of flowers...The ground came out in colors and so did our

---

[67] de Marchi, I.M.C, John. *The True Story of Fatima* [Constable, NY: The Fatima Center. Republished from the 1947 edition]: p. 37.
[68] Sr. Mary Lucia, op. cit., p. 163.
[69] de Marchi, loc.cit.

clothes. The lanterns fixed to the arch looked like gold."[70] (At the initiative of Signora Maria Carreira, the villager who since June 1917 came to the Cova on the 13th of the month, a humble wooden arch, to which was added on each side a plain lantern, was erected over the holmoak tree.)

"When the signs disappeared, the people seemed to realize that Our Lady had come and, not finding the children, had returned," as Maria Carreira would later say. "They felt that Our Lady was disappointed and hence they were exceedingly upset."[71]

Among themselves, the awed people agreed that the Lady had indeed come—with many incensed "against those who had the audacity to deprive the Most Holy Virgin of her usual confidents."[72] In fact, history records that a group of pilgrims went in search of the perpetrator or suspected accomplices, demanding the children's return.[73]

Meanwhile, over the course of three days (August 13-15, 1917), the young ones endured a roller-coaster of interrogation, enticing promises, a malicious charade of facing death should they refuse to deny seeing the Lady from Heaven, and finally, imprisonment with adult malefactors. Through it all, the three children remained faithful to what they had earlier reported, but they refused to divulge anything pertaining to the Secret.

The little ones were released to their parents on August 15, the very day on which the Church celebrates the Assumption of Mary, body and soul, into Heaven. (In 1917, the Assumption of the Virgin Mary was a Church doctrine. It was not solemnly defined as a dogma until 1950.) Our Lady unexpectedly appeared to the children on Sunday, August 19. She again promised a miracle in the last month "so that all may believe." She also told the children, "If you had not been taken away to the City, the miracle would have been greater,"[74] thus emphasizing God's revealed truth that all people are affected by every sin that wounds the Mystical Body of Christ.

Again, Lucia recorded what happened on that day: "I was accompanied by Francisco and his brother John. We were with the sheep in a place called Valinhos, when we felt something supernatural approaching and enveloping us. Suspecting that Our Lady was about to appear to us, and feeling sorry lest

---

[70] Frère Michel, *TWTF,* Vol. I, p. 224.
[71] Ibid., p. 223.
[72] Ibid., p. 224.
[73] Ibid.
[74] Ibid., p. 235.

Jacinta might miss seeing her, we asked her brother to go and call her. As he was unwilling to go, I offered him two small coins, and off he ran."

"Meanwhile, Francisco and I saw the flash of light, which we called lightning. Jacinta arrived, and a moment later, we saw Our Lady on a holmoak tree."

'What do you want of me?'

'*I want you to continue going to the Cova da Iria on the 13th, and to continue praying the Rosary every day. In the last month, I will perform a miracle so that all may believe.*' (Note that this is the **second time** the Virgin promised an October miracle.)

'What do you want done with the money that the people leave in the Cova da Iria?'

'*Have two litters made. One is to be carried by you and Jacinta and two other girls dressed in white; the other one is to be carried by Francisco and three other boys. The money from the litters is for the 'festa' of Our Lady of the Rosary, and what is left over will help towards the construction of a chapel that is to be built here.*'

'I would like to ask you to cure some sick persons.'

'*Yes, I will cure some of them during the year.*'

Then, looking very sad, Our Lady said: '*Pray, pray very much, and make sacrifices for sinners; for many souls go to hell, because there are none to sacrifice themselves and to pray for them.*'

"And she began to ascend as usual towards the east."

September: A Luminous Globe, a Pillar of Cloud, and a Shower of Flowers

On the liturgical calendar, September is the month in which the Church honors Our Lady's Nativity (Sept. 8), the Holy Name of Mary (Sept. 12), her Seven Sorrows (Sept. 15), and Our Lady of Ransom (Sept. 24).

At Fatima in 1917, September was the month *before* the promised miracle. It was also the month *after* the children were kidnapped, when—as far as the public knew—they missed their August visit with the Lady. Rather than discouraging pilgrims from the site, even more came.

Perhaps it is for all of the reasons stated above that, during the apparition of Thursday, September 13, the celestial phenomena became more pronounced. In fact, during the September Apparition, the people saw a new sign—a luminescent globe. Later, the cloud accompanying the Vision wrought itself into an incense-like pillar.

On this day, the sky was deep and blue, and entirely without a trace of cloud, as was reported by Fr. John Quaresma who, in later years, became the Vicar General of Leiria, Portugal. With two other priests, Fr. Quaresma came to Fatima, trying to ascertain the truth of the reports they had heard. He and his companions disguised themselves by wearing suit-coats. "All three were at a distance from the crowd, on the raised part of the Cova, observing events."[75]

Years later, a letter of Fr. Quaresma's, written in 1932 to another priest, provides the most details of what happened during the September Apparition. From Father's letter, we learn the following:

• For the first time, many of the onlookers saw a luminous globe, moving from east to west at midday, the exact time that the Lady always asked the children to meet her. From what is gathered by his testimony, Fr. Quaresma only saw this globe of "extraordinary light" for a brief time. Others saw it travel across the sky and descend toward the holmoak tree. As the Vision ended, witnesses again saw the globe of light, departing toward the east.

• As the globe approached the small tree, the brightness of the sun lessened, the surrounding atmosphere became a golden-yellow, and some people reported seeing stars in the sky.

• During the Apparition, a greater number of the onlookers observed a shower of small white objects—described either as petals, snowflakes, dove-shaped forms, stars, or roses—all of which gently fell from the sky and disappeared before touching the ground.[76]

• A "pleasant looking cloud formed around the rustic arch" over the holmoak tree, where Our Lady appeared.[77] "Rising up from the ground, it grew thicker and went up into the air until it was five or six meters high; then it disappeared like smoke that vanishes before the wind...A few moments later, similar curls of smoke were formed and disappeared in the same manner, and then a third time. Everything happened as though some invisible thurifers were incensing the Vision liturgically. These three 'incensations' together lasted the whole time of the apparition; that is, from ten to fifteen minutes."

Once more, Lucia testifies to what happened on this September day, where the throngs of people were larger than ever before:

"As the hour approached, I set out with Jacinta and Francisco, but owing to the crowds around us we could only advance with difficulty. The roads were packed with people, and everyone wanted to see us and speak to us. There was

---

[75] Ibid., p. 257.
[76] Ibid., p. 260.
[77] Barthas, Canon C. Cited by Frère Michel, op. cit., p. 284.

no human respect whatsoever. Simple folk, and even ladies and gentlemen, struggled to break through the crowd that pressed around us. No sooner had they reached us than they threw themselves on their knees before us, begging us to place their petitions before Our Lady. Others who could not get close to us shouted from a distance:

'For the love of God, ask Our Lady to cure my son who is a cripple!' Yet another cried out: 'And to cure mine who is blind!...To cure mine who is deaf!...To bring back my husband, my son, who has gone to the war!...To convert a sinner!...To give me back my health as I have tuberculosis!' and so on.

"All the afflictions of poor humanity were assembled there. Some climbed up to the tops of trees and walls to see us go by, and shouted down to us. Saying yes to some, giving a hand to others and helping them up from the dusty ground, we managed to move forward, thanks to some gentlemen who went ahead and opened a passage for us through the multitude.

"Now, when I read in the New Testament about those enchanting scenes of Our Lord's passing through Palestine, I think of those which Our Lord allowed me to witness, while yet a child, on the poor roads and lanes from Aljustrel to Fatima and on to the Cova da Iria! I give thanks to God, offering Him the faith of our good Portuguese people, and I think: 'If these people so humbled themselves before three poor children, just because they were mercifully granted the grace to speak to the Mother of God, what would they not do if they saw Our Lord Himself in person before them?'

"Well, none of this was called for here! It was a distraction of my pen, leading me away where I did not mean to go. But, never mind! It's just another useless digression. I am not tearing it out, so as not to spoil the notebook.

"At last, we arrived at the Cova da Iria, and on reaching the holmoak we began to say the Rosary with the people. Shortly afterwards, we saw the flash of light, and then Our Lady appeared on the holmoak.

'*Continue to pray the Rosary in order to obtain the end of the war. In October Our Lord will come, as well as Our Lady of Dolours and Our Lady of Carmel. Saint Joseph will appear with the Child Jesus to bless the world. God is pleased with your sacrifices. He does not want you to sleep with the rope on, but only to wear it during the daytime.*' (**Author's Note:** The children had been making many sacrifices, including constantly wearing under their clothing a rough bit of rope they discovered while playing. They cut the rope in thirds, each taking a part to wrap around their waists. The rope hurt and chafed terribly but, like the other penances they were offering, the three young ones kept this sacrifice for the conversion of sinners a secret among themselves.)

'I was told to ask you many things, the cure of some sick people, of a deaf-mute...'

'*Yes, I will cure some, but not others because God has no confidence in them. In October, I will perform a miracle so that all may believe.*' (Note that this is the Virgin's **third** affirmation of an October miracle.)

"Then Our Lady began to rise as usual, and disappeared."

Seeking the Meaning of the Signs

Of all the signs given to the people since June 13, the delicate cloud is a constant. Those who saw it confirmed that it rested on the holmoak tree during the Apparitions, always coming forth from, and returning to, the east. In July, it reached out to surround the children, who would see and hear the "Great Secret" of Fatima. In August, despite the children's absence, the beautiful cloud still manifested itself. And then, in September, when the sky was blue and clear, the preternatural mist once more appeared at the very site of the Apparition, thickly rising from the ground to an impressive height. Three times in September, this remarkable cloud exhibited the characteristics of blessed, burning incense which, in the Church, is used during solemn liturgies and Benediction of the Blessed Sacrament. At the last Apparition of October, 1917—the month of the prodigious Miracle of the Sun—it would do so again.

What is the meaning of the extraordinary cloud? Why did it always come forth from the east and depart hence? Why did thunder sometimes announce the Lady's approach or departure? Why were stars seen at noontime? What of the sudden atmospheric changes or mysterious flowers seen on trees, at the very height of a hot summer? Can we discover the significance of the other signs? To find the answers, we must look to the two sources of Divine Revelation—Tradition and Scripture.

CHAPTER 3

The Cloud, Sign of the Holy Trinity

"You, O Mary…are a living Tabernacle, a Monstrance, a living Temple, the permanent abode of the Most Holy Trinity, Mother of God and Our Mother…"
–Sr. Maria Lucia of the Immaculate Heart, Fatima visionary

Throughout salvation history, the signs of God indicate various purposes. A true sign can possess any one or more of the following seven functions: It confirms God's word, His goodness, authenticates prophecy, verifies God's blessings and His intervention for the sake of the elect, strengthens the faithful with hope, insures or testifies God's Presence, or declares His judgment upon sin.[78] Not only do the 1917 apparitions of the Virgin Mary at Fatima fulfill all seven functions of Scriptural signs, they also serve as a "Mariophany."

To understand what is meant by "Mariophany," we must look to the definition of "Theophany," which comes from the ancient Greek *(ή) Θεοφάνεια Theophaneia* and means "appearance of God." The *Concise Catholic Dictionary* defines "theophany" as follows: "[1] Appearances or visions of God to man or the direct communication of God with man. [2] The apparitions of God to man, usually as recorded in *Genesis* where God appeared visibly to man as Lawgiver, Judge, and Prophet. They taught that there was only one God and that God Himself was speaking to man."[79] In both Christian and Jewish usage, the word refers to "the manifestation of God to man; the *sensible sign* (i.e., one or more of the five senses, such as sight, scent, hearing, taste, or touch) by which the Presence of God is revealed."[80]

In brief, "Mariophany" may be defined as "appearances of Mary" to man. Like the word "theophany," however, there are rich, deeper meanings to this one term. "Mariophany" refers to the apparitions of Mary when she, already assumed body and soul into Heaven, appears visibly to a person (or persons) to remind all of mankind to turn to God, Who is Lawgiver, Judge, and Prophet. "Mariophany" can also mean the manifestation of Mary in which God

---

[78] For examples, please see Heb. 2:3-4; Ps. 96:17, Judg. 6:17; Josh. 24: 15-17; Isa. 7:14; Exod. 3:12; Num. 17:20.
[79] *The Concise Catholic Dictionary* [Kansas City, MO: Angelus Press. Reprinted with 1943 Nihil Obstat and Imprimatur]: p. 331.
[80] "Theophany." *Wikipedia.* [http://en.wikipedia.org/wiki/Theophany]

emphasizes her office throughout all of salvation history, from *Genesis* to the *Apocalypse*. Finally, "Mariophany" signifies God's Triune Presence *in* the Immaculate Virgin, through whom He reveals Himself via "sensible signs."

Examining the Sensible Signs at Fatima

As mentioned in the first part of this work, witness testimonies reveal the following "sensible signs" seen at Fatima over the course of five months:

• A delicate white cloud, traveling from east to west, serenely settling over a young holmoak tree. The same cloud, after resting on the tree during the entire time of the Apparition, rose and departed from whence it came–toward the east.

• In July (the month in which the Virgin gave the children a Great Secret), the cloud (mentioned above), three times curling and rising into the air during the whole time of the Apparition–as though invisible thurifers were liturgically incensing the Vision.

• Claps of thunder, either as the Lady arrived or as she departed.

• Flashes of light, as the Vision approached the small holmoak tree.

• The ground of the apparition site momentarily trembling, like the briefest of earthquakes.

• The branches and shoots of the young holmoak tree mysteriously bending to the east after the Apparition departed.

• Atmospheric changes of the sky's luminosity, similar to a solar eclipse, or changes of unusual color, from yellow gold to all the colors of the rainbow. Some people reported seeing stars in the sky at solar noon.

• A relieving drop in temperature, during the hottest days of summer, accompanied by a cool fresh breeze.

• Small, white objects described as stars, roses, or doves gently falling from the sky, only to disappear before touching the ground.

• A globe of extraordinary light that glided, from east to west, descending toward the small holmoak tree.

"Of all the signs witnessed by the people since June 13, the delicate cloud is a constant," as Chapter 1 of this book also observed. "...In July, it reached out to surround the children, who would see and hear the 'Great Secret' of Fatima. In August, despite the children's absence, the beautiful cloud still manifested itself."

"And then, in September, when the sky was blue and clear, the preternatural mist once more appeared at the very site of the Apparition, extending itself over the holmoak tree, down to the ground, only to rise up to an impressive height. Three times in September, this remarkable cloud exhibited the characteristics of blessed, burning incense. At the last Apparition of October, 1917—the month of the prodigious Miracle of the Sun—it would do so again."

The Cloud in Holy Scripture

What is the meaning of this cloud, this one recurring sign, seen by the people during every Apparition of the Lady? Since only the three young shepherd children could see a beautiful Lady dressed all in white, the people of humble and simple faith immediately concluded that the cloud revealed the presence of the Virgin Mary. Like the Scriptural theophanies wherein the Lord our God revealed His Presence in the form of a cloud or a pillar of cloud, one can say that the beautiful mist at Fatima also manifested the presence of the Holy Trinity within the Virgin Mary, who is God's living, perpetual Tabernacle.

Frère Michel of the Holy Trinity, a most astute Fatima historian and apologist, was careful to point out this biblical theophany which occurred in 1917. In discerning the meaning of the cloud, he wrote that "from the giving of the law to Moses on Sinai to the Transfiguration of Jesus on Tabor, the cloud always appears in sacred history as the symbol and sensible expression of the divine Presence." Let us look, then, to some of the Scriptures which record the Lord God manifesting His Presence in the form of a cloud or a pillar of cloud:

• "Behold, the Lord is riding on a swift **cloud** and comes to Egypt; and the idols of Egypt will tremble in his presence." (*Isaiah 19:1*) St. Jerome, St. Proclus and many early writers considered the "swift cloud" to be an opaque reference to the Virgin Mary. Since the Hebrew word "qual" means either swift or light (as in weight, not brightness), St. Jerome noted that "surely we ought to see in the light cloud holy Mary, who was not weighed down by any manly seed."[81]

• "And the Lord went before them to shew the way by day in *a pillar of* a *cloud*, and by night in a pillar of fire: that he might be the guide of their journey at both times." (*Exodus 13:21*)

• "And the angel of God, who went before the camp of Israel, removing, went behind them: and together with him the *pillar of the cloud*, leaving the forepart…" (*Exodus 14:19*)

• "And now the morning watch was come, and behold the Lord looking upon the Egyptian army through the pillar of fire and of *the cloud*, slew their host." (*Exodus 14:24*)

---

[81] Gambero, S.M., Luigi. *Mary and the Fathers of the Church* [San Francisco: Ignatius Press, 1999]: p. 211, Tractatus de Psalmo 77, 14: CCL 78, 72.

• "And when Aaron spoke to all the assembly of the children of Israel, they looked towards the wilderness: and behold the glory of the Lord appeared *in a cloud.*" (*Exodus 16:10*)

• "And the glory of the Lord dwelt upon Sinai, covering it with *a cloud* six days: and the seventh day he called him out of the midst of the cloud." (*Exodus 24:16*)

• "And when he was gone into the tabernacle of the covenant, the *pillar of the cloud* came down, and stood at the door, and he spoke with Moses." (*Exodus 33:9*)

• "And all saw that the *pillar of the cloud* stood at the door of the tabernacle. And they stood, and worshipped at the doors of their tents." (*Exodus 33:10*)

• "The Lord came down in a *pillar of the cloud*, and stood in the entry of the tabernacle..." (*Numbers 12:5*)

• "And the inhabitants of this land, who have heard that thou, O Lord, art among this people, and art seen face to face, and thy cloud protecteth them, and thou goest before them in a *pillar of a cloud* by day, and in a pillar of fire by night." (*Numbers 14:4*)

• "...and the Lord appeared there in the *pillar of a cloud*, which stood in the entry of *the tabernacle.*" (*Deuteronomy 31:15*)

• "And it came to pass, when the priests were come out of the sanctuary, that *a cloud* filled the house of the Lord." (*3 Kings: 8:10*)

• "And at the seventh time, behold, *a little cloud* arose out of the sea like a man's foot. And he said: Go up and say to Achab: Prepare thy chariot and go down, lest the rain prevent thee." (*3 Kings 18:44*)

• "So when they all sounded together, both with trumpets, and voice, and cymbals, and organs, and with divers kind of musical instruments, and lifted up their voice on high: the sound was heard afar off, so that when they began to praise the Lord, and to say: Give glory to the Lord for he is good, for his mercy endureth for ever: the house of God was filled *with a cloud.*" (*2 Paralipomenon 5:13*)

• "And in a *pillar of a cloud* thou wast their leader by day, and in a pillar of fire by night, that they might see the way by which they went." (*2 Esdras 9:12*)

• "Yet thou, in thy many mercies, didst not leave them in the desert: *the pillar of the cloud* departed not from them by day to lead them in *the* way, *and the* pillar of fire by night to shew them the way by which they should go." (*2 Esdras 9:19*)

• "He spoke to them in the *pillar of the cloud.* They kept his testimonies, and the commandment which he gave them." (*Psalms 98:7*)

• "I dwelt in the highest places, and my throne is in a *pillar of a cloud*." (*Ecclesiasticus 24:7*)

• "Who is she that goeth up by the desert, as a *pillar of smoke* of aromatical spices, of myrrh, and frankincense, and of all the powders of the perfumer?" (*Canticles 3:6*)

Of this mysterious column of cloud, St. Ambrose wrote: "That pillar of cloud did, in its outward appearance, go before the children of Israel, but as a mystery it signified the Lord Jesus, who was to come in a light cloud, as Isaiah said; that in the Virgin Mary, who was a cloud on account of the inheritance of Eve, but light because of her virginal integrity."[82] Elsewhere, St. Ambrose again compared the Virgin to a cloud: "Oh, the riches of Mary's virginity...As a cloud, she waters the earth with the rain of Christ's grace...Receive, then, receive, O consecrated virgins, the spiritual rain that falls from this cloud...Run after this good cloud, for within her she has brought forth a fountain to water the face of the earth." [83]

Centuries before the Fatima apparitions, St. Alphonsus de Liguori spoke of the Old Testament's pillar of cloud and pillar of smoke: "This stupendous pillar, at times as a cloud, at others as fire, says Richard of St. Laurence, was a figure of Mary fulfilling the double office she constantly exercises for our good. As a cloud, she constantly protects us from the ardour of Divine Justice; and as fire, she protects us from devils." In regard to the passage from Canticles 3:6 (quoted above), St. Alphonsus also said: "We gather from the sacred canticles, that on the Assumption of Our Lady, the angels asked her name three times. *Who is she that goeth up by the desert as a pillar of smoke?* Again, *Who is she that cometh forth as the morning rising?* and again *Who is this that cometh up from the desert, flowing with delights?*[84]

Considering that the biblical theophanies reveal the manifestation of the Holy Trinity in a cloud or a pillar of cloud, we must likewise consider the remarkable cloud of Fatima, which consistently appeared during the apparitions of the beautiful Lady of Fatima who, on October 13, 1917, identified herself with these words: "I am the Lady of the Rosary." Frère Michel muses, "But how can we explain the fact that a creature—even the most sublime—could manifest herself in the glorious aura of a specifically divine attribute?"

---

[82] "Ambrose." *Theotokos: A Theological Encyclopedia of the Blessed Virgin Mary*, Second Edition, s.v., p. 18. Also see Palmer, S.J., Paul F., *Mary in the Documents of the Church* [London: Burns & Oats, 1953]: p. 27.

[83] Palmer, S.J., Paul F., *Mary in the Documents of the Church* [London: Burns & Oats, 1953]: p. 27.

[84] de Liguori, St. Alphonsus. *The Glories of Mary*. Fourth Reprint Revised. [Brooklyn, NY: Redemptorist Fathers. Reprinted in 1931]: p. 261.

The answer, he notes, is also found in the Scriptures. Specifically, he writes that it is "rich in mystical significance and is taught in the *Gospel of Luke*, by way of allusion but still quite clearly: through a series of hints that the exegetes have perfectly grasped, the Evangelist identifies the Virgin Mary with the Ark of the Covenant. This Ark, hidden under the Tent, was like a moveable sanctuary, the place where Yahweh had fixed His residence, accompanying Israel in its wanderings; and the Cloud manifested His presence. As soon as the Ark was introduced, we read in the book of Exodus, 'the cloud covered the tent of the meeting, and the glory of the Lord filled the tabernacle' [Exod.40:34-35]. After the building of the Temple by Solomon, the Ark was solemnly carried in by the priests to the Holy of Holies. And finally, it is by the Cloud that Yahweh manifests that He is taking possession of His Temple, and establishes His abode there."[85]

"Mary is the sanctuary and the repose of the Holy Trinity," said St. Louis de Montfort, echoing the Church.[86] He also said, "Mary is a holy place, and the holy of holies where Saints are formed and moulded."[87] On September 13 and October 13, 1917, the Fatima Cloud rose three times like incense, just as incense is liturgically offered three times before the Blessed Sacrament at High Mass or Benediction. Frère Michel observed that these three signs not only remind us of the "triple incensation in the liturgy, [but] the Immaculate Virgin shows us that she is the Abode and the Temple of God, the Sanctuary of the Holy Trinity, and the Ark of the New Covenant."

---

[85] Frère Michel. *TWTF,* Vol. I, p. 265.
[86] de Montfort, St. Louis. *True Devotion to Mary.* [Rockford, IL: TAN Books & Publishers, 1985. Republished from the 1941 edition by the Fathers of the Company of Mary]: #5.
[87] Ibid., #218.6.

CHAPTER 4
Signs from the East

*"Look about thee, O Jerusalem, towards the east,
and behold the joy that cometh to thee from God."*
—Baruch 4:36

In continuing this concise study of the external signs seen by the crowds during the 1917 apparitions of Our Lady of Fatima, I ask the reader to keep in mind that the many "public" portents hold a "highly symbolic and mystical significance."[88] The third part of this work described the seven functions of a true sign from God, noting that the signs at Fatima fulfill all of those seven purposes.[89] It also observed that the signs of Fatima serve as a "Mariophany,"[90] and briefly illustrated how, through the sensible sign of a cloud, Our Lady of Fatima showed herself to be "the abode and Temple of God, the Sanctuary of the Holy Trinity, and the Ark of the Covenant."[91]

The graceful cloud, signifying Our Lady's presence, was seen arriving or departing to the east. In the last two months of the Fatima apparitions (September and October 1917), many in the crowd also noticed **a luminous globe**. This globe appeared in the sky, moving from east to west at midday, at the exact time that the Lady asked the three children to meet her.

Among the people, some saw the globe descend toward the holmoak tree, only to disappear while the Vision lasted. As the globe approached the little tree, the brightness of the sun lessened, the surrounding atmosphere turned a golden-yellow, and stars were seen in the sky at solar noon—a scientifically

---

[88] Frère Michel, *TWTF*, Vol. I, p. 238.

[89] As stated in Chapter 3: "A true sign can possess one or more of the following seven functions: it confirms God's word, His goodness, authenticates prophecy, verifies God's blessings and His intervention for the sake of the elect, strengthens the faithful with hope, insures or testifies God's Presence, or declares His judgment upon sin."

[90] "In brief, 'Mariophany' may be defined as 'appearances of Mary' to man. Like the word 'theophany,' however, there are rich, deeper meanings to this one term. 'Mariophany' refers to the apparitions of Mary when She, already assumed body and soul into Heaven, appears visibly to a person (or persons) to remind all of mankind to return to God, Who is Lawgiver, Judge, and Prophet. 'Mariophany' can also mean the manifestation of Mary in which God emphasizes Her office throughout all of salvation history, from *Genesis* to the *Apocalypse*. Finally, 'Mariophany' signifies God's Triune Presence *in* the Immaculate Virgin, through whom he reveals Himself via 'sensible signs.'"

[91] Frère Michel, op. cit., p. 265.

impossible occurrence if a solar eclipse is not underway. When the Lady's visit to the children ended, many witnessed that the globe or "orb" of light reappeared and serenely ascended into the sky, toward the east. Here, it is essential to emphasize that the globe (like the cloud), always came from, and departed to, the *east*.

The Luminous Orb

First, we shall consider the beautiful globe of light. Some immediately thought it a means of transport for the Virgin Mary, who is risen from the dead and assumed, body and soul, into Heaven. In other words, the globe draws attention to the Assumption of the Blessed Mother.

As Fr. H. O'Laverty wrote in his book, *The Mother of God and Her Glorious Feasts*, "...it should not be forgotten that...in the things of God, where there is but the true and the good, simplicity alone will reveal the greatest heights and the most secret depths."[92] In 1917, the Assumption of the Virgin Mary was a Church doctrine which would be solemnly **defined** as a dogma in 1950. Like the parables of Our Lord, and like the answers He gave to those who questioned Him, we must delve a little deeper to better understand the manifestation of this globe.

When reflecting on the Fatima sign of a luminous globe, one comes to the realization that at no other Church-approved Marian apparition did Our Lady exhibit any display of being "carried" from Heaven to earth. For example, in the 1830 apparitions of the Rue de Bac to St. Catherine Labouré, the Virgin suddenly appeared in the chapel; the saint could even hear the rustling of the Lady's gown. With one exception, there were no bystanders to attest to any outer signs, and so it must follow that none were given. In the one case in which the saint, at prayer with other sisters, saw the Virgin in the chapel, not one other person was aware that a heavenly vision was taking place. LaSalette was a one-time apparition; there were no witnesses except the visionaries.

The 1858 apparitions at Lourdes, France, were different because Lourdes is the first of modern apparition sites which drew onlookers. St. Bernadette Soubirous stated that "the Lady" who came to her simply appeared in the Grotto niche—but when pressed for details, she said that a "golden cloud" within the niche quickly preceded the Lady's appearance. The people who came to Lourdes during St. Bernadette's apparitions would testify to the saint's

---

[92] O'Laverty, B.A., Fr. H. *The Mother of God and Her Glorious Feasts.* [Rockford, IL: TAN Books and Publishers, reprinted in 1987 under its new title. Originally published between 1908 and 1915, under the title *The Mother of God's Glorious Feasts.* First reprinted in 1925 and later reprinted again in 1977 by Marian Publications, South Bend, Indiana]: p. 145.

demeanor during her ecstasies, but none reported any sensible signs attesting to the Vision's presence.

In other words, neither at Lourdes nor at later sites, like Pontmain and Pellevoisin, were there any "public" manifestations of the Virgin traveling to or from the apparition site—no cloud, no orb, not even the tiniest glimmer of celestial light witnessed by spectators. Neither were there other signs like those at Fatima: a flash of lightning, brief claps of thunder, trembling of the ground, a gentle rain of small white objects described as petals, doves or stars, or any atmospheric changes of color, light, or temperature. (The one-time apparition of Pontmain does have one exception, which were three stars in a triangular formation that onlookers saw only on the one night in which the Virgin appeared. The three stars were never seen again. And, of course, this observation does not include Our Lady of Knock, which was a singular appearance, witnessed by anyone who came to the site.)

In addition to the dogma of the Virgin's Assumption, it seems the Fatima globe simultaneously reminds us of the Virgin's magnificent office in the whole of salvation history. For example, St. Bernard addressed the Lady Mary as "the heavenly chariot,"[93] while St. John Geometra saluted her by saying "Hail, resplendent car!"—signifying that "she is the car in which her clients mount to heaven." St. Athanasius said, "And thou, O Lady, wast filled with grace, that thou mightest be the way of our salvation, and the means of ascent to the heavenly kingdom."[94] The orb of light attests to her own words at Fatima, when she said, "I am *of* Heaven," and not "I am *from* Heaven."

As Fr. O'Laverty wrote, "God wishes to make use of Mary for the salvation of souls."[95] The mysterious, beautiful globe confirms that the Virgin is assumed body and soul into Heaven, and it simultaneously confirms the doctrine that Our Lady is the Mediatrix between mankind and the Lord Jesus. She, herself, is "the heavenly chariot" that leads souls to Heaven when they cooperate with God's designs.

The Holy Trinity, the Virgin Mary, and the East

Second, we shall consider why both the cloud and the globe of light traveled *from the east* and *returned to the east*. To do that, we shall once more briefly look to the Scriptures, keeping in mind that the following quotations and accompanying, short commentaries merely scratch the surface of all that

---

[93] Bernard, St. *In Annunt s.1.* Cited by St. Alphonsus di Liguori, *The Glories of Mary* [Brooklyn, NY: The Redemptorist Fathers, 1931]: p. 239.
[94] de Liguori, St. Alphonsus. *The Glories of Mary,* p. 239.
[95] O'Laverty, op. cit., p. 157.

the Bible reveals to us about God, His Presence, foreshadowing, prophecies, and the many figure-types of Our Lord or Our Lady:

• "Before the tabernacle of the covenant, that is to say on the *east* side, shall Moses and Aaron camp, with their sons, having the custody of the sanctuary, in the midst of the children of Israel." (*Numbers 3:38*)

In the Old Testament, God's instructed Moses *that the Tabernacle in the wilderness must always face east*, toward the Mount of Olives, where Christ's Passion would one day begin. A figure-type for the Virgin Mary, the Old Testament Tabernacle is also a figure of the eternal Church, which Christ founded upon Peter, the Rock.

• "Who hath raised up the just one from the *east*, hath called him to follow him? he shall give the nations in his sight, and he shall rule over kings: he shall give them as the dust to his sword, as stubble driven by the wind, to his bow." (*Isaiah 41:2*)

The Just One is Our Lord and Savior, Jesus Christ. The star of His Nativity, the Star of Bethlehem, rose in the east.[96] Consider, too, that the miraculous Star was a great sign seen in the sky, as foretold in the *Old Testament* ("a star shall rise out of Jacob"–*Numbers 24:7*). Here it should be noted that, with the exception of three wise men who undertook a perilous journey to follow the star, nobody else paid the sign any attention. In a similar manner, the signs and the requests given at Fatima, coupled with the continual modern-day signs of warning given to the entire world, are for the most part ignored.

• "Arise, O Jerusalem, and stand on high: and look about towards the *east*, and behold thy children gathered together from the rising to the setting sun, by the word of the Holy One rejoicing in the remembrance of God." (*Baruch 5:5*)

Jerusalem is, of course, an ancient historical city but, like other biblical places or people or events, it also serves as a figure-type. Since the Scripture passage above cannot be interpreted literally (because the city of Jerusalem cannot arise, or stand high, or look), it is a figure-type (or rather, a personification) for both the Church and the Virgin Mary (whom the Church founded by Christ also calls the heavenly Jerusalem).

• "And the spirit lifted me up, and brought me into the *east* gate of the house of the Lord, which looketh towards the rising of the sun." (*Ezechiel 11:1*)

Thus opens the *Prophecy of Ezechiel*, which the *Douay-Rheims Bible* prefaces in this manner: "A prophecy against the presumptuous assurance of the great ones. A remnant shall be saved, and receive a new spirit, and a new heart."

---

[96] Matt. 2: 2, 9.

Such a preface soundly reminds us of our own times. Does it not make us think of the "great ones" who refuse to heed the entire message of Fatima? Should not the virtue of perseverance bid us to pray and work for the complete release of the Third Secret of Fatima and for the conversion of sinners? At the same time, does it make us deeply grateful that even now, as in the days of Ezechiel, a remnant shall be saved?

• "And the glory of the Lord went up from the midst of the city, and stood over the mount that is on the *east* side of the city." (*Ezechiel 11:23*)

This phrase, "glory of the Lord" or the "glory of God" refers to a sensible sign of God's Presence—the "Shekinah." The word "Shekinah" literally means the *dwelling* or *settling* of God, whether in a person or an object (like the Ark of the Covenant or Solomon's Temple). Furthermore, among the Hebrews, *Shekinah* was interchangeable with the word *God*.

In the Old Testament, the "Shekinah" was seen to ascend (it "went up from the midst of the city") and "stood over the mount...on the *east* side of the city." In a similar manner, both the luminous globe and the cloud seen at Fatima ascended to the *east*.

• "And he brought me to the gate that looked toward the *east*. And behold the glory of the God of Israel came in by way of the *east*...And the majesty of the Lord went into the temple by the way of the gate that looked to the *east*." (*Ezechiel 43:1-2, 4*)

Again, the Scriptures record God's preference for the symbolism of the east, for the "glory of God" (Shekinah) came in by way of the *east*. We first recall that the word "glory" refers to a sensible sign of God's Presence in a person or object, and that "Jerusalem" is also a symbol for either the Virgin or the Church. We also recall that, since Christ's death and Resurrection, the House of Israel is comprised of the faithful in the Church. Moreover, this passage calls to mind the ancient Israelite's exultant praise for Judith (an historical figure-type of Our Lady), which the entire Church ecstatically proclaims of Mary, the Mother of God, "Thou art the glory of Jerusalem, thou art the joy of Israel, thou art the honour of our people."[97]

Tradition also teaches that the **Eastern Gate** of the ancient Temple of Israel is a figure-type of Our Lady, who as the Immaculate Conception is the "glory of God." As St. Louis de Montfort wrote, "The Holy Ghost, by the mouth of the Fathers, also styles the Blessed Virgin *the Eastern Gate*, by which the High Priest, Jesus Christ, enters the world and leaves it (Ezech. 44:2-3). By it He came the first time, and by it He will (come) the second (time). The

---

[97] Jth. 15:10.

sanctuary of the Divinity, the repose of the Most Holy Trinity, the throne of God, the city of God, the altar of God, the temple of God, the world of God—all these different epithets and encomiums are most substantially true with references which the Most High has wrought in Mary."[98]

• "Thus saith the Lord of hosts: Behold I will save my people from the land of the *east*, and from **the land of the going down of the sun**." (*Zachariah 8:7*)

Zachariah's prophecy is one fulfilled in Christ, the promised Messiah, and His Church. However, since Scriptural prophecy often possesses a dual meaning, and since many Old Testament prophecies are intended for future days, it may likewise refer to the last days. This prophecy appears to be speaking of at least two nations from which God will literally save his people.

• "For as lightning cometh out of the *east,* and appeareth even into the west: so shall the coming of the Son of man be." (*Matthew 24:7*)

In the quote above, Our Lord foretells His Second Coming and the Last Judgment; the entire passage prophecies the signs that shall precede the literal last days of the world. Jesus will return from the direction of the **east**, for it has long been held that, when He ascended into Heaven, He ascended toward the **east**. As St. John Damascene wrote, "At His ascent into Heaven, He went to the East, and so do the Apostles pray to Him; He will come again as the Apostles saw Him going, and so the Lord says Himself: *For as lightning cometh out of the east...*'"[99]

The East, then, is always symbolic of Christ. It is the reason why God willed the Old Testament Tabernacle to face the east, why the Star of Bethlehem rose in the east, why Catholic altars traditionally face the east, and why, in this modern age, Our Lady of Fatima, who is hailed in the Litany of Loreto as "Gate of Heaven," arrived and departed to the east. May we remember, too, that "Russia, which is in easternmost Europe, will be the font of conversion once it is actually consecrated to the Immaculate Heart of Mary."[100]

---

[98] de Montfort, St. Louis. *True Devotion to Mary,* op. cit., #262.
[99] Damascene, St. John [c. 675-c.749 A.D.]. Cited by Michael Davies, "The Catholic Sanctuary and the Second Vatican Council." *Catholic Tradition* website [http://www.catholictradition.org/Eucharist/sanctuary1.htm]
[100] "Signs and Symbols," *Catholic Tradition* [http://www.catholictradition.org/Saints/signs3.htm]

CHAPTER 5

Stars at High Noon:
Our Lord, Our Lady, & the Church

"And there are bodies celestial, and bodies terrestrial: but, one is the glory of the celestial, and another of the terrestrial. One is the glory of the sun, another the glory of the moon, and another the glory of the stars. For star differeth from star in glory."
—I Corinthians 15:40-41

Stars appearing on a clear day at solar noon. Atmospheric changes of the sky's luminosity, similar to a solar eclipse, with hues from yellow gold to all the colors of the rainbow. A sudden and relieving drop in temperature, during the hottest days of summer, accompanied by a cool fresh breeze. Flashes of lightning and claps of thunder that made the ground tremble. These and other portents, witnessed by many onlookers to the 1917 Fatima apparitions, possess a "highly symbolic and mystical significance."[101] In particular, the Virgin Mary's visit of September 13, "in which there were more signs than ever, and the largest crowd was present, imposes itself quite especially on our attention."[102]

As already noted, in September, a new sign–a luminous globe–was seen, gliding from east to west. It descended to the holmoak tree, over which the Lady always appeared to the three children. The time was high noon and, according to a letter written by witness Fr. John Quaresma, who later became the Vicar General of Leiria, Portugal, there was not "a cloud in the deep blue sky."[103] Then, writes Fatima historian Frère Michel of the Holy Trinity, "the sun's brightness diminished, the atmosphere became golden yellow, like the other times. *Some people even reported being able to distinguish the stars in the sky.*"[104]

---

[101] Frère Michel. *TWTF*, Vol. I, p. 238.
[102] Ibid., p. 273.
[103] Ibid., p. 257.
[104] Ibid., p. 258. [Emphasis added.]

Stars in the Scriptures

According to Fr. Bernard Kramer, "In the Septuagint [the ancient Greek translation of the Hebrew Scriptures—i.e., the Old Testament—approved by the Catholic Church but rejected by orthodox Jews and Protestant sects] the word [sign] is used for celestial phenomena."[105] With the exception of the sun, which is Scripture's "day star,"[106] the symbol of Jesus who is the Son of Justice (but also representative of the Immaculate Heart of Mary, per St. John Eudes), rare is the sight of a star during the daylight hours. Writing on the invisible power behind the sign of the Star of Bethlehem, which shone in the day, St. John Chrysostom observed, "…one may see this from the time also. For it [a star] appears not in the night, but in mid-day, while the sun is shining; and *this is not within the power of a star*."[107] Such a manifestation is, however, within the omnipotent power of God, Who uses the lights of heaven when He wishes to give His people a *sign*.

The *Holy Bible* infallibly confirms that the lights of the firmament are intended for many purposes, including "for" signs:

• "And God said: Let there be lights made in the firmament of heaven, to divide the day and the night, and let them be for *signs*, and for seasons, and for days and years: To shine in the firmament of heaven, and to give light upon the earth. And it was so done. And God made two great lights: a greater light to rule the day; and a lesser light to rule the night: and the *stars*." (*Genesis 1:14-16*)

• A **STAR** SHALL RISE out of Jacob and a sceptre shall spring up from Israel…" (*Numbers 24:7*)

• "The sun, and the moon, and the *stars* being bright, and sent forth for profitable uses, are obedient." (*Baruch 6:59*)

• "Where is he that is born king of the Jews? For we have seen his *star* in the east, and are come to adore him." (*Matthew 2:2)*

• "And there shall be signs in the sun, and in the moon, and in the *stars*; and upon the earth distress of nations, by reason of the confusion of the roaring of the sea and of the waves; Men withering away for fear, and expectation of

---

[105] Kramer, Rev. H.B., *The Book of Destiny,* p. 276.
[106] For example, see 2 Pet. 1:19.
[107] Chrysostom, St. John. "Homily 6 on Matthew." Translated by George Prevost and revised by M.B. Riddle. From *Nicene and Post-Nicene Fathers, First Series, Vol. 10.* Edited by Philip Schaff. [Buffalo, NY: Christian Literature Publishing Co., 1888.] [http://www.newadvent.org/fathers/200106.htm. [Emphasis added.]

what shall come upon the whole world. For the powers of heaven shall be moved." (*Luke 21:26*)

Stars remind us that God is the Creator and that we are the created; simultaneously, they remind us that the "works of God show forth His glory, that His law is greatly to be esteemed and loved," and "that mankind cannot comprehend His power and wisdom." [108] Silently, the countless number of "jewels" in the night sky also speaks of God's majesty, love, mercy and justice:

• "Dost not thou think that God is higher than heaven, and is elevated above the height of the *stars*?" (*Job 22:12*)

• "And the *stars* have given light in their watches, and rejoiced…" (*Baruch 3:34*)

• "O Lord Our Lord, how admirable is thy name in the whole earth! For thy magnificence is elevated above the heavens… Out of the mouth of infants and of sucklings thou hast perfected praise, because of thy enemies, that thou mayest destroy the enemy and the avenger. For I will behold thy heavens, the works of thy fingers: the moon and the *stars* which thou hast founded. What is man that thou art mindful of him? or the son of man that thou visitest him?" (*Psalms 8:2-5*)

Recalling that Scripture passages often possess both a literal and spiritually figurative meaning, we also know that in the Old Testament, *stars* also signify the elect. "In *Genesis*, the patriarchs, head of the twelve tribes of Israel, are also called **stars**. And the words of *Daniel* (7:10) cannot be restricted to the priests only of the Antiochean persecution but surely embrace all martyrs of that ordeal. If the chosen people of the Old Testament are called stars, much more appropriately so the true believers of the Church of Jesus Christ,"[109]–i.e., true believers in Jesus Christ are practicing members of the one, holy, Catholic, and apostolic Church that He established. The members on earth are called the Church Militant, those in Purgatory are the Church Suffering, and those in Heaven are the Church Triumphant. The Church on earth is also called the kingdom of God on earth, the Body of Christ, and the Catholic City. The elect (the Church Militant) are also called *the just* or *the people of God*, because they are the souls of predestination, meaning the souls

---

[108] Commentator Prefaces to *The Book of Psalms*, Ch. 18, and *The Book of Job*, Ch. 8, in the *Holy Bible*, Douay-Rheims-Challoner translation.

[109] Kramer, Rev. H.B., op. cit., p. 282.

whom God knows shall remain on the narrow path of redemption and attain salvation.

St. Anthony of Padua expressed it thusly: "The saints are like the *stars*. In His providence, Christ conceals them in a hidden place that they may not shine before others when they might wish to do so. Yet they are always ready to exchange the quiet of contemplation for the works of mercy as soon as they perceive in their heart the invitation of Christ."

Even though it may seem to stand alone, each "star" (i.e., each person) has a unique and spiritual purpose to fulfill and, by doing so, adds to the beauty of "heaven" (the biblical, symbolic language for "the Church"). Moreover, God knows the names of every "star" as well as their total number. As shall be seen, we may discern depths of meaning in the following Scripture quotes, which may be literal, spiritual, figurative, prophetic, or a combination of them.

For example, in the literal sense, "stars" are the material stars observed in the night sky but, in the spiritual sense, "stars" which remain "in heaven" are human beings who shall attain everlasting life. "Jerusalem" is literally the actual ancient holy city, yet it is also a figure-type for either the Virgin Mary or the future Catholic City that would be founded by the Messiah, Jesus Christ. "Israel" denotes the elect, while "heaven" literally indicates the skies above but it, too, is spiritually symbolic for the Church:

• "I alone am not able to bear you: for the Lord your God hath multiplied you, and you are this day as the *stars* of heaven, for multitude." (*Deuteronomy 1:10*)

• "And you shall remain few in number, who before were as the *stars* of heaven for multitude, because thou heardst not the voice of the Lord thy God." (*Deuteronomy 28:62*)

• "The Lord buildeth up Jerusalem: he will gather together the dispersed of Israel. Who healeth the broken of heart, and bindeth up their bruises. Who telleth the number of the *stars*: and calleth them all by their names. Great is Our Lord, and great is his power: and of his wisdom there is no number." (*Psalms 146:3-5*)

• "The glory of the *stars* is the beauty of heaven; the Lord enlighteneth the world on high." (*Ecclesiasticus. 43:10*)

• "O ye *stars* of heaven, bless the Lord: praise and exalt him above all forever." (*Daniel 3:63*)

• "And there are bodies celestial, and bodies terrestrial: but, one is the glory of the celestial, and another of the terrestrial. One is the glory of the sun, another the glory of the moon, and another the glory of the **stars**. For **star** differeth from *star* in glory." (*I Corinthians 15:40-41*)

In the Old Testament, **stars** also symbolize kings[110] (or what we today call leaders of nations) as well as teachers of God's Laws and those of His Church. These teachers could refer not only to priests and theologians, but also to teaching nuns, lay catechists, or any Christian who instruct others in the traditional Catholic Faith:

• "But they that are learned shall shine as the brightness of the firmament: and they that instruct many to justice, as **stars** for all eternity." (*Daniel 12:3*)

In the *Apocalypse*, the Lord speaks of giving the morning star to "he that shall overcome," yet in another passage, Jesus—who is Priest, Prophet, and King—calls Himself the **Morning Star**:

• "And he that shall overcome, and keep my works unto the end, I will give him power over the nations. And he shall rule them with a rod of iron, and as the vessel of a potter they shall be broken, As I also have received of my Father: and I will give him the morning **star**. He that hath an ear, let him hear what the Spirit saith to the churches." (*Apocalypse 2: 26-29*)

• "I, Jesus, have sent my angel, to testify to you these things in the churches. I am the root and stock of David, the bright and morning **star**." (*Apocalypse 22:16*)

Elsewhere in the *Book of Revelations*, stars indicate a group who occupy offices of high estate; they symbolize the Catholic hierarchy (bishops and priests). The ordained clergy alone can offer the Holy Sacrifice of the Holy Eucharist, forgive and absolve sins, bless, etc. As *The Book of Destiny* was careful to note, "The highest function of the hierarchy is worshipping God and offering the worship of the entire membership to Him."[111]

Within the hierarchy, the first degree of rank consists of the bishops of the Church, who are also called "angels" by the Lord in the *Apocalypse* to distinguish them from priests of lesser title. Bishops are "high priests" who can administer all the Sacraments that affect the society of the Church and also perform certain sacerdotal functions that lower-ranking priests usually cannot—for example, Confirmation (which a priest can administer but only under certain circumstances and only with his bishop's permission), Holy

---

[110] Num. 24:14; Isa.14:12.
[111] Kramer, Rev. H.B., op. cit., p. 122.

Orders, and the consecration of a new church and its altar. The secondary degree is comprised of priests.[112] Thus, Our Lord speaks in the *Apocalypse* of *seven stars*, whom he also calls *angels* (bishops) of the seven churches, while the seven candlesticks represent seven churches (what we today would call seven dioceses or larger parish areas where the Church is established among the people):

  • "I am the First and the Last…Write therefore the things which thou hast seen…The mystery of the seven *stars*, which thou sawest in my right hand, and the seven golden candlesticks. The seven *stars* are the angels of the seven churches. And the seven candlesticks are the seven churches." (*Apocalypse 1:20*)

Finally, we come to the apocalyptic passage, which is mentioned many times in this book and which may be the most well known throughout the Christian world. It is also the one that many believe is the infallible prophecy foretelling the authentic Marian apparitions of the Modern Age, which opened with Our Lady's appearance at Guadalupe, began anew in 18th century Europe (especially in France), and then culminated in the public and sensible signs at Fatima in Portugal, the country long called "the land of Holy Mary":

  • "And a great sign appeared in heaven: A woman clothed with the sun, and the moon under her feet, and on her head a crown of twelve *stars*…" (*Apocalypse 12:1*)

---

[112] "The Christian law…has necessarily its priesthood to carry out the Divine Service, the principle act of which is the Eucharistic Sacrifice, the figure and renewal of that of Calvary. This priesthood has two degrees; the first, total and complete, the second an incomplete participation of the first. **The first belongs to the bishop.** This bishop is truly a priest (*sacerdos*), and even a high-priest; he has chief control of the Divine worship (*sacrorum antistes*), is the president of liturgical meetings; he has the fullness of the priesthood, and administers all the sacraments. **The second degree belongs to the priest** (presbyter), who is also a *sacerdos*, but of the second rank; by his priestly ordination he receives the power to offer sacrifice (i.e., to celebrate the Eucharist), to forgive sins, to bless, to preach, to sanctify, and in a word to fulfill the non-reserved liturgical duties or priestly functions. In the exercise of these functions, however, he is subject to the authority of the bishop to whom he has promised canonical obedience; in certain cases he even requires not only authorization, but real jurisdiction, particularly to forgive sins and to take care of souls. Moreover, certain acts of the sacerdotal power, **affecting the society of which the bishop is the head**, are reserved to the latter–e.g., Confirmation, the final rite of Christian initiation, ordination…and the solemn consecration of new temples to God. Sacerdotal powers are conferred on priests by priestly ordination, and it is this ordination which puts them in the highest rank of the hierarchy after the bishop." August Boudinhon, "Priest," *The Catholic Encyclopedia, Vol. 12.* (New York: Robert Appleton Company, 1911.) [http://www.newadvent.org/cathen/12406a.htm]

This woman is understood to be a figure-type of both the Virgin Mary and the Church; certainly, it is a prophecy rich in mystery. Of this verse, St. Louis Marie de Montfort wrote, "St. John the Evangelist saw a woman crowned with twelve stars, clothed with the sun, and the moon under her feet. According to the commentators, this woman is the Blessed Virgin Mary, with her virtues and her privileges, especially that of her divine maternity."[113]

Considering that, at Fatima in 1917, stars appeared at high noon, announcing the Blessed Mother's appearance to the people, and recalling the profound Scriptural meanings of stars as signs, is it not within faith and reason to believe that the God wishes His people to persevere in the Catholic faith, despite all the obstacles and crosses they must endure in this age of spiritual deprivation, and to contemplate and imitate the virtues of His Virgin Mother, the Queen of all Saints, who once stood at the Foot of the Cross of Jesus Christ, Our Lord and Savior?

The Lady and the Symbol of a Star

Like her Divine Son, the Virgin Mother of God is also called the Morning Star. In historic time, she appeared before her Son and she does so again before His Second Coming. Like the "morning star" of the earthly sky, she always appears before the dawn, the rising of the "day star" (the sun, which is the material symbol of her Son and Savior, Jesus Christ). St. Alphonsus de Liguori reminds us, "In the revelations of St. Bridget, Mary is called *'Star preceding the sun,'* giving us thereby to understand that when devotion towards the divine Mother begins to manifest itself in a soul that is in a state of sin, it is a certain mark that before long God will enrich it with His grace."[114]

In other words, Mary, the Morning Star is the "anticipatory star" or "demonstrative star" of Christ (the day star). At Fatima, the sensible signs given to the people, the loving and motherly message and prophecies given by the Virgin Mary to the three shepherd children, and the fulfillment of the promised sign—the Great Miracle of the Sun—reminds us again that she is indeed, the Morning Star who arrives shortly before the "Sun"—i.e., her Divine Son. All that happened at Fatima brings to mind the words of St. Peter: *"And we have the more firm prophetical word: whereunto you do well to attend, as to a light that shineth in a dark place, until the day dawn, and the day star arise in your hearts."*[115]

The Lady Mary is likewise known as the Evening Star, the brightest star in the heavens, guiding weary travelers through the darkest hours of their lifelong

---

[113] de Montfort, St. Louis. *True Devotion to Mary,* #235.
[114] de Liguori, St. Alphonsus. *The Glories of Mary,* pp. 121-122.
[115] 2 Pet. 1:19.

journey. For many reasons, the Evening Star is also hailed as "Star of the Sea." In Latin, her name *Maria* derives from "Maris," which means "sea." Her Hebrew name is *Miryam* but in Aramaic, Our Lord's and Our Lady's native language, it is *Mariam* which means "bitter" or "bitterness." According to St. Isidore of Seville (+636 A.D.), her name also means "enlightener" for she brought forth Christ, the Light of the World; the same saint also observed that in the Syriac language, her name means "Lady."

"For Mary means a bitter sea, star of the sea, the illuminated or illuminatrix," St. Bonaventure (+1274 A.D.) once penned. "Mary is interpreted as *Lady*. Mary is a bitter sea to the demons; to men, she is the Star of the Sea; to the angels, she is Illuminatrix, and to all creatures, she is Lady."

In the symbolic language of the Holy Scriptures, the bitter salt-sea (with its fluctuating waves and tempests) represents the world, as well as the "sea of humanity." Of Mary, who lived in this world but never possessed the spirit of the world, St. Aelred (+1167 A.D.) wrote: "Her name means *Star of the Sea*; no doubt the *Star of this sea* which is the world. Therefore, we ought to lift up our eyes to this Star that has appeared on earth…in order that she may lead us, in order that she may enlighten us, in order that she may show us these steps so that we shall know them, in order that she may help us so that we may be able to ascend."

St. Thomas Aquinas (+1274 A.D.) said, "Mary means Star of the Sea, for as mariners are guided to port by the ocean star, so Christians attain to glory through Mary's maternal intercession."

Finally, we have the beautiful insight of St. Louis de Montfort, who in the early 16th century wrote: "God the Father gathered all the waters together and called them the seas or *maria* (Latin, seas]. He gathered all His grace together and called it Mary or *Maria*…this immense treasury is none other than Mary whom the saints call the 'treasury of the Lord.' From her fullness, all men are made rich."[116]

The Virtues of the Virgin Mary

Among the meanings already explained, stars may also represent a plentitude of virtues and/or profound privileges. In the history of salvation, the number "12" is "the perfect number, God's number" or "the number of completion."[117] Recalling the crown of twelve stars worn by the woman of the *Apocalypse*, who is herself a "great sign appearing in heaven," we might ask ourselves: "Exactly what are the virtues of the Virgin Mary?"

---

[116] Peters, Sister Danielle. "The Most Holy Name of Mary." *Marian Library International Marian Research Institute* [http://campus.udayton.edu/mary/mostholyname.html]
[117] Kramer, Rev. H.B., op. cit., pp. 15, 400.

In making that inquiry (in the hopes of imitating Our Lord's Immaculate Mother), we recall that in the sacred history of the Church the number "12" is meant only as a *symbol* of completion. We therefore cannot literally limit Our Lady's virtues to twelve. For example, we may consider the holy insights of St. John Eudes who, in recognizing the many Marian figure-types in the Old Testament, referred to twelve *specific* types among a greater number when he wrote the following:

"Among the many images and representations of the Admirable Heart of Mary, **I can distinguish twelve of surpassing beauty**. Six of them are found in the principal divisions of the universe; namely, the heavens, the sun, the center of the earth, the inexhaustible fountain of *Genesis*, the sea and the Garden of Eden. The six others appear in six of the most important manifestations witnessed by the world from the time of Moses to the death of Our Lord. They are the burning bush of Mount Horeb, the mysterious harp of David, the magnificent throne of Solomon, the marvelous Temple of Jerusalem, the miraculous furnace of Babylon, and the holy mount of Calvary."[118]

To return to the many virtues of Our Lady—which are symbolized by the number 12—we look to a prayer known as *The Little Crown of the Twelve Stars of the Blessed Virgin Mary,* in which there is an exquisite line that simply declares, *"Thy virtues, O Virgin, surpass the stars in number."* This centuries-old prayer was offered to God by many saints including St. Joseph Calasanctius and St. John Berchmans. It is known that St. Louis de Montfort recommended this prayer to his religious foundations (the Montfort Fathers and the Daughters of Wisdom) as a morning prayer. The saint added to each *Hail Mary* a short invocation to the Virgin, and he also urged those who embraced the devotion to Jesus through Mary to pray *The Little Crown.*[119]

This prayer is divided into three sets of "crowns." The first is the Crown of Excellence, the second is the Crown of Power, and the third is the Crown of Goodness. Each crown hails a "set" of four inestimable virtues. The *Crown of Excellence* honors "the divine maternity of the Blessed Virgin, her ineffable virginity, her purity without stain, and her innumerable virtues." The *Crown of Power* honors "the royalty of the Blessed Virgin, her magnificence, her universal mediation, and the strength of her rule." The *Crown of Goodness*

---

[118] Eudes, St. John. *The Admirable Heart of Mary.* [Buffalo, NY: Immaculate Heart Publications]: p. 32.
[119] de Montfort, St. Louis. *True Devotion to Mary,* p. 200.

extols the unfathomable mercy of the Blessed Virgin toward four types of
people: sinners, the poor, the just, and the dying.[120]

The Other Signs at Fatima

It is no coincidence that the virtues honored in *The Little Crown of the
Blessed Virgin Mary* are the same holy qualities Our Lady chose to display at
Fatima. To declare that the signs and the complete message of Fatima highlight
the Virgin's virtues and privileges is certainly an understatement–for the time
has already arrived in which God wishes to establish worldwide devotion to the
Immaculate Heart of Mary.

With that said, the following sections are the signs that shall be examined:

1. Most of the witnesses who were closest to the spot where the Lady
appeared heard a far-away, indescribable sound, perceived only in response to
Lucia's words.

2. In July, just as the apparition began, the atmosphere became yellow as
gold. As one witness stated, "The luminosity of the sky noticeably decreased,
as during an eclipse, the whole time the ecstasy of the children lasted." In
August, when the children were abducted by the Masonic mayor and were not
present for the Vision, the people saw "all the colors of the rainbow, pink, red,
blue....The trees seemed to be made not of leaves but of flowers...The ground
came out in colors and so did our clothes. The lanterns fixed to the arch looked
like gold."[121]

3. At the height of a Portuguese summer, the very hot temperature suddenly
dropped to a pleasant degree, accompanied by "a cool fresh breeze."[122]

4. Also at the July 1917 apparition, a "large clap of thunder" was heard just
seconds before the eldest child, Lucia, indicated the departure of the Lady. The
thunder shook the ground, so that a small arch placed by the apparition site
"trembled as if in an earthquake." [123] In August 1917, when the children were
not present, an extremely loud boom of thunder so badly frightened the people
that many scattered and ran, thinking they would be killed.[124]

5. Again in August, a flash of lightning, following the thunder, also
garnered the attention of the now-silenced crowd. This "flash," always seen by

---

[120] Ibid, pp. 200-202.
[121] Frère Michel, *TWTF*, Vol. I, p. 183, 224.
[122] Walsh, *Our Lady of Fatima*, p. 80.
[123] Ibid.
[124] de Marchi, *The True Story of Fatima*, p. 37.

the children, served as the sign of the Virgin's approach.[125] The flash was not usually perceived by the crowd but, this time, the people saw it.[126]

6. During the Apparition of September 13, 1917, a greater number of onlookers observed a shower of small white objects–described by witnesses as either as petals, snowflakes, dove-shaped forms, stars, or roses–all of which gently fell from the sky and disappeared before touching the ground.[127]

As we shall see, all of these supernatural signs also hold a great significance in Divine Revelation. Through the intercession of the Virgin Mary, the unusual marvels at Fatima are intended to remind the Church, and all peoples of the world, that God has willed to give His graces and peace to mankind through the hands of His Immaculate Mother, who is the cause of our salvation, Jesus Christ.

---

[125] Sr. Mary Lucia, *Memoirs,* 1976 edition, p. 163.
[126] de Marchi, loc.cit.
[127] Frère Michel, op. cit., p. 260.

CHAPTER 6

Signs of Grace:
The Silent Parables of Fatima

"Through thee we have access to the Son,
O thou giver of grace, and Mother of our salvation."
—St. Bernard of Clairvaux

During His public life, Jesus spoke to great crowds of people in the form of parables, telling "plain, simple stories easily remembered by plain, simple people, even without learning or talent. In these He clothed His divine doctrines…taking His illustrations from those common and obvious objects with which they were most familiar, screening the Divine Mysteries at the same time from the ill-disposed and bigoted who listened to the parables but would not understand their meaning."[128] In a fashion similar to Our Lord's divine parables, the sensible signs witnessed by pilgrims present at the 1917 Fatima apparitions strengthened and consoled the faithful, converted souls, counteracted the doubters, and gently emphasized the divine doctrines revealed by God to His Church.

The first parts of this work concisely examined many of the wonders seen and heard at Fatima. While those signs are rich and profound in their meaning, the next two parts (Chapters 7 and 8) of this treatise shall likewise be succinct although, like St. Bernard of Clairvaux, this writer declares with filial love: "Of Mary, there is never enough." Chapter 9 examines the "Great Sign," the promised Miracle. However, from that point, Chapters 10–18 grow in detail in this continuing study of other aspects of Fatima, including our ongoing conversions (growth in the interior life, also called the spiritual life), the Third Secret, our adoration and imitation of Christ, our devotion to the Immaculate Heart of Mary, the Sacred Heart, the Precious Blood, and more. With that said, we look to the following signs given at Fatima from June–September, 1917:

• **In June and July 1917, many witnesses closest to the spot where the Lady appeared heard a far-away, indescribable sound, perceived only in response to Lucia's words.**[129] **Others said they "heard something like the**

---

[128] Prachensky, Fr. Joseph. *Divine Parables Explained.* [South Bend, IN: Marian Publications, 1973. Reprinted from the 1890 edition]: pp. 15-16.
[129] Frère Michel, *TWTF,* Vol. I, p. 183.

murmur of a very fine, but unintelligible voice."[130] What else could be this murmur other than the Virgin's voice?

In most instances, the Holy Scriptures describe a heavenly voice as *loud* or *great* or *strong*. At Fatima, however, it seems only those who first came to the apparition site (and only in the months of June and July) received the favor of "distantly" hearing Our Lady's voice. The fortunate ones included the faithful Maria Carreira, who had taken it upon herself to tidy the area around the holmoak tree, placed flowers and a silk bow upon it, and built over it a humble arch with lanterns on each side.

Years later, the exact spot of the apparition was marked by a statue of Our Lady of Fatima, standing upon a marble pillar. The statue and the pillar are directly in front of the Chapel of Apparitions (the first sanctuary built in honor of the Virgin of Fatima), and all three are now enclosed within the Basilica of Our Lady of the Rosary.

It is as though the Virgin of Fatima, the Queen of Prophets, took the prophet Zachariah's words for her own: "And they that are far off, shall come and shall build in the temple of the Lord: *and you shall know that the Lord of hosts sent me to you. But this shall come to pass, if hearing you will hear the voice of your God.*"[131]

• **In July, August, and September, when certain signs indicated the arrival of the Virgin, the atmosphere became yellow as gold.**[132]

In the history of the Fatima apparitions, July (the first time the atmosphere turned to yellow-gold) is pivotal, because Our Lady gave the three young children the Great Secret of Fatima in its three parts. It was also in July that the Mother of God promised, "In October, I will tell you who I am and what I want, and I will perform a miracle for all to see and believe."[133] As word spread of the coming miracle, the crowds grew greater each month—as did the signs at Fatima. In October, the promise was kept, the children were given the Lady's name and heard her final request, and the foretold miracle was the "great sign"—the Miracle of the Sun. So why, in the three months preceding the final "public" apparition, was the color of yellow-gold made manifest?

Gold represents the glory of God, His divine nature, and His revelation. Yellow-gold is the color of the sun, which symbolizes Jesus, the Son of God, the Lord and Savior of the world. Gold is also "the symbol of unselfish and

---

[130] Barthas, Canon C. *Fatima 1917-1968, Histoire complète des apparitions et de leurs suits* [Fatima Publications, 1969]: p. 146. Cited in *TWTF*, Vol. I: p. 160.
[131] Zach. 6:15.
[132] Frère Michel, loc. cit..
[133] Sr. Mary Lucia, *Memoirs*, 1976 edition, p. 165.

complete immolation to God"[134]–i.e., the virtue of charity, which St. Louis de Montfort called the "gold of love" and "the fulfillment of the whole law."[135] (On a vital side note, the lives of the three Fatima visionaries were those of heroic charity and sacrifice, reminding "the world that it is necessary to avoid sin, and to make reparation to an offended God, by prayer and penance."[136])

Even in ancient times, purest gold was considered a precious metal, and it was one reserved for the Ark of the Covenant, the Temple, and all the vessels that served the Lord. St. Alphonsus de Liguori wrote, "In the book of Exodus, we read that God commanded Moses to make a mercy-seat of **the purest gold**, because it was thence that He would speak to him. *Thou shalt make also a propitiatory of the purest gold...There will I give orders, and will speak to thee.*"[137]

The root of the word "propitiatory" means to pacify or placate, to conciliate, to reconcile; it also means to intercede, to calm, to mediate, or to atone. All of these verbs of "being" or action apply to both Our Lord and Our Lady. Like the Ark of the Covenant which it covered, the Old Testament propitiatory or "mercy seat" is also a figure-type for the Virgin Mary, upon whom God rests and speaks to His people–just as He did in Old Testament history and as He does again in modern times.[138]

St. John the Evangelist states in the *Apocalypse*, in which he writes of things present and future,[139] that an angel took him up in spirit to "a great and high mountain" and showed him "the heavenly Jerusalem coming down out of heaven from God,"[140] saying that the city itself is "pure gold, like to glass" and "the street of the city, as pure gold, as it were transparent glass."[141] This heavenly Jerusalem also serves as a figure-type for the Virgin Mary.

 • **As one Fatima witness stated, "The luminosity of the sky noticeably decreased, as during an eclipse, the whole time the ecstasy of the children lasted."**[142]

It was at Fatima that Mary, the Queen of Prophets, delivered a heavenly command, in a manner more majestic and striking than that of the Old Testament prophets. Our Lady of Fatima, like the prophets before her, called

---

[134] Kramer, Rev. H. B., *The Book of Destiny*, p. 192.
[135] de Montfort, St. Louis. *True Devotion to Mary*, #56-59.
[136] Sr. Mary Lucia, op. cit., p. 115.
[137] Exod. 25:17.
[138] de Liguori, St. Alphonsus. *The Glories of Mary*, p. 111.
[139] Kramer, Rev. H.B., op. cit., p. 278.
[140] Apoc. 21:10.
[141] Apoc. 21: 18, 21.
[142] Frère Michel, loc. cit.

sinners to conversion, foretold great blessings when God's commands are heeded, and warned of dire sufferings if they are not. The dimming of the sun at Fatima calls to mind that which biblical prophets called a "day of darkness"[143]—a time of tribulation and distress due to God's wrath against the multitude of sins.

A "day of darkness" can also signify the day of the Lord, of which the prophet Amos warned: "Woe to them that desire the day of the Lord: to what end is it for you? The day of the Lord is darkness, and not light."[144] In one interpretation of *Apocalypse* 8:12, wherein a great mountain (denoting a kingdom), burning with fire, slides into the sea, the star Wormwood falls, and a third part of the sun, moon, and stars darken, it is stated:

"The prophecy of our text foreshows a time of trouble for the Church and an obscuration of her splendor and her power to enlighten the world. The prophets called any misfortune that dimmed the luster of the theocracy a day of darkness. Likewise, when they prophesy defeat and humiliation for other nations they predict it by obscuration of the sun, moon, and stars. Isaias speaks thus to Babylon (XIII.10) and Ezechiel to Egypt (XXXII.7). Joel calls the coming war with the Babylonians 'a day of darkness and of gloominess' (II.2); of the temporal extinction of the theocracy in the Babylonian Captivity he says, 'the sun and the moon are darkened, and the stars have withdrawn their shining.' Ezechiel likewise calls the extinction of the theocracy 'a cloudy and dark day' (XXXIV.12)[145]...Thus Amos prophesied upon the kingdom of Israel (VIII.9)."[146] To briefly state it, then, a "sign" like the darkening of the sun foretells that God's judgment on His people (and possibly all nations) is near.

Remembering that the material sun of our solar system is also "the" symbol of Christ, the *Gospel of Luke* relates that when Christ was crucified, "there was darkness over all the earth until the ninth hour. And the sun was darkened..."[147] This darkness was supernatural, for Christ was condemned at the time of Passover, which was celebrated during the full moon—at which time a solar eclipse is not possible. The sun was darkened because Jesus, the God-man, was dying, of His own free will, to save His people from their sins.

At Fatima, the decreased sunlight, so similar to that of an eclipse, was also supernatural, lasting only during the time of the Virgin's visit. In fact, the dimming of the sun at Fatima might also be attributed to the many glories of

---

[143] For examples, see Esther 11:8; Job 15:23; Joel 2:2; and Sophonias 1:15.
[144] Amos 5:18.
[145] Kramer, Rev. H.B., op. cit., p. 206.
[146] Ibid., p. 207.
[147] Lk. 23: 44-45.

Mary, of which St Alphonsus de Liguori wrote, [148] stating that in the *Canticles*, Our Lady is called "bright as the sun."[149] St. Bonaventure said of the Blessed Mother, "She is more beautiful than the sun" and Lucia, the only Fatima visionary to reach adulthood and an elderly age, said that the Lady was "more brilliant than the sun."[150]

Perhaps, too, the diffused sun at Fatima manifested Our Lady's glory before God but also her clemency toward her Divine Son's people, for the Virgin Mother of God came to the modern world to remind us of what St. Peter taught: "But you are a chosen generation, a kingly priesthood, a holy nation, a purchased people: that you may declare his virtues, who hath called you *out of darkness into his marvellous light.*"[151]

• **At the height of a Portuguese summer, the very hot temperature suddenly dropped to a pleasant degree, accompanied by "a cool fresh breeze."**[152]

In the Holy Scriptures, when the Lord our God spoke individually to a prophet, in order to give His people a message of mercy and/or a warning of His just retribution for their infidelity, He did so in a quiet yet awesome and breath-taking way. For example, in the third book of *Kings*, we read a passage in which "the word of the Lord came unto" Elias, the prophet,[153] who lived during a perilous time when the people of Israel had again forsaken the Lord's covenant and were waging a war against God and His servants.[154] Through Elias' intercession, two miracles had already occurred on Mount Carmel, but Jezebel the queen sought to take the prophet's life.

"And he [i.e., the word of the Lord] said to him [Elias, the prophet]: Go forth, and stand upon the mount before the Lord: and behold the Lord passeth, and a great and strong wind before the Lord over throwing the mountains, and breaking the rocks in pieces: the Lord is not in the wind, and after the wind an earthquake: the Lord is not in the earthquake. And after the earthquake a fire: the Lord is not in the fire, and after the fire **a whistling of gentle air**. And when Elias heard it, he covered his face with his mantle...and behold a voice unto him."[155]

---

[148] de Liguori, op. cit., p. 214.
[149] Cant. 6: 9.
[150] Sr. Mary Lucia, op. cit., p. 159.
[151] 1 Pet. 2:9.
[152] Walsh, *Our Lady of Fatima*, p. 80.
[153] 3 Kings 19: 9.
[154] 3 Kings 19:10.
[155] 3 Kings 19: 11-13.

Is it not possible that, like the whistling of gentle air that manifested to Elias the very Presence of God, the sudden but soothing change of temperature and the gentle, cooling breeze declared the Virgin Mary's presence—she who is the Perpetual Tabernacle of the Holy Trinity? St. Louis de Montfort, when teaching that we must accomplish all of our actions *in, with,* and *through* Mary, explained that she is "the true terrestrial paradise of the new Adam" (Jesus), writing: "It is only the Holy Ghost who can make us know the hidden truth of these figures of material things. There is in this place [the Virgin Mary] **an air of perfect purity**; a **fair sun**, without shadow, of the Divinity; a fair day, without night, of the Sacred Humanity [of Jesus]; a continuing burning furnace of love, where all the iron that is cast into it is changed, by excessive heat, to gold."[156]

Finally, for the child visionaries and the thousands of pilgrims who came to Fatima, the delicate and considerate changes in the elements during Our Lady's apparitions may well have served as a foretaste of Heaven. After all, in the *Apocalypse* (7: 16-17), St. John relates: "They shall no more hunger nor thirst, *neither shall the sun fall on them, nor any heat.* For the Lamb, which is in the midst of the throne, shall rule them, and shall lead them to the fountains of the waters of life, and God shall wipe away all tears from their eyes."

---

[156] de Montfort, St. Louis, op. cit., #261.

CHAPTER 7

Rainbow Colors and Other Startling Signs:
Mother of God, Refuge of Sinners

"Now therefore children, hear me;
blessed are they who keep my ways."
—Proverbs 8:32

In this seventh part on the public, sensible signs witnessed by crowds during the May-October 1917 apparitions of Our Lady of Fatima, we look to the phenomena of thunder, the shaking of the ground, lightning, and the atmospheric changes of rainbow colors:

• In July, the month in which the Virgin Mary gave the three child visionaries the Great Secret of Fatima in its three distinct parts, a "large clap of thunder" was heard just seconds before the eldest child, Lucia, suddenly jumped up from her kneeling position, exclaiming, "There she goes! There she goes!" as the Lady departed. The thunder shook the ground, so that a small arch placed by the apparition site "trembled as if in an earthquake.[157]

• In August, when the children were not present at the apparition site because the mayor had abducted them, a great crowd gathered in anticipation of solar noon, the usual time of Our Lady's appearance. When the hour arrived, the people heard an extremely loud boom of thunder, which so badly frightened them that many scattered and ran, thinking they would be killed.[158]

• A flash of lightning, following the thunder, was also seen in August, garnering the attention of the now-silenced crowd. This "flash," always seen by the children, served as the sign of the Virgin's approach[159] but had never been previously perceived by the people.

Thunder, a Small Tremor, and Lightning
In the Scriptures, the sound of thunder, the appearance of lightning, or the trembling of an earthquake announce *a direct manifestation from the Lord or of*

---

[157] Frère Michel, *TWTF*, Vol. I, p. 238.
[158] de Marchi, *The True Story of Fatima*, p. 37.
[159] Sr. Mary Lucia, *Memoirs*, 1976 edition, p. 163.

the Lord. **Thunder** denotes God's "voice"−i.e., His irrevocable declaration of His truth, mercy and judgment: "The Lord shall thunder from heaven: and the Most High shall give forth His voice." [160] (Here it should be noted that only twice was thunder heard at Fatima−in July, after the Great Secret was divulged, and an even greater "boom" in August when the plotting mayor kidnapped the children. Recalling that thunder denotes God's voice, often in judgment, we should also remember that Our Lady would, in August, tell the children, "If you had not been taken away to the City, the miracle would have been greater.")[161]

Lightning is the sign of God's divine majesty and His wisdom and power in His wonderful works, His miracles, and His judgment.[162] In the *Book of Exodus*, thunder and lightning together announce the Holy Presence of the Lord God immediately before He gave the Ten Commandments to Moses: *"And now the third day was come, and the morning appeared: and behold thunders began to be heard, and lightning to flash, and a very thick cloud to cover the mount...and the people that were in the camp, feared.* [163]

Both thunder and lightning are likewise found in the *Psalms*, representing Divine Revelation which enlightens the interior life of the soul, when King David mysteriously addressed the Lord: *"The voice of thy thunder in a wheel. Thy lightnings enlightened the world: the earth shook and trembled."*[164] An eyewitness of the Fatima apparition in July (again, the month in which the Virgin Mary disclosed the Great Secret for the salvation of the Church and the world) inadvertently chose similar words to those of King David when, at the moment the child Lucia exclaimed the Lady's leave-taking, *"the earth trembled like an earthquake."*[165]

In searching the *Holy Bible* from the *Old Testament* to the *Apocalypse*, there are a total of 17 references to an "earthquake" or "earthquakes." In most instances, **an earthquake is the predominant sign of God's explicit action to save the faithful (spiritually and sometimes physically) even as it confounds the obstinate.**

---

[160] 2 Kings 22: 14. Also see Exod. 9:23; 1 Kings 2:10; 1 Kings 7:10; 1 Kings 12:17-18; Job 26:14; Job 37: 4-5; Job 40:4; Eccles: 43:18.
[161] Frère Michel, *TWTF,* Vol. I, p. 235.
[162] Apoc. 11:13.
[163] Exod. 19:6.
[164] Ps. 76:19.
[165] Frère Michel, loc. cit.

When the Old Testament prophet Isaiah foretold God's judgment on reprobates, he prophesied: *"And it shall be at an instant suddenly. A visitation shall come from the Lord of hosts* **in thunder,** *and* **with earthquake**... *"*[166] The *Gospel of Matthew* records an earthquake at the moment of Christ's death and a "great earthquake" at His Resurrection. [167] The *Acts of the Apostles* also tells of a great earthquake which shook the foundations of the prison in which were held Paul and Silus, released their "bands" (bonds), and opened their prison doors. [168]

In the *Apocalypse*, St. John the Evangelist alludes to lightning, voices, and thunders (together) *four* times, [169] while an earthquake (or a "great earthquake") is mentioned either alone or with other signs, a total of *five* times. [170] The first instance occurs when he is granted a vision of the Lord's throne in Heaven: *"And from the throne proceeded lightnings, and voices, and thunders; and there were seven lamps burning before the throne, which are the seven spirits of God."* [171] Lightning, voices, and thunders are not mentioned again until Chapter 8, but this time "a great earthquake" is also revealed to him: *"And the angel took the censer, and filled it with the fire of the altar, and cast it on the earth, and there were thunders and voices and lightnings, and a great earthquake."*[172]

St. John was later ordered to "measure the temple of God, and the altar and them that adore therein,"[173] and thereafter was told of the two witnesses who will publicly testify to Christ whilst resisting the actual person of anti-Christ.[174] He then wrote again of lightning, and voices, and an earthquake, which this time accompany the Ark of the Covenant (already explained as a historical figure-type of the Virgin Mary, because it was wholly consecrated to the Lord. Furthermore, it was never to be touched by any man; the Lord overshadowed the Mercy-Seat of the Ark, just as the Holy Ghost overshadowed the Virgin at the Incarnation of Christ. Like the Virgin, the Ark contained the Bread of Heaven, a figure-type for Christ):

"And the nations were angry, and thy wrath is come, and the time of the dead, that they should be judged, and that thou shouldest render reward to thy

---

[166] Isa. 29:6.
[167] Mt. 27-54; 28:2.
[168] Acts 16: 26.
[169] Apoc. 4:5; 8:5; 11:19; 16:8.
[170] Apoc. 6:12; 8:5; 11:13; 11:19; and 16:8.
[171] Apoc. 4:5.
[172] Apoc. 8:5.
[173] Apoc. 11:1.
[174] Apoc. 11: 3-13.

servants the prophets and the saints, and to them that fear thy name, little and great, and shouldest destroy them who have corrupted the earth. And the temple of God was opened in heaven: and the ark of his testament was seen in his temple, and there were **lightnings**, and **voices**, and **an earthquake**, and great hail."[175]

In addition to the symbolism of an earthquake already described, Fr. Herman B. Kramer, author of *The Book of Destiny*, stated his opinion: "Revolutions and overthrows of governments are also called earthquakes in prophetical diction."[176] The Bolshevik Revolution in Russia, which arose during the very months of the Fatima apparitions, certainly could be described as a "great earthquake," especially since Our Lady warned that, if her requests were not granted, Russia would spread her errors (plural) *throughout the world.*[177]

• **Rainbow Colors:** In July (again, the month wherein Our Lady revealed the "Great Secret"), there was an atmospheric change, in which people saw "all the colors of the rainbow, pink, red, blue...The trees seemed to be made not of leaves but of flowers...The ground came out in colors and so did our clothes. The lanterns fixed to the arch looked like gold."[178] In October, the rainbow colors would appear again during the promised miracle.

At Fatima, a humble arch had been placed in honor over the young holmoak tree, because "the Lady" always appeared upon it. As previously mentioned, a witness testified that, in July, the lanterns placed upon it appeared as gold—even though everyone and everything else were seen in rainbow colors. Why might this be?

Earlier in this work, it was explained that the color of gold represents the glory of God, His divine nature, and His revelation. Yellow-gold is the color of the sun, which symbolizes the Son of God, the Lord and Savior of the world. Gold is also "the symbol of unselfish and complete immolation to God"—i.e., the virtue of charity, which St. Louis de Montfort called the "gold of love" and "the fulfillment of the whole law." It was further explained that, even in ancient times, purest gold was considered a precious metal, and it was one reserved for the Ark of the Covenant, the Temple, and all the vessels of the Lord." At God's command to Moses, the "mercy-seat" of the Ark was likewise made of the purest gold, for from it He would give orders and speak to the prophet. Like the Ark of the Covenant which it covered, the Old Testament propitiatory or "mercy-seat" is also a figure-type for the Virgin Mary, upon whom God rests

---

[175] Apoc. 11:18-19.
[176] Kramer, Rev. H. B., *The Book of Destiny*, p. 266.
[177] Sr. Mary Lucia, op. cit., p. 162.
[178] Frère Michel, op. cit., p. 224.

and speaks to His people–just as He did in Old Testament history and as He does again in modern times.

Next, we examine the atmospheric phenomena wherein Fatima witnesses observed all the colors of the rainbow, on the ground and on their clothes. Let us consider a previous referral to the *Apocalypse*, when St. John the Evangelist was privileged to see a vision of God's throne, wherein he described it as follows: "After these things I looked, and behold a door was opened in heaven, and the first voice which I heard, as it were, of a trumpet speaking with me, said: Come up hither, and I will shew thee the things which must be done hereafter. And immediately I was in the spirit: and behold there was a throne set in heaven, and upon the throne one sitting. And he that sat, was to the sight like the jasper and the sardine stone; and *there was a rainbow round about the throne*, in sight like unto an emerald." [179]

St. Alphonsus de Liguori wrote that the rainbow encircling the throne of God is "an express figure of Mary."[180] St. Alphonsus then quoted a priest of the episcopate, known as Cardinal Vitalis: "The rainbow round the throne is Mary, who softens the judgment and sentence of God against sinners." He also cited St. Bernadine of Siena, who said "it was of this rainbow that God spoke when He promised Noah that He would place it in the clouds as a sign of peace, that on looking at it He might remember the eternal peace which He had covenanted to man. *I will set My bow in the clouds, and it shall be the sign of a covenant between Me and between the earth...and I shall see it, and shall remember the everlasting covenant.*[181] 'Mary,' says the saint, 'is this bow of eternal peace, for as God on seeing it remembers the peace promised to the earth, so does He, at the prayers of Mary, forgive the crimes of sinners, and confirm His peace with them.'"

In the tenth chapter of the *Apocalypse*, St. John revealed: "And I saw another mighty angel come down from heaven, clothed with a cloud, and a **rainbow** was on his head, and his face was as the sun, and his feet as pillars of fire. And he had in his hand a little book open: and he set his right foot upon the sea, and his left foot upon the earth. And he cried with a loud voice as when a lion roareth. And when he had cried, seven thunders uttered their voices."[182]

In an interpretation shared in *The Book of Destiny*, "This vision presents a powerful angel stepping into the wicked world to make a momentous revelation...His face shines like the face of Christ and reflects *a rainbow* from the cloud. In this apocalyptic verse, the word '**rainbow**' signifies a message of

---

[179] Apoc. 4: 1-3. [Emphasis added.]
[180] de Liguori, St. Alphonsus. *The Glories of Mary*, p. 203.
[181] Gen. 9:13.
[182] Apoc. 10: 1-3.

mercy although it forebodes the direst of all God's judgments upon the world."[183]

We might also recall that a rainbow usually boasts *seven* colors–red, orange, yellow, green, blue, purple (indigo), and violet (sometimes perceived as a deep pink, because, depending on the individual, it is possible to see the various hues within a rainbow). In the Church, there are seven Sacraments, seven gifts of the Holy Ghost, the Seven Last Words of Christ, the Seven Sorrows of Mary, the Seven Joys of Mary, the Seven Spiritual Works of Mercy, and the Seven Corporal Works of Mercy.

It is also intriguing to discover an observation made by Fr. James L. Meagher, a priest of the 19th century: "All through the *Bible* runs the sacred number *seven*, and in sevens the *Gospels* were written in the original Greek."[184]

Lastly, according to Fr. Herman Bernard Kramer's discernment of Catholic symbolism, the number "7" is considered as God's sacred number, the number of spiritual perfection, and the fundamental number of the *Apocalypse*.[185]

---

[183] Kramer, Rev. H. B., op. cit., pp. 239-240.

[184] Meagher, D.D., Fr. James L. *How Christ Said the First Mass.* [Rockford, IL: TAN Books & Publishers, 1984. Reprinted from the 1906 edition by Christian Press Association Publishing Co., NY, Reprinted several times, beginning in 1975, by Marian Publications, South Bend, IN]: p. 139.

[185] Kramer, Rev. H.B., op cit., p. 51.

CHAPTER 8

A Shower of Petals:
Our Lady of the Rosary, Mediatrix of All Graces

"...after Christ, we find in Mary the end of the law
and the fulfillment of the figures and oracles."
—Pope St. Pius X, "Ad Diem Illum Laetissimum," 1904 A.D.

"When will people learn that it is very easy to secure the friendship of Mary and that her protection destroys all the wiles of the devils?" asked Fr. H. O'Laverty, the author of *The Mother of God and Her Glorious Feasts*. "The friendship of Mary is not passing, like so many worldly friendships, which is based often on love of self rather than on love of others. Our Blessed Lady only wishes to bestow graces upon us and to bring us within the Sacred Heart of Jesus."[186]

It may seem strange to call the Mother of God "our friend," but did not Jesus call the Apostles His friends? *"I will not now call you servants: for the servant knoweth not what his lord doth. But I have called you friends: because all things whatsoever I have heard of my Father, I have made known to you."*[187]

To state a truth in the most simple of terms, the 1917 Fatima apparitions highlight the motherly solicitude and the friendship of Mary, who inevitably identified herself as the Lady of the Rosary while revealing herself as the Mediatrix of All Graces. In this section on the public, sensible signs manifested to the witnesses of the Fatima apparitions, we look at two signs yet to be examined:

• Onlookers to the third Apparition, which occurred on July 13, 1917 (the day the Virgin Mary gave to the children the Great Secret in its three distinct parts), testified to atmospheric changes, in which people saw "all the colors of the rainbow, pink, red, blue....*The trees seemed to be made not of leaves but of flowers*..."

• During the Apparition of September 13, the month before the promised Miracle, the sensible signs increased and included a shower of small white objects—described either as *petals, snowflakes, dove-shaped forms, stars, or*

---

[186] O'Laverty, *The Mother of God and Her Glorious Feasts,* p. 185.
[187] Jn. 15:15.

roses—all of which gently fell from the sky and disappeared before touching the ground.[188]

Flowering Trees at the Height of Summer

"The trees seemed to be made not of leaves but of flowers…" In this one sign alone, we will see that the flowers are a multi-faceted emblem of both the Virgin Mary and the Catholic Church established by Our Lord Jesus Christ, which alone offers the spiritual means to gain eternal salvation, and the heavenly garden of Paradise.

• Firstly, it is thought-provoking when one notices that witnesses of the July apparition never mentioned a likeness to a specific type of flower—for example, an apple, peach, pear, or cherry blossom. Instead, they simply used the generic term "flowers." The significance? All beautiful flowers symbolize the Virgin Mary's holiness and divine prerogatives.

To cite only a limited number of examples, the white *lily* (also known as the "Annunciation Lily") is a symbol of Our Lady's Immaculate purity; *impatiens* (called "Our Lady's Earrings") denote the Virgin's ears which heard God's word and kept it; the small *violet* reminds us of Mary's humility; the lovely *"Lady's Slipper"* flower calls to mind the Virgin's charity when she traveled on foot to the hill country to assist her elder cousin, St. Elizabeth, the mother of St. John the Baptist; the *columbine* represents the Holy Ghost overshadowing Our Lady; the *strawberry*, in flower and yet simultaneously bearing fruits, symbolizes the Perpetual Virginity of Mary, and the *marigold* ("Mary's Gold") signifies the glories of Mary, "a woman clothed with the sun" in the *Apocalypse*.[189]

• Secondly, the Old Testament's *Prophecy of Isaias* foretells, in figurative language, the budding and blossoming of God's kingdom on earth, the Catholic Church, despite the constant onslaughts against it from without and within: *"The land that was desolate and impassable shall be glad, and the wilderness shall rejoice, and shall flourish like the lily.* **It shall bud forth and blossom,** *and shall rejoice with joy and praise: the glory of Libanus is given to it: the beauty of Carmel, and Saron, they shall see the glory of the Lord, and the beauty of our God."*[190]

The Virgin Mary, Mother of the Church, came to Fatima with the most urgent of messages to save the Church from the wasteland of desolation, the

---

[188] Frère Michel, *TWTF*, Vol. I, p. 260.
[189] Stokes, Jr., John S. "Flower Theology." *Catholic Culture* website. [http://www.catholicculture.org/culture/library/view.cfm?recnum=5855]
[190] Prophecy of Isaias 35:2.

abomination of desolation. There may also be an implicit allusion to the *Apocalypse,* for the woman crowned with twelve stars flees to the wilderness. It has been shown that the royal woman of the *Apocalypse* is a figure-type, sometimes for the Virgin Mary and other times for the Church. One could truthfully state that Our Lady has been "chased" out of the Church, for in a great number of parishes there rarely exists any public devotion to her. The apocalyptic dragon, after chasing the woman into the wilderness, then goes out to seek war with her children—those who are still faithful to Christ and His Church, who still hold and practice a filial devotion to the Sacred and Immaculate Hearts.

• Thirdly, since flowers on trees produce fruits, it follows that celestial flowers are the signs of graces, given by God through the hands of Our Lady, strengthening the elect in practicing the supernatural virtues. St. Louis de Montfort taught: "If Mary, who is the tree of life, is well cultivated in our soul by fidelity to the practices of this devotion [to Jesus through Mary], she will bear her fruit in her own time, and her fruit is none other than Jesus Christ." [191] Pope Leo XIII expounded on the doctrine of Mary as Mediatrix of All Graces when he wrote: "With equal truth may it be also affirmed that, by the will of God, Mary is the intermediary through whom is distributed unto us this immense treasure of mercies gathered by God, for mercy and truth were created by Jesus Christ. Thus as no man goeth to the Father but by the Son, so no man goeth to Christ but by His Mother." [192]

However, just as Jesus could work no miracles in Nazareth due to unbelief, Fr. H. O'Laverty wrote that "Mary cannot give her gifts to those who will not receive them. How many pass by graces or refuse them, with the result that countless souls are lost. Every grace accepted means the increase of grace in others. Every soul sanctified means the sanctification of countless other souls." [193] This explanation appears to be another reason for the flowering of the trees, for God primarily acts in the world through people—that is, God acts through those who accept and use well the graces He sends, for the good of their own souls and that of others.

Thus the heavenly flowers which briefly replaced the trees' natural leaves, an event witnessed at the height of summer (when trees do not blossom but are already growing fruit) and lasting only through the time of Our Lady's Apparition, also appear to represent the Gifts of the Holy Ghost. Hence, the flowering trees represent the virtues and good works necessary for salvation,

---

[191] de Montfort, St. Louis. *True Devotion to Mary,* #218.

[192] Pope Leo XIII, *Octobri Mense* (On the Rosary, September 22, 1891): para. 4.

[193] O'Laverty, op. cit., p. 183.

which are never out of season. "By a voice he saith: Hear me, *ye divine offspring*, and bud forth as the rose planted by the brooks of waters. Send forth flowers, as the lily, and yield a smell, *and bring forth leaves in grace*, and praise with canticles, and bless the Lord in his works."[194]

• Fourthly, when explaining why we must accomplish all of our actions "in" the Virgin Mother of God, St. Louis de Montfort, known as the apostle of "true devotion to Jesus through Mary," wrote: "Thoroughly to understand this practice, we must first know that Our Blessed Lady is the true terrestrial paradise of the New Adam, and that the ancient paradise was but a figure of her...It is in this earthly paradise that *there is the true tree of life*, which has borne Jesus Christ, the Fruit of Life, and the tree of the knowledge of good and evil, which has given light unto the world. There are in this divine place *trees planted by the hand of God and watered by His divine unction*, which have borne and daily bear fruits of a divine taste. There are flowerbeds adorned with beautiful and varied *blossoms of virtues*."[195]

Almost two centuries later, Blessed John Henry Newman said, "A garden is a spot of ground set apart for trees and plants, all good, all various, for things that are sweet to the taste or fragrant in scent, or beautiful to look upon, or useful for nourishment; and accordingly in its spiritual sense it means the home of blessed spirits and holy souls dwelling there together, *souls with both the flowers and the fruits upon them*, which by the careful husbandry of God they have come to bear, *flowers and fruits of grace*, flowers more beautiful and more fragrant than those of any garden, fruits more delicious and exquisite than can be matured by earthly husbandman."[196]

He continued, "All that God has made speaks of its Maker; the mountains speak of His eternity; the sun of His immensity, and the winds of His Almightiness. In like manner *flowers and fruits speak of His sanctity, His love, and His providence*; and... since they are found in a garden, therefore a garden has also excellences which speak of God, because it is their home."[197] This mystical garden of Paradise is likewise a figure-type of the Virgin Mary.

"*My sister, my spouse is a garden enclosed, a fountain sealed up.*"[198] Those are the words of the Holy Ghost, speaking of His Beloved—the Virgin

---

[194] Eccles. 29: 17-19. [Emphasis added]
[195] de Montfort, op. cit., #261.. [Emphasis added.]
[196] Newman, Blessed John Henry. "Meditations on the Litany of Loreto, for the month of May: On the Immaculate Conception, Meditation #5: Mary is the '*Rosa Mystica*,' the Mystical Rose." *Newman Reader: Meditations and Devotions* website [http://www.newmanreader.org/works/meditations/meditations1.html] [Emphasis added.]
[197] Ibid. [Emphasis added.]
[198] Cant. 4:12.

that would bear Christ. St. Sophronius (560-638 A.D.) remarked, "Mary was this enclosed garden and sealed fountain, into which no guile could enter, against which no fraud of the enemy could prevail, and who always was holy in mind and body." Almost six centuries later, St. Bernard said something similar when addressing the Blessed Virgin: "Thou art an enclosed garden, into which the sinner's hand has never entered to pluck its flowers."[199]

• Finally, Blessed Newman reminds us that "our first parents were placed in 'a garden of pleasure' shaded by trees, 'fair to behold and pleasant to eat of,' with the Tree of Life in the midst, and a river to water the ground. Thus Our Lord, speaking from the cross to the penitent robber, calls the blessed place, the heaven to which He was taking him, 'paradise,' or a garden of pleasure. Therefore St. John, in the *Apocalypse*, speaks of heaven, the palace of God, as a garden or paradise, in which was the Tree of Life giving forth its fruits every month."[200]

A Shower of Signs in September

Other than the Miracle of the Sun, the final sensible sign to examine is the shower of small white objects, described either as *petals, snowflakes, dove-shaped forms, stars, or roses*, all of which gently fell from the sky and disappeared before touching the ground.

• **White:** The color white represents purity of mind, heart, and will. It is the symbol of prayer and good works for the conversion of sinners. Additionally, white is comprised of all seven colors of the rainbow and therefore signifies the whole of God's plan of Redemption.

• **Snow:** In the *Book of Proverbs*, we read: *"She shall not fear for her house in the cold of snow: for all her domestics are clothed with double garments,"* a passage that refers to the Virgin. St. Alphonsus de Liguori reminds us that these "domestics" are Mary's clients, and then he cites Cornelius à Lapide who said this double clothing "'consists in her adorning her faithful servants with the virtues of her Son and with her own,' and thus clothed they persevere in virtue."[201]

• **Doves:** *"Those who are led by the Spirit of God are the children of God."* [202] From the time of antiquity, a white dove is the symbol of the Holy Ghost, the Spirit of God. The dove is seen in representations of the Annunciation (the Incarnation of Jesus Christ), the Lord's Baptism, and the descent of the Holy Ghost upon Mary and the Apostles at Pentecost. The dove

---

[199] de Liguori, St. Alphonsus. *The Glories of Mary,* p. 306.
[200] Newman, loc. cit.
[201] de Liguori, op. cit., p. 93.
[202] Rom. 8:14.

is also the symbol of the Sacrament of Confirmation, which means the sacrament of "strengthening," through which the confirmed person is then called "a soldier of Christ because he is especially deputed to profess the faith strongly and fight for it."[203]

The dove is also the symbol of the Virgin Mary. St. Alphonsus explained: "Mary was prefigured by the dove which returned to Noah in the Ark with an olive branch in its beak, as a pledge of the peace which God granted to men. And on this idea St. Bonaventure thus addresses Our Blessed Lady: 'Thou art the most faithful dove; thou was a sure mediatress [sic] between God and the world, lost in a spiritual deluge; thou, by presenting thyself before God, hast obtained for a lost world peace and salvation.' Mary, then, was the heavenly dove which brought to a lost world the olive-branch, the sign of mercy, since she in the first place gave us Jesus Christ, who is the source of mercy; and then, by His merits, obtained all graces for us."[204]

Again, the saint tells how Mary is likened to a dove in the *Canticles*, wherein it is written: "There are…young maidens without number. *One is my dove, my perfect one* (in the Hebrew, it is *"my entire, my immaculate one"*) is *but one, she is the only one of her mother.*"[205] St. Alphonsus continued: "All just souls are daughters of divine grace; but amongst these Mary was the *dove* without the gall of sin; the *perfect* one without spot in her origin, the *one* conceived in grace."[206]

• **Stars**–as mentioned in a previous chapter–remind us that God is the Creator and that we are the created; simultaneously, they remind us that the "works of God show forth His glory, that His law is greatly to be esteemed and loved," and "that mankind cannot comprehend His power and wisdom."[207]

Recalling that Scripture passages often possess both a literal and spiritually figurative meaning, we also know that in the Old Testament, *stars* also signify the elect–i.e., true believers in and of the Church, the Body of Christ. "In *Genesis*, the patriarchs, head of the twelve tribes of Israel, are also called **stars**. And the words of *Daniel* (7:10) cannot be restricted to the priests only of the Antiochean persecution but surely embrace all martyrs of that ordeal. If the

---

[203] *Baltimore Catechism and Mass #3*, Lesson 25: Confirmation, #330.
[204] de Liguori, op. cit., p. 203.
[205] Cant. 6:7, as cited by St. Alphonsus de Liguori, Ibid., p. 307.
[206] de Liguori, op. cit., p. 307.
[207] Commentator Prefaces to *The Book of Psalms*, Ch. 18, and *The Book of Job*, Ch. 8, in the *Holy Bible*, Douay-Rheims version.

chosen people are called stars, much more appropriately so the true believers of Jesus Christ."[208]

In the *Apocalypse*, the Lord speaks of giving the morning star to "he that shall overcome," yet in another passage, Jesus—who is Priest, Prophet, and King—calls Himself the *Morning Star*.[209] Elsewhere in the *Book of Revelations*, *stars* indicate a group who occupy offices of high estate; they symbolize the Catholic hierarchy (bishops and priests).[210]

Finally, again is repeated the reference to the apocalyptic passage that may be the one most well known throughout the world. It is also the one that many believe is the infallible prophecy foretelling the authentic Marian apparitions of the modern age—and specifically those of Our Lady of Fatima: "And a great sign appeared in heaven: A woman clothed with the sun, and the moon under her feet, and on her head a crown of twelve *stars*..."[211]

• **Roses:** Finally, the white rose is the symbol of pure love (charity) and beauty of soul, which explains why it is the foremost symbol of the Virgin Mary, who is called the Mystical Rose of Heaven. As the rose is also considered the Queen of Flowers, so Our Lady is hailed as the Queen of Heaven. The rose is likewise an emblem of the Holy Faith, martyrdom, and the secrecy of the Sacrament of Penance, while five roses grouped together symbolize the Five Wounds of Christ, from whence all graces flow.[212]

---

[208] Kramer, Rev. Herman Bernard, *The Book of Destiny*, p. 282.
[209] Apoc. 2: 26-29; 22:16.
[210] Apoc. 1:20.
[211] Apoc. 12:1.
[212] Morrow, Bishop Louis LaRavoire. *My Catholic Faith: A Manual in Religion*. [Kansas City, MO: Sarto House. Republished from the 1954 edition by Sarto House, January 2000]: p. 396.

CHAPTER 9

October: The Promised Sign

"For she is more beautiful than the sun, and above all the order of the stars: being compared with the light, she is found before it."
—Wisdom 7:9

As we have seen, from May through October 1917, the hamlet of Fatima, Portugal was graced by the presence of the Virgin Mother of God. Shining brighter than the sun, veiled and gowned in white, adorned with the Star of Esther and a luminous necklace from which hung a brighter orb, with a Rosary suspended from her right arm, the Lady promised three shepherd children, "In October, I will tell you who I am and what I want, and I will perform a miracle so that all may see and believe."[213] The vow was fulfilled with the most stupendous *public* miracle since the parting of the Red Sea. Symbolizing Christ, the Great Miracle of the Sun (like the Star of Esther on Our Lady's gown), is a "figure-type," illustrating once more that "the miracles of Our Lord and the signs accomplished by Our Lady of Fatima are not only extraordinary facts which bear witness to their supernatural origin, they are also symbols rich in meaning, the sensible expressions of mystery."[214]

Our Lady in the Modern Age

"The intervention of God in human history through the Fatima events was predicted in the Bible and is God's definitive response to the revolt of many nations and peoples away from the revelation and rule of Jesus Christ," explained Father Joseph de St. Marie, Professor of Theology at the Pontifical Faculty of Saint Theresa in Rome. "The revolt against God is the 'mystery of iniquity' of which Saint Paul speaks, saying that it is already in operation."[215]

Let us then consider the Great Revolt of the "Modern Age," which began in the 1500's near the end of the Renaissance era and continues to our times. Of great import to the Church and the faithful, each heinous step of this Revolt occurred two hundred years apart, the last of them coinciding with Our Lady's

---

[213] Frère Michel, *TWTF*, Vol. I, p.181.
[214] Ibid., p. 262.
[215] de St. Marie, Fr. Joseph (Professor of Theology, Pontifical Faculty of Saint Theresa, Rome). "Our Lady of Fatima is the Fulfillment of Biblical Prophecy." [http://www.worldenslavementorpeace.com/e1cp2.asp]

appearances at Fatima: the revolt of Luther (1517), the public establishment of Freemasonry (1717), and the birth of Bolshevism (1917).

Note also how the Great Revolt against the Church, which began in 1517, is comprised of **three distinct parts**—just like its antidote, the Great Secret of Fatima, which opened with a vision of hell because so many souls condemn themselves to eternal perdition. Thus the first step of the Revolt marks the 16th century as "the epoch of humanism and also of the Lutheran drama, of the Protestant revolt. Humanism was a cultural movement admittedly, but it was also a return to paganism under the color of culture. As for Luther, he was at the very beginning of the division of Christian Europe. He was the great divider: *'Gott ist im Himmel, du bist auf Erden' ('God is in His Heaven; you are on earth').* Between heaven and earth, Luther establishes an impassable abyss. He denies all mediations. In the end Luther, who talks so much about Christ, denies the mediation of Christ's Humanity. A *fortiori,* he denies the mediation of Christ's Mother, His Co-Redemptrix."[216] Herein lies the essential significance of the 16th Century: "The affirmation of man, of rupture between heaven and earth by the denial of the mediations which unite them: Christ, Mary, and first of all the Church. Such is the beginning of the revolt of modern times against God."[217]

To this first revolt of the Modern Age, the hierarchy of the Church ultimately responded at the infallible Council of Trent (1570). Still, the evil continued to spread into the 17th century. Heresy insidiously spread throughout Christendom, finally reaching France, "the eldest daughter of the Church," so-called because it was the first nation to publicly proclaim Catholicism as the state religion. Although condemned as a heresy, Jansenism rippled throughout the country, which explains the French bishops' resistance to St. Louis de Montfort's apostolate of *True Devotion to Jesus through Mary.* The Jansenist crisis, however, led to a worse one.

Near the end of the 17th century, Our Lord attempted to save the Church and France by His direct intervention via the Sacred Heart apparitions at Paray-le-Monial, France. Jesus asked for reparation to His Sacred Heart, especially in the form of the Nine First Fridays, and He also sent a special request to the King of France. Above all, as He offered His Divine Mercy, He spoke of the ingratitude of sinners which would soon demand His Justice.

St. Margaret Mary revealed, "Our Lord showed Himself to me covered with wounds, His body all bleeding and His Heart torn with grief; He seemed overcome with fatigue. I threw myself at His feet, filled with a great fear, and I

---

[216] Ibid.
[217] Ibid.

dared not say a word to Him. He said to me: 'Behold to what I am reduced by My chosen people whom I had called to appease My justice, and they persecute Me in secret. If they do not mend their ways, I will punish them severely; I will withdraw the good, and the rest I will devote to My just wrath, which will flame up against them.'"[218]

Not thirty years later, in 1717, Freemasonry was born. A secret society, it bears a special hatred for the Catholic Church, "and its avowed aim to destroy the Church is confirmed in Catholic and Masonic documents alike [219] ... Within 50 years, Masonry's well-known battle cry was 'to overcome Throne and Altar'—that is, monarchies and Catholicism."[220]

Still, the patient Lord waited for the members of His Church to repent and offer reparation, but not enough did so. He waited for the king of France to heed Him—but to no avail. "The 18th Century saw a further expansion of rebellion which reached its climax in the French Revolution, the first great act of organized political rebellion against God."[221]

Deeply offended, the Merciful "Heart of Christ somehow withdrew behind the Heart of Mary" for "men had refused to respond, or had given insufficient response, to the appeal" [222] of the Sacred Heart. The passion of France began in July 1789, commencing exactly **100 years to the day** that Our Lord made known to St. Margaret Mary Alacoque a special request: To save France from the enemies of the Church, the Catholic monarch must solemnly consecrate himself and the country to His Sacred Heart, thus publicly proclaiming that France placed her trust in God. [223] For 100 years, the kings ignored the request; the tragic result was the French Revolution. France, "eldest daughter of the Church," succumbed to the Masonic Revolution's savagery and its pernicious attack against altar and throne.

In many ways, the doom of 18th century France prefigures both the Third Secret Vision of Fatima and the reign of apocalyptic anti-Christ. Here will be mentioned the **three** most pertinent parallels:

• **First,** the line of Catholic monarchs who failed to honor the Sacred Heart's consecration request, a rejection which eventually led to the apostasy in

---

[218] "The Hour of Reparation," *Home with God* website. [http://our.homewithgod.com/sacredheart/sacred4/]

[219] Vennari, John. *The Permanent Instruction of the Alta Vendita.* [Rockford IL: TAN Books and Publishers; Copyright 1999 by the author]: p. 14.

[220] Ibid., p. 38.

[221] de St. Marie, op. cit.

[222] Ibid.

[223] Gheon, Henri. "The Secret of Saint Margaret Mary." *Secrets of the Saints* [Garden City, NY: Image Books: 1963]. Republished on the *Catholic Information Network* (CIN) website. [http://www.cin.org/sstmargm.html]

France [historically prefiguring the failure of a line of Catholic Stewards of the Catholic City—the Popes—to command the bishops of the world to participate in a solemn, collegial consecration of Russia to the Immaculate Heart of Mary];

• **Second,** the rightful king's imprisonment, which ended in his unjust and public execution, lasted 3 ½ years (the length of time in which anti-Christ will persecute the faithful);

• **Third,** the cruel deaths of the monarch, his queen, and the little Dauphin, all of which were both preceded and followed by the martyrdoms of those who were faithful to Catholicism and to the kingly office [so like the Third Secret Vision in which "a bishop dressed in white" and others before and after him are killed, most likely as martyrs for Christ and also for their fidelity to the papal office].

The 19th century was a "catastrophe for the Church and for the Faith…God could tolerate no more: He could no longer permit men's crimes to go without chastisement; yet neither could He cease to seek to spare us through pure mercy."[224] So it was that Our Lord sent His Mother to the world.

Beginning with the Rue-de Bac in Paris (1830), Our Lady also appeared at Blangy (1840), LaSalette (1846), Lourdes (1858), Pontmain (1871), Pellevoisin (1876), and Knock, Ireland (1879). With the exception of Our Lady of Guadalupe in Mexico (1531), the others that followed in Europe and Ireland became the very first Marian apparitions of modern times. With the 1830 series of apparitions to St. Catherine Labouré, Our Lady gave the world the "Medal of the Immaculate Conception" (commonly known as "the Miraculous Medal"), with its inscription, "O Mary, conceived without sin, pray for us who have recourse to thee." At each of the apparitions, she always showed herself the Mother of Mercy and the Mediatrix of All Graces.

The year of Our Lord 1917 marked the third year in which the world suffered from the first universal war. It should be noted that Our Lady did not again come to earth until that year, when the third part of the Great Revolt was imminent. The Secrets of Fatima, "in their known contents" as Cardinal Ratzinger phrased it in 1984, allow us to reasonably deduce that the Virgin came to warn the Church that mankind had entered a critical juncture in history—specifically, the "revolt" [literally, "apostasy"] that must come first, as foretold by St. Paul.[225] It is this last Revolt that possesses the ability to lead the entire world into the age of great distress among all nations, thus initiating an even greater, three-fold chastisement, prophesied by St. Luke in his eschatological discourse and by St. John in the *Apocalypse*.

---

[224] Ibid.
[225] 2 Thess. 2.

Bolshevism, arising in 1917, completed the "trinity of errors" of the "Modern Age." As we have already seen, the first part of the Great Revolt consists of philosophical error (which departs from the Church's philosophy of scholasticism). From this error sprang the other two—theological ambiguity and political-social secularism.[226] "And let it be noted; at the very moment when, as a consequence of the Bolshevik victory, the '*Red Dragon*' emerged at one extremity of Europe in Leningrad, which then was still Petrograd, at the other extremity of Europe, at Fatima…there appeared the '*Woman Clothed with the Sun*,' the Immaculate Heart of Mary. Such was the miracle of October 13, 1917, the Miracle of the Sun, a miracle which calls for an entire book to itself…But, dear friends, this sun is the symbol of Christ."[227]

The Effects of Divine Mercy

Thrice foretold in the preceding three months, witnessed by 70,000-100,000 people, the astounding Miracle of the Sun marks Fatima as unique amongst all Church-authenticated Marian apparitions. The "Great Sign," given on October 13, 1917, majestically summarizes the whole Fatima message of God's Divine Mercy and Justice, which are inseparable.

"Among the effects of Divine Mercy," said St. John Eudes, "we must enumerate three principal realities, which in turn embody numberless effects. **The first** is the Incarnation of the God-Man; **the second**, his Mystical Body, namely Holy Church; **the third** is the Mother of the God-Man, namely the Most Blessed Virgin Mary. These constitute three admirable masterpieces of Divine Mercy."[228] Possessing theological and Mariological depths which no one could hope to fully explore, these *three* principal masterpieces nevertheless resonate throughout the Fatima revelations. They are manifested in the Great Secret (in three distinct parts) and the Great Miracle (in three marked phases). Conversely, the Great Revolt's three parts utterly oppose these holy realities.

During the whole night and morning of Oct. 12-13, 1917, a "thin, persistent rain fell, wetting the fields, muddying the ground, and penetrating with its cold humidity"[229] all those making their way to Fatima. No doubt, Heaven had many reasons for sending this permeating rain, which might be summed up as a chance to offer as a sacrifice for the conversion of sinners that which the Lord

---

[226] Chojnowski, Dr. Peter. "The Miracle of the Sun as Proclamation of the Universal Queenship of Mary." *Catholic Family News*, November 2007: p.16.
[227] de St. Marie, op. cit.
[228] Eudes, St. John. "Divine Mercy Mirrored in Mary's Heart," excerpted from *The Admirable Heart of Mary*, Part Five, Chapter I.
[229] Frère Michel, op. cit., p. 287.

allows us to suffer and as a "sensible sign" of the graces God wishes to dispense through the hands of the Immaculate One.

Many people expected the miracle to begin promptly at noon, according to the clock, not realizing that the Lady appeared at the solar noon hour–that is, according to the sun's time. In October, the difference between solar time and clock time was that of an hour and a half, which explains why witnesses would later say that the children arrived just before one o'clock (11:30 a.m. by the sun's time) or that they saw the cloud around 1:30 p.m. (solar noon), which occurs in the following account.

"I am going to relate to you in a brief and concise manner, without any statements which would conceal the truth, what I saw in Fatima on 13 October, 1917," wrote Dr. Joseph Almeida Garrett, Professor of Natural Sciences at Coimbra University, who penned his witness account in December, 1917. "I arrived at midday. The rain which had fallen persistently all morning, combined with a blustery wind, continued fretfully, as if threatening to drown everyone. The dull and heavy sky, its dark-grey clouds water-laden, predicted abundant rain for a long time to come."

"I remained on the road in the shelter of the hood of my car, looking rather disdainfully towards the place where they said the apparition would be seen, not daring to step on the sodden and muddy earth of the freshly-ploughed field. I was a little more than a hundred meters [about 330 feet] from the high wooden posts mounted by a rough cross, seeing distinctly the wide circle of people who, with their umbrellas open, seemed like a vast arena of mushrooms. A little after one o'clock, the children to whom Our Lady, as they declare, appeared and appointed the place, day and hour of the apparition, arrived at the site. Hymns were intoned and sung by the people who gathered about them. At a certain moment, this immense mass of people, so varied and compact, closed their umbrellas and uncovered their heads in a gesture that could have been one of humility or respect, but which left me surprised and bewildered, because now the rain, with a blind persistency, poured down on their heads and drenched them through. Later, I was told that this crowd, who finished up by kneeling in the mud, had obeyed the voice of a child." Indeed, it was true that Lucia, in anticipation of the Virgin's imminent arrival, had asked the people to close their umbrellas.

"It must have been about half-past one when there rose up, on the precise spot where the children were, a pillar of smoke, a delicate, slender, bluish column that went straight up to about two meters, perhaps above their heads and then evaporated. The phenomenon lasted for some seconds and was perfectly visible to the naked eye…It was repeated yet a second and third time. On these three occasions, and especially on the last one, the slender posts stood out distinctly in the dull grey atmosphere."

Note that Dr. Joseph Almeida Garrett carefully observed the wondrous pillar of smoke and yet wrote in his account that he had been "looking at the spot of the apparitions, in a serene, if cold, expectation of something happening and with diminishing curiosity because **a long time had passed without anything to excite my attention**."[230]

One may well consider the professor's latter words, pondering if the oppressive difficulties of the perseverant faithful—thousands of people exhaustedly making their way through persistent rain and wind that was at first annoying but then chilled them to the bone, spattered and then bogged down with the heavy mud of this earth, mocked by others and yet filled with hope—and who perhaps, like Dr. Garrett, also felt that a "long time had passed without anything to excite [their] attention" are symbolically indicative of the years and the many spiritual trials the Church Militant shall continually endure until *all* of Our Lady's requests are finally heeded. For although a long time has indeed passed since the Mother of God made her requests, we know that their accomplishment will immediately result in the fruition of the Virgin's promise: "In the end, my Immaculate Heart will triumph. The Holy Father will consecrate Russia to me and she will be converted and an era of peace will be granted to the world."

What the Children Saw on October 13, 1917

The cloud which appeared indicated the Virgin's arrival and, as usual, Lucia asked the Lady what she wanted. She revealed to the three children who she is and what she sought: *"I want a chapel to be built here in my honor, for I am the Lady of the Rosary. Continue to say the Rosary every day. The war will end soon and the soldiers will return to their homes."*

Lucia said she had many things to ask of the Lady, "to heal some sick people, and to convert some sinners, etc." To this general request, the Virgin gravely responded: *"Some, yes; others, no. People must amend their lives and ask pardon for their sins."* Growing sadder, she said, *"Do not offend the Lord our God any longer; He is already deeply offended.* [231]

---

[230] Johnston, Francis. *Fatima: The Great Sign.* [Rockford, IL: TAN Books & Publishers, 1980. With Nihil Obstat, Fr. Vincentius Codina, C.M.F. and Imprimatur, Alberto Cosme de Amartal, Bishop of Fatima]: p. 61.
[231] Sr. Mary Lucia, *Memoirs,* 1976 edition, pp. 172-173.

"Then, opening her hands, Our Lady made them reflect on the sun and, as she ascended, the reflection of her own light continued to be projected on the sun itself." [232]

Here, as with other manifestations at Fatima (like the mysterious pillars of cloud thrice arising from the holmoak tree upon which Our Lady stood,[233] a phenomenon mentioned, 60 years later, when the Cardinal Patriarch of Lisbon publicly stated at the 8th Fatima Congress at Kevelaer, Germany, on September 18, 1977, "While the death of God is proclaimed with arrogant glee, Fatima appears to be a supernatural light. It is God who reveals Himself with the impressive majesty of Sinai"[234]), we recognize anew that incredible Mariophany of which Sr. Lucia would later write, addressing the Virgin as "a living tabernacle, a Monstrance, a living Temple, the permanent abode of the Most Holy Trinity." [235] Surely those words of Sr. Lucia's grant a breath-taking glimpse into the "lights about this mystery" (the Holy Trinity) that she later received as a young nun but was not permitted to reveal. [236]

Lucia continued, "After Our Lady had disappeared into the immense distance of the firmament, we beheld St. Joseph with the Child Jesus and Our Lady robed in white with a blue mantle, beside the sun. St. Joseph and the Child Jesus appeared to bless the world, for they traced the Sign of the Cross with their hands."

"When, a little later, this apparition disappeared, I saw Our Lord and Our Lady; it seemed to me that it was Our Lady of Sorrows. Our Lord appeared to bless the world in the same manner as St. Joseph had done."

"This apparition also vanished, and I saw Our Lady once more, this time resembling Our Lady of Mt. Carmel."[237]

At the precise moment, Our Lady cast her own light upon the sun, the drenching rain suddenly stopped, the brooding clouds dispersed, and the sky became clearer. The sudden change immediately attracted attention of the great crowd of thousands.

---

[232] Ibid.

[233] Frère Michel, op. cit., p. 260.

[234] Johnston, op. cit., p. 70.

[235] Sr. Maria Lucia of the Immaculate Heart, "Letter on the Rosary," April 12, 1970. Published by S. Martina dos Reis, *Uma Vida*: pp. 372-373. Cited in Frère Michel, *TWTF*, Vol. 1: p. 284.

[236] Frère Michel, *TWTF*, Vol. II. [Buffalo, NY: Immaculate Heart Publications, English translation copyright 1989 by the author]: pp. 461-500.

[237] Frère Michel,. *TWTF*, Vol. I, pp. 293-294.

What the People Saw

Many witnesses, both poor and rich, uneducated or cultured, believers or scoffers, testified to what happened next. First among them is the faithful Ti Marto, the father of Blessed Jacinta and Blessed Francisco: "We looked easily at the sun, which did not blind us. It seemed to flicker on and off, first one way and then another. It shot rays in different directions and painted everything in different colors... What was most extraordinary is that the sun did not hurt our eyes at all. Everything was still and quiet; everyone was looking upwards..."[238]

O Dia, the Libson newspaper, described the Miracle in this way: "At midday by the sun, the rain stopped. The sky, pearly grey in color, illuminated the vast arid landscape with a strange light. The sun had a transparent gauzy veil so that the eye could easily be fixed on it. The grey mother-of-pearl tone turned into a sheet of silver which broke up as the clouds were parted and the silver sun, enveloped in the same gauzy grey light, was seen to whirl and turn in the circle of broken clouds. A cry went up from every mouth and people fell on their knees in the muddy ground...The light turned a beautiful blue as though through the window of a cathedral. The blue faded slowly and then the light seemed to pass through yellow glass. Yellow stain fell on white handkerchiefs against the dark skirts of the women. The colors were repeated on the stones and the serra."[239]

Perhaps most astonishing is the report published in *O Seculo*, the anti-Catholic, Masonic daily paper of Lisbon, Portugal, written by none other than the paper's Editor-in-Chief, Avelino de Almedia. We must give credit to this man who, despite his leanings, honestly reported what he witnessed regardless of the heckling and derision that he knew he would receive from his employers and fellow journalists:

"...one could see the immense multitude turn toward the sun, which appeared at its zenith, coming out of the clouds."

"It resembles a dull silver disc, and it is possible to fix one's eyes on it without the least damage to the eye. It does not burn the eyes. It does not blind them. One might say that an eclipse was taking place."

"An immense clamor bursts out, and those who are nearer to the crowd hear a shout: 'Miracle! Miracle! Prodigy!...Prodigy!'

"The attitude of the people takes us back to biblical times. Stupefied and with heads uncovered, they watch the blue sky. Before their dazzled eyes the sun trembled, the sun made unusual and brusque movements, defying all the

---

[238] Ibid., p. 292.
[239] Johnston, op cit., pp. 62-63.

laws of the cosmos, and according to the typical expression of the peasants, *'the sun danced'...*"

Fifteen days later, after receiving the expected mocking, Almedia enumerated previously omitted details: "What did I see at Fatima that was even stranger? The rain, at an hour announced in advance, ceased falling; the thick mass of clouds dissolved; and the sun–a dull, silver disc–came into view at its zenith, and began to dance in a violent and convulsive movement, which a great number of witnesses compared to a serpentine dance, because the colors taken on by the surface of the sun were so beautiful and gleaming."[240]

Dr. Garrett also described "a disc, with a clear cut rim, luminous and shining, but which did not hurt the eyes. I do not agree with the comparison which I have heard made in Fatima–that of a dull silver disc. It was a clearer, richer, brighter color, having something of the lustre of a pearl. It did not in the least resemble the moon on a clear night because one saw it and *felt it to be a living body*...It looked like a glazed wheel made of mother-of-pearl."[241]

"A Wheel of Fire"

As witnesses testified, the "dance of the sun" was repeated *three* times, with many likening its movements to a "a wheel of fire, "a bicycle wheel," a "captive ball of fire," etc. For ten to twelve minutes, the people stood transfixed in wonder, before their amazement turned to terror as the sun suddenly crashed toward the earth:

• "As if from a bolt from the blue, the clouds were wrenched apart, and the sun at its zenith appeared in all its splendor. It began to revolve vertiginously on its axis, like the most magnificent *firewheel* that could be imagined, taking on all the colors of the rainbow and sending forth multi-coloured flashes of light, producing the most astounding affect. This sublime and incomparable spectacle, which was repeated three distinct times, lasted for about ten minutes. The immense multitude, overcome by the evidence of such a prodigy, threw themselves on their knees. The Creed, the Hail Mary, Acts of Contrition burst from all lips, and tears, tears of thanksgiving and repentance sprang from their eyes." (Dr. Formigão, professor of the seminary at Santarem)[242]

• "It seemed like a *wheel of fire* which was going to fall on the people." (Maria Carreira)

• "...it spun like a *firewheel*." (Maria do Carmo Marques da Cruz Menezes)

• "...it spun round upon itself in a *mad whirl*." (Dr. Almeida Garrett)

---

[240] Frère Michel, op. cit. pp. 323-324.

[241] Ibid., p. 336.

[242] Johnston, op. cit., p. 63.

• "It came down as if to the height of the clouds and began to whirl giddily upon itself like a *captive ball of fire*." (Fr. Pereira da Silva)

• "I saw the sun spinning round and it seemed about to come down on us. It revolved like a *bicycle wheel*. Afterward, it returned to its place…I wasn't afraid, but I heard people cry out: 'Oh, we're going to die! We are going to die!'" (John Carreira, the crippled son of Maria Carreira, and later sacristan of the Fatima shrine)[243]

• "I saw the sun, as if it were a *ball of fire*, begin to move in the clouds. It had been raining all morning and the sky was full of clouds, but the rain stopped. It lasted for several seconds, crushingly pressing down on us. Wan faces, standing here, from every side great ejaculations, acts of contrition, of the love of God. An indescribable moment! We feel it. We remain dominated by it. But it is not possible to describe it." (Carlos Mendes, a lawyer)[244]

• "At a certain moment, the sun seemed to stop and then began to move and dance." (Ti Marto, father of Francisco and Jacinta Marto)

• "However, the sun stops, only to begin the strange dance again after a brief interruption, whirling upon itself, giving the impression of approaching or receding." (Dr. Pereira Gens of Batalha)[245]

• "Then suddenly, one heard a clamor, a cry of anguish breaking from all the people. The sun, whirling wildly, seemed to loosen itself from the firmament and advance threateningly upon the earth, as if to crush us with its huge and fiery weight. **The sensation during those moments was terrible**." (Dr. Almeida Garrett)[246]

• "At a certain moment, the sun seemed to stop and then began to move and dance until it seemed that *it was being detached from the sky and was falling on us*. **It was a terrible moment**." (Ti Marto)[247]

• "It suddenly seemed to come down in a zig-zag, menacing the earth. **Terrified**, I ran and hid myself among the people, who were weeping and expecting the end of the world to come at any moment." (Fr. Lourenco, who witnessed the Miracle as a schoolboy.)[248]

• "I looked at the sun and saw it spinning like a disc, rolling on itself. I saw people changing color. They were stained with colors of the rainbow. The sun

---

[243] Ibid.
[244] Ibid., pp. 63-64.
[245] Frère Michel, op. cit., p. 337-338.
[246] Ibid., p. 339.
[247] Ibid.
[248] Ibid., p. 343.

seemed to be falling from the sky…The people said that the world was going to end…They were afraid and screaming." (Antonio de Oliveiro, farmer)[249]

- "I saw the sun turn upon itself; it seemed to fall from the sky…The people around me were crying that the world was going to end." (Maria dos Prazeres, widow)[250]

- "The sun started to roll from one place to another and changed to blue, yellow—all colors. Then we saw the sun coming towards the children. Everyone was crying out. Some started to confess their sins because there was no priest around here…My mother grabbed me to her and started to cry, 'It is the end of the world!' And then we see the sun come right into the trees…" (Dominic Reis, in a 1960 television interview)[251]

- "Suddenly the rain stopped and a great splendor appeared and the children cried, 'Look at the sun!' I saw the sun coming down, feeling that it was falling to the ground. At that moment, I collapsed." (Maria Candida da Silva)[252]

- "I looked and saw that the people were in various colors—yellow, white, blue. At the same time, I beheld the sun spinning at great speed and very near to me. I at once thought: I am going to die." (Rev. Joao Menitra)[253]

- "The sun at its zenith whirled upon itself; it detached itself in descending towards the right, all the while whirling with sudden movements never seen before, to the right and the left; having almost arrived at the horizon line, it went back up to the zenith on the left, *tracing a sort of winding ellipse as it went.*" (Baron de Alvaiazere)[254]

The frightened people, watching the sun return to its place in the heavens, had not yet noticed that their drenched and mud-soaked clothing was now clean and dry. Certainly, one can ponder even this prodigy, which reminds us of God's abiding Providence. So many pilgrims had for days traveled to Fatima, and then faced a downpour that led them through mud up to two feet deep. Their shoes and lower apparel were caked with muck, their hair and clothes soaked, their bodies thoroughly chilled—and then within the ten to twelve minutes during the Miracle of the Sun, they were spotless, warm, dry, restored. This wonder, however, was not what moved them to instinctively raise their voices in an ecstasy of exultation.

---

[249] Johnston, op. cit., p. 64.
[250] Ibid.
[251] Ibid.
[252] Ibid.
[253] Ibid.
[254] Frère Michel, op. cit., p. 340.

"What could be more overwhelming in impact than the sun plunging like fire from Heaven while tens of thousands lay writhing in the mud, screaming for mercy, convinced that the end of the world had arrived?" asked Francis Johnston, a Catholic writer on Marian apparitions. "At Fatima, we have 100,000 eyewitnesses of all faiths and none, united in their conviction that this indeed was the end of the world. And afterwards, when they found themselves alive and safe, but quivering with fear, they were seized by the realization that God had stamped His Mother's words with a colossal preview of His Second Coming. Why then should we not ponder their unanimous testimony and take seriously to heart the crucial message which the solar Miracle so heavily underscored?"[255]

"We have seen the Sign of God!" the crowd cried in joy and thanksgiving, "spontaneously using the most exact biblical term, which also evokes the mysterious prophecy of the *Apocalypse...A great sign appeared in heaven, a woman clothed with the sun...*(Apoc.12:1)"[256]

Virgin of Fatima & the *Apocalypse:*
The Great Sign in Heaven
The apocalyptic verse above continues "...and the moon under her feet, and on her head a crown of twelve stars. And being with child, she cried travailing in birth, and was in pain to be delivered. *And there was seen another sign in heaven*: and behold a great red dragon, having seven heads, and ten horns: and on his head seven diadems: And his tail drew the third part of the stars of heaven, and cast them to the earth: and the dragon stood before the woman who was ready to be delivered; that, when she should be delivered, he might devour her son. And she brought forth a man child, who was to rule all nations with an iron rod: and her son was taken up to God, and to his throne."[257]

"Before the eyes of the Seer [St. John], a great sign, the first of the 'signs,' a portent of something momentous, appears *in the Church*. It is a sign of divine origin," explains Rev. Herman Bernard Kramer in *The Book of Destiny*.[258] Previously, it was explained that, in apocalyptic symbolism, the word "heaven" (in the singular sense) means "the Church," which is the kingdom of God on earth.[259] It follows that the great sign of "a woman clothed with the sun" appears *in the Church*.

---

[255] Johnston, op. cit., pp. 69-70.
[256] Frère Michel, op. cit., p. 356.
[257] Apoc. 12: 1-4.
[258] Kramer, Rev. H.B., *The Book of Destiny*, p. 275.
[259] Ibid., p. 200.

It shall also be repeated that, throughout salvation history, the signs of God indicate various purposes. **A true sign** can possess any one or more of the following seven functions: It confirms God's Word, His goodness, authenticates prophesy, verifies God's blessings and His intervention for the sake of the elect, strengthens the faithful with hope, insures or testifies to God's Presence, or declares His judgment upon sin.

"Signs in prophetical terminology are ominous revelations of what is about to happen," as Rev. Kramer wrote in his commentary on *Apocalypse*, Chapter 12. "Therefore the apostles asked Our Lord for the 'sign' of His coming.[260] The Pharisees demanded 'a sign from Heaven' as a proof of Our Lord's claim to divinity."[261] In the sense intended by the Pharisees, a sign is a miracle from Heaven. [262] However, Rev. Kramer adds a sobering insight: "The word furthermore denotes the wonders wrought by evil powers."[263]

In considering Rev. Kramer's phrasing, along with the seven purposes of signs as they are given in the Scriptures, [264] three things are understood, as follows: **1)** signs, in and of themselves, are either good or evil, the good coming from God but the evil only permitted by God, 2) signs are "ominous," a word which can mean "portentous, significant, promising, ill-omened, threatening, or boding evil," and **3)** the actual appearance of the sign reveals "what is about to happen."

Rev. Kramer continued, "In the Septuagint, the word is used for *celestial phenomena.*[265] The sign [of "a woman clothed with the sun"] appearing here is GREAT, because it will indicate the time of the judgment that shall proclaim the 'Great Day' of Almighty God. *It will herald the near approach of the events narrated in chapters eleven and thirteen.* Appearing in heaven, it will point to the center of the whole desperate struggle for the possession of the world by Satan and his hordes. **When this sign appears in the Church, the advent of Antichrist is near...The interpretation of this 'sign' is thus very important.**"[266]

Since the *Apocalypse* is not necessarily written as a chronology—that is, as an exact order of events—Rev. Kramer's view that the great sign of *Apocalypse*

---

[260] Matt. 24:3.
[261] Mc. 8:11; Mt. 16:1, as footnoted by Rev. H. B. Kramer, op. cit.
[262] Lk.11:16.
[263] Kramer, Rev. H. B., loc. cit.
[264] For New Testament examples, see Mt. 12: 39; Mt. 24:30; Mt. 26:48; Lk. 2:12; Lk. 2:34; Lk. 11:30; Rom. 4:11; 1 Cor. 14:22; Apoc. 9:4; Apoc. 15:1. There are many others in the Old Testament.
[265] Gen. 1: 14.
[266] Kramer, Rev. H.B., loc. cit.

Chapter 12:1 **precedes** those matters recorded in Chapters 11 and 13 leads us to note that Chapter 11 foretells the measuring of the temple and the appearances of the two witnesses, commonly believed to be Henoch and Elias. Chapter 13 prophesies the beast with the seven heads and ten horns, coming out of the sea, as well as the second beast, "coming up out of the earth, and he had two horns, like a lamb, and he spoke as a dragon." A horn is the biblical symbol for either a man or an object consecrated to God; horns are also the sign of what the Bible calls "kings" who possess spiritual and/or earthly authority over a nation or nations. (For examples, see Exod. 27:2; Lev. 4:7; Ps. 74:11; Daniel 7:24; Dan. 8:20; Amos 6: 14; Zach. 1:21; but there are many others.) Kings may be good or evil, as the Bible has often shown.

Our resurrected Lord in Heaven is described by St. John in *Apocalypse 5:6* in the following manner: "And I saw: and behold in the midst of the throne and of the four living creatures, and in the midst of the ancients, a Lamb standing as it were slain, having seven horns and seven eyes: which are the seven Spirits of God, sent forth into all the earth." The descriptive number of seven indicates God's spiritual perfection, because He is God, the King of kings.

In a word, *horns* are Scriptural emblems of power, authority, dominion, glory, intensity, or ferocity. The "two horns, like a lamb" are very telling; for they infallibly predict a living man who holds a high office of authority, who poses as a lamb (a Christian) but who speaks as "a dragon," meaning his doctrines are those of hell. That said, it seems apparent that this man will be either one of two things: an ordained bishop or a cardinal (both wear "two-horned" mitres which denote spiritual authority) *or* he might be the leader of a nation (a lay person) who holds a position of great authority in the world and who presents himself to the world as a Christian leader. St. John relates in his Gospel (Jn. 21: 15-17) that Our resurrected Lord, when speaking to St. Peter, twice told the Prince of the Apostles, "Feed my lambs," Christ's reference to the laity or possibly His "little ones" (the humble), and then "Feed my sheep," Jesus' reference to the other apostles, the hierarchy. Whoever will be this allegedly Christian "lamb" with authority, he will appear righteous and humble, but he will speak "as a dragon" because he is a liar and a traitor to the Lord.

A Royal Woman, Clothed with the Sun

Whom or what is represented by "a woman clothed with the sun"? That the woman is royal is evident—she is clothed with the sun, she wears a crown of twelve stars, and she stands upon the moon. As we already know, there is found within the Church two main interpretations: one claims that she is the Virgin Mary and another believes that she personifies the Church. We shall see that she is both.

For example, Pope St. Pius X declared to the bishops of the Church, "Everyone knows that this woman signified the Virgin Mary, the stainless one who brought forth our Head. The Apostle continues: '*And, being with child, she cried travailing in birth, and was in pain to be delivered* ' (Apoc.12: 2). John therefore saw the Most Holy Mother of God already in eternal happiness, yet travailing in a mysterious childbirth. What birth was it? Surely it was the birth of us who, still in exile, are yet to be generated to the perfect charity of God, and to eternal happiness. And the birth pains show the love and desire with which the Virgin from heaven above watches over us, and strives with unwearying prayer to bring about the fulfillment of the number of the elect."[267]

In defining the dogma of the Assumption of the Virgin Mary, Pope Pius XII pronounced: "Moreover, the scholastic Doctors have recognized the Assumption of the Virgin Mother of God as something signified, not only in various figures of the Old Testament, but also in that *woman clothed with the sun* whom John the Apostle contemplated on the Island of Patmos."[268]

In the *Douay-Rheims Bible*, an accompanying footnote for the *Apocalypse*, Chapter 12:1, summarizes another interpretation, one that favors "a woman" as a symbolic image of the Church: " '*A woman* '...The church of God. It may also, by allusion, be applied to Our Blessed Lady. The church is clothed with the sun, that is, with Christ: she hath the moon, that is, the changeable things of the world, under her feet: and the twelve stars with which she is crowned, are the twelve apostles: she is in labour and pain, whilst she brings forth her children, and Christ in them, in the midst of afflictions and persecutions."

Since the Blessed Virgin Mary painlessly brought forth only one Child,[269] Who is the Christ, the Lord and Savior of the world, it seems reasonable that "ancient interpreters beginning with Hippolytus and Methodius understood this ['a woman clothed with the sun' who is in pain to be delivered] to be a figure of the Church."[270]

---

[267] Pope St. Pius X, *Ad Diem Illum Laetissimum* (On the Immaculate Conception, Feb. 2, 1904): para. 24.

[268] Pope Pius XII, *Munificentissimus Deus* (Apostolic Constitution Defining the Dogma of the Assumption of the Blessed Virgin Mary, Nov. 1, 1950): para. 27.

[269] Brookby, Peter, ed. *Virgin Wholly Marvelous: Praises of Our Lady from the Popes, Councils, Saints, and Doctors of the Church* [Cambridge, MA: The Ravengate Press, 1981]. Cited in "Woman Clothed with the Sun," *Just for Catholics* website in quoting Pope Alexander III speaking about the virginal conception of Our Lord, the painless birth of Christ, and the Virgin's departure from this life without corruption: "Mary conceived without detriment to her virginity, gave birth to her Son without pain, and departed hence without being subject to corruption." [http://www.justforcatholics.org/a131.htm]

[270] Kramer, Rev. H. B., op. cit., p. 276.

However, if the woman represents the Church and *only* the Church, the latter interpretation raises a necessary question, as follows:

Why would St. John describe, in symbolic language, the Church ("a woman clothed with the sun") as appearing *in the Church* ("in heaven")? In other words, why would the Church appear as a "great sign" within herself?

The Great Sign at Enmity with the Dragon

Likewise considering that the whole of Scripture contains figure-types [271] of New Testament archetypes (such as Christ, Our Lady, or the just versus the reprobates), is it not possible that this "great sign" foretells the age in which Mary (assumed into Heaven), appears *in the Church?*

It is already known that the Virgin Mary is herself a sign from God. In the Old Testament, the infallible Scriptures reveal: "Therefore, the Lord Himself shall give you a sign. Behold a virgin shall conceive and bear a son and His name shall be called Emmanuel."[272]

The Virgin Mother is also "Woman," the title by which Jesus Christ called His Virgin Mother. [273] He called her "Woman" at Cana, and He immediately performed His first miracle at her request. As He was dying on the Cross, He again called her "Woman," saying, "Woman, behold thy son." Then speaking to John, He said simply, "Behold thy mother." Our Lord's last directive from the Cross entrusted the Virgin Mary to St. John as *Mother*, for St. John in his person represented the faithful of the Church. (Additionally, might we momentarily consider that St. John was the only one of the Apostles to stand with the Virgin at the Foot of the Cross, the only Apostle privileged to take Christ's Mother "to" his own, and the only Apostle who beheld the great visions which he was instructed by Heaven to write, a record which became known as the *Apocalypse?)*

By calling His Mother "Woman," another mystery of grace is revealed: *The Word* Incarnate[274] revealed *by* His Word that His Mother, the Virgin Mary, is "the Woman" foretold in the *proto-evangelium* (the first Good News) of *Genesis 3:15*. God Himself pronounced to the serpent (the devil) that HE (the Lord) would place enmities (i.e., hostilities, antagonisms, animosities) between the evil one and "the woman." God made clear His Holy Will that "the woman" is the one who crushes the head of the serpent and all his plots: "*I* will put

---

[271] In the Old Testament, a **figure-type** is a person, place, thing or event *foreshadowing* a New Testament **archetype** (a perfect model or type). The New Testament **archetype** is always greater than its Old Testament figure-type.

[272] Isa. 7:14.

[273] Jn. 2:4, Jn. 19:26.

[274] Jn. 1:1.

enmities between thee and *the woman*, and thy seed and her seed: she shall crush thy head, and thou shalt lie in wait for her heel." [275]

Illustrating that the Church's Tradition has long recognized the Virgin Mary as the Woman of *Genesis,* Blessed Pope Pius IX quoted the first eight words of *Genesis 3:15*, when defining the Immaculate Conception.[276] More than a century before that solemn definition, St. Louis de Montfort (the great saint who so well taught true devotion to Jesus through Mary), fully grasped the true meaning of "the woman" prophesied in the *proto-evangelium* of *Genesis 3:15*, writing:

"God has established only one enmity—but it is an irreconcilable one, which will last and *even go on increasing to the end of time.* That enmity is between Mary, His worthy Mother, and the devil, between the children and the servants of the Blessed Virgin and the children and followers of Lucifer."

"Thus the most fearful enemy that God has set up against the devil is Mary, His holy Mother. From the time of the earthly paradise, although she existed then only in His mind, He gave her such a hatred for His accursed enemy, such ingenuity in exposing the wickedness of the ancient serpent and such power to defeat, overthrow and crush this proud rebel, that Satan fears her not only more than angels and men but in a certain sense more than God Himself. This does not mean that the anger, hatred and power of God are not infinitely greater than the Blessed Virgin's, since her attributes are limited. It simply means that Satan, being so proud, suffers infinitely more in being vanquished and punished by a lowly and humble servant of God, for her humility humiliates him more than the power of God."[277]

The Woman and the Church

Our Lady, as "*the* woman," is God's chosen one who shall crush the serpent's head, which means she is victorious over the very same entity typified as the red dragon of the *Apocalypse*. As "*the* woman," the Virgin Mary is the Immaculate and living archetype of the authoritative, infallible, and indefectible Church.[278] As the Mother of God the Son and Spouse of the Holy Ghost, she is also the Mother of the Church.

---

[275] Gen. 3:15.

[276] Pope Pius IX, *Ineffabilis Deus (*Apostolic Constitution Defining the Dogma of the Immaculate Conception, December 8, 1854): para. 52.

[277] de Montfort, St. Louis. *True Devotion to Mary,* #52.

[278] *Authoritative*: By the authority of the Catholic Church is meant that the Pope and the bishops, as the lawful successors of the apostles, have power from Christ Himself to teach, to sanctify, and to govern the faithful in spiritual matters. *Infallibility of the Church:* By the special help of the Holy Ghost, the Church cannot err when it **defines** a matter of faith or morals to be held by all the faithful. [See Vatican Council I, Session 4, Chapter 4—"The

The Church, as "*a* woman clothed with the sun," is the Spotless Bride of Christ. As such, the eternal Church is given unique attributes. She herself is sinless, but her impeccability is slandered by the sins of those who profess to be her children and by those who boldly hate her. Like the Virgin Mary, the eternal Church is sinned against by those whom she would save, her name and all of her divinely-given prerogatives trampled and blasphemed, and she, too, is in constant battle with the dragon.

The Woman who appeared at Fatima was described by Sr. Lucia, eldest of the three shepherd children, as "a Lady all dressed in white. She was more brilliant than the sun, and radiated a light more clear and intense than a crystal glass filled with sparkling water, when the rays of the burning sun shine through it."[279] Lucia's account of the Beautiful Lady who "appeared in heaven" (the Church) aptly describes that of "a woman clothed with the sun."

"And let it be noted, at the very moment when, as a consequence of the Bolshevik victory, the '*Red Dragon*' emerged at one extremity of Europe in Leningrad, which then was still Petrograd, at the other extremity of Europe, at Fatima...there appeared the '*Woman Clothed with the Sun*,' the Immaculate Heart of Mary," as we have already seen explained by Fr. Joseph de St. Marie, Professor of Theology at the Pontifical Faculty of Saint Theresa in Rome.[280]

Just as the *Apocalypse* foretold, in 1917 it was the Woman who *first* appeared as "a great sign" in the Church. "And there was seen another sign in heaven—and behold, a great red dragon, having seven heads, and ten horns: and on his head seven diadems." This sign is not "a great sign" like the Woman clothed with the sun, but it is *another* sign, one that is in stark contrast against the woman, an ominous sign that appears *in the Church*. This infallible warning appears to indicate that Satan will both persecute and infiltrate the Church, just as he persecuted the first twelve apostles; he also infiltrated them by drawing Judas further into his own weak inclinations and Judas, as we know, unwittingly betrayed Christ and then died by his own hand.

This terrible sign of "a great red dragon" with seven heads, ten horns (leaders of nations), and seven diadems reminds us that Our Lady said Russia will spread her errors (plural) throughout the world. The great red dragon is the spirit of anti-Christ already risen, the spirit behind the heresy of universal salvation which redefines the word *catholic* (i.e., universal) as it applies to the

---

Infallible Teaching Authority of the Roman Pontiff"]; *Indefectible*; meaning the Church, as Christ founded it, will last until the end of time. [Mt. 16:18; Matt. 28:20; 1 Cor.11:26] For further explanations, see Denzinger, *The Sources of Catholic Dogma* or *The Baltimore Catechism #3*, Part One: The Creed, "Lesson 12: The Marks and Attributes of the Church."
[279] Sr. Mary Lucia. *Memoirs,* 1976 edition, p. 159.
[280] de St. Marie, loc. cit.

true Church, the spirit behind the creation of a universal world-government that seeks to totally abolish the Social Reign of Christ the King, and the spirit behind a "new order" which inverses the order of God's Church and God's world. It is the spirit paving the way for the actual person of anti-Christ. To counter that evil spirit, the Fatima Virgin asked specific requests of the entire Church, one being that the Pope and the hierarchy make an act of solemn, collegial consecration of Russia to her Immaculate Heart.

Only at Fatima did the Lord, through the Virgin Mary, perform a *public* miracle so great that those who saw it called it "the sign of God."[281] The child Lucia had asked Our Lady for a sign, not for herself but for the scoffing unbelievers, like those who challenged Our Lord, "What **sign** therefore dost thou shew, **that we may see, and may believe thee**? What dost thou work?"[282]

To see and to believe—the faithful believe without seeing, but unbelievers always demand a sign. For the sake of the Message and the Great Secret, which are given for the conversion of sinners, Our Lady of Fatima assured Lucia and her two younger cousins, "In October, *I will tell you who I am* and *what I want*, and *I will perform a miracle for all to see and believe.*"

On October 13, 1917, the Woman who is more brilliant than the sun kept her promise with the Miracle of the Sun. Witnessed by at least 70,000 people, the "great sign" was seen in the heavens, recalling Rev. Kramer's observation: "**In the Septuagint, the word [sign] is used for** *celestial phenomena.*"[283]

Thus, it seems there does exist a dual-symbolism in *Apocalypse*, Ch. 12:1, in which the Virgin Mary not only appears as "a great sign" in the Church, in order to assist the Church as her prophesied travail approaches—but she, through the power of God, also gave "a great sign" to those who live in these very troubled times.

The Message and the Miracle:
A Private Revelation?

The Miracle of the Sun is "the great eschatological sign, the answer of God to the errors of the present time," said Bishop Rudolf Graber of Regensburg. Pope Paul VI said of the falling sun at Fatima, "It was eschatological in the sense that it was like a repetition or an *annunciation of a scene at the end of time for all humanity assembled together.*"[284]

---

[281] Frère Michel, *TWTF*, Vol. 1, p. 356.
[282] Jn. 6:30.
[283] Kramer, Rev. H. B., op. cit.
[284] Johnston, loc. cit., p. 69. [Emphasis added.]

Eschatology is the study of the end of days, which is also called the Day of Judgment, the latter days, the great and terrible day, or the last days of the world. Therefore, in reflecting that the Miracle is "the great eschatological sign," it is necessary to keep in mind that the Great Secret of Fatima (in three parts) and the Great Miracle (in three phases) are Heaven's responses to the ongoing Great Revolt (in three stages), which rebels against God and His one, holy, Catholic, and apostolic Church. It is also important to recall the revelations of the Sacred Heart at Paray-le-Monial, stressing the necessity of mankind's repentance and reparation for sin, and the Lord's desire to grant us Divine Mercy rather than chastisement. Finally, one cannot forget Our Lady's many intercessions since the year 1830 to save souls.

It is likewise reasonable and prudent to reflect and assent to the truth that Fatima (in its signs witnessed by others for five successive months, in its entire message, its Great Secret and Great Miracle) is not a mere "private revelation" which can be airily dismissed with the alleged excuse that Catholics need only adhere to Divine Revelation (Tradition and Scripture), otherwise known as the Deposit of Faith. Such a claim is not reasonable because it actually *contradicts* Divine Revelation.

The Scriptures themselves proclaim: "Extinguish not the spirit. Despise not prophecies. But prove all things; hold fast to that which is good" (1 Thess. 5:19-20). No Pope has ever insisted that Fatima is a private revelation but rather, as this book's first chapter noted, Pope Benedict XVI spoke of Fatima's "prophetic mission" and Pope John Paul II said, "Fatima places an obligation on the Church."[285] Before them, Pope Pius XII had said that the time for doubting Fatima was past, and that it was time to take action. Again, Popes do not say such things of "private revelations."

"Frequently, objections are made to Fatima as being a sort of magic word in theology," as Bishop Rudolf Graber said on September 23, 1973 in his address to the Fatima Congress at Freiburg, Germany. "Fatima, they say, is after all only a private revelation and is therefore not binding in conscience, except for the person to whom it was given. [People claim] we only accept the great revelation of God [i.e., Divine Revelation of Tradition and Scripture] which ended definitively with Christ and the Apostles. Why then such an outcry against Fatima?

"It is to be noted that this objection comes principally from those who neither respect the great revelation of God, nor of Christ, and who even want to eliminate some fundamental truths of Faith, such as the virgin birth of Jesus, His Resurrection, His miracles, and even His very Divinity…It is absolutely

---

[285] Pope John Paul II, *Sermon at Fatima*, May 13, 1982.

certain that revelation as such was completed with Christ and His Apostles. **What happens then if these private revelations confirm and emphasize certain truths that are found in this great revelation?**

"This is exactly what happens with Fatima. Fatima confirms the existence of angels and demons that Modernists try to eliminate. Fatima confirms the mystery of the Eucharist which Modernists have stripped of all meaning. Fatima confirms the existence of Hell, which is simply denied today. Fatima requires prayer and sacrifice, values to which people today feel themselves far superior and from which they consequently dispense themselves. Nevertheless, all through the Old and New Testament, this penance is spoken of…Today, much is spoken about fraternity, which naturally is not understood so much on a supernatural level, but almost exclusively in the social field and in technical developments.

"Once again, we affirm that revelation proper ended with Christ and His Apostles. **But does that mean that God has to remain silent, that He can no longer speak to His elect? Does it mean, as some believers think, that He should remain apart and leave the world abandoned to itself?** Would not this be a very strange kind of God indeed! Did He not expressly say through His prophet that He would 'pour forth of His Spirit on all flesh, that sons and daughters would prophesy, that old men would have visions in dreams? Even upon servants and handmaids, He would pour forth His spirit.' (Acts 2:17; John 3:1-5) Is such a prophecy to be limited only to the first Pentecost? Certainly not. Wherefore hear the word of the Prophet Amos: 'The trumpet sounds in the street, men do well to be afraid; if peril is afoot in the city, doubt not it is of the Lord's sending. Never does he act, but His servants, the prophets, are **in the secret.**' (Amos 3:6) Should we not thank God with our whole heart, Who even today speaks to us, especially when any danger is approaching?"

"At an opportune moment," the bishop continued, "an eminent theologian called attention to the fact that we ought to distinguish exactly between private revelations which are given only to a privileged person, and others that contain a message for the Church or even for the whole world. We need not preoccupy ourselves with the first kind, but we should take serious account of the latter, since to reject them or not to be interested in them would mean a reprehensible despising of the Word of God, and a grave lack of responsibility towards the world. For these the word of the prophet holds good: 'But what if the sentry, when he sees the invader coming, sounds no alarm to his neighbor to warn his neighbor? Here is some citizen overtaken by the enemy; well, his guilt deserved it. But for his death, I will hold the sentry accountable' (Ezechiel 33:6)."

It was then that Bishop Graber said that Miracle of Fatima represents "the great eschatological sign, the answer of God to the errors of the present time. The world finds itself on the eve of tremendous happenings breaking forth from the East. Hell seems to be let loose. The maternal Heart of Mary offers to save the world...May this depreciatory allegation that 'these are only private revelations' not become the norm for dismissing the subject. Naturally, Mary's words at Lourdes and Fatima are not on the same level as the general (Divine) revelation...But this does not mean that God and Mary are prohibited from speaking again. God speaks once more today and in a manner all the more intelligible **as His Second Coming draws nearer, and this is precisely what Fatima seems to indicate.**"[286]

Another theologian, Fr. G. Van Noort, wrote in his book *Dogmatic Theology* (Vol. 3, p. 215): "Such a revelation ought to be believed by both the one who receives it and by those for whom it is destined. The rest of the faithful cannot outrightly deny it without some sort of sin." [287] (This, of course, is after the local bishop has investigated the event and only if he has judged it to be "worthy of belief.")

"There are other things besides the solemn teaching authority of the Church that bind a person to accept something," explained Fr. William A. Hinnebusch, O.P. of the Dominican House of Studies in Washington, D.C., in a letter published by the *Northern American Voice of Fatima* (November 10, 1963). "A creature endowed with reason is obliged by his own intelligence to bow to evidence when it is present. To resist evidence is obstinately anti-intellectual. Furthermore, when reliable witnesses testify to an event or fact which seems incontrovertible, a reasonable man must give assent. To say he may refuse assent without blame is a questionable position. When a person of such outstanding authority as the late Pope Pius XII says 'the time for doubting Fatima is past; it is now time for action,' then reasonable men must stop and question whether good evidence offered by reliable witnesses is behind the conviction. For a Catholic to deliberately close his mind to such a statement can hardly be without blame...a reasonable man accepts the evidence of reliable witnesses. When he refuses to do so, he does violence to his own reason."[288]

"As a professional philosopher, what I find most remarkable in the event of Fatima is that it is a heavenly intervention in the history of mankind in order to redirect history," wrote Abbé André Richard, D.D., of Paris in *Soul* magazine's

---

[286] Johnston, op. cit., pp. 3-4.
[287] Ibid., p. 4.
[288] Ibid.

January-February 1979 issue. "Fatima is...an intervention to change the march of the entire caravan of mankind, which is on the road to a precipice over which it would inevitably fall unless its route is changed. Fatima concerns not only the pious Christian, but the man in the street–every man in the world. And as a theologian, what impresses me about Fatima is its reaffirmation of the entire *Gospel* and its emphasis on the source of moral evil: offenses against God which today mount even to the ultimate offense of militant atheism...How can any of us fail to be conscious of Our Lady appearing in the sky, reminding us of the great sign in chapters 11 and 12 of the *Apocalypse*? How can any of us consider Fatima to be less than the presentation of that apocalyptic message of Our Lady, dressed with the sun and announcing her triumph over Satan?"

  Commenting on the Fatima miracle and the *Apocalypse*, Fr. Louis Kondor, S.V.D, the vice-postulator for the causes of canonization of Francisco and Jacinta (who are now Blessed) and editor of the book, *Fatima in Lucia's Own Words*, wrote in his regular bulletin, *Seers of Fatima* (July-August 1975), "In view of this similarity, which seems a telling fulfillment of *Apocalypse* 12, who would venture any longer to speak of a private revelation? Fatima is...an eschatological sign that reveals the saving victory of the 12th chapter of the *Apocalypse*." Later in the same bulletin, he also stated that "we can consider Fatima as the *great eschatological sign* given by God to our times, so that we will not deserve the rebuke that Our Lord made to the Jews: 'You know how to read the face of the sky, but you cannot read the signs of the times.' (Matt. 16:4) Fatima is a sign of the times. The lightning flash that preceded each of Mary's apparitions at Fatima is an announcement of the lightning that will flash from east to west before the coming of the Son of Man (Matt. 24:27). And the remaining atmospheric phenomena which belong to the complexity of Fatima are a presage of those signs in the sun, in the moon and the stars that Our Lord speaks of in His eschatological discourse (Luke 21:25). Fatima is a great sign of the times."

  Finally, the dogmatic Vatican I council affirmed that "in order that the 'obedience' of our faith should be 'consonant with reason' [cf. Rom. 12:1], God has willed that to the internal aids of the Holy Spirit there should be joined external proofs of His revelation, namely: **divine facts, especially miracles and prophecies** which, because they clearly show forth the omnipotence and infinite knowledge of God, **are most certain signs of a divine revelation**, and are suited to the intelligence of all." This same council also condemned those who insist "that divine revelation cannot be made credible by external signs" and "that miracles are not possible, and hence all accounts of them...are to be banished among the fables and myths; or, that miracles can never be known with certitude."[289]

The signs and secrets of Fatima are one, integral whole and cannot be separated. Fatima was proven by the Church to be worthy of belief, and so its "miracles and prophecies...are most certain signs of a divine revelation." As we have also seen in this section, certain men within the Church hierarchy referred to the Great Miracle of the Sun as a "sign of the times" and an "eschatological sign," thus opposing liberal "theologians" who have, for decades, tried in diverse ways to trivialize or dismiss the whole of the Fatima Message and the Miracle. The Miracle was the clear, wondrous, and then terrifying sign given by God so that all would believe and heed the Virgin's messages; therefore, it is directly connected to the Great Secret in its three distinct parts. To further explore these matters, however, we must also examine a sign seen only by the children—the Star of Esther on the Virgin's floor-length tunic.

---

[289] Denzinger, Henry. *The Sources of Catholic Dogma.* [London: B. Herder Book Co., 1957]: #1790, #1812, #1813.

Hidden Revelations:

The Star of Esther & the Secrets of Fatima

"We must do all our actions *with* Mary."

—St. Louis de Montfort

It is said that the best place to hide something is in plain sight.

When Sr. Lucia, the last Fatima visionary, was called into eternity on February 13, 2005, both the Catholic and mainstream media sought the significance of the date. Most sources tied-in to May 13, noting the "13" in the anniversary date of the Fatima apparitions (1917), the papal assassination attempt (1981), and John Paul II's world consecrations and entrustments to the Immaculate Heart (1982, 1984, and 2000). Ultimately, the mainstream efforts implied that Sr. Lucia's death was a sign that Fatima is finished. Yet when an incredible Scriptural connection to February 13th and Fatima is examined as a whole, the opposite conclusion is made: While the date of Lucia's death is definitely a sign, it is one alerting the world that we have reached the most critical chapter of the Fatima revelations.

Heretofore, it was never noticed that the date of Sr. Lucia's passing links to a small yellow star, worn by Our Lady of Fatima. This star is a profound symbol long recognized by tradition as the "Star of Esther." It points to an Old Testament history called *The Book of Esther*, which relates the story of a Jewish queen whose intercession saved her people from annihilation. Queen Esther's mediation allowed the ancient Hebrews "to gather themselves together, and to stand for their lives" on "the 13th day of Adar."

Until Lucia's passing, the magnitude of "the 13th of Adar" could not be realized, even by Fatima scholars. Her death signals that, like the Jews who stood for their lives on the 13th of Adar, our own great battle against annihilation is begun. The secret significance of Lucia's date of death has been right before our eyes all the time: It occurred exactly 40 minutes before **sunset,**[290] on the 13th of **February**[291] of the Gregorian calendar—but in the Hebrew month of **Adar.**[292]

---

[290] Sunrise and Sunset in Coimbra, timeanddate.com
[http://www.timeanddate.com/worldclock/astronomy.htm]

P.S. to the Message of Fatima

Thus it seems that even Lucia's death accentuated the entire Fatima message, manifesting a kind of heavenly post-script: "Hear, O foolish people, and without understanding: who have eyes, and see not: and ears, and hear not."[293]

In the Scriptures, the 13th day of Adar is one with historical portent. First, it marks the battle throughout the Persian Empire during the reign of Esther (Esther 9:1); second, it was the date of the Machabees' liberation of the Holy Land after a four-year combat (1 Mach. 7:3), and third, it is the eve of the anniversary of the infant Moses' circumcision (through whom God would give His law and whom the Jews have always revered; because he freed his people from centuries of bondage, Moses is a figure-type of Christ).[294] **The theme becomes obvious**: An epic battle of God's *ecclesia* against her enemies.

Because there are no insignificancies in God's designs, there are great reasons for the Star of Esther adorning Our Lady of Fatima. On February 13, 2005, its purpose was again emphasized when God willed that Lucia should leave this world on a date directing our attention to both Esther and Our Lady of Fatima.

---

[291] "Last Fatima Witness Sister Lucia Dies at 97." *CathNews*. [http://www.cathnews.com/news/502/80.php]
*According to the Portuguese news agency **Lusa**, Sr. Maria Lucia of the Immaculate Heart, born in 1907 as Lucia de Jesus dos Santos, died of old age at the Carmelite convent of St. Teresa of Coimbra in central Portugal, at 5:25 pm local time.*

[292] Hebrew Date Converter
[http://www.hebcal.com/converter/] Let it be noted that the Gregorian calendar is solar-based, while the Hebrew (or Jewish) calendar is lunar-based. In October of 1582, Pope Gregory XVI advanced the solar calendar date by 11 days. Thus, according to the Gregorian calendar, which is used almost universally, Lucia died on the 13th of February. By the Jewish lunar calendar of 2005, she died on the 4th of Adar II. It is the author's conjecture, which is submissive to the Church's ultimate judgment, that God wished to highlight the 13th day of the universal Gregorian calendar, which would call the attention of Catholics familiar with the story of Our Lady of Fatima. However, by calling Lucia's soul from this life in the Hebrew month of Adar, He also called attention to the sign of the Star of Esther on the robe of Our Lady of Fatima.

[293] Jer. 5:21.

[294] "Timeline: Adar in Jewish History." *Wikipedia*.[http://en.wikipedia.org/wiki/Adar]. Also see "Moses." Jewish Encyclopedia.[http://www.jewishencyclopedia.com/articles/11049-moses] and Janicki, Tobi. "eRosh Blog: The Birth and Death of Moses." [http://ffoz.org/blogs/2008/02/erosh_blog_the_birth_and_death_1.htm]

Figure Types: *Of Mary, There is Never Enough*

Just as the star adorning Our Lady of Fatima points to *The Book of Esther*, so does *The Book of Esther* point to all of the Fatima apparitions. Esther's theme centers on secrets and revelations, suggesting that *The Book of Esther* is a figure-type for the *Apocalypse* (Greek for Revelations).

The Book of Esther appears to encapsulate what Fatima highlights about both the Virgin's and the Church's singular office in salvation history. Esther's Star on Our Lady's gown directs the Church to "the history of Queen Esther, who was herself a great [figure] type of our Queen Mary!" as St. Alphonsus de Liguori reiterated.[295]

But first, what is meant by a figure-type? In its application to the whole of Scripture, an Old Testament **figure-type** is a person, place, thing or event foreshadowing a New Testament **archetype** (a perfect model or type). The New Testament archetype is always greater than its Old Testament figure-type.[296]

Our Lord Himself plainly alluded to Scriptural figure-types when, after His Resurrection, He appeared to two disciples on the road to Emmaus. "And beginning at Moses and all the prophets, he expounded to them in all the scriptures the things that were concerning him." Our Lord used similar words when He subsequently appeared to the Apostles.[297]

So, too, "Mary appears on every page of the Old Testament," said St. Bernard.[298] As we have already seen, in *Genesis 3:15*, God Himself literally prophesied Our Lady as "**the** woman," but she is foreshadowed in many figure-types—including but not limited to Miriam, Sarah, the foot-shaped cloud of Mt. Carmel, Ruth, Anna, Judith, and Esther; in the Gebirah (queen mothers of the Davidic kings); in the mother of the seven Machabees; in the spouse of the *Canticle of Canticles*, the daughter of Zion, the burning bush on Mt. Sion, the Ark of the Covenant, the Root of Jesse, the City of God, and the Temple of Jerusalem.

---

[295] de Liguori, St. Alphonsus. *The Glories of Mary*, p. 39.
[296] Stanley, Bob. "Types, Antitypes, Signs and Shadows are Absolutely Indispensable for Proper Scriptural Interpretation." *Catholic Treasure Chest*. [http://www.thecatholictreasurechest.com/type.htm]
[297] Lk. 24:27.
[298] Stokes, Jr., John S. "Bible Gardens Revisited." Republished on the *Mary Gardens* website. [http://www.mgardens.org/JS-BGR-MG.html]

In the *Apocalypse,* **the** Woman (the Virgin Mary) is prefigured by a "type within type"–"a woman clothed with the sun, with the moon under her feet, and on her head a crown of twelve stars." [299] This woman is a type of the Church, but the eternal Church is herself a type of Mary. With these examples, one begins to see what is meant by "types within types."

The *Book of Esther* and the *Book of Revelations*

Among the many women who are figure-types of the Virgin, Esther is foremost for three reasons: she interceded for her people; her Star appeared on Our Lady's dress; and the number "13" is central to her history. There exist depths in *The Book of Esther's* figure-types, who were living persons in history. That said, the following comparisons are those most pertinent for the purposes of this study.

In the Old Testament, the fourth chapter of *The Book of Esther* relates the history of a "fair and exceedingly beautiful" virgin named Edissa, "who by another name was called Esther." [300] In the Old Testament of the Hebrew text, her name was Hádássah–meaning myrtle, a white, five-pointed, **star**-shaped flower. [301]

• An orphan, Esther was raised by her uncle Mardochai, whose immediate ancestors were carried away from Jerusalem to Persia at the onset of the Babylonian Exile. Esther was in her uncle's care from the time she was a "**little one**" [302] –a "figure-type" phrase foreshadowing the Virgin Mary's sublime humility.

• Mardochai himself is an enigmatic "type within type." He seems to embody in his person the faithful in exile, St. Joseph (chaste guardian of the Virgin) but also a "vizier" or vicar, if not the Vicar of Christ. Esther and Mardochai lived in Susan, Persia's capital city. The Persian king was Assuerus (a figure-type for God) and his queen was Vasthi.

The Book of Esther, permeated with figure-types, opens with the historical narration of the king's feast. To grasp the types, one must understand that the first chapter of Esther alludes to the glory of the heavenly kingdom, the hierarchy of creation, the princes of the kingdom (the angels), and the Garden of Paradise, even to the first woman, Eve:

---

[299] Apoc. 12:1.
[300] Esther 2:7.
[301] Goodman, Philip. *The Purim Anthology.* [Philadelphia: Jewish Publication Society, 1988 pages]: 126-27. *Jewish Heritage Online Magazine.*
[http://www.jhom.com/calendar/adar/names.html]
[302] Esther 2:20.

"Now in the third year of his reign, he made a great feast for all the princes, and for his servants, for the most mighty of the Persians, and the nobles of the Medes, and the governors of the provinces, that he might show the riches of the glory of his kingdom, and the greatness, and boasting of his power, for a long time, to wit, for a hundred and fourscore days. And when the days of the feast were expired, he invited all the people that were found in Susan, from the greatest to the least: and commanded a feast to be made seven days, in the court of the garden, and of the wood, which was planted by the care and the hand of the king."[303]

At the time, "Vasthi the queen made a feast for the women in the palace, where the king Assuerus was used to dwell."[304] However, on the seventh day of the second feast, she disobeyed the king's solitary command "to show her beauty to all the people and the princes; for she was exceedingly beautiful. But she refused, and would not come at the king's command."[305]

Vasthi, the first queen, is a historical figure-type for the Lady Eve, queen of the earthly Paradise where God Himself "used to dwell." Like Eve, Vashti forever lost her office when she refused the King's singular command. No more is said of Vasthi's fate other than the words of an edict proclaiming she could "come in no more to the king, but another, that is better than her, be made queen in her place."[306]

"After this, when the wrath of King Assuerus was appeased, he remembered Vasthi, and what she had done and what she had suffered." [307] In the Old Testament, a phrase like "he remembered" signaled that the very next action, no matter how innocuous or unconventional, is an immediate manifestation of God's mercy. This Divine intervention looks like a natural human event, but it is always God Who is behind it. Knowing this helps us understand why one moment the king remembered Vasthi but, in the very next sentence, he issued an edict summoning all the most beautiful virgins of the land, so that he might select a new bride. The virgins were brought to the capital, and "were delivered to Egeus the eunuch; Esther also among the rest of the maidens were delivered to him to be kept in the number of the women."[308]

---

[303] Esther 1:5.
[304] Esther 1:9.
[305] Esther 1:11-12.
[306] Esther 1:19.
[307] Esther 2:1.
[308] Esther 2:8.

Figure-types within Figure-types

It was not until the twelfth month that "every virgin's turn came to go in to the king, after all had been done for setting them off to advantage."[309] This "going in to the king" represents spiritual union "in God," which requires grace, time and merits. *The Book of Esther* relates that the virgins were given a year's preparation before "going in to" the king, "so that for six months they were anointed with oil of myrrh, and for [sic] other six months they used certain perfumes and sweet spices."[310] All of the virgins underwent this preparation. As shall be seen, a total of four years passed from the time of the king's edict before Esther's turn arrived.

The maidens, who typify the entire line of the Old Testament's holy women, were prepared for a total of 12 months, which is the symbolic number of completion (12 patriarchs from Adam to Jacob, 12 tribes of Israel, 12 loaves of proposition, 12 judges of Israel, 12 months of the year. Additionally, the New Testament, especially *The Book of Apocalypse*, is replete with the number 12: Twelve apostles, 12 legions of angels to whom Jesus refers in the Garden of Gethsemane, 12 fruits of the Holy Ghost, 12 foundation stones in the New Jerusalem and, of course, *Apocalypse* 12:1, prophesying the "great" sign who wears a crown of 12 stars: "And a great sign appeared in heaven: A woman clothed with the sun, and the moon under her feet, and on her head a crown of twelve stars"). Like the virgins presented to and accepted by Asserus, the holy women of God were accepted by the Lord, and yet they were not chosen as His queen.

Again, we see figure-types within figure-types. In the Old Testament, myrrh is first mentioned in *The Book of Exodus* and it is used in the "oil of unction," which God commanded Moses to prepare immediately before the building of the Ark of the Covenant, another figure-type of the Virgin Mary. Myrrh (Arabic, "bitter") was used for the healing of wounds and bruises. Myrrh was also a symbol of self-sacrifice.[311]

How striking, then, is the six month's anointing with oil of myrrh during the virgins' preparation. Likewise, the other perfumes and sweet spices in the second six months' preparation are reminiscent of the ingredients in the holy incense, which God ordered Moses to set before the tabernacle of the testimony. In all of the Fatima revelations, the need for *prayer* and *sacrifice* was stressed repeatedly.

---

[309] Esther 2:12.
[310] Ibid.
[311] Exod. 30: 23.

When Esther's turn came to "go in to the king…she sought not women's ornaments, but whatsoever Egeus the eunuch the keeper of the virgins had a mind, he gave to adorn her. For she was exceedingly fair, agreeable and amiable in the eyes of all…And the king loved her more than all the women, and she had favor and kindness before him above all the women, and he set the royal crown on her head, and made her queen instead of Vasthi."

This event took place "in the tenth month which is called Tebeth, in the seventh year of the king's reign."[312] Thus, since the king's feast took place in the third year of his reign, we know that four years passed and a great number of maidens were presented to the King until Esther's appearance before him.

In this passage, we can easily see why Esther is a figure-type of the Virgin Mary, she who is "full of grace" and blessed amongst all women.[313]

• The time between Vasthi's fall to Esther's appearance before the king is a span of four years. These four years prefigure the four centuries of Advent.[314]

• Tebeth correlates with the Gregorian calendar's twelfth month of December, [315] the month in which we commemorate the Feast of the Immaculate Conception.

• When Our Lady, Esther's archetype, appeared at Fatima, she also wore no adornments other than those symbolizing that with which God Himself adorned her.

The Secrets of the Star

Thus Esther became the Queen of Persia, but for a reason established by the Lord. In obedience to her uncle, Mardochai, she revealed to the king neither her ancestry, nor her Hebrew name, nor their kinship. The Hebrew texts relate that she gave her name as *Hester* (in Persian, *Esther*—which means "star."). As we shall see, this change in name was more than a translation.

• The alteration from *Hádássah* to *Hester* refers to a secret, because **Hester** (emphasis on the letter "H") translates to "hidden [meaning of the] star." [316] Esther had **three** secrets, as does Our Lady of Fatima.

• The Hebrew name for *The Book of Esther* is *Megillat Hester*—e.g., **"revelation of [that which is] hidden**."[317] By displaying the Star of Esther, it seems Our Lady of Fatima not only wishes to "discreetly suggest a hidden and

---

[312] Esther 2:15-17.
[313] Lk. 1:28.
[314] Lk. 1:3, 2:16.
[315] "Introduction to the Jewish Calendar." *JewishGen.*
[http://www.jewishgen.org/InfoFiles/m_calint.htm]
[316] "Girls Names." *Jewish Literacy.*
[http://www.aish.com/literacy/lifecycle/Girls_Names.asp]
[317] "Purim." *Wikipedia.* [http://en.wikipedia.org/wiki/Purim]

sublime aspect of her unique vocation"[318] as Mediatrix but also "secrets within secrets" or "revelations within revelations."

• The word play of *Megillat Hester* suggests another meaning: **God is hiding His Face.** The Hebrew text of *The Book of Esther*, which ends with Ch. 10:3, lacks any mention of God's name. Jewish scholars refer to the Lord's role as *Hester Panim* or "hidden Face."[319] Clearly, the implications for our own times are staggering.

The plot in Esther builds because her uncle Mardochai did not attend her marriage banquet; rather, he "stayed at the king's gate."[320] This one reference is a figure-type of some depth: The royal marriage banquet foreshadows the Virgin as the Bride of the Divine Spouse and the Church as the Bride of Christ; it reminds us of St. Joseph, the chaste protector of the Virgin Mary (the Eastern Gate, the King's Gate) and the Child Jesus, who is the King of Kings. Mardochai standing at the king's gates typifies he who guards the kingdom of God on earth, as well as the faithful in the kingdom; the gates themselves refer to both the Virgin (Gate of Heaven) and the Church (the Narrow Gate).

So it was that by lingering at the gate, Mardochai overheard a conspiracy to kill the king. He told Esther, who told the king in Mardochai's name, thus saving the king's life. [321]

Soon afterward, the king advanced Aman, of the race of Agag (a race which was at perpetual enmity with the Jews), setting him above all the princes. The king's servants bent their knees and worshiped Aman–all but Mardochai. Aman became so obsessed with Mardochai's fidelity to the First Commandment that he plotted revenge against him and all the Jews.[322]

Cunningly employing his position in the royal court, Aman issued a decree that all Jews living throughout Persia would be massacred on one day, down to the last man, woman, and child. To choose the month of this annihilation, lots were cast into an urn. The month chosen was the twelfth month, called Adar.[323] Some believe that it was Aman (an anti-Christ figure) who chose the day–the 13th day, [324] possibly in homage to the demon-god Nergal.[325]

---

[318] Frère Michel, *TWTF,* Vol. I, p. 147.
[319] Levanon, Rabbi David Dov. "Ester and the Dawn." *The Torah World Gateway.* [http://www.yeshiva.org.il/midrash/shiur.asp]
[320] Esther 2:19.
[321] Esther 2: 21-22.
[322] Esther 2:6.
[323] Esther 3: 7.
[324] Esther 3:12.
[325] "Nergal." *Wikipedia* [http://en.wikipedia.org/wiki/Nergal]

The Intercession of the Queen

The Scriptures relate that Mardochai asked Esther to intervene with the king, but Esther explained that the king had proclaimed none could enter his inner court without being called; those who dared were immediately put to death unless the king showed his clemency by holding out his golden scepter. Mardochai reminded her, "Think not that thou mayest save thy life only, because thou art in the king's house, more than all the Jews...And who knoweth whether thou are not therefore come to the kingdom, that thou mightest be ready in such a time as this?"[326] This passage also foreshadows Christian doctrine, for the Virgin Mary is placed above all others for the sake of all.

Hearing Mardochai's plea, Esther for the first time commanded her uncle, saying, "Go...gather together all the Jews...and pray ye for me. Neither eat nor drink for three days and three nights: and I with my handmaids will fast in like manner, and then I will go in to the king, against the law, not being called, and expose myself to death and danger."[327]

Thus Esther, her maidens, and the faithful throughout all of Persia prayed and fasted. How tragically apt **to our own day** are these words from Esther's prayer for the people:

"...We have sinned in thy sight, and therefore thou hast delivered us into the hands of our enemies, for we have worshiped their gods. Thou are just, O Lord. And now they are not content to oppress us with most hard bondage, but attributing the strength of their hands to the power of their idols, they design to change thy promises, and destroy thy inheritance, and shut the mouths of them that praise thee, and extinguish the glory of thy temple and altar..."[328]

In the meantime, Aman planned Mardochai's death, preparing a gibbet upon which he would be hanged. Aman had every reason to believe he would succeed, but his secret goal was the king's usurpation. However, armed with prayers and sacrifices to God and the king's love for her, Esther revealed her secrets to Assuerus, denounced Aman, and pled for her people. [329] "If I have found favor in thy sight, oh king, give me my people for which I request."[330]

"But the king being angry rose up from the place of the banquet into the garden set with trees. Aman also rose up to entreat Esther the queen for his life, for he understood that evil was prepared for him by the king. And when the king came back...he found Aman was fallen upon the bed on which Esther

---

[326] Esther 4:12, 14.
[327] Esther 4: 15-17.
[328] Esther 14: 6-9.
[329] Esther 7: 5-6.
[330] Esther 7:23.

lay…" [331] Seeing this and thinking that Aman's audacity knew no limits, the king ordered his death on the very gibbet prepared for Mardochai. [332] Assuerus then placed Mardochai in Aman's place, making him second in authority after the king–another emphasis that Mardochai is the figure-type of a "vicar," who is the steward of a king. [333]

Aman, as a figure-type, suggests a high-level infiltration within the kingdom (the Church), which plots to overthrow the King by first executing the steward of the monarch (the Pope, Vicar of Christ the King). To accomplish this, he and others lay plans to also destroy the king's true allies (the elect who, in Esther's time, were the faithful Jews but who are, since Jesus' death and Resurrection, the loyal Catholics). Aman's act of throwing himself upon Esther implies a great offense against the Virgin, resulting in the wrath of God.

The Faithful Must Stand for Their Lives

To save the Jews, the king gave Mardochai liberty to issue a new edict commanding the Jews "to gather themselves together, and to stand for their lives."[334] After the battle of the 13th of Adar, the king was told the number of those slaughtered, which included Aman's ten sons, and then asked Esther, "What wilt thou have me to command to be done?"[335] Esther asked that it be granted to the Jews "to do tomorrow in Susan as they have done this day and that the ten sons of Aman may be hanged on gibbets."[336] So it was that the Jews defended themselves in the capital city on both the 13th and 14th days of Adar. But in other areas of Persia, the battle occurred only on the 13th. [337]

From the human standpoint, the requests of Mardochai and Esther appear vindictive but, when understood as figure-types, we better follow the meanings. The Jews represent the ecclesia of the Old Dispensation saved from annihilation. Esther's request to the king signifies the Virgin's desire to save God's people and also completely eradicate all of the heresies afflicting the Catholic City, while the death of Aman and his ten sons suggests the defeat of the apocalyptic anti-Christ and the ten horns of the Beast.[338]

The doctrine of Mediatrix of all Graces is foreshadowed in Esther, the mediatrix of her people. Thus, Esther is a great figure-type for the Virgin Mary, especially under her title *Our Lady of Fatima*. Like Esther, the Virgin of

---

[331] Esther 7: 7-8.
[332] Esther 7: 10.
[333] Esther 8:2.
[334] Esther 8: 11.
[335] Esther 9: 11-12.
[336] Esther 9: 13.
[337] Esther. 7-18.
[338] Apoc. 13:1.

Fatima acts to save her people from annihilation, first asking that the pope, bishops and the lay faithful heed all of her requests. Unlike Esther, however, the Virgin Mary does not need our prayers and sacrifices for her own sake, but for ours.

Sr. Lucia and the 13th of February

In the Biblical sense, the date, day and time of Lucia's death on February 13, 2005 are **three great signs** from heaven. As already seen, February 13 directs us to the history of Queen Esther, and all that it signifies. The third sign is the day of Lucia's passing, which fell just before sunset on the first Sunday in Lent, the liturgical season dedicated to prayer and self-sacrifice. (According to the Gregorian calendar month, the date was February 13, which on the Jewish lunar calendar of that year was the 4th of Adar II. In this day and month, we see a "meshing" of dates in salvation history because, with few exceptions, today the Gregorian calendar is utilized throughout the world.) With Lucia's passing, it seems that God wished to again draw attention to at least three things: **1)** Sunday, the Sabbath, which is the day that the Lord commanded the elect to keep holy; **2)** the 13th day, which is associated with both Our Lady of Fatima and Queen Esther's history; and **3)** the connection in Esther's story to the Hebrew month of Adar, the month chosen by lot to destroy the Old Testament's elect. Surely, Our Lady's words to the child Lucia have proven true in every aspect: "Jesus wishes to use you to make me known and loved. He wants to establish in the world devotion to my Immaculate Heart. To whoever embraces this devotion, I promise salvation; these souls shall be dear to God, as flowers placed by me to adorn His throne."[339]

This devotion throughout the world has not yet occurred, because there has been no solemn collegial consecration of Russia to the Virgin's Immaculate Heart. For this singular, constant offense against her request, Heaven has already warned that what awaits us is a horrific victory of the incessant Revolt against the Church and the Holy Father. The culmination is rapidly approaching.

Certain words of Our Lord's to Sr. Lucia strongly indicate that the ominous portent of the Third Secret of Fatima may occur within fifteen years' time (by June 13, 2029, which marks the centenary of Our Lady's return to Lucia to tell the Holy Father that the "the moment" had come when God Himself asked for the collegial consecration of Russia, promising to save that country by this means.). This probable tragedy alone should inspire those who possess confidence in Our Lady of Fatima to courageously accept our collective obligation to declare the entire Fatima message throughout the Catholic world.

---

[339] Frère Michel, op. cit., pp. 158-159.

A particular warning of Our Lord's to Sr. Lucia about the collegial consecration brings to our attention the apparitions of the Sacred Heart to St. Margaret Mary Alacoque in Paray-le-Monial, France. Through this saint, Our Lord gave the world the devotion of the Nine First Fridays with its Twelve Promises. Yet there is another serious matter surrounding these apparitions to the saint, one which is very little known.

St. Margaret Mary was told by the Lord that she was to "**inform the King of France, 'Eldest son of His Sacred Heart,' that the Sacred Heart wished 'to reign in his palace, to be painted on his standard, to be engraved on his arms,' and that it [public homage] will make him 'triumphant over all the enemies of Holy Church,' if the King obeyed Christ's command on these matters.**" However, as history relates, "Either Louis XIV never received the letter or he refused to reply. **But the command still stands.**"[340]

On **June 17, 1689**, Our Lord also told the saint to tell the Catholic King Louis XIV that France must be solemnly consecrated to His Sacred Heart. This command, too, was ignored by the king and his heirs. As a result, France, called "the first daughter of the Church" because it was the first country in which the Catholic Faith was recognized as the nation's religion, succumbed to the "enemies of the **Church**."

The Time Limit Expired

Exactly one hundred years later, on **June 17, 1789**, the godless "Third Estate" declared itself a national assembly, lawlessly stripping the reigning Catholic monarch (Louis XVI) of his authority. Thus the Reign of Terror went into full motion; the king, his queen, and other innocents were martyred. Due to the ravenous "Mademoiselle Guillotine" and her devotees, the streets literally ran ankle-deep in blood because apostasy reigned.[341]

To think of what France—and with it, the Church—could have been spared, if only one of the reigning kings had obeyed the simple command of Our Lord!

Christ our King wished to establish the public consecration and devotion to His Sacred Heart in order to save France, "First Daughter of the Church," and with it, Christendom. As we now know through the apparitions to Sr. Lucia of Fatima, the Sacred Heart also wills the collegial consecration of **Russia** to the Immaculate Heart of Mary—this time to save the entire world from the punishments it deserves for its many sins.

---

[340] Ghéon, Henri. "The Secret of Saint Margaret Mary," loc. cit.
[341] Laux, M.A., Fr. John. *Church History*. [Rockford, IL. TAN Books and Publishers. Republished from the original 1930 edition]: pp. 522-526.

Our Lord also made it known to Sr. Lucia that He wishes to have the whole world acknowledge that Russia and the world will be saved by the collegial consecration, so that the Immaculate Heart of His Mother will honored beside His Sacred Heart.

If You Love Me, Keep My Commandments

In briefly reviewing the tragic history of the French Revolution, especially the fates of the Catholic monarchs and thousands of innocents, we fully understand how the Lord's apparitions and requests at Paray-le-Monial are linked to Our Lady's requests at Fatima.

On July 13, 1917, Our Lady said to the child Lucia: "...I shall come to ask for the consecration of Russia to my Immaculate Heart, and the Communion of Reparation on the First Saturdays. If my requests are heeded, Russia will be converted and there will be peace; if not, she will spread her errors throughout the world, causing wars and persecutions of the Church. The good will be martyred, the Holy Father will have much to suffer, various nations will be annihilated. In the end, my Immaculate Heart will triumph. The Holy Father will consecrate Russia to me, and she will be converted, and an era of peace will be granted to the world."[342]

She kept her promise that she would return to formally ask for the two acts mentioned above, but she did so on two separate occasions. First, on December 10, 1925, Our Lady appeared to Lucia, showing her a Heart encircled by thorns. By her side on a luminous cloud stood the Child Jesus, Who said: "Have compassion on the Heart of your Most Holy Mother, covered with thorns, with which ungrateful men pierce it at every moment, and there is no one to make an act of reparation to remove them."

Then the Virgin spoke to Lucia: "Look, my daughter, at my Heart, surrounded with thorns with which ungrateful men pierce me at every moment by their blasphemies and ingratitude. You at least try to console me and say that I promise to assist at the hour of death, with the graces necessary for salvation, all those who, on the first Saturday of five consecutive months, shall confess, receive Holy Communion, recite five decades of the Rosary, and keep me company for fifteen minutes while meditating on the fifteen mysteries of the Rosary, with the intention of making reparation to me."

Eleven years, eleven months after her first notification in 1917, the Virgin again appeared to Lucia—on June 13, 1929—to make the formal request regarding the consecration of Russia. Sr. Lucia was making a Holy Hour from

---

[342] Frère Michel, op. cit., pp. 182-183.

11 p.m. until midnight from Thursday to Friday. Alone in the chapel, Lucia said, "The only light was from the sanctuary lamp."

"Suddenly a supernatural light illumined the whole chapel and on the altar appeared on a cross of light which reached to the ceiling.

"In a brighter part could be seen, on the upper part of the Cross, the face of a man and His body to the waist. On His breast was an equally luminous dove. And nailed to the cross, the body of another man.

"A little below the waist, suspended in mid-air, was to be seen a Chalice and a large Host onto which fell some drops of Blood from the face of the Crucified and from a wound in His breast. These drops ran down over the Host and fell into the Chalice.

"Under the right arm of the Cross was Our Lady with her Immaculate Heart in her hand. (It was Our Lady of Fatima with her Immaculate Heart, in her left hand, without a sword or roses, but with a crown of thorns and flames.)

"Under the left arm [of the Cross] some big letters, as it were of crystal clear water running down over the Altar, formed these words: 'Grace and Mercy.'

"I understood that it was the mystery of the Holy Trinity that was shown to me, and I received lights about this mystery which I am not permitted to reveal."

"Then Our Lady said to me:

'**The moment has come when God asks the Holy Father to make, in union with all the bishops of the world, the consecration of Russia to my Immaculate Heart, promising to save it by this means.'**

'**So numerous are the souls which the Justice of God condemns for sins committed against me, that I come to ask for reparation. Sacrifice yourself for this intention and pray.'**

Lucia then related, "I gave an account of this to my confessor, who ordered me to write what Our Lord willed to be done."[343] Two years passed, but Sr. Lucia's endeavors proved fruitless. Those with the authority to fulfill the command would not comply.

In August 1931, Our Lord Himself spoke to Sr. Lucia, referring to **His** command for the collegial consecration of Russia. By the choice of God's own words, He left no doubt that the request of His Mother was also His own command and Will: **"Make it known to My ministers that given they follow the example of the King of France in delaying the execution of My request,**

---

[343] Frère Michel, *TWTF*, Vol. II, p. 247 and pp. 463-464.

they will follow him into misfortune. It will never be too late to have recourse to Jesus and Mary." [344]

With only the release of the Third Secret Vision (which did not include Our Lady's words elucidating it), Our Lord's warning to Sr. Lucia in 1931 makes itself tragically clear. Like the Kings of France who for 100 years disobeyed the heavenly King's command by delaying the solemn consecration of France to the Sacred Heart, the Savior Himself has warned that His religious ministers who do the same in regard to the collegial consecration of Russia to the Immaculate Heart of Mary "will follow the French king into misfortune." Like the countless numbers who also followed the King of France and his family "into misfortune" by their deaths at the guillotine, the Third Secret Vision of Fatima makes it clear that, if Our Lady's requests are not heard, "a bishop dressed in white" (generally understood to be the Bishop of Rome, the Pope) will die at the hands of soldiers who bear both guns and arrows, followed by a long line of faithful Catholics from all states in life. [345]

In regard to the long-awaited collegial consecration of Russia to the Immaculate Heart, is it not possible that Our Lord was also telling us that, "like the King of France," He will again allow **exactly** 100 years for His ministers to completely obey Him?

If so, will the 100 years conclude either on **July 13, 2017** (the anniversary of the Great Secret of Fatima, when the Virgin said she would, in the future, come to ask for the consecration, as well as for the First Five Saturdays of Reparation) or on **June 13, 2029** (the centenary of the date when Our Lady returned to request the collegial consecration)? Should the 100 years close on the latter date (and reason concludes it to be so, since it was on June 13, 1929 that the Virgin said, "The moment has come"), the time limit expires only 15 years hence from this book's 2014 publication.

---

[344] Ibid., pp. 543-544.
[345] *The Message of Fatima.*

CHAPTER 11

The Signs and the Traces of Hidden Things

"The light and the sun rose up, and the humble were exalted…"
-Esther 11:11

At Fatima, Our Lady's distinct words provided Heaven's counsel and admonition, while the accompanying signs and symbols fulfilled all seven purposes that authentic prodigies may hold. While scholars examine the text from and about Fatima in regard to the Third Secret and the collegial consecration, we must also study the Fatima signs. That God wills the elect to understand His signs, at the proper time, is supported by inerrant Scripture: "For the Lord knoweth all knowledge, and hath beheld the signs of the world, he declareth the things that are past, and the things that are to come, and **revealeth the traces of hidden things.**"[346]

The Seven Purposes of Signs
Chapter 3 of this book stated: "Throughout salvation history, the signs of God indicate various purposes. A true sign can possess any one or more of the following seven functions: It confirms God's Word, His goodness, authenticates prophesy, verifies God's blessings and His intervention for the sake of the elect, strengthens the faithful with hope, insures or testifies to God's Presence, or declares His judgment upon sin."[347] The **signs of the world** oppose the Catholic City, both in her human and divine nature, leading souls to revolt against God, mimicking but falsifying God's Word, undermining true prophecy, weakening or destroying the virtues by employing their imitators as replacements, and working contrary to God's Will.[348] In sum, God's signs and the world's signs contradict each other. This explains why "the whole truth about Fatima," specific to the salvation of souls living in this era, remains contradicted by the world.

Fatima follows the pattern of Scriptural prophecy, which is given by visions, words, types and signs. Regarding the Church's practice as it concerns Scriptural interpretation, the usual course is to first seek the literal meaning of the text of its prophecy and only then seek its symbolic meaning. As most

---

[346] Eccles. 42:19.
[347] Heb. 2:3-4; Ps. 96: 17; Judg. 6:17; Josh. 24:15-17; Isa. 7:14; Exod. 3:12; Num. 17:20.
[348] Pope Pius XII, *Humani Generis* (Concerning Some False Opinions Threatening to Undermine Christian Doctrine, August 12, 1950).

Catholic biblical exegetes agree, "When the generations for whom it was chiefly intended would come into being, the true author of all true prophecy, the Holy Spirit, would in his own ways allow his elect to take from the text the knowledge that had from the beginning been concealed therein. In this, then, is to be found the reason why the magisterium of the Church, which is based directly on tradition in all matters of faith and morals, must depend largely on experience and the interpretation of signs when there is a question of unfulfilled or only partially fulfilled prophecy."[349]

What St. Justin the Martyr said in relation to the Old Testament which prophesied Jesus as the Son of God can also be applied to the public revelation and prophecies of Fatima: We are "compelled to belief by those who prophesied before the events. With our own eyes, we are witness to things **that have happened and are happening**, just as they were predicted. And this, we think, will appear to you as the strongest and surest proof."[350]

Fatima, judged by the Church as "worthy of belief," [351] prophesied "things that have happened and are happening." Above all, Fatima has proven to be in perfect accord with Church dogma and doctrine, which is the supreme test of any revelation. The validity of the Virgin's merciful message and apocalyptic warnings—and, principally, the solution to avert the latter from fulfilment—was authenticated by miraculous signs, from the seemingly small to the stupendous.

The Mother of God vs. Modernism

The Virgin Herself is a sign: "*Therefore the Lord himself shall give you a sign. Behold a virgin shall conceive and bear a son and his name shall be called Emmanuel.*"[352] Our Lady is the same Woman foretold in *Genesis* who will crush the serpent and his plots: "*I will put enmities between thee and the woman, and thy seed and her seed: she shall crush thy head, and thou shalt lie in wait for her heel.*"[353]

This same Virgin, who came to Fatima, concisely underscored dogma, doctrine, sacred history and Scriptural prophecy in the dates she appeared, the place she chose, the distinct dress and adornments she wore, the succinct words she uttered, the visions and secrets she revealed, and the many signs she gave.

---

[349] Kramer, Rev. H. B., *The Book of Destiny*, p. 40. [Emphasis added.]
[350] Jurgens, William A. *The Faith of the Early Fathers*, Vol. One. [Collegeville, MN: The Liturgical Press, 1970]: p. 53.
[351] De Marchi, I. M.C., John. *Fatima from the Beginning*. [Missões Consolata, Fátima, 1986]: p. 227.
[352] Isa. 7:14.
[353] Gen 3:15.

Together they form a consistent whole, fortifying the Secret given in three parts, applying to: first, the salvation of souls; second, the salvation of the nations and of Christendom, which shall result in the peace of the world; and third, the preservation of the Catholic Faith and the salvation of the Church. For, as previously stated: "These three themes, which are joined by an indissoluble bond, reveal to us the extraordinary mystical, moral, political, ecclesial, and dogmatic implications of the Secret of Fatima."[354]

Not long before the first Fatima apparition, Pope St. Pius X had issued *Pascendi Dominici Gregis (1907)* against the modernists and *Our Apostolic Mandate (1910)*, in which within the latter document the sainted Pope declared:

"We must repeat with the utmost energy in these times of social and intellectual anarchy when everyone takes it upon himself to teach as a teacher and lawmaker—**the City cannot be built otherwise than as God has built it**; society cannot be set up unless the Church lays the foundations and supervises the work; no, civilization is not something yet to be found, nor is the New City to be built on hazy notions; it has been in existence and still is: it is Christian civilization, **it is the Catholic City**. It has only to be **set up and restored continually against the unremitting attacks of insane dreamers, rebels and miscreants**. OMNIA INSTAURARE IN CHRISTO. (To restore all things in Christ)"[355]

Because the heresy of Modernism is insubordinate to Tradition and Scripture, it redefines *everything* pertaining to sacred dogma and doctrine, leaving no stone of the Catholic City unturned. It is especially defiant against Vatican I, which affirmed the "sacred dogmas must be perpetually maintained, which Holy Mother Church has once declared; and there must never be a recession from that meaning *under the pretext of a deeper understanding*."[356] As the prophetic *Pascendi* expounded, modernism pretends that dogmas are merely symbols instead of absolute truths. "Thus the way is open to the intrinsic evolution of dogma. Here we have an immense structure of sophisms [false reasoning] which ruin and wreck all religion."[357]

Modernism, the "synthesis of all heresies," [358] is an insidious sign of apostasy that lives in the souls of men, wherein should reside the kingdom of God.[359] It is the heresy of inversion, spawned by the same evil entity behind

---

[354] Frère Michel, *TWTF*, Vol. II: pp. 9-10.
[355] Pope St. Pius X, *Our Apostolic Mandate* (Letter to the French Bishops and Archbishops on the "Sillon," August 25, 1910): para. 11.
[356] Vatican Council I, can. 3.
[357] Pope St. Pius X, op. cit., para. 12-13.
[358] Ibid., para. 39.
[359] Lk. 17:21.

liberalism, which brought forth the "Enlightenment," the French Revolution, and "The Age of Reason." However, throughout salvation history, when the elect are (or soon shall be) insidiously besieged, God manifests His Divine Intervention in diverse ways—as did the Sacred Heart in the visions of Paray-le-Monial before liberalism and rationalism began to sweep Christian Europe.

The year 1830 initiated the prelude to "The Age of Mary," in which the Virgin Mother of God herself began to earnestly entreat Her children, giving us a repeated message of prayer and penance, and sacramentals like the Medal of the Immaculate Conception, the Badge of the Immaculate Heart (the Green Scapular), and the miraculous water at Lourdes. Yet Fatima is the crown of all, with its message and its signs to the world, culminating in the Miracle of the Sun.

The First Sign:
Immaculate Spouse of the Holy Ghost,
Figure of the New Israel, the Church

The smallest of the Fatima signs are two adornments of the Virgin. The ornaments, however, speak for themselves, if only we have the eyes to see: *"For it is good to hide the secret of a king, but honourable to reveal and confess the works of God."*[360]

The first symbol was a waist-length yellow necklace, from which hung a luminous orb or ball of light; the orb shone even brighter than the radiating light of Our Lady's risen and glorious body.[361] The second ornament was a small yellow star, suspended on Our Lady's long gown between knee and hem.[362] There is no extant record that Our Lady or Sr. Lucia, the last surviving visionary who died in 2005, ever explained these two adornments, although Lucia obviously described their appearance. Might her silence on them be connected to the Third Secret?

Of the necklace and the shining orb, Fatima historian and expert Frére Michel of the Holy Trinity wrote, "...in the light of the liturgy, itself completely saturated with Holy Scripture, it seems to us that we can easily guess the symbolic meaning of this ornament. Does it not remind us of the 'jewels,' the traditional attribute of the spouse? *Sicut sponsam ornatum monilibus suis*—'As a bride adorned with her jewels,' continues the canticle of Isaiah, which the Church places on the lips of the Immaculate One."

"Is it not in this sense that we must look for the most profound significance of this mysterious jewel described by Lucia? Several verses of the Canticle

---

[360] Tob. 12:7.
[361] Frère Michel, *TWTF,* Vol. I, p. 145.
[362] Ibid., p. 149.

seem to invite us to do so; thus the divine Spouse [is] speaking to the Bride, the figure of Israel and of the Church, personified in the Blessed Virgin: '*You have ravished my heart, my sister, my bride, you have ravished my heart with a glance of your eyes, with one jewel of your necklace. How sweet is your love, my sister, my bride!*' (Cant. 4:9-10)"[363]

The Second Sign:
The Mediatrix of All Graces

The meaning of the jewel and necklace is intertwined with the little yellow star, which we have already seen is "The Star of Esther," and which "points to a particular Old Testament history called *The Book of Esther*, which relates the story of a Hebrew queen whose intercession saved her people from annihilation...Just as the star adorning Our Lady of Fatima points to *The Book of Esther*, so does *The Book of Esther* point to all of the Fatima apparitions. Esther's theme centers on secrets and revelations, suggesting [it] is a figure type for *The Apocalypse* (Greek for Revelations)...*The Book of Esther* appears to encapsulate what Fatima highlights about both the Virgin's and the Church's singular office in salvation history."

Centuries ago, St. Alphonsus agreed with St. Albert who noted Queen Esther[364] as a figure type of the Virgin Mary. Since the Star of Esther was one of the Fatima Virgin's adornments, it is clear that *The Book of Esther* calls for a thoroughly traditional, theological study. That said, it must also be noted that no Church Doctor ever attempted a complete examination of this canonical, historical book. For those of us living in the Fatima era, the proper interpretation of *Esther* is vital. The interpretation must be in accord with Church dogma and doctrine, the constitution of the Church, apostolic tradition, and the study of history with a "Catholic conscience"[365] of that same history. Such a venture includes "studies into the spiritual, moral, social, political, educational, economic and cultural conditions of the times,"[366] employing the truths of Faith and scholastic reason.

Both of the Virgin's adornments reveal the "secrets" of Mary and about Mary, which are carefully hidden in the Old Testament and apocalyptic figure types. As to the method prescribed for the interpretation of Scripture (which, with Tradition, is one of the two sources of Revelation), Pope Pius IX clarified

---

[363] Ibid., p. 146.
[364] de Liguori, St. Alphonsus. *The Glories of Mary*, p. 39.
[365] Belloc, Hilaire. *Europe and the Faith*. [Rockford, IL: Tan Books and Publishers. Retypeset and republished 1992. Originally published in New York: The Paulist Press, 1920]: p. 3.
[366] Kramer, Rev. H. B., op cit., p. 17.

that "the rules which the holy Synod of Trent salutarily decreed concerning the interpretation of Divine Scripture in order to retrain impetuous minds, are wrongly explained by certain men. We, renewing the same decree, declare this to be its intention: that, in matters of faith and morals pertaining to the instruction of Christian Doctrine, that must be considered as the true sense of Sacred Scripture which Holy Mother Church has held and holds, whose office it is to judge concerning the true understanding and interpretation of the Sacred Scriptures; and, for that reason, no one is permitted to interpret Sacred Scripture itself *contrary* to the sense, or even *contrary* to the unanimous agreement of the Fathers..."[367]

Regarding the literal and mystical sense of Scripture, Pope Pius XII taught, "In this work, let interpreters keep in mind that their greatest care should be to discern and define what the so-called literal sense of the Bible is."[368] In obedience to Trent's decree, this examination of *The Book of Esther* will hold to the sense held by the Church and the Fathers, recalling what St. Augustine stated: "**What lies hidden in the Old Testament is made manifest in the New.**"[369]

The Central Figures in Esther

Before continuing, a brief recap on the story of Esther is necessary. Almost five hundred years before Christ, God raised up a Hebrew virgin, an orphan adopted and educated by her uncle Mardochai, to save the Israelites from annihilation. Through an unusual series of events, she became the queen of ancient Persia, living in its capital city of Susan.

The very name of this Hebrew queen, who was loved by the king above all others, refers to "hidden things." To repeat from the previous section, she was "named Edissa, 'who by another name was called Esther.' In the Old Testament of the Hebrew text, her name was **Hádássah**—meaning *myrtle*, a white, five-pointed, star-shaped flower. The Hebrew texts also relate that she gave her name as *Hester* (in Persian, *Esther*—which means 'star.')...The alteration from **Hádássah** to **Hester** refers to a secret, because **Hester** translates to 'hidden [meaning of the] star.'" In addition, the "Hebrew name for *The Book of Esther* is *Megillat Esther*—e.g., "revelation of [that which is] hidden."

Intriguing as a figure type is Assuerus, Esther's spouse, the unfathomable Persian monarch apparently serving as a figure type of God. Modern-day Iran

---

[367] Denzinger. *The Sources of Catholic Dogma.* "Pius IX," #1788. [Fitzwilliam, NH: Loreto Publications, 1954]: p. 444.

[368] Ibid., "Pius XII," #2293; p. 621.

[369] Pope, Hugh T. "Angels," *The Catholic Encyclopedia,* Vol. 1. [New York: Robert Appleton Company, 1907] [http://www.newadvent.org/cathen/01476d.htm]

is the heart of ancient Persia, even to the city of Susan (Susa). Is it not possible that Our Lady's choices to appear at Fatima, a village named after a Mohammedan woman who converted to Catholicism, and to display of Esther's Star provide many traces of the Third Secret's hidden things? **After all, *The Book of Esther* centers on secrets and revelations, a plot among nations against one kingdom and the elect, prayer and sacrifice, and the final triumph of the Queen.**

Esther's history may prefigure the world's punishments by further persecutions of the Church and the Holy Father in the form of war against crumbling Christendom by Mohammedanism, as well as by nations under the influence of Russia, which has "spread her errors throughout the world."[370] Also contemplate the description of the Third Secret Vision, which depicts soldiers bearing "guns and arrows"[371] and consider which soldiers today use both of these weapons. Like Esther who softened the Persian king's wrath and changed his heart, we can be confident that Our Lady of Fatima will, after the collegial consecration of Russia to her Immaculate Heart and the papal promulgation of the Five First Saturdays, also convert many souls, including the hearts of those who now hold to Islam.

In *The Book of Esther*, however, Assuerus' Persian kingdom appears to represent the kingdom of God on earth but also the heavenly kingdom. His first queen, Vasthi, represents Eve while Esther, his second queen, prefigures the Virgin Mary. Mardochai, uncle of Esther, is "an enigmatic 'type within type.' He seems to embody in his person the faithful in exile but also a 'vizier' or vicar, if not the Vicar of Christ."[372] As Esther's guardian, he is also figurative of St. Joseph, guardian and chaste spouse of the Virgin, archetype of Esther and the Church. As we know, St. Joseph briefly appeared during the Miracle of the Sun at Fatima to bless the world with the Christ Child.

Finally, there is Mardochai's nemesis, Aman "of the race of Agag."[373] This reference is yet another trace—this time to the struggles between Esau and Jacob, the twin sons of Isaac and Rebecca (another type of the Virgin). These brothers prefigure two nations or "cities"—the first of reprobates and the second of Jesus Christ and the elect.[374] The race of Agag are also known as Amalcites and Edomites (descendants of Esau[375]), about whom God Himself prophesied **"the war of the Lord shall be against Amalec, from generation to**

---

[370] Frère Michel, op. cit., pp. 182-183
[371] *The Message of Fatima.*
[372] Frère Michel, loc. cit., p. 15.
[373] Esther 3:1.
[374] de Montfort, St. Louis. *True Devotion to Mary*, #185-#212.
[375] Gen. 36: 1-43; Jer. 49: 7-8.

generation."[376] Due to their pride and treachery against Jacob, God revealed in a vision to Abdias the eventual destruction of Esau's line. As punishment, the Edomites would never experience a final triumph over Jacob;[377] rather, they would be eventually reduced to "stubble," until there "shall be no remains of the house of Esau."[378] Astonishingly, in Abdias' vision, the Lord asked, "How have they searched Esau, **how have they sought out his hidden things?**"[379]

Returning to Aman, King Asseurus' first vizier, he was called "our father" and "was worshipped by all as the next man after the king," [380] a worship that defies the First Commandment in lieu of appropriate honor of a high office. However, from the beginning of his appointment, Aman secretly schemed, first against the king and later, due to his personal hatred of Mardochai the Jew, against the entire nation of the Hebrews.

It follows that Aman also appears to serve as a "a type within type" of treason against God and His Kingdom—e.g., as Lucifer-turned-Satan (the highest angel in the hierarchy of angels who revolted against God and tried to ascend to His throne), an anti-Christ figure, and one who gains and then abuses the authority of his high position by plotting against "the three necessary societies"—the family, civil society, and the Church.[381] As illustrated in the Old Testament, his perfidious qualities—including lying, conspiracy, hypocrisy, soothing words, deceit, feigned indulgence and favor—are always those of the traitor.[382] These traits are also descriptive of Judas,[383] once Christ's apostle and friend, as well as of many Christians in the end times.[384]

In a word, Aman prefigures treachery "not from without but from within"[385] the earthly kingdom of God, against the Lord and His people. In relation to Fatima and the Star of Esther, his role as nemesis against the elect must be taken seriously. The Old Testament makes clear that the Israelites were the elect, but today's elect are the faithful Catholics. As St. Justin the Martyr explained, since the time of Christ, "The true spiritual Israel, descendants of

---

[376] Exod.17: 14-16.
[377] Abdias 1.
[378] Abdias 17.
[379] Abdias 6.
[380] Esther 16:11.
[381] Pope Pius XI, *Divini Illius Magistri* (On the Christian Education of Youth, December 31, 1929): para. 3.
[382] Gen. 34: 13-31; Jud. 9:1-5; 1 Sam. 18: 17-19; Dan. 6:1-8.
[383] Lk. 6:16.
[384] 2 Tim. 3:4.
[385] Pope St. Pius X, op cit., para: 3.

Judah and Jacob and Isaac and Abraham…are we who have been led to God through this crucified Christ."[386]

The Consolation of the Elect

The imagery found in *Esther* and the *Apocalypse*, both among the Church's infallible canonical books, bear great similarities. *Esther* appears to prefigure the *Apocalypse*, which "is chiefly the grand finale of the Kingdom of God on earth, the completion of all prophecies in a final synthesis."[387] Both books console the elect "in the hardships of a virtuous life and in the dangers of practicing their religion with persecutions facing them."[388] In *Esther*, for example, the dream of Mardochai relates:

"**Behold there were voices**, and **tumults**, and **thunders**, and **earthquakes**, and **a disturbance** upon the earth. And **behold two great dragons came forth ready to fight one against another**. And at their cry all nations were stirred up to fight against the nation of the just. And that was a day of darkness and danger, of tribulation and distress, and great fear upon the earth. And **the nation of the just was troubled** fearing their own evils, and was prepared for death. And they cried to God: and as they were crying, **a little fountain grew into a very great river, and abounded into many waters**."

"**The light and the sun rose up, and the humble were exalted**, and they devoured the glorious. And when Mardochai had seen this, and arose out of his bed, he was thinking what God would do: and he kept it fixed in his mind, desirous to know what the dream should signify." [389]

This dream was later interpreted by Mardochai, who waited a decade before its meaning was made manifest:

"**The little fountain which grew into a river, and was turned into a light, and into the sun, and abounded into many waters, is Esther**, whom the king married, and made queen. But the two dragons are I and Aman. **The nations that were assembled** are they that endeavoured to destroy the name of the Jews. And my nation is Israel, who cried to the Lord, and **the Lord saved his people**: and he delivered us from all evils, and **hath wrought great signs and wonders among the nations**: And he commanded that there should be **two lots**, one of the people of God, and the other of all the nations. And both

---

[386] Jurgens, op. cit., p. 59.
[387] Kramer, Rev. H. B., op. cit., p. 6.
[388] Ibid., pp. 8-9.
[389] Esther 11: 5-12.

lots came to the day appointed already from that time before God to all nations: *And the Lord remembered his people, and had mercy on his inheritance.*"[390]

Since Esther is a great Marian figure type, should we not carefully consider the "types within types" of Mardochai's dream, especially the parts which he later understood symbolized the Queen? Note also that **it was only** when in terror and preparing for death that the **nation of the just** first "cried to God," and it was as they were crying that this little fountain grew into a great river. Might this dream prefigure what will happen in our own day? **Must the Third Secret Vision come to pass before the nation of the just cry to God for His intercession, which must be accomplished through the Mediatrix of All Graces?**

The Holy Spirit says of the Virgin: "My sister, my spouse, is a garden enclosed, a fountain sealed up."[391] In the Scriptures, a fountain symbolically prefigures fear of the Lord, wisdom, the law of the wise, understanding, God's blessings, or the Virgin Mary.[392] A river may designate the prosperity of the saints, affliction, Christ or the Virgin, God's Presence, the Holy Ghost, and God's Love.[393] The Sun or its light indicates grace, God's Presence, His Glory and Justice, or the glory of the just.[394] At Fatima, the Virgin—the Fountain Enclosed, the River of Grace—shone with a light more brilliant than the sun, and it was she who gave the spectacular sign of the Miracle of the Sun.

Finally, the first sentence describing Mardochai's dream includes the elements:

• "Behold there were **voices**, and **tumults**, and **thunders**, and **earthquakes**, and **a disturbance** upon the earth."[395]

So does the very last sentence of the *Apocalypse's* eleventh chapter mention the elements, immediately before "a woman clothed with the sun" is described:

• "And the temple of God was opened in heaven: and **the ark of his testament was seen in his temple**, and there were **lightnings**, and **voices**, and **an earthquake**, and **great hail**."[396]

There are other parallels between *Esther* and the *Apocalypse*, with the following only a sampling: allusions to the kingdom of God; all the classes of

---

[390] Esth. 10: 6-12.
[391] Cant. 4:12.
[392] Prov. 14: 27; Prov. 16:22; Prov. 18: 4, Jer. 2:13; Cant. 4:12.
[393] Ps. 1:3; Ps. 124:4; Isa. 32: 1, 2; Isa. 33:21; Jn. 7: 38-39; Apoc. 22: 4-5.
[394] Ps. 19: 4-7; Mt. 17:2; Mt. 13:43.
[395] Esther 11: 5-12.
[396] Apoc. 11: 19.

mankind; the patience of the elect in exile; a wedding feast, persecutions of the elect by other nations (the reprobates); false worship; apostasy; penance and sackcloth; the ancient Persians (modern-day Iranians); great signs and wonders among the nations; "a woman" of royalty; a dragon or dragons (one in the *Apocalypse*, "a great red dragon," but two in *Esther*, which Mardochai eventually understood represented he and Aman); water; the sun; voices, tumults, tribulations, thunder; and earthquakes.

The Continuing Tale of Two Cities

In fine, both books tell "the tale of two cities" from the beginning of the world—*Esther* in abridged form, *The Apocalypse* in its entirety. As St. Augustine wrote:

"**Accordingly, two cities have been formed by two loves**: the earthly by the love of self, **even to the contempt of God**; the heavenly by the love of God, **even to the contempt of self**. The former, in a word, glories in itself, the latter in the Lord. For the one seeks glory from men; but the greatest glory of the other is God, the witness of conscience. The one lifts up its head in its own glory; the other says to its God, 'Thou art my glory, and the lifter up of mine head.'

"In the one, the princes and the nations it subdues are **ruled by the love of ruling**; in the other, the princes and the subjects **serve one another in love**, the latter obeying, while the former take thought for all. **The one delights in its own strength**, represented in the persons of its rulers; **the other says to its God**, 'I will love Thee, O Lord, my strength.'

"And therefore the wise men of the one city, **living according to man**, have sought for profit to their own bodies or souls, or both, and those who have known God 'glorified Him not as God, neither were thankful, but became vain in their imaginations, and their foolish heart was darkened; professing themselves to be wise,'—that is, **glorying in their own wisdom**, and being **possessed by pride**—'they became fools, and changed the glory of the incorruptible God into an image made like to corruptible man, and to birds, and four-footed beasts, and creeping things.'

"'**For they were either leaders or followers of the people in adoring images**, and **worshipped and served the creature more than the Creator**, who is blessed forever.' **But in the other city there is no human wisdom**, but only godliness, which offers due worship to the true God, and looks for its reward in the society of the saints, of holy angels as well as holy men, 'that God may be all in all.'"[397]

Only the Lady Queen Can Help You

We recall that, once Esther was aware of Aman's decree to annihilate the entire Jewish nation throughout Persia, her uncle appealed her aid. She privately sent a message to Mardochai—a command to him and all the people to pray and fast for her intention, taking no food or water for three days, before she interceded with the king. [398] She and her maidens did likewise.

In her prayer to God, the Queen acknowledged that the punishments so far forthcoming were due to the **apostasy** among her people. [399] But now they were faced with total annihilation and their only hope was the Queen—just as Our Lady of the Rosary at Fatima said of herself in the third person, "Only she can help you." Thankfully, the king heard Esther's plea and the elect were saved.

In light of Fatima, we must wonder—**what would have happened if the elect had ignored the Queen's command?** What if they doubted that she could intercede with the king for their sake?

At the conclusion of *The Book of Esther*, we find the probable outcome to those questions in the king's letter, favoring the Jews and condemning the executed Aman, who was once second after the king. If the people disregarded Esther's command for prayer and penance, which allowed her to intercede and soften the king's heart, **the ultimate outcome would have been the elect annihilated and the kingdom overtaken by secret enemies.**[400]

Sr. Lucia once referred to chapters 8-13 of the *Apocalypse*, which exhibits the same theme of treachery, apostasy, and a final attempt to annihilate the Church and the elect, in order to usurp the Kingdom of God. It is also strongly suggested in the Vision of the Third Secret with the martyrdom of "a bishop dressed in white" and all the faithful who die in the same manner. As Sr. Lucia revealed, when asked about the Third Secret, "It's in the *Gospel* and the *Apocalypse*. Read them!"[401]

---

[397] St. Augustine. *The City of God*. "Excerpts on the Two Cities." *Medieval Sourcebook* website. [http://www.fordham.edu/halsall/source/aug-city2.html]
[398] Esther 4: 15-17.
[399] Esther 14: 6-9.
[400] Esther 16: 3-16.
[401] Fellows, Mark. *Fatima in Twilight*. [Niagara Falls, U.S. and Canada: Marmion Publications, 2003]: p. 295.

CHAPTER 12

Fatima and the Great "Et Cetera":
Traces of the Third Secret Message

"Truly, it is the greatest of errors
to neglect the business of eternal salvation."
−St. Eucherius

That the entire Third Secret, given in July 1917, remains hidden is clear to many Catholics. The disclosure of the Third Secret's Vision contradicts those who claim that the "veil is removed from the greatest mystery of the twentieth century"[402] and that events leading to the Third Secret "now seem a part of the past."[403] Despite various papal consecrations of the *world* and acts of entrustment made from 1942 to 2013, at least three of the Fatima prophecies have come to pass, while the third−the martyrdom of the good−continues. Daily news reports alone should convince all Catholics that to avoid the fulfillment of the Third Secret, the Holy Father and the world's bishops must consecrate Russia to the Immaculate Heart of Mary.

Our Lady's messages and prophecies to the Church are too often treated by clergy and laity as a few redundant reminders. Casually dismissed is the truth that the Three Secrets of Fatima are firmly founded on Divine Revelation and authentic prophecy. Based on Faith and facts, the following is apparent: 1) world-wide devotion to the Immaculate Heart of Mary (which includes the papal promulgation of the Five First Saturdays of Reparation) has not come to fruition, 2) the collegial consecration of *Russia* has not been made 3) the entire Third Secret *Message* is not yet revealed, and 4) if the first three requests are not heeded, the tragedies of the past century will reach their apex in the Third Secret *Vision's* fulfillment and the annihilation (the complete destruction) of various nations.

It is reasonable−although painfully so−to reach these conclusions because there are objective, coinciding reasons for them. First, there has been no papal promulgation of the Five First Saturdays, although there is sometimes mention of praying the Rosary. Second, there has never been any specific mention of

---

[402] Bertone, Cardinal Tarcisio (with Giuseppe De Carli). *The Last Secret of Fatima.* [New York: Doubleday, English translation copyright 2008]: p.162.

[403] *The Message of Fatima.*

Russia in any papal consecration or entrustment. Third, the world's bishops did not join the popes who made those acts. Fourth, the world has not yet experienced the prophesied "era of peace" promised by Our Lady. So let us look once more for the "traces of hidden things."

Fatima and the Significance of the 13th

Catholics may wonder why Our Lady first appeared at Fatima on May 13, as well as the 13th day of each month through October, 1917 (with the singular exception of August 19, 1917, due to the Fatima visionaries' imprisonment on August 13).

• First and foremost, May 13 was originally dedicated to Our Lady of the Martyrs. On May 13, 609 A.D., Pope St. Boniface IV (608-615),[404] converted the Roman Pantheon into a basilica, dedicating the edifice to Our Lady under her title, *St. Mary of the Martyrs.*

In 1561, this basilica,[405] built in the very heart of the Baths of Diocletian (an emperor by whom the early Christians suffered the most vicious persecutions and martyrdoms), "received its [current] official name, St. Mary of the Angels *and* the Martyrs."[406]

Correlation: Both the date and place of Our Lady's first Fatima appearance silently emphasized her title as *St. Mary of the Angels and the Martyrs*, for the Cova da Iria (the Cove of Irene) appears to be named for the virgin martyr, St. Irene of Tomar.[407] It was on July 13 that Our Lady gave the Three Secrets, warning that if her requests were not heeded, "the good will be martyred, various nations will be annihilated."[408] The description of the Third Secret *Vision* also includes two angels who gather the blood of martyrs.[409]

• There is another striking link between the basilica named in honor of *St. Mary of the Angels and the Martyrs* and the appearances of Our Lady of Fatima, which have to do with **the sun.** Almost one thousand years after the

---

[404] Oestereich, Thomas. "Pope St. Boniface IV." *The Catholic Encyclopedia,* Vol. 4. [New York: Robert Appleton Company, 1907] [http://www.newadvent.org/cathen/02660c.htm]
[405] "From Antiquity to the Present," *The Basilica of St. Mary of the Angels and the Martyrs Official Website*
[http://www.santamariadegliangeliroma.it/paginamastersing.html?codice_url=antiquity_to_pr esent&ramo_home=Basilica&lingua=INGLESE]
[406] Loc cit., "Basilica"
[http://www.santamariadegliangeliroma.it/paginamastersing.html?codice_url=basilica&lingu a=INGLESE&ramo_home=Basilica]
[407] Frère Michel, *TWTF,* Vol. 1, p. 123.
[408] *The Message of Fatima.*
[409] Ibid.

basilica's dedication, Pope Clement XI[410] (reigning 1700-1721), the same Vicar of Christ who declared the Feast of the Immaculate Conception as a holy day of obligation, commissioned Francesco Bianchini–an astronomer, mathematician, archeologist, historian, and philosopher–to build inside the church a "meridian line" for the city of Rome. (A beautiful example of science combined with Catholic culture, this meridian line is known as "The Clementina," named after the pope who ordered its construction). To track the path of the sun, Bianchini made careful calculations, then created a small hole in the southern wall of the basilica, and laid into the marble floor the meridian line, which runs exactly north to south. The result is that, when the sun reaches its zenith (called solar noon or solar time), light shines through the hole on the wall, casting its light on the meridian line. By the clock, however, this event[411] takes place near 12:15 p.m. (1:15 p.m. in the summer)[412]

The meridian lines' purpose was to check the parameters[413] of the solar-based "Gregorian Calendar," so named after Pope Gregory XIII, who advanced the Catholic Restoration after the Protestant Revolt. To exactly predict Easter, which is based on the vernal equinox, Pope Gregory XIII also revised the Julian solar-based calendar. As a result, the Gregorian calendar is "so nearly exact that there will be an error of one day only in 35 centuries."[414] Pope Gregory officially promulgated the solar-based calendar, which took effect on October 4, 1582, thus immediately advancing the calendar date by 11 days.

Correlation: The first basilica ever named after **Our Lady of the Martyrs** also tracks **the sun**, which is a symbol of the **Sun of Justice**, Our Lord Jesus Christ. At Fatima, Our Lady always appeared at the **noon** hour, an hour of great significance, since it is the time in which Our Lord was actually crucified and hung on the Cross. The noon hour may also indicate how much time is left

---

[410] Loughlin, James. "Pope Clement XI." *The Catholic Encyclopedia*, Vol. 4. [New York: Robert Appleton Company, 1908] [http://www.newadvent.org/cathen/04029a.htm]
[411] "Santa Maria degli Angeli e dei Martiri," *Wikipedia*.
[http://en.wikipedia.org/wiki/Santa_Maria_degli_Angeli_e_dei_Martiri]
[412] In January, 1972, CUT, replacing Greenwich Mean Time, introduced a "leap second" at irregular intervals, in which one minute becomes 61 seconds, to compensate for the earth's slowing rotation. "Coordinated Universal Time," *Wikipedia*.
[http://en.wikipedia.org/wiki/Coordinated_Universal_Time]
[413] "Science with the Clementine Gnomon." *The Basilica of St. Mary of the Angels and the Martyrs Official Website*
[http://www.santamariadegliangeliroma.it/paginamastersing.html?codice_url=science_with& ramo_home=La_Meridiana&lingua=INGLESE]
[414] Laux, M.A., Fr. John. *Church History*. [Rockford, IL: TAN Books and Publishers, republished from 1930 original text]: p. 486.

before *the world's* sunset. That Sr. Lucia died 40 minutes before sunset, on February 13, 2005–in the Hebrew month of Adar–is another sign.[415]

On October 13th, the day of the Miracle of the Sun, witnesses stated that Our Lady appeared exactly at **solar noon**–not by the clock's time but by the sun's time. [416] Both the adjusted Gregorian calendar dates and the time of the Virgin's appearances at solar noon prove that **heaven acknowledged Pope Gregory's authority** in the calendar reform. This acknowledgement also underscores the pope's authority, as the Vicar of Christ, to command the collegial consecration of Russia to the Immaculate Heart of Mary. That heaven acknowledged the Gregorian calendar is also proven by the next fact.

• Centuries earlier, on May 13, 1391 (before the Gregorian reform of the calendar), Pope Boniface IX (reigning 1389-1404) acquiesced to the request of King John I of Portugal and ordered that all Portuguese cathedrals should be named in honor of the Virgin.[417] On August 13, 1385, the Virgin had previously answered the King's prayer, made at Fatima, for his smaller army to reign victorious against a much larger force; now the King wished to further honor the Virgin throughout all of Portugal.[418]

Correlation: Exactly 526 years later, the Virgin first appeared at Fatima on May 13, 1917–on the "new" May 13 of the Gregorian calendar. Coincidentally, the length of time in years between these two events (526) equals "13" when the numbers are added as individual digits (i.e., 5+2+6 =13).

• May 13 was also the Feast of Our Lady of the Blessed Sacrament.[419] This salutary title of the Blessed Mother's became more well-known due to St. Peter Julian Eymard and a mission given to him by the Virgin Mary. She made him aware that no religious order was named in honor of her Divine Son's Real Presence in the Blessed Sacrament. With the encouragement of Pope Pius IX, the saint founded the Congregation of the Most Blessed Sacrament in Paris, France on May 13, 1856. In 1921, the Sacred Congregation of Rites authorized May 13 as the annual solemn commemoration of *The Feast of Our Lady of the Blessed Sacrament.*

Correlation: Before Our Lady appeared at Fatima, the children were granted visions of an angel who taught them special prayers of adoration and supplication to the Holy Trinity and the Blessed Sacrament.

---

[415] Please refer to Chapter 10.

[416] Frère Michel, op. cit., p. 332.

[417] Just, S.J., Ph.D., Felix. *An Overview of Christian History.* [http://catholic-resources.org/Courses/Christianity-Gilles.htm]

[418] Frère Michel, op. cit., p. 9.

[419] O'Laverty, *The Mother of God and Her Glorious Feasts*, p. 125.

• October 13 (the day of the wondrous yet terrifying Miracle of the Sun in 1917) is believed by many scholars to be the actual date of St. Peter's martyrdom in Rome under the tyrant Nero, who is unquestionably a figure-type of the anti-Christ. The date's conclusion is based on the detailed research of Margherita Guarducci (+1999), a remarkable epigraphologist and archeologist, who participated in the study of excavations under St. Peter's Basilica which were ordered by Pope Pius XII on June 28, 1939 (eve of Ss. Peter and Paul).

It was Guarducci who first realized that certain bones found were those of Peter, the first Pope; she was also the first to establish October 13, 64 A.D. as the date of the martyred saint's crucifixion. In 1960, her outstanding book, *The Tomb of St. Peter*, was translated into English and published. Eight years later, another of her written works, "The Date of Peter's Martyrdom," was published in Naples (in the original Italian) in *Words from the Past* in the *Antiquity Studies Review*, No. 267. That latter work was summarized in 1996 by Giovanni Ricciardi and published in "30 Days" magazine, Issue No. 3. For the purposes of this book, the following excerpts of Ricciardi's synopsis of Guarducci's 1968 work are included:

"The most authoritative text informing us of Peter's martyrdom in Rome is the first letter of Saint Clement the Roman to the Corinthians, generally dated at about 96 AD. In its turn, Clement's letter cannot be read apart from one famed passage of Tacitus' 'Annales' (XV, 38-45), in which the historian speaks of the famous fire that flared in Rome on the night of July 18-19, 64 [A.D.] and of its consequences. A comparison of these two testimonies seems to show that Peter was martyred during the anti-Christian persecution campaign unleashed by Nero after the fire and that the place of his martyrdom was the Vatican's 'horti.' The information Tacitus provides is undoubtedly very authoritative because the author of the 'Annales' was writing not long after the events and he was able to quote eyewitnesses as well as from first-hand documents, such as the 'Acta senatus' and the 'Acta diurna'—respectively the minutes of Senate sessions and the official diaries of the Roman State.

"According to Tacitus, then, the Christians whom he—as others do—describes as a 'considerable multitude' ('multitudo ingens'), were condemned to death not so much for causing the fire but because they were guilty of **'hatred towards the human race'** ('odium human,' generic). This was **a serious charge because the identification of the human race with the empire itself meant that anyone so charged was considered an enemy of the empire.**"

(**Author's Note**: In 1996, when Ricciardi wrote this summation of Guarducci's written research, it could not be foreseen that before 20 years had passed, the term "**hate crime**" would be coined and hurled by liberals of all types against Catholics who loyally adhere to Christ and His Church's traditional doctrines, dogmas, articles of faith, and traditional views on moral issues; this malevolent phrase is also used against anyone who holds to "old-fashioned" values. Shockingly, the term "hate crime" appears to be a modern-day resurrection of Nero's false judgment against the early Catholics of "hatred towards the human race," which resulted in the subsequent penalty of a cruel death.)

To continue: "The execution of the condemned, according to Tacitus' information, took place during grandiose circus spectacles ('circense ludicrum'), for which Nero made available his own circus in the Vatican that was the principal adornment of his 'horti.' It is true, too, that the Vatican circus would have been a natural choice since, after the fire, it was the only area left in Rome for the kind of spectacle Nero desired. In fact, the Circus Maximus—the usual venue for Rome's 'circensia ludrica'—could not be used because of fire damage.

"Tacitus goes on to add an interesting detail: Nero himself honored the Vatican spectacles with his presence, mixing with the crowd disguised as a chariot driver and racing around the circus track. The spectacles lasted for several days. The question now was establishing exactly when they were held."

As for the month of October in the year 64 (A.D.):

"Tacitus has no hesitation in establishing the year 64 for these events. If we look at the series of events the historian lists as having happened between the fire of Rome (July 18-19) and the end of the year, we can establish that the Vatican spectacles took place in the first half of October. Nor is it difficult to prove that between the end of 64 and Nero's death on June 9, 68 [A.D.], there are no other periods in which there was anti-Christian persecution of the type that Tacitus and Clement describe. It is also useful to note that the period between the end of September 66 [A.D.] and the beginning of 68 [A.D.] can be excluded without doubt since that was the period of Nero's travels in Greece.

"But, confirming the dating proposed for the circus spectacles and, therefore, for Peter's martyrdom, are two other important, anonymous, texts in Greek contained in a papyrus conserved in Vienna today. They are the *Apocalypse of Peter* and the *Ascension of Isaiah*. I believe that these texts (belonging to the so-called 'apocraphal literature,' a very common category between the end of the first century and the first half of the second which used prophetic and symbolic language to interpret historical events of the time) are so well informed on the history of the Neronian period that they must have been written not long after events in 64 (not after the year 80, perhaps). I also believe that they are the fruit of the same Judeo-Christian environment. After addressing Nero's infamies, the authors of the two texts announce his punishment as imminent. According to the author of the *Apocalypse* [of Peter], **it would be none other than Peter's martyrdom that would mark the beginning of the emperor's end.** This statement is echoed in the *Ascension* [of Isaiah] text which affirms that Nero's kingdom would last for 'three years, seven months and 27 days' after the apostle's death. If we calculate three years, seven months and 27 days from Nero's death (June 9, 68), we arrive at the year 64 [A.D.] and October 13 to be precise: this date falls perfectly within the period in which, according to the Tacitus passage, we have set the unleashing of Nero's persecutions."

On Nero's *dies imperii*

"The date calculated chronologically three years, seven months and 27 days after Nero's death is confirmed by another decisive point. October 13 was not just any ordinary day. It was the anniversary of Nero's ascent to the throne, his *dies imperii*. Moreover October 13, 64 [A.D.] was the tenth anniversary of his reign (*decennalia,* October 13, 54/October 13, 64).

"The *dies imperii* was an important date in the Romans' official calendar at the time of the empire. Numerous sources certify that between the first and fourth centuries, it was celebrated more or less solemnly with sacrifices, feasts, contests and donations to the public by the emperor. Regular features of these festivities were sacrifices and exhibitions of bloodletting according to the ancient belief that bloodshed was to the advantage of the living. In fact, it has been pointed out that in Rome the most important feasts concerning the person of the emperor—birthdays (*dies natalis*) for example, and anniversaries of his ascent to the throne—often coincided with exhibitions of bloodletting, gladiator fights, displays of the condemned (*venationes*). It has also been noted that it was on the occasion of these anniversaries that Jews and Christians would often be sacrificed. Thus for example, Jews of Alexandria were sacrificed on Caligula's *dies natalis*. Saint Polycarp's martyrdom coincides with the *dies imperii* of Antoninus Pius and that of the Christians of Lyons with the *dies imperii* of Marcus Aurelius. It is highly likely, then, that the Emperor Nero, who loved manifestations to be as spectacular as possible, would have promoted cruel spectacles for his *decennalia* (a feast when, in the person of the emperor made a god, the majesty of the Roman Empire was exalted). It is highly likely that he would have organized the execution of Christians who were already condemned on charges of being enemies of the empire.

"From a study of this whole series of testimonies, we can draw two significant conclusions. Firstly the hypothesis, founded on Tacitus' testimony that Nero's persecution in which Peter also suffered martyrdom happened in October 64, is confirmed. Secondly, it appears extremely likely that we must set the date of the martyrdom of the Prince of the Apostles at October 13 that year."

In addition, there is the following and alarming observation made by Margherita Guarducci in her book, *The Tomb of St. Peter*, wherein she noted "a singular coincidence" that she discovered in the two apocryphal works, the *Apocalypse of Peter* and the *Ascension of Isaiah*:

"This latter work deals with the Emperor Nero. In language which is symbolic but sufficiently clear, **he is portrayed as possessed by the devil and resolved to persecute the Twelve Apostles of Christ, one of whom (Peter) will eventually fall into his hands.** There are other allusions to the misdeeds suggested by Lucifer to the Emperor, and finally two little sentences appear, little for sure, but how precious! I quote them from the French translation of the Ethiopian text, given by Cardinal Eugene Tisserant:

'*And he will set up his image in the sight of all the cities. And he will rule for three years, seven months and twenty-seven days.*'

"What could be the meaning of this particular indication of three years, seven months and twenty-seven days?" Guarducci rhetorically asks, and she answers: "The images set up in every city are certainly the statues of the Emperor customarily erected in the various cities of the Empire."

Then came Guarducci's surprising yet reasonable conclusion: "And so the *Ascension of Isaiah* led me back to the first half of October 64 [A.D.], the very same when, according to my other research, the Vatican spectacle and Peter's martyrdom would have taken place. **But what is the significance of this date of October 13, which is presented as the day of the Apostle's martyrdom?** In the other prophetic book, the *Apocalypse of Peter*, this martyrdom is regarded as the beginning of the ruin of Nero. 'There we have it,' I said to myself, 'the beginning and the end of the three year, seven month and twenty-seven day period of calamities! It opens with the martyrdom of Peter, the culminating point of the persecution, and closes with the death of the tyrant.'"

Correlation: October 13 was the day of the final apparition at Fatima, Portugal. It was the day on which occurred the Miracle of the Sun in 1917 and, as we have seen, there is good cause to believe it is also the anniversary of the first Pope's martyrdom, which an innumerable number of faithful also suffered with him on that same day in the year of Our Lord 64. In the "Great Secret" given to the children on July 13, 1917, the Third Secret's Vision revealed a half-ruined city (which might be Rome), the bodies of the dead, the souls for whom "a bishop dressed in white" prayed as he made his halting, painful way, the death (by gunshots and arrows) of the bishop (who may or may not be the reigning Pope), and a countless number of people who are killed in the same manner. **Thus we recognize themes in regard to the 13th day:**

First, May 13 reinforces the dogma of the "hidden Jesus," as the Fatima children called the True Presence of Jesus–Body, Blood, Soul and Divinity–in the Blessed Sacrament of the altar.

Second, May 13 signifies Our Lady as Queen of Angels *and* of Martyrs, underlining the Virgin's prophecies at Fatima *if she is not heeded*, especially that **"the good will be martyred."**

Third, this is also true with the date of October 13, which is the likely date of Pope St. Peter's martyrdom and with him many of the faithful, under the Emperor Nero, one of the most infamous, historical figure-types of anti-Christ, the son of perdition.

Finally, the history of May 13, in relation to the Gregorian calendar and heaven's acknowledgement of it, reinforces the pope's special prerogatives, not only as bishop of Rome but as the reigning Supreme Pontiff of Christ's kingdom on earth, the Catholic Church.

Five Scourges, Five Blasphemies, Five First Saturdays

Since "the very nature of true prophecy is that it unerringly predicts what comes to pass,"[420] we must also recall that authentic prophecy from God is given for our edification and instruction. As St. Paul taught, we must "despise not prophecy, but prove all things; hold fast that which is good."[421] The Church found Fatima "worthy of belief,"[422] and its prophecies have proven true. Therefore, we must hold fast to the requests the Mother of God made at Fatima, and despise not the prophecies she gave to the Church.

Too, we cannot forget Our Lady foretold that, if her requests were ignored–a circumstance that could only happen due to the hierarchy's dismissal of them–five scourges would afflict the world. The first three of the following five sufferings have *unquestionably* occurred:

1. Russia will spread her errors throughout the world.

2. A second and worse war, which will begin during the reign of Pius XI (World War II).

3. The good will be martyred.

4. Persecutions of the Church and of the Holy Father.

5. The annihilation of nations.

The five points above are one example of how, for a mysterious reason, the number "five" plays an important role of the Fatima Message. To illustrate, Our Lady of Fatima first appeared in May, which is the fifth month of the year.

---

[420] Ferrara, Christopher. *The Secret Still Hidden.* [Pound Ridge, NY: Good Counsel Publications, 2008]: p. 11.

[421] 1 Thess. 5: 20-23.

[422] De Marchi, I. M.C., John. *Fatima from the Beginning*, p. 227.

May 13, 1981 marked the assassination attempt against Pope John Paul II, a terrible example of the hatred held against the Church and her Vicar. The pope attributed Our Lady of Fatima's intercession for saving his life, an admission that "definitively removed the Fatima apparitions from the so-called 'private revelation' by a series of papal acts."[423] In the fifth year of the new century, first Sr. Lucia and then Pope John Paul II passed away, and Pope Benedict XVI (now Bishop Emeritus of Rome who may be, as we shall see, the "bishop dressed in white" of the Third Secret Vision) ascended the chair of Peter.

In sum, Our Lady asked or showed she wanted five things of all the faithful: prayers of the daily Rosary (with each mystery containing five decades), the wearing of the Brown Scapular, the faithful accomplishment of daily duty as Catholics and in our states of life, sacrifice for sinners, and the Five First Saturdays. Specific to the Holy Father, she asked that he command and lead the collegial consecration of Russia to her Immaculate Heart.

On the night of May 29-30, 1930, Our Lord revealed to Sr. Lucia five reasons for the Five First Saturdays of Reparation:

"My daughter, the reason is simple. There are five kinds of offenses and blasphemies uttered against the Immaculate Heart of Mary:
• "Blasphemies against the Immaculate Conception."
• "Blasphemies against Her perpetual Virginity."
• "Blasphemies against Her divine Maternity, while refusing at the same time to recognize Her as Mother of men."
• "The blasphemies of those who publicly seek to place in the hearts of children indifference or scorn, or even hatred towards this Immaculate Mother."
• "The offenses of those who outrage her directly in her holy images."[424]

Two Means to Save the Church Militant
Exactly sixty-eight years before (May 30, 1862), St. John Bosco related his incredible dream, noted as "The Two Columns in the Sea," [425] in which frequent Communion and Marian devotion are the Church's pillars and to which the Barque of Peter—after many battles and much confusion—securely ties itself.

In his dream, the details of which should not be glossed over, St. Bosco stood on an isolated rock, unable to see any other patch of land other that under his feet. From this spot, he saw "a vast sheet of water" with "an innumerable

---

[423] Ferrara, op. cit., p. 14.
[424] Frère Michel, *TWTF,* Vol. II., p. 265.
[425] Bacchiarello, S.D.B, Fr. J. *Forty Dreams of St. John Bosco, the Apostle of Youth.* [Rockford, IL: TAN Books and Publishers, 1996}: pp. 205-211.

fleet of ships in battle array. The prows of the ships are formed into sharp, spear-like points so that, wherever they are thrust, they pierce and completely destroy. These ships are armed with cannons, with lots of rifles, with incendiary materials, with other arms of all kinds, and also with *books*, and they advance against a ship very much bigger and higher than themselves and try to dash against it with the prows or burn it or in some way to do it every possible harm."

"As escorts to the majestic, fully equipped ship, there are many smaller ships, which receive commands by signal from it, and carry out movements to defend themselves from the opposing fleet."

In the sea's midst stood "two mighty columns of great height." Upon the taller pillar rested a Host of great size, the "Salvation of the Faithful," and upon the shorter one stood a statue of the Immaculate Virgin, "Help of Christians." The saint also related, "The Supreme commander on the big ship is the Sovereign Pontiff."

After the pontiff calls a council, the captains of the smaller ships board his vessel and hold a meeting, but "the wind and the waves gather in storm, so they are sent back to control their own ships. There comes a short lull; for a second time, the pope gathers the captains together around him, while the flag-ship goes on its course. But the frightful storm returns. The pope stands at the helm and all his energies are directed to steering the ship toward those two columns, from the top of which and from every side of which are hanging numerous anchors and big hooks, fastened to chains."

The great ship's adversaries maintain a relentless battle to stop and sink the great ship. At times, the great ship suffers "large, deep gaps in its side," but "a gentle breeze blows from the two columns and the cracks close up and the gaps are stopped immediately." The enemies' weapons are blown up or broken, and many of their ships shatter or sink. "Then, the frenzied enemies strive to fight, hand-to-hand, with fists, with blows, with blasphemy and with curses."

"All at once, the pope falls gravely wounded. Immediately those who are with him run to help him and they lift him up. A second time the pope is struck; he falls again and dies. A shout of victory and of joy rings out amongst the enemies; from their ships an unspeakable mockery arises. But hardly is the Pontiff dead than another pope takes his place. The pilots, having met together, have elected the pope so promptly that the news of the death of the pope coincides with the news of the election of the new successor."

It is the immediately-elected pope who puts the enemies to route and "guides the ship right up to the two columns and comes to rest between them," securely fastening the barque—first to the pillar of the Host and then to the pillar of the Virgin.

St. John Bosco asked Fr. Rua, one of his fellow priests, his opinion of the dream. Fr. Rua responded, "It seems to me that the pope's ship might mean the Church; of which he is the head; the ships, men; the sea, this world. Those who defend the big ship are the good, lovingly attached to the Holy See; the others are her enemies, who try with every kind of weapon to annihilate her. The two columns of salvation seem to be devotion to Mary Most Holy and to the Blessed Sacrament and the Eucharist."

"You are right!" said St. Bosco. "Only I ought to correct one expression. The enemy ships are persecutions. The most serious trials for the Church are near at hand. That which has been so far is almost nothing in the face of that which must befall. Her enemies are represented by the ships that tried to sink the principal ship if they could. **Only two means are left to save her amidst so much confusion: DEVOTION TO MARY MOST HOLY and FREQUENT COMMUNION**, making use of every means and doing our best to practice them and having them practiced everywhere and by everybody."

Next to consider is Fatima's Third Secret Vision, wherein "the Holy Father passed through a big city half in ruins and half trembling with halting step, afflicted with pain and sorrow, he prayed for the souls of the corpses he met on his way; having reached the top of the mountain, on his knees at the foot of the big Cross he was killed by a group of soldiers who fired bullets and arrows at him, and in the same way there died one after another the other Bishops, Priests, men and women Religious, and various lay people of different ranks and positions. Beneath the two arms of the Cross there were two Angels each with a crystal aspersorium in his hand, in which they gathered up the blood of the Martyrs and with it sprinkled the souls that were making their way to God."[426]

The fate of a future pope was also related by none other than Pope St. Pius X: "I saw one of my successors **by name** fleeing over the corpses of his brethren. He will flee to a place for a short respite where he is unknown; but he himself will die a cruel death."[427]

In the Third Secret Vision, the pope walks "half trembling and with halting step," indicating advanced age. As for Pope St. Pius X's vision, it may be that a future pope will take the name of Pius, but there is another consideration: Pope St. Pius X's baptismal name was Giuseppe Sarto. In Italian, *Giuseppe* means *Joseph*—the baptismal name of Joseph Ratzinger, who became Pope Benedict XVI and is now Bishop Emeritus of Rome—a bishop who dresses in white.

---

[426] *The Message of Fatima.*
[427] Culleton, Rev. R. Gerald. *The Prophets and Our Times.* [Rockford, IL: TAN Books and Publishers, 1974. First published by the author in 1941 & 1943]: p. 216.

Revealing Remarks
about the Third Secret and the Consecration

Comparing what is known of the public Fatima revelations to the visions of two great saints, at least three themes appear: the Holy Eucharist and Marian devotion; increasing persecutions of the Church and the Holy Father, with the last one likened to hand-to-hand combat; and a pope's death at the hand of enemies. Current world circumstances—including an elderly bishop, who resigned from the papal office but appears as "a bishop dressed in white" and whose baptismal name is Joseph—are additional indicators that we are now in the final stages leading to Fatima's Third Secret Vision.

What we can reasonably conclude about the Third Secret *Message*, still undisclosed, issues from commentary by Sr. Lucia and others in a position to know:

• **Cardinal Eugenio Pacelli** (the future **Pope Pius XII**), who was the Vatican Secretary of State in 1931 when he wrote the following in a letter (published in *Pie XII Devant L'Histoire*, pp. 52-53): "I am worried by the Blessed Virgin Mary's messages to Lucia of Fatima. This persistence of Mary about the dangers which menace the Church is a divine warning against the suicide of altering the Faith, in her liturgy, her theology, and her soul." Note that there is nothing in any **known** part of the Great Secret addressing these themes, and yet the Vatican Secretary of State said his concerns came from the Virgin's messages to Lucia, and that Our Lady was persistent "about the dangers which menace the Church," etc. His words reiterate what is now known of the Fatima history: Sr. Lucia was still acting as Heaven's messenger, and the message was urgent.

• **Pope John Paul II, 1980**: "Given the seriousness of the contents, my predecessors in the Petrine office diplomatically preferred to postpone publication so as not to encourage the world power of Communism to make certain moves. On the other hand, it should be sufficient for all Christians to know this: *if there is a message in which it is written that the oceans will flood whole areas of the earth, and that from one moment to the next millions of people will perish,*[428] truly the publication of such a message is no longer something to be desired...We must prepare ourselves to suffer great trials before long, such as will demand of us a disposition to give up even life, and a

---

[428] These words call to mind those of Our Lady of Akita on Oct. 13, 1973: "As I told you, if men do not repent and better themselves, the Father will inflict a terrible punishment on all humanity. It will be a punishment greater than the deluge, such as one never seen before. *Fire will fall from the sky and will wipe out a great part of humanity, the good as well as the bad, sparing neither priests nor faithful. The survivors will find themselves so desolate that they will envy the dead.*" The Akita apparitions were approved as worthy of belief by Bishop Ito.

total dedication to Christ...With your prayer and my prayer, it is possible to mitigate this tribulation, but it is no longer possible to avert it, because only thus can the Church be effectively renewed. How many times has the renewal of the Church sprung from blood? This time, too, it will be otherwise. We must be strong and prepared, and trust in Christ and His Mother, and be very, very assiduous in praying the Rosary."[429] (**Author's note**: Of course, it *is* possible to avert this great trial, by means of the collegial consecration of Russia to the Immaculate Heart.)

• **Sr. Lucia, May 13, 1980,** when asked during an interview, "Has Our Lady ever spoken to you about the consecration of *the world* to her Immaculate Heart?" responded: "No... *Never!* At the Cova da Iria in 1917, Our Lady had promised: *I shall come to ask for the Consecration of Russia...*In 1929, at Tuy, as she had promised, Our Lady came back to tell me that the moment had come to ask the Holy Father for the consecration of that country (Russia)."[430]

• **Sr. Lucia, March 19, 1983** confirmed in the presence of three witnesses, including the Papal Nuncio, Archbishop Portalupi, that Pope John Paul II's 1982 world consecration did *not* fulfill Our Lady's request. As reported in an article by Father Pierre Caillon of Centre Saint Jean 61500 Sees, (Orne) France, and which was published by the monthly periodical *Fidelite Catholique* of Auray Cedex, France, Sr. Lucia explained: "In the act of offering of May 13, 1982, Russia did not appear as being the object of the consecration. And each bishop did not organize in his own diocese a public and solemn ceremony of reparation and Consecration of Russia. Pope John Paul II simply renewed the consecration of the world executed by Pius XII on October 31, 1942. From this consecration we can expect some benefits, but not the conversion of Russia."

• **Sr. Lucia, March 22, 1984,** who had already received and read the text of the pope's consecration formula planned for March 25, 1984, when asked about it, made a negative sign and declared, "That consecration cannot have a decisive character."[431]

• **Pope John Paul II, March 25, 1984**, immediately following his "act of offering" the world to Our Lady, said: "**Enlighten especially the peoples of which you yourself are awaiting our consecration and confiding.**"[432] These words clearly reveal the pope's awareness that Russia had not been explicitly consecrated to the Immaculate Heart nor in the way Our Lady requested.

---

[429] *Stimme Des Glaubin* (Voice of Faith), October 1981.

[430] *L'Osservatore Romano*, May 12, 1982 edition.

[431] Des Anges, (Frère) Francois de Mari. *Fatima: Intimate Joy World Event, Book IV: Fatima: Tragedy and Triumph.* [Buffalo, NY: Immaculate Heart Publications, 1994]: pp. 167-168.

[432] *L'Osservatore Romano*, March 26, 1984 edition.

• **Cardinal Joseph Ratzinger, late 1984** on why the Third Secret was still not made public: "Because, according to the judgment of the Popes, it adds nothing to what a Christian must know from Revelation – i.e., a radical call for conversion; the absolute importance of history; *the dangers threatening the faith* and the life of the Christian and therefore the world. And also *the importance of the last times*...But the things contained in this Third Secret correspond to what is announced in Scripture and are confirmed by many other Marian apparitions, beginning with the Fatima apparitions themselves in their known contents. Conversion, penance are essential conditions to salvation."[433]

• **Cardinal Silvio Oddi, March 17, 1990** said of the Third Secret: "The Blessed Virgin was alerting us against apostasy in the Church."[434]

• **Cardinal Luigi Ciappi, 1995**, serving for 40 years as papal theologian to all the popes from Popes Pius XII through John Paul II: "In the Third Secret it is foretold, among other things, that the great apostasy in the Church begins at the top."[435]

• **Pope Benedict XVI, May 11, 2010**: "Beyond this great vision of the suffering of the Pope, which we might in essence attribute to John Paul II, there is indicated that the reality of the future of the Church which will gradually develop and demonstrate itself. Namely, it is true that beyond the moment indicated in [the Third Secret] vision, **it is spoken, it is shown**..."[436] In other words, the former Pope definitely revealed that there are words ("it is spoken") that accompany the Third Secret Vision ("it is shown").

The Dogma of the Faith and the Great "Et Cetera"

In 1943, when asked about the contents of The Third Secret, Sr. Lucia said, "In a certain way, I have already revealed it."[437] How so? In her *Fourth Memoir,* she implicitly disclosed it in a sentence of substantial importance: "**In Portugal, the dogma of the Faith will always be preserved,** *etc.*"[438] This sentence, which ends with the intriguing "et cetera," is the prelude to the Third Secret Message—the part of the secret still hidden.

---

[433] *Jesus* Magazine, November 11, 1984 issue, p. 79.

[434] *Il Sabato*, Rome, March 17, 1990, cited in Ferrara, p. 42.

[435] Miguel, Aura. *Totus Tuus: Il Segreto di Fatima nel Pontificato de Giovanni Paolo II* [Itaca: Castel Bolognese, 2003]: p. 137, cited in Ferrara, p. 43.

[436] English translation by the author (M. Bartold) from the original Italian article by Gian Guido Vecchi, "Le Parole del papa: <<*Nonostante la famoso nuvola siami qui...>>*," *Corriere della Sera*, May 11, 2010.

[437] Alonso, Fr. Joaquin. *La verdad sobre el Secreto de Fátima*, p. 61; see also Frère Michel, *The Whole Truth about Fatima,* Vol. III, p. 684.

[438] Frère Michel, op. cit., pp. 749-750.

"*The* dogma of the Faith" is a telling phrase, one which addresses the Church's primary dogma, thrice-defined: "Outside the Church, there is no salvation."[439] Today, this singular dogma *about* the Church is either unknown or rejected *within* the Church, which is another sign of Fatima's veracity, lending further credence that the Third Secret's smothered Message centers on "an apocalyptic crisis of the faith in the Church starting from the top"[440]–namely, the revolt which St. Paul said must come first.[441]

"In" Portugal, Not "Throughout" Portugal

In light of Our Lady's promise, the faithful are confused by unfolding religious and political events in Portugal, including the desecration of the original, majestic Fatima basilica–accomplished with its rector's awareness and permission–and the construction of a concrete monstrosity, a "colossal monument dedicated to diabolic disorientation."[442]

How can such things happen, when Our Lady prophesied, "In Portugal, the dogma of the Faith will always be preserved, etc.?"

It is because even the faithful have interpreted Our Lady's opening phrase, "*In* Portugal" to mean "*Throughout* Portugal." Previously understanding that the sentence indicated apostasy throughout the rest of the world while Portugal remained faithful, we now begin to more deeply grasp its meaning: Only *parts* of Portugal will preserve the dogma of the faith, while many other formerly Catholic countries will abandon this foremost dogma–a terrible indictment to how widespread the apostasy has become.

Why is this so? Our Lord revealed to Sr. Lucia certain chastisements of Portugal, previously protected from the ravages of WWII because the country's bishops collegially consecrated it to the Immaculate Heart in 1931, renewing the act in 1938 and 1940:

"But in spite of this, the Hearts of Our Good Lord and Our Good Mother are sad and grieved. Portugal in its majority does not correspond either to Their graces or love. They [the Holy Hearts of Jesus and Mary] frequently complain about the sinful life of the majority of the people, even of those who call themselves practical Catholics. But above all, They complain very much about

---

[439] Pope Innocent III, Fourth Lateran Council, 1215; Pope Boniface VIII, the bull *Unam Sanctam*, 1302; Pope Eugene IV, the bull *Cantate Domino*, 1442.

[440] Socci, Antonio. *Il Quarto Segreto di Fatima* (The Fourth Secret of Fatima), p. 82, cited in Ferrara, op. cit.,
p. 223.

[441] 2 Thess 2:3.

[442] Vennari, John. "A Colossal Monument to Diabolic Disorientation." *Catholic Family News*, November 2007.

the lukewarm, indifferent and extremely comfortable life of the majority of the priests and members of religious congregations."

"The number of souls He meets through sacrifice and intimate life of love is extremely small and limited. These confidences lacerate my heart, mainly because I am one of those unfaithful souls. Our Lord doesn't restrain Himself in setting me there, showing me the mountain of my imperfections that I recognize with huge confusion..."

"Nevertheless, Our Lord goes on communicating with my soul. He seems concerned about the destiny of some countries and wishes to save Portugal, but she is guilty, too."[443]

This revelation is a startling testimony to the doctrine of the Mystical Body of Christ. It reminds us of a previous declaration of the universal Church, "The times in which we live demand action–but action which consists entirely in observing with fidelity and zeal the divine laws and the precepts of the Church, in the frank and open profession of religion, in the exercise of every kind of charitable works, without regard to self–interest or worldly advantage."[444]

The entire Church Militant must follow Our Lady's five requests. The Holy Father and the bishops must effect the solemn, public consecration of Russia to the Immaculate Heart, and all must respond to the other four requests, recalling that "the Church is built of living stones. It is built of saints. And saints are made only by the grace of God and the infused virtues and gifts of the Holy Ghost, not by speeches and publicity and campaigns, which are all doomed to sterility without the essentials of **prayer and sacrifice**."[445]

---

[443] Frère Michel, loc. cit.
[444] Pope St. Pius X, *E Supremi* (On the Restoration of All Things in Christ, October 4, 1903): para. 14.
[445] Chautard, O.C.S.O., Dom Jean-Baptiste. *The Soul of the Apostolate*. [Garden City, NY: Image Books, 1961]: p. 17.

CHAPTER 13

Our Lady of Akita
and the Third Secret of Fatima

"...it is necessary for each one of us to begin to reform himself spiritually. Each person must not only save his own soul but also the souls that God has placed on our path."
—Sr. Maria Lucia of the Immaculate Heart, Fatima visionary

Cardinal Ratzinger (now Bishop Emeritus of Rome) once made an astonishing remark that the messages of Fatima and Akita "are essentially the same."[446] It was not the first time that someone in a position to know provided such crucial hints. By examining certain aspects concerning the Fatima and Akita revelations, we will find abundant proof that the entire message of Fatima—especially the Third Secret Message, a text still concealed by the Vatican—is of universal and apocalyptic proportion.

Foremost amongst the proofs are the prudent but urgent disclosures of Sr. Lucia. Refusing to disclose the Third Secret on her own authority, in various ways she pointed to an unimaginable crisis for the Church and the world. On two different occasions, Lucia's response intimated the Third Secret's connection to Divine Revelation when she stated it was in the *Gospel* and the *Apocalypse*—"Read them!"[447]

In another encounter, she was unexpectedly open about the Third Secret's contents when she specified chapters 8-13 of the *Apocalypse*. Three years before the Third Secret's anticipated 1960 release, Lucia was consulted by Father Augustin Fuentes, postulator of the causes for beatification of Francisco and Jacinta, who later published a report of this candid interview with "every guarantee of authenticity and episcopal approval, including that of the Bishop of Fatima."[448] In this revealing interview, Sister Lucia introduced new concepts

---

[446] *Catholic World News*, October 11, 2001. In 1998, Howard Dee, the former Philippine ambassador to the Vatican, revealed that "Bishop Ito was certain Akita was an extension of Fatima, and Cardinal Ratzinger personally confirmed to me that these two messages are essentially the same."

[447] Fellows, *Fatima in Twilight*, p. 295.

[448] Alonso, Fr. Joaquin. *La verdad sobre el Secreto de Fatima*, pp. 110-112. Cited in Frère Michel, *TWTF*, Vol. III, p. 503.

that can only be the essence of the Third Secret, even as she recalled "the essence" of the First and Second Secrets.[449]

"This is the third part of the Message of Our Lady, which will remain secret until 1960," Lucia concluded after frankly remarking, "Father, how much time is there before 1960 arrives? It will be very sad for everyone, not one person will rejoice at all if beforehand the world does not pray and do penance. I am not able to give any other details because it is still a secret."

Lucia also spoke of Our Lady's sadness "because no one has paid any attention to her Message, neither the good nor the bad. The good continue on their way but without giving any importance to her Message. The bad, not seeing the punishment of God actually falling upon them, continue their life of sin without even caring about the message. But believe me, Father, God will chastise the world and this will be in a terrible manner. The punishment from Heaven is imminent."[450]

During the interview, Sr. Lucia mentioned *worldwide* but conditional scourges, both spiritual and material, due to mankind's constant offenses against God: the annihilation of nations, a diabolical attack on consecrated souls which also affects the laity, and the grave danger of the eternal loss of souls due to obstinate sins. "Tell them, Father," said Lucia, "that **many times** the Most Holy Virgin told my cousins Francisco and Jacinta, as well as myself, that *many nations will disappear from the face of the earth.* She said that Russia will be the instrument of chastisement chosen by Heaven to punish the whole world if we do not beforehand obtain the conversion of that poor nation."[451]

Lucia made mention of "the fall of religious and priestly souls," which so afflict the Hearts of Jesus and Mary: "The devil wishes to *take possession of consecrated souls.* He tries to corrupt them in order to lull to sleep the souls of laypeople and thereby lead them to final impenitence. He employs all tricks, even going so far as to suggest the delay of entrance into religious life. Resulting from this is the *sterility of the interior life*, and among the laypeople, coldness regarding the subject of renouncing pleasures and the total dedication of themselves to God."[452]

The Cause of Our Lady's Sadness

Again Lucia mentioned Our Lady's sadness, which was the reason behind the great sacrifices of her cousins Francisco and Jacinta, "because in all the

---

[449] Frère Michel, *TWTF,* Vol. III, p. 508.
[450] Ibid., p. 504.
[451] Ibid., p. 505. [Emphasis added.]
[452] Ibid. [Emphasis added.]

apparitions of the Most Holy Virgin, they always saw her very sad. She never smiled at us. This sadness, this anguish which we noted in her, penetrated our souls. This sadness is caused by the offenses against God and the punishments which menace sinners…The other thing which sanctified these children was to see the vision of hell."

"Father, that is why my mission is not to indicate to the world *the material punishments which are certain to come* if the world does not pray and do penance beforehand. **No**, my mission is to indicate to *everyone* the *imminent danger we are in of losing our souls for all eternity* if we remain obstinate in sin."[453]

Lucia spoke of the dire need for each soul's spiritual reform and conversion. She urged that "we should not wait for an appeal to the world to come from Rome" to do penance. We should not wait for a call to penance from the Holy Father, the bishops, or religious congregations because "Our Lord has already very often used these means and the world has not paid attention. That is why now, **it is necessary for each one of us to begin to reform himself spiritually. Each person must not only save his own soul but also the souls that God has placed on our path**…The devil does all in his power to distract us and to take away from us the love of prayer; we shall be saved together or we shall be damned together."[454]

Near the end of the interview, Lucia spoke of "the last times of the world," saying, "Father, the Most Holy Virgin did not tell me that we are in the last times of the world but she made me understand this for three reasons." As will be seen, these three reasons correspond with certain remarks made 27 years later by Cardinal Joseph Ratzinger when he was asked why, in 1984, the Third Secret had still not been made public.

Although he appeared to dismiss its importance, he encapsulated its essence by connecting it to Divine Revelation: "Because, according to the judgment of the Popes, it adds nothing to what a Christian must know from Revelation—i.e., a radical call for conversion; *the absolute importance of history; the dangers threatening the faith and the life of the Christian* and therefore *the world*. And also *the importance of the last times*…But the things contained in this Third Secret correspond to what is announced in Scripture and are confirmed by many other Marian apparitions, beginning with the Fatima apparitions in their known contents. Conversion and penance are essential conditions to salvation."[455]

---

[453] Ibid., pp. 503-505. [Emphasis added.]
[454] Ibid., p. 506. [Emphasis added.]
[455] *Jesus* Magazine, November 11, 1984 issue, p. 79. [Emphasis added.]

What are the three reasons that made Lucia understand we are in the last times?

"The first reason," said Lucia, "is because she told me that the devil is in the mood for engaging in a decisive battle against the Virgin. And a decisive battle is the final battle where one side will be victorious and the other side will suffer defeat. Hence from now on we must choose sides. Either we are for God or we are for the devil. There is no other possibility."

"The second reason is because she said to my cousins as well as to myself that God is giving two last remedies to the world. These are the Holy Rosary and the Devotion to the Immaculate Heart of Mary. These are the last two remedies which signify that there will be no others."

"The third reason is because in the plans of Divine Providence, God always, before He is about to chastise the world, exhausts all other remedies. Now, when He sees that the world pays no attention whatsoever then, as we say in our imperfect manner of speaking, He offers us, with a certain trepidation, the last means of salvation, His Most Holy Mother. It is with a certain trepidation because if you despise and repulse this ultimate means, we will not have any more forgiveness from Heaven because we will have committed a sin which the *Gospel* calls the sin against the Holy Spirit. This sin consists of openly rejecting, with full knowledge and consent, the salvation which He offers."

"Let us remember that Jesus Christ is a very good Son and that He does not permit that we offend and despise His Most Holy Mother. We have recorded through many centuries of Church history the obvious testimony which demonstrates, by the terrible chastisements which have befallen those who have attacked the honor of His Most Holy Mother, how Our Lord Jesus Christ has always defended the honor of His Mother."

Finally, Lucia emphasized that "the two means to save the world are prayer and sacrifice," another reference to the spiritual efforts of individual souls as well as to the prayers and the Sacrifice of the Mass. Implicitly underlining the doctrine of Mary as Mediatrix of All Graces, Lucia stated, "Look, Father, the Most Holy Virgin in these last times in which we live has given a new efficacy to the recitation of the Rosary...There is no problem, no matter how difficult it is, that we cannot resolve by the prayer of the Holy Rosary. With the Holy Rosary, we will save ourselves. We will sanctify ourselves. We will console Our Lord and obtain the salvation of many souls."[456]

---

[456] Frère Michel, op. cit., pp. 507-508.

Further Hints of the Third Secret's Message

On February 8, 1960 (coincidentally or not, the date then commemorated the Feast of the Most Pure Heart of Mary)[457] the Portuguese news agency, A.N.I.[458] at Rome, released a communiqué from anonymous Vatican sources who declared "the Secret of Fatima will never be disclosed" and "that it is most likely that *the letter* will never be opened, in which Sister Lucia wrote down *the words* which Our Lady confided as a secret to the three little shepherds in the Cova da Iria."[459] This announcement verifies that the Third Secret is not only a Vision but also includes a Message ("*the words* which Our Lady confided"). It is also indicative of an internal Church struggle, already existing, since no Vatican source publicly assumed authority for the statement or ever denied it. Still, the Vatican silently confirmed A.N.I.'s announcement because the Third Secret was not released in 1960.

Within the course of the 12 years following 1960, various remarks (of which the following are a mere handful) made by Sr. Lucia and others provide further insights into the Third Secret (with all emphasis below mine):

• Sr. Lucia would emphasize, "We must pray a great deal and **beg God** not to chastise us and **save us in time and for eternity**."[460] She would also write "many times to reliable witnesses of a '**diabolical disorientation'** in the Church and the world of which Our Lady warned her."[461]

• Pope Paul VI would lament, "Through some crack, the smoke of Satan has entered the temple of God."[462]

• Bishop Venancio of Leiria-Fatima would issue a pastoral letter for the July 1966 Fatima Jubilee, alluding to "*a Church...continually threatened by the mystery of iniquity 'which is already at work.'* (II Thess. 2, 7)"[463]

---

[457] Holweck, Frederick. "Feast of the Most Pure Heart of Mary." *The Catholic Encyclopedia*, Vol. 10. [New York: Robert Appleton Company, 1911.] [http://home.newadvent.org/cathen/10600a.htm]

[458] Agencia Nacional de Informacão.

[459] Frère Michel, op. cit., p. 578.

[460] Ibid., p. 509.

[461] Ferrara, *The Secret Still Hidden*, p. 35.

[462] Pope Paul VI, June 29, 1972 (Feast of St. Peter and Paul).

[463] Frère Michel, op. cit., p. 778. Bishop Venancio's pastoral letter stated, "Fatima has not yet said its last word...Neither has Fatima come to give reason to the prophets of imaginary world catastrophes. Fatima cannot be reduced to sensational prophecies of frightful wars...We affirm that Fatima is something much more serious that all that. Fatima, really, in this too, 'actualizes' the whole evangelical meaning of a Church launched eschatologically towards a future which is, to be sure, most assuredly in God's hands, but which, however, is continually threatened by the mystery of iniquity 'which is already at work.'" (II Thess. 2, 7).

• Providing astute commentary on the Third Secret Message, which opens with Our Lady's words, "In Portugal, the dogma of the Faith will always be preserved, etc.," Fr. Joaquin Alonso, official Fatima archivist, would say, "The phrase most clearly implies a critical state of Faith…**In the period preceding the great triumph of the Immaculate Heart of Mary, terrible things are going to happen**. These form the content of the third part of the Secret. What are they?"

"If '*in Portugal the dogma of the Faith will always be preserved,*'" he continued,"…it can be clearly deduced from this that in other parts of the Church these dogmas are going to be obscure or even lost altogether. Thus it is quite possible that in this intermediate period which is in question (after 1960 and before the triumph of the Immaculate Heart of Mary), **the text** [of the Third Secret Message] **makes concrete references to the crisis of the Faith of the Church and to the negligence of the pastors themselves**."

"One conclusion does indeed seem to be beyond question: the content of the unpublished part of the Secret does not refer to new wars or political upheavals, but to **happenings of a religious and intra-Church character**, which of their nature are still more grave."[464]

• At yet another time, Fr. Alonso wrote "…Does the unpublished text speak of concrete [e.g., tangible, actual] circumstances? It is very possible that it speaks not only of a real crisis of the faith in the Church during this in-between period but, like the secret of LaSalette, for example, there are more concrete references to the **internal struggles of Catholics or to the fall of priests and religious**. Perhaps it even refers to the **failures of the upper hierarchy of the Church**. For that matter, **none of this is foreign to other communications Sister Lucia has had** on this subject."[465]

From Fatima to Akita: Part of the Third Secret Revealed

As previously mentioned, Lucia had spoken of the Fatima Virgin's anguish and sadness "caused by the offenses of God and the punishments which menace sinners." In 1973, Our Lady would also speak of the cause of her sadness, this time to a nun long afflicted by various illnesses and almost totally deaf, Sister Agnes Katsuko Sasagawa in Akita, Japan: "The demon will be especially implacable against souls consecrated to God. *The thought of the loss*

---

[464] Alonso, op. cit., p. 70. Cited in Frère Michel, *TWTF,* Vol. III, p. 687.
[465] Alonso, Fr. Joaquin. *The Secret of Fatima: Fact and Legend.* Cited in Frère Michel, *TWTF,* Vol. III, p. 705.

of so many souls is the cause of my sadness. If sins increase in number and gravity, there will be no longer pardon for them."[466]

After a thorough investigation of eight years by Bishop John Shojiro Ito, the Akita apparitions and events, which center around a three-foot high statue of Our Lady placed in the chapel of the Eucharistic Handmaids of the Sacred Heart, were found to be of supernatural origin. In addition to the messages, the statue perspired, wept tears, and issued blood from its right hand—in total 101 times. This same bishop, who authorized the veneration of the Blessed Virgin Mary of Akita, later said, *"The message of Akita is the message of Fatima."*[467]

What, then, is the Message of Akita? Like Fatima, it is comprised of three distinct parts, but at Akita Our Lady did not impart them as secrets. Like Fatima, each sentence and manifestation reveals profound doctrinal or dogmatic depths, especially in regard to the Mystical Body of Christ. Perhaps most incredible is that Akita's Third Message is either a part of or central to Fatima's Third Secret Message.

Our Lady of Akita's First Message addresses reparation for the sins of men, the True Presence of Jesus in the Blessed Sacrament, and consecration to Jesus through Mary, emphasizing Our Lady's role as Mediatrix of All Graces.

The Second Message again asks for reparation and refers to Mary as Mediatrix but also mentions "a great chastisement" from the Heavenly Father: "If you love the Lord, listen to what I have to say to you. It is very important; you will convey it to your superior. Many men in this world afflict the Lord. I desire souls to console Him to soften the anger of the Heavenly Father. I wish, with my Son, for souls who will repair by their suffering and their poverty for the sinners and ingrates. In order that the world might know His anger, the Heavenly Father is preparing to inflict a great chastisement on all mankind. I have intervened so many times to appease the wrath of the Father. I have prevented the coming of calamities by offering Him the sufferings of the Son on the Cross, His Precious Blood, and beloved souls who console Him forming a cohort of victim souls. Prayer, penance and courageous sacrifices can soften the Father's anger..."[468]

The Third Message of Akita, given on October 13, 1973 (the 56th anniversary of the Miracle of the Sun at Fatima, Portugal), is tragically compatible with the evidence, already examined, that the last Fatima Secret

---

[466] "Sr. Agnes Sasagawa," EWTN Online.
[http://www.ewtn.com/library/MARY/AKITA.HTM]
[467] "Our Lady of Akita," Holy Mother Mary website.
[http://www.holymothermary.org/apparitions/akita.htm]
[468] "A Terrible Warning: The Message of Our Lady of Akita (1973-1981)." Our Lady of the Rosary Library. [http://www.olrl.org/prophecy/akita.shtml]

foretells widespread apostasy throughout the Church and the world, an apostasy centering on "the dogma of the Faith," consequently evoking even greater retributions from God. It also explains why the Vatican refuses to release the text of the Third Secret Message. Even further, Akita's third message simultaneously corresponds with Sr. Lucia's warning, "God will chastise the world and this will be in a terrible manner" as well as Fr. Alonso's thesis, "In the period preceding the great triumph of the Immaculate Heart of Mary, terrible things are going to happen. These form the content of the third part of the Secret."

Thus follows the third Message of Akita:

"As I told you, if men do not repent and better themselves, the Father will inflict a terrible punishment on all humanity. **It will be a punishment greater than the deluge,** *such as one will never have seen before*. Fire will fall from the sky and wipe out a great part of humanity, the good as well as the bad, sparing neither priests nor faithful. The survivors will find themselves so desolate that they will envy the dead. The only arms that will remain for you will be the Rosary and the Sign left by my Son. Each day recite the prayers of the Rosary. With the Rosary, pray for the Pope, the Bishops, and the Priests."

"The work of the devil will infiltrate even into the Church in such a way that one will see cardinals opposing cardinals, bishops against bishops. The priests who venerate me will be scorned and opposed by their confreres. Churches and altars will be sacked; the Church will be full of those who accept compromises and the demon will press many priests and consecrated souls to leave the service of the Lord."

"Pray very much the prayers of the Rosary. I alone am able to save you from the calamities which approach. **Those who place their confidence in me will be saved**."[469]

The *opening* lines of the third Akita message directly tie to the oft-overlooked *opening* of Fatima's Third Secret *Vision*, wherein Lucia wrote "at the left of Our Lady and a little above, we saw an Angel with a **flaming sword** in his left hand; flashing, it gave out flames that looked as though they would **set the world on fire**; but they died out in contact with the splendour that Our Lady radiated towards him from her right hand: pointing to the earth with his right hand, the Angel cried out in a loud voice: 'Penance, Penance, Penance!'"[470] As can be seen, the Akita message reinforces what is now known of Fatima's Third Secret *Message*, although its text remains suppressed.

---

[469] "Our Lady of Akita," loc. cit.
[470] *The Message of Fatima.*

In the Third Secret of Fatima *Vision*, Our Lady's *right hand* signifies the great power of her intercession because the angel, while thrice crying the word "Penance," is already prepared to set the world on fire with the sword of Divine Justice.

At Akita, on July 6, 1973, the statue's *right hand* issued blood. Before that, on the vigil of the Feast of the Sacred Heart in June, Sister Agnes received a cross-shaped stigmata in her *left hand*, causing her great pain and suffering. (On that same occasion, Sr. Agnes' guardian angel taught her a prayer she had never before heard. Later, she would learn it was the "O my Jesus" prayer which Our Lady of Fatima said was to be prayed after every Rosary decade: *"O my Jesus, forgive us our sins, save us from the fires of hell. Lead all souls to heaven, especially those with the greatest need of Thy mercy."* At that time in Japan, the prayer was not well-known. Through the Akita apparitions, the "Fatima Decade Prayer" spread throughout the country.)

That Sr. Agnes and the chapel statue of the Virgin, now known as Our Lady of Akita, bore similar marks on opposite hands must be a sign of theological implications. Of the blood issuing from the Akita statue's right hand, Sr. Agnes was told by an angel, "This flowing of blood is significant. It *will* be shed for the conversion of men and in reparation for sins. **To the devotion to the Sacred Heart, add the devotion to the Precious Blood.**"[471] The prophecy that "blood *will* be shed for the conversion of men and in reparation for sins" reveals that the Fatima Virgin's warning that "good people will be martyred" will continue unabated and most likely increase, culminating in the martyrdoms seen in the Third Secret Vision, when an even greater massacre of Catholics occurs after "a bishop dressed in white" is killed–all because the Virgin's simple requests at Fatima remain ignored.

The Hidden, Bitter Star

It cannot be denied that Our Lady of Akita's description of a fiery, worldwide cataclysm which destroys a large part of humanity literally indicates an apocalyptic chastisement. As we've already seen, further lights on the Third Secret and "the seriousness of the contents" were expressed by the late Pope John Paul II who, when speaking to a select group in Fulda, Germany, surprised everyone by describing a devastating and universal deluge, saying, "…it should be sufficient for all Christians to know this: *if there is a message in which it is written that the oceans will flood whole areas of the earth, and that from one moment to the next millions of people will perish,* truly the publication of such a message is no longer something to be desired…"[472]

---

[471] "Our Lady of Akita," loc. cit.
[472] *Stimme Des Glaubin* (Voice of Faith), October 1981.

Consider three things: **1)** The Third Secret *Vision* describes an angel with a flaming sword, **2)** the Akita message warns that "fire will fall from the sky," **3)** but John Paul II, when asked about the Third Secret, specifically mentioned *flooding*. What could be the cause of **both** worldwide fire and flood? Recalling the movements of the "day star" of the celestial heaven (the Miracle of the Sun at Fatima), and also bearing in mind Lucia's specificity that the Third Secret can be found in the *Gospel* and the *Apocalypse*, we take into account the following Scriptures:

• "And there shall be signs in the sun, and in the moon, and in the stars; and upon the earth distress of nations by reason of confusion of the **roaring of the sea and of the waves**; Men withering away for fear, and expectation of what shall come upon the whole world. **For the powers of heaven shall be moved**..."[473]

• "And the second angel sounded the trumpet: and as it were a great mountain, **burning with fire**, was cast into the sea, and the third part of the sea became blood: And the third part of those creatures died, which had life in the sea, and the third part of the ships was destroyed. And the third angel sounded the trumpet, and **a great star fell from heaven, burning as it were a torch, and it fell on the third part of the rivers, and upon the fountains of waters: And the name of the star is called Wormwood**. And the third part of the waters became wormwood; and many men died of the waters, because they were made bitter."[474]

Too, there exist various prophecies that appear to foretell the onset of a comet (suggested at Akita), and those which definitely predict a pope's exile (as seen in the Third Secret Vision), of which only two shall here be mentioned: "A powerful wind will rise in the North carrying heavy fog and the densest dust by divine command, and it will fill their throats and eyes so they will cease their savagery and be stricken with great fear... Before the comet comes, many nations, the good excepted, will be scourged by want and famine...By its tremendous pressure, the comet will force much out of the ocean and flood many countries, causing much want and many plagues. All coastal cities will live in fear, and many of them will be destroyed by tidal waves, and most living creatures will be killed, and even those who escape will die from horrible diseases. For in none of those cities does a person live according to the laws of God." (St. Hildegard, 12th century)[475]

---

[473] Lk. 21:25-26.
[474] Apoc. 8: 8-11.
[475] Dupont, Yves. *Catholic Prophecy: The Coming Chastisement*. [Rockford IL, TAN Books and Publishers, 1973]: pp. 16-17.

And the second:

"For seven days, the great star shall be seen,

As if two Suns in the sky should appear.

The big Mastiff (Islamic or Arab powers) shall be howling all night

When the Pontiff shall go into exile." (*Michel de Nostredame*, "Michael of Our Lady")[476]

Although we cannot be certain, an asteroid or comet of great magnitude seems to be the plausible explanation for these prophecies of a devastating star. In Greek, "*aster*" or "*astro*" is etymologically rooted to "*ester*," calling to mind the Star of Esther on Our Lady of Fatima's dress. Again, this star directs us to *The Book of Esther*, providing "the traces of hidden things"[477] that Fatima is an annunciation of Divine Revelation as found in the *Gospel* and the *Apocalypse*. It has been mentioned repeatedly that Queen Esther is a great figure type for the Virgin—especially as the Fatima Virgin. However, the main facts bear repeating, since they may indicate another surprising link to the Third Secret.

Once more we will recall that, in the Old Testament of the Hebrew text, Esther's birth name of Hádássah referred to myrtle, a star-shaped flower. The word *myrtle* shares the same etymological root as *myrrh* ("bitter"). [478]The Hebrew text relates that Esther (in Persian, "star"), who became queen of Persia, changed her name to *Hester*, which translates to "hidden star" or "hidden [meaning of the] star." Together, the various philological traces of Esther's name also indicate "**hidden bitter star**."

Thus, in addition to all else that it means to the Church, the Star of Esther may also symbolize the "hidden bitter star" which the *Apocalypse* names as **Wormwood**. If so, it reinforces the Fatima message that the Pope, the bishops and the entire Church must do their duty and heed all of the requests of the Morning Star, who wishes to grant an era of peace to mankind—or soon face the chastisement of God's avenging star.

In concluding this section, these are the main factors to take into account:

• The revelations of the Sacred Heart at Paray-le-Monial, stressing the necessity of mankind's repentance and reparation for sin and the Lord's desire to grant us Divine Mercy rather than chastisement;

• All of the incredible "hidden revelations" inherent in the Star of Esther which adorned the Fatima Virgin's gown;

---

[476] Ibid., p. 108.

[477] Eccles. 42:19.

[478] *Etymology Dictionary*.[http://www.etymonline.com/index.php?l=m&p=26]

• *The Book of Esther* itself, which "centers on secrets and revelations, a plot among nations against one kingdom and the elect, prayer and sacrifice, and the final triumph of the Queen;"

• The themes found in *The Book of Esther* suggest it is a figure type for the *Apocalypse*, reinforcing Sr. Lucia's statement that the Third Secret of Our Lady of Fatima may be found in the *Gospel* and Chapters 8-13 of the *Apocalypse*.[479]

• Too, there is the Hebrew name for *The Book of Esther* (Megillat Hester), which translates to "revelation [of that which is] hidden" or "hidden revelation" but also "hidden revelation of the star." Thus, the book's name is itself an indication that the star on the Fatima Virgin's gown is another trace to the *Apocalypse*.

• The opening lines describing the Third Secret Vision of Fatima ("an Angel with a flaming sword in his left hand");[480]

• The later prophecy of Our Lady of Akita ("Fire will fall from the sky");[481]

• And so, "in addition to all else it means to the Church, the Star of Esther may also symbolize the 'hidden bitter star' which the *Apocalypse* names as Wormwood."

• At Fatima, Our Lady made use of the great Star of Heaven (the sun) as a reminder of God's greatness but also as an image of the end of the world.[482]

In studying the *Apocalypse's* chapters 6-11, we find it "portrays the great distress among the nations on account of the calamities which the Lamb allows to overtake the world in punishment for unbelief," as Fr. R. Gerald Culleton explained. "These calamities are in origin *terrestrial* (Ch. 6), *celestial* (Ch. 8), and *infernal* (Ch. 9). Even a foretaste of hell is given to mankind before the great day of reckoning. Also in St. Luke's eschatological chapter, there is a clear distinction made between ordinary wars and insurrections on the one hand, and **universal war**, calamity, famine, and death on the other. The latter is the sign of the coming judgment (Lk. 21:9-11)."

He continued, "The period of great distress coincides with the 'Major Apostasy' of *2 Thess. 2:3* and with the end of the 'Time of the Gentiles.' After describing the destruction of Jerusalem, Jesus said: 'And Jerusalem will be trodden down by the Gentiles until the times of the nations to be fulfilled' (Luke 21:24). The great distress brought physical death to many on earth, but like the days of the flood (see 1 Peter 3:20), many found repentance before

---

[479] Fellows, *Fatima in Twilight*, p. 295.
[480] *The Message of Fatima*.
[481] "Our Lady of Akita," loc. cit.
[482] Frère Michel, op. cit., p. 364.

death and washed their robes in the blood of the Lamb, and an innumerable crowd remained faithful to Him until death (Apoc. 7: 9-14)."[483]

It is no small wonder that the last words of Our Lady on October 13, 1917 were the motherly plea: "Do not offend the Lord our God any longer. He is already deeply offended." At present, the world is already chastised with a terrible terrestrial calamity—the Great Revolt, which still runs its course. Its three historical stages directly link to the reasons Our Lady came to Fatima, the Great Secret's three distinct parts, and the Great Miracle's three-fold twirl.

As for the celestial calamity foretold in the *Apocalypse*, it also seems prefigured in the "dancing" Star of Heaven, which advanced and receded *three* times before its final, soul-shaking tumble. The Scriptures are clear that the sun or its light indicate God's Grace, His Presence, His Glory and Justice, or the glory of the just.[484] Symbol of the Sun of Justice, the sun at Fatima was shaken from its heavenly moorings, revolving like "a captive *ball of fire*," suddenly plunging to the very horizon line, and finally "tracing a sort of winding ellipse as it went" back to its zenith—suggesting the path of an asteroid in the heavens. Was the sudden fiery plummet, so like a "wheel of fire," the sensible sign of the *celestial* chastisement of the *Apocalypse's* "bitter" star, Wormwood? Did it portend Our Lady of Akita's warning that came exactly 56 years later to the day, "Fire will fall from the sky..."?[485]

Each of us must make this heartfelt prayer our own: "I must ardently desire to have Him as my Savior, Whom I am unable to withstand as my Judge."[486] The Church [that is, her human element] and the world still have a choice between repenting and asking for God's Mercy or remaining obstinate in sin and facing His Wrath. Each of us can do our part, following and spreading the whole truth about Fatima and the meaning of its magnificent Miracle. We must pray, sacrifice and work for the happy day of triumph, when Russia is collegially consecrated to the Virgin's Immaculate Heart. Through it all, **"Look to the Star! Call Mary!"** *(St. Bernard of Clairvaux)*

---

[483] Culleton, Rev. R. Gerald. *The Reign of Antichrist: A Sourcebook of Catholic Prophecies About "The Man of Sin."* [Rockford, IL: TAN Books and Publishers, 1974; originally issued in 1951]: pp. 6-7.

[484] Ps. 19:4-7; Matt. 17:2; Matt. 13:43.

[485] "Our Lady of Akita," loc. cit.

[486] Prayer of St. Ambrose.

CHAPTER 14

What Pope Benedict XVI Revealed:
The Third Secret is Spoken

"In all ages, men have been divinely instructed in matters expedient for the salvation of the elect...and in all ages there have been persons possessed of the spirit of prophesy, not for the purpose of announcing new doctrines, but to direct human actions."
-St. Thomas Aquinas, Summa Theologica II-II, Q. 174, Art. 6

Three simple but remarkable words from Pope Benedict XVI during an in-flight interview reveal that there is more to the Third Secret of Fatima than a startling but inexplicable Vision. A careful examination of the Pope's response to a question, asked and answered in Italian, show that—not once, but *twice*—the Pope made clear that the Third Secret is also spoken.[487]

Flying en route to Portugal on May 11, 2010, Pope Benedict made a crucial revelation to a group of journalists, the press corps of the papal entourage. As is the usual practice, Vatican protocol asks correspondents who will travel with the Pope to submit their questions *days in advance*.[488]

Of all the inquiries, the Pope chose to answer only three, all of which were formally presented by Vatican spokesman Fr. Frederico Lombardi. On the same day, the complete question-and-answer session (an exchange made and published in Italian) was quickly transcribed by journalist Gian Guido Vecchi for *Corriere della Sera*.

As it turned out, the last of these pre-selected questions was actually a three-part inquiry about the Fatima apparitions and the Third Secret, the last of three distinct parts of "the Great Secret" given by the Virgin Mary to three shepherd children on July 13, 1917.

In comparing the various English renditions of the on-board press conference, one will find a few inaccuracies or mistranslations. To a certain

---

[487] Bartold, Marianna. "Pope Benedict on the Third Secret: 'It is Spoken,'" *Keeping It Catholic–The Blog!,* May 27, 2010.
[http://keepingitcatholic.blogspot.com/2010/05/pope-benedict-on-third-secret-it-is.html]
[488] Allen, Jr., John L. "On the Crisis, Benedict Changes the Tone." *National Catholic Reporter* website, May 11, 2010.
[http://ncronline.org/blogs/examining-crisis/crisis-benedict-xvi-changes-tone]

degree, this is understandable, as any translator would attest. On the other hand, some things lost in translation are too important to lose. My research into the original Italian articles discovered that the English translations were askew; as a result, I published the correct translation on my blog because every single journalist, in print or online, had missed something both startling and imperative.

What follows, then, is my *literal* translation from Italian-to-English of the Fatima/Third Secret question and the incredibly relevant section of the Pope's response (all following emphasis mine): [489]

[**Author's translation begins**]: "Holiness, what significance have we today for the apparitions of Fatima? And when you presented the text of the Third secret (sic), in the Vatican Press Office, in June 2000, it was asked if the Message could be extended ["broadened" or "widened"], beyond the attack on John Paul II, also to the additional [or "other"] sufferings of the *popes*? And is it possible, in your opinion [or "according to you"], to frame also in that vision the sufferings of the Church of today for the sins of the sexual abuse of minors?"

Pope Benedict XVI's Response: "*Beyond this great vision* of the suffering of the pope, which we *might* in *essence* attribute to John Paul II, there is indicated the reality of the future of the Church which [will] gradually develop and demonstrate [itself]. Namely [also rendered as either "That is" or "In other words"] it is true that *beyond* the moment indicated in the vision, **it is spoken**, it is shown [there is] the necessity of the passion of the Church which, naturally [or "of course"], is reflected in the person of the Pope, but the Pope is in the Church, and therefore it is the sufferings of the Church that are *announced*...*"[490] [**End of author's translation**]

The remainder of this substantial section of the Pope's response to the Third Secret question is as follows, "As for the new things we may find today

---

[489] Please note that, in order to make better sense of the exact English-language translation, bracketed words or phrases in my translation indicate either an alternative meaning of the preceding word or phrase, or a necessary grammatical English structure not explicitly expressed in the original Italian.

[490] English translation by the author (M. Bartold) from the original Italian article by Gian Guido Vecchi, loc. cit. Pope Benedict's original response, in Italian, was phrased as follows: **"Oltre questa grande visione della sofferenza del Papa**, che possiamo in sostanza riferire a Giovanni Paolo II sono indicate realtà del futuro della Chiesa che man mano si sviluppano e si mostrano. **Cioè è vero che oltre il momento indicato nella visione, si parla, si vede la necessità di una passione della Chiesa**, che naturalmente si riflette nella persona del Papa, ma il Papa sta nella Chiesa **e quindi sono sofferenze della Chiesa che si annunciano."**

in this message, it is also that the attacks on the Pope and the Church not always come from the outside, but the sufferings of the Church actually come from *within* the Church, from the sin that exists in the Church. This has always been known, but today we can see it in a really terrifying way: the greatest persecution of the Church does not come from outside enemies, but it is *from sin within the Church*. And the Church now has a deep need to relearn penance, accept purification, learn to forgive, but also a need for justice."[491]

In those preceding words, one discerns a slight echo of Pope St. Pius X in his landmark encyclical, *Pascendi Dominici Gregis* (On the Doctrine of the Modernists, September 8, 1907): "...they put into operation their designs for her undoing, not from without but from within. Hence, the danger is present almost in the very veins and heart of the Church, whose injury is the more certain from the very fact that their knowledge of her is more intimate."

The Third Secret: "It is spoken..."

• **First**, closer attention must be paid to the pivotal sentence: "Namely, it is true that *beyond* the moment indicated in the vision, *it is spoken* (the briefest pause, almost as if the Holy Father caught himself), *it is shown*..." and later in the same sentence he stated "...it is the sufferings of the Church that are *announced.*"

In highlighting that one sentence, Pope Benedict XVI made a staggering and critical revelation. In June of 2000, the Vatican released a description of the Third Secret Vision, but not the Virgin's words that pertain to it.[492]

Since that time, less than a handful of influential Vatican prelates insist there is nothing left to reveal of the Third Secret, evoking a collective, common-sense response from many Catholics: "That's it?" This includes Mother Angelica, the founder of EWTN (Eternal World Television Network), who, when speaking to a priest on her program on May 16, 2001, said: "As for the Secret [the Third Secret of Fatima], well, I happen to be one of those individuals who thinks we didn't get the whole thing. I told you! I mean, you have the right to your own opinion, don't you, Father? There, you know, that's my opinion. Because I think it [the Third Secret] is scary."

Then, in May 2010, Pope Benedict XVI submitted a crucial piece of evidence that there is more to the Third Secret, when he unexpectedly admitted that "beyond...the vision...**it [the Third Secret] is spoken**."

---

[491] Vennari, John. "Pope Resurrects Third Secret." Posted on *Catholic Family News* website, May 19, 2010, and subsequently published in the June 2010 issue of *Catholic Family News*. [Emphasis added.] [http://www.cfnews.org/b16-3rd-sec.htm]

[492] *The Message of Fatima.*

• **Second**, one critical fact cannot be forgotten: Pope Benedict XVI was the first pope to ascend the papal throne, already possessing full knowledge of the Third Secret of Fatima. [493] In light of the fact that Benedict XVI had at least 26 years (if not longer) to ponder the full Third Secret, the manner in which the Pope expressed himself on May 11, 2010 indicates either a purposefully discreet admission or a momentary slip.

To provide a brief summary: During a 1984 interview, Cardinal Ratzinger (who became Pope Benedict XVI in 2005) disclosed that he had already read the Third Secret. However, he did not say when or under what circumstances the Secret was made known to him. Also in 1984, Cardinal Ratzinger, when asked why the Third Secret had still not been revealed, provided an amazing six-point summary of its contents, a topic addressed in the next section.

• **Third**, the specific inquiry about the Third Secret initially asked "if the Message could be extended…to the additional sufferings of the *popes.*"

Initially, it should be noted that Pope Benedict did not object to the plural word, *"popes."* Moreover, the Holy Father's reply also reveals that the pope of the Third Secret Vision is not necessarily the late Pope John Paul II: *"Beyond this great vision of the suffering of the pope, which we might in essence* attribute to John Paul II…"

The entire "Great Secret," in fact, addresses the role of the Holy Father many times. The papacy is absolutely central to complete the Virgin Mary's requests to, and on behalf of, the Church. While the Secret concerns (meaning "is of concern to") the Holy Father, it is not only *about* the Holy Father. These two points are made clear by Our Lady's words in the Second Fatima Secret, by Heaven's later and repeated insistence to Sr. Lucia, and, logically, by the hidden text of the Third Secret, which the Virgin wanted revealed to the world no later than 1960.

The "person of the pope," mentioned by Benedict XVI, means the individual in the office of the papacy, whether past, present, or future. Uncomfortable as it is to admit, the "other sufferings of the popes" is of their own tragic making, due to their baffling and dreadful refusals to obey the explicit commands of God, given by Our Lady of Fatima.

Furthermore, John Paul II was not the only pope to be victimized by a murderous attack. The Holy Father seen in the Third Secret Vision "is killed by

---

[493] Cardinal Ratzinger, who became Pope Benedict XVI, was interviewed by Vittorio Messori on August 15, 1984. On that date, he disclosed that he had indeed read the Third Secret, although he never stated **when** he read it. The August 1984 interview was later published in *Jesus* magazine, November 1984, p. 79.

a group of soldiers who fired bullets and arrows at him."[494] Surely, Benedict XVI knew "the attack in 1981 [an assassination attempt made against John Paul II] stands with respect to that vision exactly as the other attempts suffered by popes—for example, the attack on Paul VI on November 27, 1970, when he was stabbed in the abdomen by a lunatic in Manila."[495] Furthermore, bullets and arrows together were not used against either Paul VI or John Paul II.

Still, even in hindsight, no Vatican prelate attributed the lethal attempt against Paul VI as a fulfillment of the Third Secret, but only to John Paul II. Now Benedict's recent words refute that interpretation.

• **Fourth**, Pope Benedict XVI never clarified that the Third Secret's indicated "reality of the future of the Church" is *conditional*, whether for good or for evil.

In accord with Divine Revelation, the Virgin Mary qualified these conditions in the Second Part of "the Great Fatima Secret": "If what I say to you is done…"—"To prevent this…" *and* "If my requests are heeded, Russia will be converted and there will be peace"—*but*, "If not, she [Russia] will spread her errors throughout the world, causing wars and persecutions against the Church. The good will be martyred. The Holy Father will have much to suffer. Various nations will be annihilated."[496]

Our Lady's words, then and later, left no doubt of God's will. In fact, due to the incomplete 1942 consecration of Russia made by Pope Pius XII, Sr. Lucia "would say more than once, and with deliberate emphasis, **'What Our Lady wants is that the Pope and all the bishops in the world shall consecrate Russia to her Immaculate Heart on one special day. If this is done, she will convert Russia and there will be peace. If it is not done, the errors of Russia will spread through every country in the world.'**"[497]

In July 1917, the Mother of God also promised, "In the end, my Immaculate Heart will triumph. The Holy Father will consecrate Russia to me, and she will be converted, and an era of peace will be granted to the world." [498] This is *the Promise* in which all must keep hope.

As previously mentioned, credible Fatima scholars agree, as would anyone who understands the rules of grammar, that the Promise concludes the Second Secret, and the Third Secret begins with Our Lady's next sentence, "In

---

[494] *The Message of Fatima.*

[495] Socci, Antonio. *The Fourth Secret of Fatima.* [Loreto Publications: Fitzwilliam, NH, 2009]: p. 33.

[496] Frère Michel, *TWTF*, Vol. II, pp. 281-282.

[497] Walsh, *Our Lady of Fatima*, p. 221. [Emphasis added.]

[498] Sr. Mary Lucia, *Memoirs*, 1976 edition, p. 165.

Portugal, the dogma of the Faith will always be preserved, etc."–the *etc.* added by Sr. Lucia, who indicated that explanatory words followed.

• **Fifth**, Benedict XVI said there is "need for the passion of the Church, which naturally reflects itself on the person of the pope..."

To the contrary, it was precisely to avoid this ongoing passion (beginning anew with the post-WWI era) that Our Lady came to Fatima, there to warn against many future dangers and give the means to avoid them all.

Again, the Virgin at Fatima repeatedly emphasized through her requests and prophecies (especially in the still unexplained but ominous Third Secret Vision) that the present and future are fully dependent upon the Church's fidelity to Divine Revelation. That fidelity, however, depends on "the person of the pope," the man whose office is entrusted by God with the duty and obligation to guard the Deposit of Faith and faithfully transmit it to Christ's flock.

In the words of the great saint, Pope St. Pius X, "One of the primary obligations assigned by Christ to the office divinely committed to Us of feeding the Lord's flock is that of guarding with the greatest vigilance the deposit of the faith delivered to the saints, rejecting the profane novelties of words and the gainsaying of knowledge falsely so called."[499]

Tragically, waning papal vigilance has marked the past decades of Church history. God, Who knows all things, foresaw the failure of those hierarchs who simply would not wholly fulfill all of Heaven's directives given at Fatima. Part of Lucia's mission was to transmit God's commands to the hierarchy, which they in turn were to fulfill for the benefit of the universal Church and the world.

From the beginning, however, her first superior, Bishop de Silva, repeatedly rejected the responsibility of the Third Secret placed upon him. This bishop was given the authority to read and disseminate the Third Secret, but he obstinately refused to do so.[500]

As a result, various misunderstandings and capitulations rippled throughout the hierarchy in regard to many important facets of Fatima. The consecrations of Pope Pius XII, Paul VI, and Pope John Paul II were incomplete; the other popes (Pius XI and John XXIII) did not even make the attempt. Sadly, Benedict XVI also did not endeavor to make the collegial consecration.

---

[499] Pope Pius X, loc. cit., para. 1.

[500] The details of these events are fully documented in the monumental works of Frère Michel, *The Whole Truth about Fatima,* Volumes I, II, and III. One particular example of Bishop de Silva's refusal is found in Vol. II, *The Secret and the Church* [Buffalo, NY: Immaculate Heart Publications, Revised Edition 2001]: p. 40.

An appropriate observation was made by Antonio Socci, author of *The Fourth Secret of Fatima*, who wrote, "All of the history of Fatima and of this century resides in this dramatic incapacity of Peter, of the men of the Church, and of humanity to entrust themselves fully to she who is 'omnipotent by grace'–the incapacity to trust in her truly and totally, almost as if the possibility of salvation could come from Peter (alone) by his own initiatives, from Vatican politics."

• **Sixth**, Benedict XVI subsequently remarked, "…but the Pope is in the Church, and therefore it is the sufferings of the Church that are *announced*." These words accomplish two things: 1) they make a second verification that the Third Secret is indeed spoken, and 2) they express a vital truth of Catholic doctrine regarding the Pope and the Church.

Jesus Christ said to the first pope, "And I say to thee: Thou art Peter, and upon this rock I shall build my Church, and the gates of hell shall not prevail against it."[501] Since the meaning of individual words is significant, this essay now turns to the connotation of the word "church," as explained by the Catholic priest and scholar, Msgr. Joseph Clifford Fenton:

"What Our Lord promised, and what He actually accomplished, was thus the continuation of a social unit which had been in existence since the beginnings of the human race, but a continuation of this unit in a new status and under new conditions. In this new status, the *ecclesia* was to be established or founded upon St. Peter. In other words, this man and his successors were to be the source of the unity and stability of this *ecclesia* of the new dispensation. The society of Our Lord's disciples was the 'Church' of the new dispensation. It was and, until the end of time, it will continue to be the assembly of the chosen people, the people of the covenant, the kingdom of God in this world. By reason of its association with Our Lord, it is designated as His Mystical Body."[502]

With this definition in mind, the entire Church, from the Holy Father to the laity, must recall the great yet terrible "secret of the Catholic City," as it is taught in the infallible Scriptures:

"Unless the Lord build the house, they labor in vain that build it. Unless the Lord keep the city, he watcheth in vain that keepeth it."[503]

---

[501] Matt. 16:18.
[502] Fenton, Msgr. Joseph Clifford. "The Meaning of the Name 'Church.'" *The American Ecclesiastical Review*, Vol. CXXXI, No. 4, October 1954: p. 272.
[503] Ps. 126:1.

CHAPTER 15

The Six Themes
of the Third Secret of Fatima

"We had enough exhortations to be silent. Cry out with a hundred thousand tongues! I see that the world is rotten because of silence."
—St. Catherine of Siena

We have seen how, in choosing to answer a "Third Secret question," which was really a three-part inquiry, Pope Benedict XVI unexpectedly revealed that the Third Secret consists of both a verbal Message from Our Lady as well as a Vision. In fact, when the Pope said the Third Secret is spoken and shown, his words correlate with other proofs that this last Secret is comprised of *two* parts.

To cite only one example, let us momentarily turn to what was said decades ago by Fr. Joseph Schweigel. This priest, upon his return from an important mission given to him by Pope Pius XII to make inquiries of Sr. Lucia about unfulfilled parts of the Fatima Message (the Third Secret, the consecration of Russia, etc.), was briefly questioned by a curious colleague about the Third Secret. Fr. Schweigel responded in the following manner:

"I cannot reveal anything of what I learned at Fatima concerning the Third Secret, but I can say that it has two parts: *one concerns the Pope.* The other, logically—although I can say nothing—would have to be the continuation of the words: *In Portugal, the dogma of the Faith will always be preserved.*"[504]

The colleague pressed a little further, asking, "The present Pope or the next one?" However, as the interrogator himself attested in a written letter, "To this question, Fr. Schweigel made no reply."[505]

Only a few years later, Fr. Schweigel would also say that the Third Secret "seems to suppose a victorious, triumphant, but difficult and heroic decision" of a Pope's.[506] In considering the purpose of Fr. Schweigel's papally-directed mission in questioning Sr. Lucia and in light of the tragic circumstances in which the Church Militant finds itself today, one can reasonably presume that, sometime in the future, a Pope will make a "difficult and heroic decision" under circumstances in which he faces vehement, if not physically violent, opposition to his unique prerogatives in his office as Vicar of Christ when he

---

[504] Frère Michel, *TWTF,* Vol. III: p. 710. [Emphasis added.]
[505] Ibid.
[506] Loc. cit., p. 351, footnote 39.

decides to comply with at least one, if not all, of Our Lady's unfulfilled requests at Fatima.

Since Our Lady still awaits three particular actions to be made by the Pope and the bishops of the Catholic Church, it appears that Fr. Schweigel's description of a "victorious, triumphant, but difficult and heroic decision," made by the present Pope or a future one, lends further insight into Our Lady's promise, "In the end, my Immaculate Heart will triumph."

Because they deserve repeating, what are these three things in which the Queen of the Catholic City so gently insists? Our Lady first asks the Pope to command (not invite) and lead the world's bishops in a public and solemn collegial consecration of *Russia* to the Immaculate Heart of Mary. Secondly, the Virgin Mary also desires the release of the complete Third Secret Message (which will then make clear the meaning of the Third Secret Vision). Third, the Pope must promulgate the Five First Saturday devotions, which are acts of reparation for five specific blasphemies against the Immaculate Heart of Mary.

What must never be forgotten is that the last Secret of Fatima, like the first Two Secrets, is intended by God to be publicly disseminated to the entire Church and likewise followed, for it also is given for the salvation of souls living in these days of great peril. To insist on the release of the Third Secret and the other two things for which the Virgin Mary asks is neither a matter of satisfying mere curiosity nor is it one of overly sentimental piety; these are matters of obedience to God Himself, Who sent the Immaculate Virgin Mother to Fatima with an apocalyptic warning and the means to avoid its fulfilment.

To grasp the general idea "of what" the Third Secret consists, it is entirely appropriate to attentively review an earlier disclosure by Cardinal Joseph Ratzinger, made many years before he became the Pope.

It has been previously mentioned that in a 1984 interview with Vittorio Messori, Cardinal Ratzinger was asked if he had read the Third Secret of Fatima. When he answered, "Yes, I have read it," it was then inquired as to why the Secret had still not been released. A careful examination of the Cardinal Ratzinger's answer reveals a total of six "themes" to the Third Secret:

"Because, according to the judgment of the Popes, it adds nothing (literally: "nothing different") to what a Christian must know concerning what derives from Revelation: i.e., a radical call for conversion; the absolute importance of history; the dangers threatening the faith and the life of the Christian, and therefore of the world. And then the importance of the *'novissimi'* [the last events at the end of time]. If it is not made public—at least for the time being—it is in order to prevent religious prophecy from being mistaken for a quest for the sensational (literally: 'for sensationalism'). But the things contained in this 'Third Secret' correspond to what has been announced in Scripture and has been said again and again in many other Marian apparitions, beginning with the Fatima apparitions in their known contents. Conversion and penitence are the essential conditions for 'salvation.'"[507]

Since Cardinal Ratzinger spoke of the "Novissimi" (the last events at the end of time), one might ask: Could these six themes of the Third Secret direct our attention to one or more of the 'six signs' of the last times, given by Christ Himself?

When Our Lord prophesied to His Apostles the destruction of Jerusalem (which occurred in 69 A.D. but also serves as a figure-type for the end of the world), He said, "These things which you see, the days will come in which there shall not be left a stone upon a stone that shall not be thrown down. And they asked him, saying: Master, when shall these things be? and what shall be the sign when they shall begin to come to pass? Who said: Take heed you be not seduced; for many will come in my name, saying, I am he; and the time is at hand: go ye not therefore after them. And when you shall hear of wars and seditions, be not terrified: these things must first come to pass; but the end is not yet presently. Then he said to them: **Nation shall rise against nation, and kingdom against kingdom. And there shall be great earthquakes in divers places, and pestilences, and famines, and terrors from heaven; and there shall be great signs.**"[508] Those infallible words of Our Lord's are the last six events of the end times.

Consider, then, the six themes found in Cardinal Ratzinger's disclosure about the Third Secret's contents:

1.) The Third Secret of Fatima adds "nothing different" to what derives from Divine Revelation (of which the two sources are Tradition and Scripture). Of course, this remark might be considered superfluous, because the Church cannot approve any apparition or locution as "worthy of belief" *unless* it is in perfect accord with Divine Revelation. However, if a Church-approved revelation adds "nothing" different from Revelation," then it must be derived *from either Tradition or Scripture , or both.*

2.) The Third Secret is a "radical" (i.e., a drastic, profound, or extreme) call for conversion and penance. As the Church's long history proves, whenever God chose to make such a "radical" call through His chosen prophets, that same call was always intended to be given to His people for their salvation. God's message to a prophet is never solely intended for the prophet alone.

---

[507] Ratzinger, Cardinal Joseph as quoted by Vittorio Messori, "Here is Why the Faith is in Crisis," *Jesus* Magazine, November 11, 1984: p. 79. [Emphasis added.]
[508] Lk. 21: 6-11. [Emphasis added.]

For example, St. John the Evangelist was commanded by God, "What thou seest write in a book, and send to the seven churches…"[509] As we know, the beloved disciple also wrote what he *heard* in that same collection of writings, now known as the *Apocalypse*. This example again reminds us that Sr. Lucia herself said that the Third Secret is in the *Gospel* and the *Apocalypse*.

3.) The Third Secret refers to "the absolute importance of history," which the Church refers to as either "sacred history" or "salvation history." Sacred history centers on two things: The Incarnation of Christ, when Our Lord came to offer Redemption and Mercy to fallen mankind, and His Second Coming, when He will come as Just Judge. Sacred history records the unfolding of events, which depend on mankind's acceptance or rejection of God's Will.

4.) The Third Secret alerts the Church and the world "to the dangers threatening the Faith, the life of the Christian, and therefore the world." What "dangers" are seen in the Third Secret *Vision* that could simultaneously threaten the Faith, a Christian's life, and the entire world? As tragic as the Vision appears to be, the events in the "half-ruined city" (which might be Rome) cannot threaten the entire world—or can they? If so, then *how* so? The missing words of Our Lady are the only explanation for Cardinal Ratzinger's words in 1984. The omitted text of the Virgin's must be about the spiritual and material dangers of "the revolt," foretold by St. Paul, which he said must come first before "the man of sin be revealed, the son of perdition" (2 Thess. 2:3). Surely, then, the nature of these unknown threats revealed in the Third Secret Message is most grave, since Cardinal Ratzinger appeared to suggest their essence in the next point.

5.) The Third Secret relates "the importance of the *Novissimi*," a theological term with two "simultaneous" definitions: the four "last things" as they pertain to every human soul (death, judgment, heaven, hell) and "the last things" (meaning the last events at the end of time), in which all peoples will witness the Second Coming of Christ, the universal judgment, and the literal ending of the material world. The *Novissimi* could also pertain to the time immediately preceding Christ's Second Coming—the days of the great apostasy, which are then followed by the "son of perdition," the anti-Christ. As Cardinal Ratzinger used the term in 1984, the *Novissimi* is not only about each soul's individual death, judgment, and final fate, for that would have no bearing on the importance of salvation history, or the "dangers threatening the Faith, the life of the Christian, and, therefore, the world."

6.) Although it could be mistaken for sensationalism, the Third Secret is a "*religious prophecy* corresponding to Scripture and confirmed by many other

---

[509] Apoc. 1:11.

Marian apparitions," *beginning* with the Fatima revelations in their "known contents."

This last point is Cardinal Ratzinger's final affirmation that the Third Secret is in accord with Scripture (and also corresponds with Sr. Lucia's declaration, mentioned previously, that the Third Secret is in the *Gospel* and the *Apocalypse*)–but it is also confirmed as well by other "private" Marian revelations, starting with what is already publicly known of Fatima but was not then, in 1984, or later, in 2000, fully revealed. The Cardinal summarized these Church-approved apparitions by stating them in their most basic but essential message: "Conversion and penitence are the essential conditions for salvation."

One may reasonably ask: **Where are seen those six themes in the Third Secret *Vision*,** the only part of the Third Secret finally released 40 years after its final due date of 1960? Perhaps the fourth theme is represented, but the others are not. Cardinal Ratzinger's words in 1984 confirm that the Secret later revealed in June, 2000 was not the entire Third Secret. Again, the whole of Fatima is complete, from the first message to the Miracle of the Sun. It makes no sense to opine, as some do, that the Mother of God left the third part of the Great Secret unexplained and, as it were, hanging, while expecting the men of the Church to interpret only the Third Secret but not the first Two Secrets. As with the vision of hell, the Virgin must have stated more which completes both the opening sentence of the Third Secret Message, "In Portugal, the dogma of the Faith will always be preserved, *etc.*" **and** the Third Secret Vision that opens with an angel and a flaming sword of justice. Let's again consider the description of the Third Secret *Vision*:

"...at the left of Our Lady and a little above, we saw an Angel with a flaming sword in his left hand; flashing, it gave out flames that looked as though they would set the world on fire; but they died out in contact with the splendour that Our Lady radiated towards him from her right hand: pointing to the earth with his right hand, the Angel cried out in a loud voice: 'Penance, Penance, Penance!'"

"And we saw in an immense light that is God: 'something similar to how people appear in a mirror when they pass in front of it;' a Bishop dressed in White 'we had the impression that it was the Holy Father.' Other Bishops, Priests, men and women Religious going up a steep mountain, at the top of which there was a big Cross of rough-hewn trunks as of a cork-tree with the bark; before reaching there the Holy Father passed through a big city half in ruins and half trembling with halting step, afflicted with pain and sorrow, he prayed for the souls of the corpses he met on his way; having reached the top of the mountain, on his knees at the foot of the big Cross he was killed by a group of soldiers who fired bullets and arrows at him, and in the same way there died one after another the other Bishops, Priests, men and women Religious, and various lay people of different ranks and positions. Beneath the two arms of the Cross there were two Angels each with a crystal aspersorium in his hand, in which they gathered up the blood of the Martyrs and with it sprinkled the souls that were making their way to God."

Finally, of the relatively few Church-approved Marian revelations since the time of Fatima, it must be remembered that it was Cardinal Ratzinger who said that the two messages of Fatima and Akita (with its very serious subject matter, including warnings of an apocalyptic nature) "are essentially the same."[510] In considering all that he knows, it is no small wonder that Benedict XVI (who resigned from the papacy in 2013) said on May 13, 2010 (the 93rd anniversary of the first Fatima apparition): "We would be mistaken to think that Fatima's **prophetic mission** is complete."

---

[510] *Catholic World News*, October 11, 2001. Howard Dee, the former Philippine ambassador to the Vatican, revealed in 1998 that "Bishop Ito was certain Akita was an extension of Fatima, and Cardinal Ratzinger personally confirmed to me that these two messages are essentially the same."

CHAPTER 16

Our Lady and the Apostles
of the Latter Times

"One must strive to maintain a strong spiritual life.
If one lacks this, one lacks everything."
—*St. Vincent de Paul*

The Church will soon observe the 100th anniversary of the 1917 Fatima apparitions, in what we hope shall be a wondrous and universal celebration commemorating the Triumph of Mary's Immaculate Heart. The year 2029 (again, only fifteen years hence from the date of this book's publication) will mark the centenary of the day the Virgin returned to say that the moment had come when the Lord God Himself asked the Holy Father to command and lead the consecration of Russia to the Virgin's Immaculate Heart. Today, however, as the human race descends into a chaos unparalleled in world history, one wonders what the coming years will bring. Are these the times foretold by St. Louis de Montfort, the days which will bring forth "the apostles of the latter times"?[511]

Thirty years after Our Lady gave the Great Secret of Fatima, the Church canonized St. Louis Marie de Montfort, the apostle of "true devotion to Jesus through Mary."[512] "The mainspring of his apostolic ministry," as Pope Pius XII said at the canonization, "**his great secret** of attracting and giving souls to Jesus, was his devotion to Mary. All his activity was founded upon her, all his confidence rested in her. In opposition to the joyless austerity, melancholy, fear and depressing pride of Jansenism, he promoted the filial, trustful, ardent and expansive love-in-action of a slave of Mary."[513]

St. Montfort, now a candidate to be recognized as a Doctor of the Church, authored *True Devotion to Mary, The Secret of Mary,* and *The Secret of the Rosary.* Even before his canonization, St. Montfort's writings positively influenced three popes—Pope Leo XIII, Pope St. Pius X, and Pope Pius XII. In fact, Pope St. Pius X granted an Apostolic Blessing to all who read *True*

---

[511] de Montfort, St. Louis. *True Devotion to Mary,* p. 34.
[512] On July 20, 1947, Pope Pius XII canonized St. Louis-Marie de Montfort.
[513] Pope Pius XII, *A.A.S.,* 39, 413.

Devotion to Mary, stating, "There is no surer or easier way than Mary in uniting all men in Christ."[514]

Parallels: Our Lady of Fatima and St. Louis de Montfort

St. Louis de Montfort "knew that Mary is the *pathway* to her Son, leading souls quickly and securely to Jesus Christ, the Eternal Wisdom."[515] In a most striking parallel two hundred years after the saint's death, Our Lady herself said at Fatima, "Don't lose heart. I will never forsake you. My Immaculate Heart will be your refuge, and *the path* that leads you to God."[516]

Too, there are other interesting similarities in religious authorities' acceptance or resistance toward St. Montfort's mission and the later Fatima revelations (especially the third part of the Great Secret, the collegial consecration of Russia to the Immaculate Heart, and the papal promulgation of the Five First Saturday devotions in reparations for sins of blasphemy against the same Immaculate Heart). For example:

• Modernism, the synthesis of all heresies, is the central obstruction to the Fatima Virgin's six requests. It is the particular cause explaining the resistance against the collegial consecration of Russia to her Immaculate Heart. Although the modernist heresy has been condemned by many popes (and vehemently so by Pope St. Pius X over 100 years ago[517]), there is still an overwhelming number of people in all states and ranks of life who have embraced it.

Similarly, St. Montfort's "greatest problem was the opposition he encountered from the propagators of the Jansenist heresy...Although Jansenism had been condemned by the Church twice even before St. Louis de Montfort's birth, its teachings continued to spread and to influence people for a century."

• At Fatima, Our Lady prophesied what would happen, dependent upon whether or not her requests were heeded. Ardent promoters and defenders of the whole truth of Fatima are pitted in a constant battle against detractors who either insist that ongoing historical events leading to the Third Secret "now seem a part of the past"[518] or who implicitly persecute Our Lady by casting various doubts upon the witness of Sr. Lucia (now Servant of God), the last Fatima visionary, who died in 2005.

---

[514] *Museo San Pio X* website. [http://www.museosanpiox.it/]
[515] de Montfort, op. cit., p. xiii.
[516] Sr. Mary Lucia, *Memoirs*, 1976 edition, p. 163.
[517] Pope St. Pius X, *Pascendi Dominici Gregis* (On the Doctrines of the Modernists, Sept. 8, 1907).
[518] *The Message of Fatima.*

Likewise, St. Montfort during his lifetime was "at once persecuted and venerated everywhere,"[519] because his "preaching, his writing and his conversation were all impregnated with prophecy and with anticipations of the later ages of the Church."[520]

• Finally, there exists overwhelming evidence that the Third Secret of Fatima is not yet "fully" released.[521] While the Third Secret *Vision* may now be known (but obfuscated with various interpretations, with none of them binding on the faithful), its accompanying Message, which explains the Vision, remains buried by Vatican officials who still refuse to obey the Mother of God.

In a similar fashion, St. Montfort prophesied about his treatise, *True Devotion to Mary*, "I clearly foresee that raging brutes will come in fury to tear with their diabolical teeth this little writing and him whom the Holy Ghost has made use of to write it; or at least to envelop it in the silence of a coffer, in order that it may not appear."[522]

"This prediction was fulfilled to the letter," explains one of four introductions and prefaces to *True Devotion*. "Throughout the whole 18th century, the spiritual sons of St. Louis de Montfort were persecuted by the Jansenists for their zeal in spreading this devotion; the precious manuscript of de Montfort remained hidden during the troubled times of the French Revolution and was brought to light only in 1842, when it was found in a chest of old books by a Montfort Father."[523]

For the reasons stated above, it may be no coincidence that only 13 years after St. Montfort's canonization, the Bishop of Leiria, Msgr. Joao Venancio, blessed and installed a statue of the saint on October 13, 1960 (the 43rd anniversary of the Miracle of the Sun). This statue "now stands above the colonnade of the [original Fatima] basilica," commemorating the bishop's appeal to his brother bishops throughout the world, "inviting them to organize days of prayer and penance on October 12 and 13, in union with the pilgrims to the Cova da Iria, in a spirit of reparation and consecration to the Holy Hearts of Jesus and Mary."[524]

---

[519] "Fr. Faber's Preface," *True Devotion to Mary*, p. xix.

[520] Ibid., p. xx.

[521] See Antonio Socci, *The Fourth Secret of Fatima* and Christopher Ferrara, *The Secret Still Hidden.*

[522] "Fr. Faber's Preface," op. cit., p. xx.

[523] Ibid., p. xii.

[524] Brother François de Marie des Anges of the Little Brothers of the Sacred Heart. *The Whole Truth of Fatima*, Vol. IV. [http://www.catholicvoice.co.uk/fatima4/] On May 17,

Mary Forms the Great Saints of the Consummation

One cannot properly repeat the saint's emphasis on devotion to the Incarnation of Christ (which is also the first Rosary mystery, the Annunciation) or his explanations as to why the Virgin Mary is necessary to God's plan for the salvation of souls. What follows, then, is an "overview," illustrating key points of what the saint taught in his book, *True Devotion to Mary* about Our Lady and her "apostles of the latter times":

• "It was only through Mary that God the Father gave His only-begotten Son to the world…The world was unworthy, says St. Augustine, to receive the Son of God directly from the Father's hands. He gave Him to Mary in order that the world might receive Him through her." [525]

Explaining the action and conduct of each Divine Person of the Holy Trinity toward Mary in regard to the Incarnation and the first coming of Jesus Christ, the saint wrote, "They still pursue [it] daily, in an invisible manner, throughout the whole Church, and They will pursue it even to the consummation of ages in the last coming of Christ."[526]

• "**Mary has produced, together with the Holy Ghost, the greatest thing which has been or ever will be—a God-Man**; and she will consequently produce the greatest saints that there will be in time. **The formation and the education of the great saints who shall come at the end of the world are reserved for her**.[527]

• "It is Mary alone who has found grace before God (Lk. 1:3) without the aid of any other mere creature; it is only through her that all those who have since found grace before God have found it at all, and it is only through her that all those who shall come afterward shall find it."[528] (Here we might observe that St. Bernard said something similar, explaining that when the angel greeted Mary at the Incarnation, he said "thou hast found grace with God," meaning she who was previously addressed as "full of grace" had also *found* grace for the conversion of sinners.) [529]

1960, the "Bishop of Leiria, Msgr. Joao Venancio, launched an appeal to all the bishops of the world, inviting them to organise [sic] days of prayer and penance on October 12 and 13, in union with the pilgrims to the Cova da Iria, in a spirit of reparation and consecration to the Holy Hearts of Jesus and Mary… About three hundred bishops responded to his appeal. This was scarcely fifteen per cent of the world episcopate. Nevertheless their letters indicated that, in numerous countries, people would be uniting themselves with the ardent supplications of the pilgrims in Fatima."

[525] de Montfort, op. cit., p. 11.
[526] Ibid., p. 14.
[527] Ibid., p. 21.
[528] Ibid., p. 25.
[529] St. Bernard, cited by St. Alphonsus de Liguori, *The Glories of Mary*, p. 73.

• "It was through Mary that the salvation of the world was begun, and it is through Mary that it must be consummated. Mary hardly appeared at all in the first coming of Jesus Christ, in order that men, as yet but little instructed and enlightened on the Person of her Son, should not remove themselves from Him in attaching themselves too strongly and too grossly to her…But in the Second Coming of Jesus Christ, Mary has to be made known and revealed by the Holy Ghost in order that, through her, Jesus Christ may be known, loved and served. The reasons which moved the Holy Ghost to hide His spouse during her life, and to reveal her but very little since the preaching of the *Gospel*, exist no longer."[530]

• "Being the way by which Jesus came to us the first time, she will also be the way by which He will come the second time, though not in the same manner." (This anticipated era before Our Lord's Second Coming is one which many call "**The Age of Mary**.")[531]

• "Mary must shine forth more than ever in *mercy*, in *might* and in *grace*, in these latter times: **in mercy**, to bring back and lovingly receive the poor strayed sinners who shall be converted and shall return to the Catholic Church; **in might**, against the enemies of God, idolaters, schismatics, Mahometans, Jews and souls hardened in impiety, who shall rise in terrible revolt against God to seduce all those who shall oppose them and to make them fall by promises and threats; and finally, she must shine forth **in grace**, in order to animate and sustain the valiant soldiers and faithful servants of Jesus Christ, who shall battle for His interests."[532]

• "And lastly, Mary must be terrible to the devil and his crew, as an army arranged in battle, principally in these latter times, because the devil, knowing that he has but little time, and now less than ever, to destroy souls, will every day redouble his efforts and his combats. He will presently raise up cruel persecutions and will put terrible snares before the faithful servants and true children of Mary, whom it gives him more trouble to conquer than it does to conquer others."[533]

• "**But the power of Mary over all the devils will especially shine forth in the latter times, when Satan will lay his snares against her heel**; that is to say, her humble slaves and her poor children, whom she will raise up to make war against him. They shall be little and poor in the world's esteem, and abased before all like the heel, trodden underfoot and persecuted as the heel is by the other members of the body. But in return for this, they shall be rich in the grace

---

[530] de Montfort, op. cit., p. 28.
[531] Ibid., p. 29.
[532] Ibid., p. 30.
[533] Ibid.

of God, which Mary shall distribute to them abundantly. They shall be great and exalted before God in sanctity, superior to all other creatures by their lively zeal, and so well sustained with God's assistance that, with the humility of their heel, in union with Mary, they shall crush the head of the devil and cause Jesus Christ to triumph."[534]

• "In a word, God wishes that His holy Mother should be at present more known, more loved, more honored than she has ever been. This, no doubt, will take place if the predestinate enter, with the grace and light of the Holy Ghost, into the interior and perfect practice which I will disclose to them shortly. Then they will see clearly, as far as faith allows, that beautiful Star of the Sea. They will arrive happily in harbor, following its guidance, in spite of the tempests and the pirates....they will have recourse to her in all things, as to their dear advocate and Mediatrix with Jesus Christ. They will know what is the surest, the easiest, the shortest and the most perfect means of going to Jesus Christ; and they will give themselves to Mary, body and soul, without reserve, that they may thus belong entirely to Jesus Christ."

• **"But who shall those servants, slaves, and children of Mary be?** They shall be the ministers of the Lord who, like a burning fire, shall kindle the fire of divine love everywhere. They shall be 'like sharp arrows in the hand of the powerful' Mary to pierce her enemies (Ps. 126:4). They shall be sons of Levi, well-purified by the fire of great tribulation, and closely adhering to God (1 Cor. 6:17), who shall carry the gold of love in their heart, the incense of prayer in their spirit, and the myrrh of mortification in their body. They shall be everywhere the good odor of Jesus Christ to the poor and to the little, while at the same time, they shall be an odor of death to the great, to the rich and to the proud worldlings."

"They shall be clouds thundering and flying through the air at the least breath of the Holy Ghost; who, detaching themselves from everything and troubling themselves about nothing, shall shower forth the rein of the Word of God and of life eternal. They shall thunder against sin; they shall storm against the world; they shall strike the devil and his crew; and they shall pierce through and through, for life or for death, with their two-edged sword of the Word of God (Eph. 6:17), all those to whom they shall be sent on the part of the most High."

• **"They shall be the true apostles of the latter times**, to whom the Lord of Hosts shall give the word and the might to work marvels and to carry off with glory the spoils of His enemies. They shall sleep without gold or silver and, what is more, without care, in the midst of the other priests, ecclesiastics,

---

[534] Ibid. All quotes from this point are found on pp. 32-35.

and clerics (Ps. 67:14); and yet they shall have the silvered wings of the dove to go, with the pure intention of the glory of God and the salvation of souls, wheresoever the Holy Ghost shall call them. Nor shall they leave behind them, in the places where they have preached, anything but the gold of charity, which is the fulfillment of the whole law (Rom. 13:10)."

"**In a word, we know that they shall be true disciples of Jesus Christ,** walking in the footsteps of His poverty, humility, contempt of the world, charity; teaching the narrow way of God in pure truth according to the *Holy Gospel,* and not according to the maxims of the world; troubling themselves about nothing; not accepting persons; sparing, fearing and listening to no mortal, however influential he may be..."

"These are the great men who are to come; but **Mary is the one who, by order of the Most High, shall fashion them** for the purpose of extending His empire over that of the impious, the idolaters and the Mahometans. **But when and how shall this be?** God alone knows."

As we pray and sacrifice for the Immaculate Heart's Triumph via the Church hierarchy's obedience to her Fatima requests, we can say with St. Montfort, "As for us, we have but to hold our tongues, to pray, to sigh, and to wait: '*With expectation I have waited*' (Ps. 39:2)."[535]

---

[535] de Montfort, Ibid., p. 35.

CHAPTER 17
Fatima's Foremost Request

"Make it known to the Holy Father that I am always awaiting the Consecration of Russia to my Immaculate Heart. *Without the Consecration,* Russia will not be able to convert, nor will the world have peace."
—Our Lady of Fatima to Sr. Maria Lucia, May, 1952

October 13, 2017 marks the 100th anniversary of the Miracle of the Sun at Fatima, the most-well known of all true Marian apparitions of the Modern Age. In August, 2013, most Catholics heard that on October 13, 2013, the 96th anniversary of the Miracle, Pope Francis would repeat the consecration of the world (but not Russia, specifically) to the Immaculate Heart of Mary. That news brought forth a world-wide flurry of wasted commentary because, ultimately, Pope Francis neither *consecrated* the world nor Russia. Rather, his words of "entrustment" indicated that he (and perhaps those present who wished to unite themselves with him) offered a prayer of appeal to the "Blessed Virgin Mary of Fatima," which, while laudatory, is not the required response to the Holy Mother's consistent request for a *collegial* act of solemn *consecration* of *Russia* to her under the **specific** title, **"Immaculate Heart of Mary."**

As mentioned above, it began on August 13, 2013 when the Fatima Sanctuary's official website published the following announcement, which some now claim was erroneously translated because the word "consecration" did not appear in the original Portuguese: "In response to the desire of Holy Father Francis, the Statue of Our Lady of the Rosary of Fatima, venerated in the Little Chapel of Apparitions, will be brought to Rome on October 12/13 to be present at the Marian Day promoted by the Pontifical Council for the Promotion of the New Evangelization. On October 13, next to the Statue of Our Lady, Pope Francis will make the consecration of the world to the Immaculate Heart of Mary."

"[The] Marian Day is one of the great pontifical events marked down on the calendar of celebrations of the Year of Faith which will bring to Rome hundreds of movements and institutions connoted with Marian devotion."

"In a letter addressed to Bishop Antonio Marto, of Leiria-Fatima, the President of the Pontifical Council for the Promotion of the New Evangelization, [Archbishop] Rino Fisichella, informs that 'all ecclesial entities of Marian spirituality' are invited to take part in this Marian day, a gathering which includes, on the 12th, a pilgrimage to the tomb of Apostle St. Peter and other moments of prayer and meditation and, on the 13th, a Mass presided over by Pope Francis, in St. Peter's Square."

"In that letter, [Archbishop] Fisichella wrote: 'The Holy Father strongly desires that the Marian Day may have present, as a special sign, one of the most significant Marian icons for Christians throughout the world and, for that reason, we thought of the beloved original Statue of Our Lady of Fatima.'"

"Therefore, the Statue of Our Lady will depart from the Shrine of Fatima on the morning of October 12 and return on the afternoon of October 13. Scheduled to take its place in the Little Chapel of Apparitions is the first Pilgrim Statue of Our Lady of Fatima, which is enthroned in the Basilica of Our Lady of the Rosary since December 8, 2003."[536]

On the internet, online news sources repeated the report above, and the inquiries and comments immediately began. One question that consistently arose was similar to the following: "What about *Russia?* The world has already been consecrated to the Immaculate Heart of Mary, but Our Lady specifically said *Russia.*" The second was: "What about the bishops? Are they going to join in the consecration? Will any of them tell the Pope that it is *Russia* they together must solemnly consecrate?"

For example, one comment to a news article stated: "Pope Francis' consecration of the world to the Immaculate Heart of Mary in October, is another repetition of the consecrations of the world to the Immaculate Heart of Mary, made by John Paul II in 1982, 1984 and again in 2000. If these previous acts of consecration of the WORLD met the requirements of heaven to consecrate RUSSIA, where is the promised Triumph of Mary and WORLD PEACE? It is outrageous to suggest that heaven accepted the acts of consecration by John Paul II as valid, but God then failed to fulfill the promises attached to a valid act of consecration. If Our Lady desired the CONSECRATION OF THE WORLD, WHY DID SHE ASK FOR THE CONSECRATION OF RUSSIA? Surely, the Mother of God knows the difference between the two? Why the disconnect between heaven's request and the response of the Popes? And, since the previous consecrations of the world

---

[536] "Imagem de Nossa Senhora de Fátima será levada à Jornada Mariana a pedido do Papa," *Santuário de Fátima* website.
[http://www.santuario-fatima.pt/portal/index.php?id=66425; English translation posted on the Rorate Caeli blog, "In October, at the Vatican, Pope Francis will consecrate the world to the Immaculate Heart of Mary." [http://rorate-caeli.blogspot.com/2013/08/in-october-at-vatican-pope-francis-will.html]

didn't produce the promises attached to a valid consecration of Russia, why is this one going to be any different?"[537]

These questions are just and reasonable. Both Pope Pius XI (in 1930 and again in 1937) and Pius XII (in April 1940) learned through Sr. Lucia of the Virgin's specific requests. In those ten years, she was met with silence, so that her superior, Bishop de Silva, suggested that she change the conditions to consecrating the world, with a special mention of Russia. Although she resisted the concept, she eventually mentioned it but made it clear that it was the bishop's idea and not Our Lady's request.

On October 31, 1942, *"the Church and the peoples of the world"* were consecrated to the Immaculate Heart of Mary in a "Radio Address" by Pope Pius XII. A decade later, in his *Apostolic Letter to the Peoples of Russia* (July 7, 1952), he wrote that "just as a few years ago, We consecrated the entire human race to the Immaculate Heart of the Virgin Mary, Mother of God, so today We consecrate and in a most special manner We entrust all the peoples of Russia to this Immaculate Heart," etc. It's clearly evident that neither a radio address nor an apostolic letter is a solemn and public act of consecration, much less a collegial one.

Pope Pius XII's 1942 consecration of the Church and the peoples of the world (which occurred near the height of World War II) shortened what Our Lord called "the current distress" (the war), but it did not bring about the promised conversion of Russia, which is exactly what Christ had forewarned Lucia would occur since the Pope did not do exactly as he was asked. WWII ended three years later—which makes one wonder how much longer it would have lasted without the benefit of the uncalled-for consecration of the *world*, or how much faster the war would have ended, not to mention how quickly Russia's conversion and the world-wide era of peace would have commenced— if only the Pope and bishops followed Our Lady's very simple "request" to consecrate *Russia* to her Immaculate Heart.

Instead, three more years ensued before WWII's terrible conclusion, during which time millions had died in service, in battles on ground, ship, or plane, and in blitzes on civilian cities, and by atrocities in concentration camps. Finally—lest we forget—WWII only came to an end with not one but *two* atomic bombs on civilians in Hiroshima and Nagasaki, Japan.

---

[537] "Pope Francis to Consecrate the World to Mary's Immaculate Heart." *Catholic News Agency.*
[http://www.ncregister.com/daily-news/pope-francis-to-consecrate-the-world-to-marys-immaculate-heart#ixzz2f2YIGp80]

As would be later reported by *Il Pellegrinaggio Della Meravigle* in Rome, 1960, published under the auspices of the Italian episcopate, two months before Pius XII made the July 1952 "consecration," Our Lady appeared to Sr. Lucia, saying, "Make it known to the Holy Father that I am always awaiting the Consecration of Russia to my Immaculate Heart. *Without the Consecration, Russia will not be able to convert, nor will the world have peace.*" The report also affirms that this message was communicated to Pope Pius XII in June but, for reasons never understood, he chose not to heed it. In 1967, seven years after this report became public, Canon Barthas mentioned the May, 1952 apparition in his communication *De Primoridiis cultus mariania, Acta congressus mariologici-mariana in Lusitania anno 1967 celebrati* (p. 517) to the Mariological Congress of Lisbon-Fatima.

The sufferings of the 1930's, World War II and all following wars, the contagion of the modernist heresy, the spread of false religious sects, the persecution of Christians, the immoral culture in which we are now forced to live and from which we all suffer, the increasing family dissensions and the sorrows that come with them, and so much more, could have been avoided if only Pope Pius XI or Pope Pius XII had done exactly what the Virgin asked in 1929.

Those Popes are not alone. Pope Paul VI and Pope John Paul II followed suit, making solitary acts of consecration (or a renewal or an entrustment) of the *human race* or of the *world* (but never Russia) to the Immaculate Heart of Mary and without the participation of the world's bishops. None of those deeds were what the Virgin asked of a Pope, and so the ultimate grace of Russia's conversion and a world-wide era of peace have not yet been granted.

Tragically, the October 13, 2013 papal act did not even consecrate the world, as news sources around the globe had earlier announced. That which was done by Pope Francis was again not the fulfillment of Our Lady's repeated requests that the Pope and the bishops *solemnly* **consecrate** *Russia* to her Immaculate Heart. In fact, it was even less. It was a kind of "entrustment," but it was not a **consecration, which is an act of blessing a person** (as when a priest is consecrated as a bishop)**, place** (like a church)**, or thing** (like an altar and its vessels) **because it is being set aside for a sacred purpose in the service and worship of God**. That said, Vatican Radio posted the text of Pope Francis' 2013 entrustment, which is translated as follows:

"Blessed Virgin Mary of Fatima, with renewed gratitude for Your maternal presence we unite our voice with that of all the generations who call You blessed."

"We celebrate in You the great works of God, Who never tires to incline with mercy on humanity, afflicted by evil and wounded by sin, to heal it and save it."

"Accept with the compassion of a Mother the act of entrustment which today we make with confidence, before this Your image to us so dear."

"We are certain that each one of us is precious to Your eyes and that nothing which dwells in our hearts is unknown to You."

"Let us reach Your sweet gaze and receive the consoling caress of Your smile. Guard our life in Your arms: bless and strengthen every good desire; revive and foster faith; sustain and illumine hope; create and enliven charity; guide all of us in the path of holiness."

"Teach us Your same preferential love for the small and the poor, for the excluded and the suffering, for sinners and the lost: gather all under Your protection and give all of us to Your beloved Son, Our Lord Jesus. Amen."[538]

As one can see by the words above, not once was the title "Immaculate Heart" or the word *world* (in Italian, "mundo") expressed by the Pope. The "act of entrustment" was a personal one and had nothing to do with the Virgin's requests at Fatima, other than the selected date of October 13 and the transportation of the Pilgrim Virgin statue. Thousands had flocked to Rome on that day, happy and ecstatic in expecting, at the least, a renewal of previous world consecrations made by previous popes. Even that did not happen.

Simply stated, Our Lady of Fatima has waited almost 100 years for the Vicar of Christ to heed her requests for the following:

• **Worldwide devotion to the Immaculate Heart of Mary.**

• **Papal promulgation of the Five First Saturdays of Reparation for the five major blasphemies committed against the Virgin's Immaculate Heart.**

• **The public dissemination of the Third Secret Text.**

• **The solemn and public collegial consecration of Russia (and Russia alone) to the Immaculate Heart of Mary.**

Individual Catholics can and do respond to the other requests made by the Blessed Mother at Fatima (daily Rosary, daily duty offered in penance, making sacrifices for the conversion of sinners, the wearing of the Brown Scapular, conscientiously striving not to offend the Lord our God any longer, and taking part in First Saturday devotions where they might be offered, or otherwise

---

[538] "Santa Messa Celebrata Dal Santo Padre Francesco Per La 'Giornata Mariana' in Occasione dell'Anna Della Fede." *News. VA*, Official Vatican Network. [http://www.news.va/it/news/151094]

privately making the intention of reparation to the Immaculate Heart of Mary at a Saturday Mass when the intention is not publicly stated by the priest; the requirements include Confession, Holy Mass, Rosary, and 15 additional minutes on the 15 Rosary Mysteries of the Redemption).

However, *only a Pope* can take action to fulfill the other requests of the Virgin. *Only a Pope* can command and lead the bishops to join him in a solemn, public act of consecration of Russia to Our Lady's most pure Heart. *Only a Pope* can universally promote the Five First Saturday devotions, and now (at this point in history, since in 1957 the Vatican ordered Lucia's bishop, who was entrusted to release the Third Secret in 1960, to send it and all other Fatima documents to Rome) *only a Pope* can ensure that the Third Secret Text is fully released to the entire world.

Red Herrings: Flotsam and Jetsam in the Mainstream

In response to inquiries about the collegial consecration of Russia, the usual red herring remarks arose like flotsam and jetsam swirling through the Catholic mainstream's news, blog articles, and commentary. What is most curious is the amount of time devoted and the consistent hardline resistance made by those who, in one way or the other, employ the most unreasonable pretexts to summarily reject the Virgin's specific requests.

Despite the facts of history and the mounds of documentation (spanning from 1917 to the present), critics who are provided with all the proofs which objectively counter their erroneous claims decide to ignore them, instead choosing to refute the facts with *ad hominem* attacks. Those who are familiar with and keep abreast of the ongoing debate over the collegial consecration of Russia to the Immaculate Heart can easily anticipate the usual red herrings:

• "The Pope [meaning John Paul II] said he did it." Actually, Pope John Paul II never made such a statement. Others tried to imply it, but he himself never said it. Furthermore, this same claim that only John Paul II's actions matter implicitly deems as irrelevant the world consecrations to the Immaculate Heart made by Pope Pius XII and Paul VI.

•"You're disobedient to the Pope!" That is a judgmental conclusion concerning the state of another's soul, which Christ Himself forbade. One usually finds that this accusation is an *ad hominem* tactic used by those who do not know the entire history regarding the Fatima apparitions and are not interested in learning it, but still wish to debate its most important points. Too, such critics are otherwise quick to claim "thou shalt not judge" when discussing Catholic moral issues with which they disagree. Their stance also shows a tragic ignorance of the Church's defined dogma on papal infallibility. And again, no pope ever stated that he fulfilled the Virgin's requests.

• "This is the stuff of conspiracy theorists (or malcontents)." This is a negative emotional response. The consecration discussion is usually divided between those who can objectively–that is, impartially, fairly, neutrally– examine facts and those who allow their emotions to rule over their reason. Furthermore, faithful Catholics will never disregard the words of the Mother of God uttered in apparitions which the Church approved as worthy of belief, or the accolades of many Popes for Our Lady of Fatima, or the words of Lucia who, both as a child and as a cloistered nun, proved herself a faithful witness.

• "Lucia said it was done." Also not true; the claim contradicts decades of her testimony, including her remarks made before and after the consecrations of the 1980's. Furthermore, Lucia was commanded to absolute silence from 1958 after her revealing interview with Fr. Fuentes until her death on February 13, 2005. She was not allowed to have visitors without the Pope's explicit permission. Even her confessor was halted from seeing her.

If all was done as Our Lady of Fatima requested, there was no need to keep Sr. Lucia smothered by such an extreme command of silence or required permission for visitors, any more than that which was included in the Rule of the Carmelites. Like those who dared to put words in Pope John Paul II's mouth, others have made false claims on Lucia's behalf.

"I'm convinced that Sister Lucia continued to have conversations, or whatever you want to call them: apparitions, visions, inner locutions, with Our Lady. She had them for decades, *all through the eighties and beyond*," states Cardinal Bertone in his book, *Last Secret of Fatima*, published in 2008. One can reasonably ask: If everything was done with Pope John Paul II's consecrations and entrustments, then why did Heaven continue to communicate with Lucia all through the 1980's and beyond? Furthermore, Cardinal Bertone said, "During our meetings, she referred to a *whole sequence* of dates between 1985 and 1989."[539]

A whole *sequence* is a chain or succession of events, which apparently for Sr. Lucia began anew in 1985, the year *following* the March 1984 consecration of the world but a year *before* the 1986 pan-religious Assisi, Italy event. This particular sequence continued for at least four years, but it should be kept in mind that the Cardinal also said Lucia had messages "beyond" the 1980's.

---

[539] Bertone, Cardinal. *The Last Secret of Fatima*, p. 83.

First consider that it was immediately after publicly reciting the text prepared for the 1984 consecration that Pope John Paul II spontaneously added a revealing sentence, saying, "Enlighten especially the peoples whose consecration and entrustment by us you are still awaiting." Within the following year, John Paul II, waiting for the era of peace to arrive due to his previous acts, decided he needed to do something more. That conclusion resulted in his arrangement and participation of the 1986 Assisi pan-religious, "ecumenical" prayer meetings with world leaders of false religions, which scandalized many in Rome and elsewhere in the Church. Although Bertone claimed that Lucia revealed she had a "whole sequence" of heavenly apparitions and/or locutions between 1985 and 1989, he soon followed it with a curious remark that Lucia was "evasive about her continuing conversations with Mary, and she would change the subject whenever it was brought up." This, of course, makes little sense, but Cardinal Bertone has previously shown himself confused about many things regarding the Third Secret and the need for the collegial consecration of *Russia* to the Virgin's Immaculate Heart.

• "Russia is included in the world, so to insist that Russia must be specifically mentioned is hair-splitting." Russia is part of the world, but the world is not a part of Russia, and Russia alone is the nation to be consecrated.

• "The era of peace is on its way because John Paul II did what he could; we just have to do our part" or "Russia is converting; see how it is trying to instill Christian values?" Sadly, perhaps even blasphemously, this view makes a liar of the Virgin, the Queen of Prophets. She was quite clear about the specific conditions that would fulfill her promise of Russia's conversion to the Roman Catholic Faith and immediately usher in the era of peace and the triumph of her Immaculate Heart.

• "Fatima is a private revelation so we aren't obligated to believe in it or act on the requests." Incorrect, on many counts, and which this book elsewhere covers. However, a few points shall here be mentioned: First, we have to consider the comments of popes about Fatima, from Pius XII, "The time for doubting Fatima is past; it is time to take action" to John Paul II's "Fatima places an obligation on the Church" to Benedict XVI's stunning 2010 remark that Fatima's prophetic mission is not complete. Second, six popes have publicly recognized Fatima, with two of them, Pope John Paul II and Pope Benedict XVI, traveling there in public homage to the Mother of God. Furthermore, Fatima's "prophetic mission," as Benedict XVI called it, warns of the commencement of certain apocalyptic chapters, but it also offers a specific remedy with particular directions to the Church hierarchy to save the *visible* Church and therefore save even more souls in the world.

The two most recent "short baits" added to the bucket of red herrings are rather incorrigible assertions against the Virgin's words that the collegial consecration of Russia will bring about that nation's conversion and an era of peace for the world. The first absurdity claims that to believe a collegial consecration of *Russia* can do "all that" is akin to believing in magic (*"Abracadabra and Hocus Pocus! Whoosh, now Russia is converted!"* as one commentator phrased it) and second, Russia never asked any pope for any such consecration, which invalidates the Virgin's request.

Conspicuously missing are similar remarks about "magic" or "invalidity" when a Pope decides to consecrate the *world* to Mary's Immaculate Heart. Why, then, are they made when given the reminder of Our Lady's request that *Russia* is to be consecrated by the Pope and the bishops?

For example, what is conveniently (and consistently) overlooked (even when reminded) are decades of evidence proving Our Lady's insistence that her requests are heeded. In fact, one notes a "heavenly determination" from both Christ and the Virgin regarding the collegial consecration of Russia to the Immaculate Heart. Of all the requests, the collegial consecration of Russia is one which Heaven kept repeating.

What is also ignored is that which was mentioned above—the late Pope John Paul II's remark that "Fatima places an obligation on the Church" and the revelation made in May 2010 by Benedict XVI, now Bishop Emeritus of Rome: "We would be mistaken to think that Fatima's prophetic mission is complete."[540] Meanwhile, as many cling to superfluous and unproven claims that either Pope John Paul II or Sr. Lucia said the world consecrations fulfill Our Lady's request, what was and still is never acknowledged are Sr. Lucia's frequent remarks about the "diabolical disorientation" afflicting the world, including those within the Church. In a word, presented facts are ignored because, as St. Thomas Aquinas said, "Against a fact, there is no argument."

The Meaning of Consecration

For the purposes of this section, I will not set out to prove that Fatima does not fall into the realm of private revelation but is a fulfillment of Divine Revelation and so it is what some describe as a prophetic and public revelation. Again, that topic was previously covered in this book. Nor shall I here respond *in-depth* to any of previous red herrings since many other objective authors have previously done so. Instead, let us briefly look at the last two counter-claims that insist that any belief in swift and positive results from the requested

---

[540] *Pope: we would be mistaken to think that Fatima's prophetic message is complete*, Asia News, May 13, 2010.

consecration is akin to believing in magic, and that Our Lady's request regarding Russia cannot be valid because Russia has not asked for that honor.

Unfortunately, those who contribute such bizarre commentary against the facts that the Virgin's insistence on the collegial consecration of Russia to her Immaculate Heart remain unfulfilled clearly do not understand that Christ is King and Mary is Queen and that both have dominion over the Church and the world. They do not grasp that a reigning Pope is the Vicar of Christ, the Steward of the Church, which is God's kingdom on earth, and that the Catholic bishops are princes of the same Church. Since Mary is Queen, and not only a Queen Mother (which would mean, at least in the earthly sense, that hers is only an honorary title with no real authority), she has the right to make requests of her Son's Steward and princes, and she has the right to expect their obedience.

It therefore follows that objectors to the collegial consecration of Russia cannot grasp the four following issues regarding the Virgin's requests: **1)** The Virgin's office in salvation and her right to ask for devotion to her Immaculate Heart (which includes understanding the depths of that title and all else that such devotion implies), **2)** the nature, duty, authority, jurisdiction, and scope of the Pope's leadership as Christ's Steward on earth; and **3)** the duty and authority of the bishops who are joined in union with the Pope and subject to him, and **4)** the Catholic definition of the word "consecration." In a brief response to these four points:

1) "Jesus is King of the Eternal Ages by nature and by right of conquest; *through* Him, *with* Him, and *subordinate* to Him, Mary is Queen by grace, by divine relationship, by right of conquest and by singular election. And her kingdom is as vast as that of her Son and God, since *nothing is excluded from her dominion*."[541] (These two topics–Jesus as King, Mary as Queen–are later covered in this book.)

2) A reigning Pope possesses supreme authority (because only God possesses *absolute* authority). "Not only did Christ constitute St. Peter head of the Church but in the words 'Whatsoever thou shalt bind on earth, it shall be bound also in heaven; and whatsoever thou shalt loose on earth, it shall be loosed in heaven,' He indicated the scope of this leadership."[542] Furthermore, "The Church is a perfect society. She is not dependent on the permission of the State for her existence, but holds her charter from God. As a perfect society,

---

[541] Pope Pius XII, Radio Message to Fatima, May 13, 1946, Bendito seia, AAS 38.266. [Emphasis added]

[542] Joyce, George. "The Pope." *The Catholic Encyclopedia*, Vol. 12. [New York: Robert Appleton Company, 1911] [http://www.newadvent.org/cathen/12260a.htm]

she has a right to *all those means which are necessary for the attaining of her end.*[543]

The Church has the right to exist because Jesus Christ, Lord and Savior, founded her. What is the purpose of the Church? To adore God and save souls. Therefore to protect herself, her children, and those in the world who may yet be spiritually saved, the Church has the duty and the corresponding *right* to obey the Virgin of Fatima and consecrate Russia to the Immaculate Heart of Mary, without asking anyone's permission. This, of course, always applies to the reigning Pope, who has the duty and its corresponding right to order the world's bishops to join him in the necessary act of consecration without asking for either their consent or Russia's. After all, the few previous popes who made solitary attempts to consecrate or entrust the world to the Immaculate Heart did not ask for the approval of every nation in the world.

3) "Bishop is the title of an ecclesiastical dignitary who possesses the fullness of the priesthood to rule a diocese as its chief pastor, *in due submission to the primacy of the pope.*"[544] The Pope, as Bishop of Rome, is not only "first among the bishops" in the sense of being the eldest brother, but he is the supreme head of the Church; the Supreme Pontiff, the Vicar of Christ, the monarch-steward of Our Lord's kingdom on earth. Heaven wants every bishop, from the Pope in Rome to the bishop of the most humble diocese, to participate in a literally universal (which in Greek means Catholic) act so that the entire world will know of it. When a Pope finally commands the world's Catholic bishops to join him in the "collegial" consecration of Russia to the Immaculate Heart, the bishops must obey him, just as he, as Steward, will be obeying the command of God, given through the Queen through her chosen messenger, Sr. Lucia. Should some bishops choose not to obey the Holy Father, the fault will be theirs, but not the Pope's. Despite the chance of such disobedience, the Supreme Pontiff still must carry through with the bishops who yet submit to him and, together with them, undertake the solemn and public consecration of Russia to the Virgin's Immaculate Heart.

4) The word **"consecration"** literally means "to associate with the sacred." The *Catholic Encyclopedia* explains: "Consecration, in general, is an act by which a thing is separated from a common and profane to a sacred use, **or by which a person or thing is dedicated to the service and worship of God** by prayers, rites, and ceremonies."[545] Any nation that is thus consecrated by the

---

[543] Joyce, Ibid. [Emphasis added.]
[544] Van Hove, Alphons. "Bishop." *The Catholic Encyclopedia*, Vol. 2. [New York: Robert Appleton Company, 1907] [http://www.newadvent.org/cathen/02581b.htm]
[545] Schulte, Augustin Joseph. "Consecration." *The Catholic Encyclopedia*. [Vol. 4. New York: Robert Appleton Company, 1908]

Pope and the world's bishops to the Virgin's Immaculate Heart should humbly consider itself as highly favored to be placed under the Mother of God's protection and intercession before the Most Holy Trinity. Finally and to repeat: Among all of Our Lady's requests, it is clear that a Pope who commands and leads the collegial consecration of Russia is the most imperative act.

What we do know with certainty is that both Christ and the Virgin many times repeated the necessity of the consecration of Russia by the Pope and the world's bishops. Such insistence on the part of God and His Holy Mother makes it clear that the consecration is Heaven's foremost request. As Our Lord said in 1931 to Sr. Lucia (and through her, to us), **"Pray much for the Holy Father**. He will do it, but it will be late. Nevertheless, the Immaculate Heart of Mary will save Russia. It has been entrusted to her."

[http://www.newadvent.org/cathen/04276a.htm].[Emphasis added.]

CHAPTER 18

The Woman and the Battle
of the Latter Days

"For those who believe in God,
no explanation is necessary.
For those who do not believe in God,
no explanation will suffice."

Now and in the days ahead, the Church Militant must not place its faith in mere human means to restore the Church. "Modern times are dominated by Satan and will be more so in the future," as St. Maximilian Kolbe said. "The conflict with hell cannot be engaged by men, even the most clever. The Immaculate alone has from God the promise of victory over Satan."[546]

Those words echo the revelations of the Queen of Heaven, who came to Fatima, revealing in essence that Christ reserves to her the final triumph in the battle of the latter days. In that combat, all that the children of Mary need do is heed the requests of Our Lady—it is as simple as that.

To quote the character of Lord Elrond in *The Fellowship of the Ring*, "This quest may be attempted by the weak with as much hope as the strong. Yet such is oft the course of deeds that move the wheels of the world; small hands do them because they must, while the eyes of the great are elsewhere."[547]

Two Handmaidens to Sanctity

When events and circumstances leave us feeling helpless, we may find ourselves saying, "There is nothing I can do but pray," momentarily forgetting that **prayer *and* sacrifice** are the lot of the elect. Prayer and sacrifice are the two spiritual handmaidens to sanctity; they are always the conditions required by God Himself to obtain favors.

Our Lord foresaw that, for the faithful of the Modern Age, daily life would be a heavy cross. Throughout our sacred history, it is always the same story—an age of increased sin, affecting not only the sinner but everyone. The difference between our age and former times is that mortal sin is prevalent, officially

---

[546] Sharkey, Don. *The Woman Shall Conquer.* [Kenosha, WI: Prow Books/Franciscan Marytown Press, revised 1976]: Back cover.
[547] Tolkien, J.R.R., *The Fellowship of the Ring.* [New York: Ballantine Books. Published by arrangement with the Houghton Mifflin Company, 1982]: p. 323.

endorsed by almost all governments and, tragically, encouraged and committed even by those within the Church.

Our Blessed Mother's constant intercession for this sinful age is the reason **Heaven made clear that the prayer of our times must be the Rosary.** It seems nothing can stop the madness, for the Church's human element is infiltrated with the sins of modernism—and that reality explains why Our Lord said that life as a faithful Catholic would be our *true* penance.

When on a great scale mankind abandons God and tempts Him to turn His face from us, Our Lady's continual intercession is the last means to save souls; that is the reason why God wishes to establish devotion to the Immaculate Heart. When we are tempted to think we have nowhere to go for help, we cannot forget Our Lady of Fatima's consoling words, "My Immaculate Heart will be your refuge, and the path that leads you to God."

Our Mother, Mediatrix, and Queen

Numerous are the battlefronts in the great spiritual war of the latter days. The world news worsens with tragic reports—martyrdoms of the faithful, scandals, murders, terrible accidents, thefts, and increasing revolts against the Church and the Holy Father. Too, the number of "natural" cataclysms like earthquakes, floods, and volcanic eruptions seem to be rising.

The faithful may continue to fight the good fight, declaring their outrage against the persecutions of their fellows, signing petitions, writing letters of protest against all kinds of scandals, joining marches in defense of morality, and engaging those who ardently resist the Tridentine Rite's restoration in every parish and diocese. Still, despite our best efforts, we must admit that, as Pope Pius IX once declared, **"up till now reasonable demands and repeated protests have availed nothing to *remove* these evils."**[548]

Our Lady also wants *conversions*, which includes advancement in the interior life of the soul. The Rosary prayers and the sacrifices of the faithful have not yet been enough to bring worldwide devotion to the Immaculate Heart. Only that devotion, with the collegial consecration of Russia to the same Pure Heart, will bring the era of peace to all mankind and the conversion of Russia, who has spread her errors throughout the world.

Our own efforts are not enough, perhaps due not only to our lack in numbers but also to our lack of confidence. As Our Lady said at Akita, "Those who place their confidence in me will be saved."[549] Why?

---

[548] Pope Pius IX, bulla *Ineffabilis Deus* (The Immaculate Conception, December 8, 1854). Cited by Pope Pius XII, *Ad Caeli Reginum* (On Proclaiming the Queenship of Mary, Oct. 11, 1954): para. 50. [Emphasis added.]
[549] "Our Lady of Akita," Holy Mother Mary website.

She is Our Mother and Mediatrix: "With a heart that is truly a mother's does she approach the problem of our salvation," wrote Blessed Pope Pius IX, "and is solicitous for the whole human race; made Queen of heaven and earth by the Lord…standing at the right hand of her only Son, Jesus Christ Our Lord, she intercedes powerfully for us with a mother's prayers, obtains what she seeks, and cannot be refused."[550]

She loves us and desires our salvation: As Pope St. Leo declared, "It has been her unremitting concern to see to it that the Catholic Faith stands firmly lodged in the midst of the people, there to thrive in its fertile and undivided unity."[551]

She is the cause of salvation: Pope Pius XII quoted St. Irenaeus in saying, "she has been constituted the cause of salvation for the whole human race."[552]

She is the Virgin Queen and Mother of the King: "Because the Virgin Mary was raised to such a lofty dignity as to be the mother of the King of kings," held St. Alphonsus Liguori, "it is deservedly and by every right that the Church has honored her with the title of 'Queen.'" [553]

She is the Queen of Peace: As Blessed Pius IX urged, "Whoever, therefore, reverences the Queen of heaven and earth—and let no one consider himself exempt from this tribute of a grateful and loving soul—let him invoke the most effective of Queens, the Mediatrix of peace; let him respect and preserve peace…**to its safeguarding and growth the gentle urgings and commands of the Virgin Mary impel us.**"[554]

Our Lady came to Fatima as Mother, Mediatrix and Queen, there to affirm the Church's central doctrines. With a supreme and royal dignity, she also gave commands in the gentle way befitting our true Lady and Queen.

The Virgin's specific requests, while simple, give us frequent opportunities to practice the virtues we need most: **1)** The daily Rosary, **2)** daily duty as true penance, **3)** sacrifice for the conversion of sinners, **4)** the Five First Saturdays devotion, and **5)** the necessity of wearing the Brown Scapular (the Scapular of Our Lady of Mt. Carmel), since Our Lady held it out during the Miracle of the Sun.

[http: www.holymothermary.org/apparitions/akita.htm]

[550] Blessed Pius IX, Ibid., para. 42.

[551] Pope Leo XIII, *Adiutricem* (On the Rosary. Sept. 5, 1895), para. 11.

[552] Pope Pius XII, *Ingruentium Malorum* (On Reciting the Rosary, Sept. 15, 1951), para. 6.

[553] de Liguori, St. Alphonsus. *Le glore de Maria (The Glories of Mary)*, p. I, c. I, §1. Cited by Blessed Pius IX, *Ad Caeli Reginum*, para. 25.

[554] Pope Pius XII, *Ad Caeli Reginam* (On Proclaiming the Queenship of Mary, Oct. 11, 1954): para. 51.

Incidentally: The Scapular should be blessed (or the recipient enrolled in the Confraternity of Our Lady of Mt. Carmel by a Catholic priest; when enrolled, this means that each new Scapular need not be blessed since the blessing is carried by the person, who still must wear the Scapular). To obtain the Sabbatine Privilege associated with the Brown Scapular (wherein Our Lady promised centuries ago, "I, the Mother of Grace, shall descend on the Saturday after their death and whomsoever I shall find in Purgatory, I shall free, so that I may lead them to the holy mountain of life everlasting"), there are three conditions: **1)** it must be worn (within reason; one can remove it when taking a bath or shower, for example), **2)** live chastely according to one's state in life, and **3)** Pray *the Little Office of Our Blessed Mother*, which can be substituted by the Rosary with a Catholic priest's permission.

There is also the sixth request, comprised of two parts. For the Holy Father and the bishops of the world, God Himself commands the collegial consecration of Russia to the Immaculate Heart of Mary. The request's second part is the universal establishment of the Communion of Reparation (the Five First Saturdays Devotion), which is founded on Confession, the Holy Sacrifice of the Mass, the Rosary and meditation on the Psalter's 15 mysteries in reparation for blasphemies against Our Lady's Immaculate Heart.

The solemn act of consecration will bring the era of peace and world-wide conversion, because it will firmly establish true devotion to Our Lady's Pure Heart, that path that will lead us to God. No one but the Holy Father can order the bishops to join him in that solemn act, so we must always pray and sacrifice for that intention. As for the Five First Saturdays of Reparation, we ourselves can make this devotion every month of the year for those who do not, as Sr. Lucia did all of her life.

The Virgin said, "If my requests are heeded, Russia will be converted and there will be peace; if not, she will spread her errors throughout the world, causing wars and persecutions of the Church. The good will be martyred, the Holy Father will have much to suffer, various nations will be annihilated... In the end, my Immaculate Heart will triumph. The Holy Father will consecrate Russia to me, and she will be converted, and an era of peace will be granted to the world."[555] To save souls from hell in this age of spiritual chaos, the Lady revealed that God "wills to establish in the world devotion to my Immaculate Heart...To whoever embraces this devotion, I promise salvation; those souls will be cherished by God, as flowers placed by me to adorn His throne...If what I say to you is done, many souls will be saved and there will be peace."[556]

---

[555] Frère Michel, *TWTF*, Vol. I, pp. 182-183.
[556] Ibid., p. 182.

The Sacred and Immaculate Hearts

The Immaculate Heart devotion has long been willed by Christ. Almost seven centuries ago, the Sacred Heart made clear to St. Mechtilde (Matilda) that He Himself is "the herald of this devotion [to His Mother's Heart], which He teaches to us both by word and example." [557] In modern times, Our Lord told Sr. Lucia the reason why the solemn, public collegial consecration of Russia to the Virgin's Heart is His Will: "Because I want My whole Church to acknowledge that Consecration as a triumph of the Immaculate Heart of Mary so that it may extend its cult later on and put the devotion to this Immaculate Heart beside the devotion to My Sacred Heart..." [558]

Many saints have insisted that devotion to the Sacred Heart is itself a sign of the last days. As St. Gertrude once said, "The love of the Incarnate Word as exemplified by His Divine Heart is reserved for the last ages to be made known, so that the world, carried away by follies, may regain a little of the warmth of early Christian charity by learning of the love of the Sacred Heart." [559]

The Fatima revelations are also a sign of what Sr. Lucia, Servant of God, called "the last times of the world." It is not hard to see with eyes of Faith that Scriptural prophecy came to pass at Fatima when *a great sign appeared in Heaven: a woman clothed with the sun, with the moon under her feet, and upon her head a crown of twelve stars.* [560]

We have seen that, in the *Apocalypse*, "a woman" is a symbol of the Church while, in *Genesis 3:15*, "the woman" is the Virgin Mary, foretold by God Himself. It was *the Woman* who appeared at Fatima as the apocalyptic sign that the greatest battle of our own age, the one between *a woman clothed with the sun*" (the Virgin Mary and the Church on earth) and the dragon (Satan), had begun. That spiritual battle is one we will never win by our own efforts or designs, but only when all we do is "*with* Mary, *in* Mary, *through* Mary, and *for* Mary." [561]

The Woman of *Genesis*, who came to Fatima, was even brighter than the sun, clad in a white gown and veil, the veil's light making it appear as if it was trimmed in gold. Here it must be noted that white is considered "the color of mourning" worn *only* by Catholic queens, while gold is everywhere recognized as the color of royalty.

---

[557] Eudes, St. John. *The Admirable Heart of Mary*, p.101.
[558] Frère Michel, *TWTF*, Vol. II, pp. 543.
[559] Culleton, Rev. R. Gerald. *The Prophets and Our Times*, p. 151.
[560] Apoc. 12:1.
[561] de Montfort, St. Louis. *The Secret of Mary*. [Bay Shore, NY: Montfort Publications, Revised Edition, 1993]: p. 35.

As already examined, the Lady wore two ornaments, one a long yellow necklace from which dangled a bright orb or jewel, symbolizing her bridal attributes as reigning consort of the Divine Spouse. Her other ornament was the Star of Esther, symbol of the Old Testament's virgin queen who saved the entire nation of the elect from annihilation.

St. John Eudes explained, "Mary's peerless heart is a fountain of light, that was foreshadowed in the person of Queen Esther, who is represented in Sacred Scripture as a small fountain that becomes a great light and is turned into the sun. *'The little fountain which grew into a river and was turned into a light, and into the sun...'* It is the fountain of the sun, *fons solis*, mentioned in chapters fifteen and seventeen of the *Book of Josue*." The saint continued, "Truly the heart of Mary is the foundation of the sun, because Mary is the Mother of the Sun of Justice, and this Divine Sun is the fruit of Mary's heart."[562] St. John Eudes' words give us more to ponder about the Virgin and the Miracle of the Sun, the "Great Sign" that would convince many to believe and again turn to God, thus saving their souls while avoiding the greatest sin threatening mankind, final apostasy.

In his commentary on St. Luke's eschatological discourse of the great apostasy, St. Ambrose interpreted the symbols of sun, moon and stars in this way: "Many apostatizing from Christianity, the brightness of the Faith will be dimmed by this cloud of apostasy: since **the heavenly Sun grows dim or shines in splendour according to my Faith**. And as in its monthly eclipse **the moon**, by reason of the earth coming between it and the sun, disappears from view, so likewise the holy Church, *when the vices of the flesh stand in the way of the celestial light*, can no longer borrow the splendour of His divine light from the Sun of Christ. And in the persecutions, it was invariably the love of this life that stood in the path of the Divine Sun. **Also the stars—that is, men** surrounded by the praise of their fellow Christians—**shall fall**, as the bitterness of persecution mounts up; which must however come to pass, until the number of the faithful be made up; **for so the good are proved and the weak made known**."[563]

The Example of St. Joan of Arc

If we genuinely know the whole truth of Fatima, why is there any doubt that Fatima is truly the fulfillment of prophecy from Divine Revelation? Why is it that *all the faithful* are not following Our Lady's counsels to restore the Church, but instead fight the battle in ways we prefer?

---

[562] Eudes, op. cit., p. 42.
[563] St. Ambrose, cited in *The Sunday Sermons of the Great Fathers*. [http://books.google.com/books?id=MCX6nTwu8U8C]. [Emphasis added.]

How much would God be pleased should we imitate St. Joan of Arc, the virgin of Orleans, who was another figure-type of Our Lady.

"'To St. Joan's mind the coronation and anointing of the King of France were ever present, because that anointing did homage to the universal Kingship of Christ,'" said Pope St. Pius X.[564]

Like Our Lady who, by God's will, leads the army of the Church Militant, St. Joan also led an army by God's command. Like Our Lady, St. Joan insisted that her soldiers stop offending God, avail themselves of the Sacraments of Confession and Holy Eucharist, pray often and do well their daily duty.

In our turn, we must be like St. Joan, our minds ever fixed on the collegial consecration of Russia to the Immaculate Heart, because it will restore the Social Reign of Christ the King. **What each one of us need to do—every day—is heed and promote every request of Our Lady of Fatima.**

"Therefore, whilst we have time, let us work good to all men, but especially to those who are of the household of faith." (Gal. 6:10)

---

[564] Pope St. Pius X. *Discourse on the Beatification of St. Joan of Arc.* Cited by Rev. Denis Fahey, C.S. SP., B.A., D. PH., D.D., *The Kingship of Christ: According to the Principles of St. Thomas Aquinas* [Palmdale, CA: Christian Book Club of America, 1990 republication. First published in 1931]: p. 164.

~SECTION IV~
CHAPTER 19
The Age of Mary
and the Lost Meaning of Conversion

"One purpose for which the Blessed Mother was created Mother of God is that she may obtain the salvation of many who, on account of weakness and wickedness, could not be saved according to the rigor of divine justice, but might be so with the help of this merciful Mother's powerful intercession."

-St. John Chrysostom

In these latter days of the Modern Age, Our Lady has appeared on earth more than in any other time in history.[565] As the spiritual war between good and evil intensifies, the Mediatrix of All Graces pleas with us to pray and do penance, even as she continues to intercede for us before the throne of God. In the ongoing epic battle for souls, each true Marian apparition in the Modern Age is, in the chronicles of sacred history, another chapter intended to remind all peoples—from practicing Catholics to those separated from God in diverse ways—of **the lost meaning of conversion**.

Just over one hundred years ago, the *Catholic Encyclopedia* provided **four definitions of conversion**, as follows: "a moral change, a turning or returning to God and to the true religion, in which sense it has passed into our modern languages. (For example, the conversions of St. Paul, of Constantine the Great, and of St. Augustine.) In the Middle Ages, the word conversion was often used in the sense of forsaking the world to enter the religious state. Thus St. Bernard speaks of his conversion. The return of the sinner to a life of virtue is also called a conversion. More commonly do we speak of the conversion of an infidel to the true religion, and most commonly of the conversion of a schismatic or heretic to the Catholic Church."[566]

Already lost was the fifth and most crucial definition of *conversion*: the three ages of the interior life. Dom Jean-Baptiste Chautard, author of *The Soul of the Apos*tolate, defined the interior life as "the state of activity of a soul who

---

[565] Sharkey, *The Woman Shall Conquer*, p. 5.
[566] Guldner, Benedict. "Conversion." *The Catholic Encyclopedia*, Vol. IV. [New York: Robert Appleton Company, 1908]

strives against its natural inclinations in order to regulate them and endeavors to acquire the habit of judging and directing its movements in all things according to the light of the *Gospel* and the example of Our Lord."[567]

As the Dominican theologian Fr. Reginald Garrigou-Lagrange emphatically taught, "The interior life is for all the one thing necessary. It ought to be constantly developing in our souls…The interior life is lived in the depths of the soul…it is important to us not only as individuals, but also in our social relations; for it is evident that we can exert no real or profound influence upon our fellow-men unless we live a truly interior life ourselves."[568]

True Conversion in Three Stages

"Scripture often recalls, even to those who are in the state of grace, the necessity of a more profound conversion toward God," explained Fr. Garrigou-Lagrange. [569] Our Lord, Who desires not the death of the sinner, wills that every soul should travel the path of the **three conversions**. This is **the secret** to which the lives of the Apostles and all the saints attest: *In all the labors of life, that of the interior life is the most important.*

The three stages are transitions or conversions, known as the **Purgative Way** (beginners), the **Illuminative Way** (proficients), and the **Unitive Way** (the perfect). Very simply stated, the three interior conversions might be called an increase in the life of sanctifying grace, which is a gratuitous gift from God and which we will lose when we lack humility, a spirit of mortification, confuse our pride or cowardice with virtues, etc.

The life of grace, said Fr. Garrigou-Lagrange, "is there, hidden within you, like the grain of mustard seed, like the leaven which will cause the whole of the meal to rise, like the treasure hidden in a field, like the source from which gushes a river of water that will never fail."[570] He also taught, "We are thus able to appreciate something of the importance of true conversion, by which a man passes from the state of mortal sin to the state of grace."[571] This is the important first step of conversion, "the entrance into the kingdom of God,

---

[567] Chautard, O.C.S.O., Dom Jean-Baptiste. *The Soul of the Apostolate.* [Garden City, NY: Image Books, 1961]: p. 34.

[568] Garrigou-Lagrange, Fr. Reginald. *The Three Conversions in the Spiritual Life* [Rockford, IL: TAN Books and Publishers, 1977. Reprinted from the original; copyright 1938 by Burnes Oates & Washbourne Ltd.]: p. 1.

[569] Garrigou-Lagrange, Fr. Reginald. *The Three Ages of the Interior Life, Volume Two* [Rockford, IL: TAN Books and Publishers. Reprinted from the original; copyright 1948 by B. Herder Book Co., St. Louis and London]: p. 21.

[570] Lagrange, op. cit., p. 15.

[571] Ibid., p. 16.

where the docile soul begins to reign with God over its own passions, over the spirit of the world and the spirit of evil."[572]

A great crisis in the soul—which may or may not issue from a crisis in practical life—is the defining mark of transition from one stage to another. St. John of the Cross speaks of the imperfections being winnowed out, especially in the first two stages. Yet not all souls progress when the crisis comes. Many fall back, either by giving up the struggle or in becoming complacent and quite satisfied with Self.

Conversion is neither a one-time matter, nor is it enough to live the exterior life of a practicing Catholic or even, perhaps, to be involved, even in small ways, in any apostolate. The signs of an advancing interior life have nothing to do with zealous activity, even for a good cause. Necessary for any Catholic, including those leading or participating in an apostolate, is "to fight against an excessive exteriorization through good works"[573] or, to phrase it another way, to reject "love of action for action's sake."[574] The interior life is one of inner recollection of God's Presence at every moment of the day.

Conversion is an ongoing process; thus, we will recognize how the five meanings of conversion are directly connected to the five ways of sanctification and salvation. St. Louis Marie de Montfort reminds us that these five means are "are laid down in the *Gospel*, explained by the masters of the spiritual life, practiced by the saints, and necessary to all who wish to be saved and to attain perfection. They are: *humility of heart, continual prayer, mortification in all things, abandonment to Divine Providence, and conformity to the Will of God.*"[575]

Our Lady: Devotion and Conversion

When the Virgin came to Fatima, God deigned to give the Catholic peoples of the world another incentive toward further conversion of their interior lives or—for those who fell away from or were outside of the Church instituted by Christ—to their initial conversions, the first "age" or "stage" of the life of grace. While the complete Fatima Message, the Great Secret, and the Miracle reveal many dogmatic themes, Fatima's ultimate thesis, the initial secret which the children at first kept to themselves, is true devotion to the Immaculate Heart of Mary, by which many souls will be converted and saved for all eternity.

---

[572] Ibid., p. 17.
[573] Chautard, op. cit., p. 28.
[574] Ibid., p. 42.
[575] de Montfort, St. Louis. *The Secret of Mary*, p. 11.

"Jesus Christ, the only begotten Son of God, chose the incomparable Virgin Mary from among all creatures to be His Mother and deigned to be nourished and governed by her," explained St. John Eudes. "In His infinite goodness, He also gave her to us to be our Queen, our Mother and our sure Refuge in all our needs. He therefore wishes us to honor her as He honors her and to love her as He loves her."[576]

The saint continued, "According to the Apostle Saint Paul, Christ is the Head of His Mystical Body, the Church, and we are the members. [577] We must therefore be animated by His Spirit; we must follow His inspirations, walk the path He has traced, and continue, as it were, His life on earth by practicing the virtues which were His Own. It follows that our devotion to His Holy Mother must be a continuation of His devotion to her."

Understanding that the "human will is not, however, moved to love a fellow creature unless the intellect first knows what renders it worthy of respect and esteem," St. John Eudes immediately noted, "The infinite zeal, with which the Son of God is inflamed for all that concerns His dear Mother, has urged Him to reveal to us through the inspired words of Sacred Scripture and through the writings of the Fathers some small measure of the perfections with which He has enriched her. The reality far surpassing our knowledge of her in this vale of darkness will be revealed only in Heaven, the land of unclouded light."[578]

Particularly compelling is the saint's initial selection from Sacred Scripture, a passage which he describes as "a compendium of all the great things that can be said or thought of our marvelous Queen."[579] Moreover, according to the general law of preparation, a term coined by St. Bonaventure to describe the distinctly Catholic doctrine foreshadowed in the Old Testament, it is "God's Way not to allow the fullness of revealed truth to break upon the world suddenly. There is a long period of adaption, as it were, during which the way is prepared gradually for the final Revelation," which closed with the death of St. John the Evangelist. [580] Understanding this general law assists those of us who live in the Modern Age to receive **a glimmer of understanding** in

---

[576] Eudes, St. John. *The Admirable Heart of Mary*, p. 3.

[577] 1 Cor. 12, 27; Eph. 5, 30. Cited by St. John Eudes, Ibid.

[578] Eudes, loc. cit.

[579] Ibid., p. 4.

[580] St. Bonaventure notes this law, which refers to the way God provided Divine Revelation to make ready the human race for His "undoing of the awful consequences of Original Sin, taken in conjunction with man's response to God's overtures." Also see Smith, D.D., Ph.D., Canon George D. *The Teaching of the Catholic Church: A Summary of Catholic Doctrine*, Vol. I [New York: The MacMillan Co., 1959]: p. 115.

how St. John Eudes' explanations for this passage (and others) apply to the Immaculate Heart as she manifested herself at Fatima (brighter than **the sun**) and the sign that she gave (**the Miracle of the Sun**).

To illustrate the Lord's revelations about His Virgin Mother, St. John Eudes first chose *Apocalypse*, Chapter 12:1, *"A great sign appeared in Heaven: A woman clothed with the sun, and the moon under her feet, and on her head a crown of twelve stars."*

"What is this great sign?" the saint queried. "Who is this miraculous woman? Saint Epiphanius, Saint Augustine, Saint Bernard, and many other holy doctors agree that the woman is Mary, the Queen among women, the Sovereign of angels and men, the Virgin of Virgins. She is the woman who bore in her chaste womb the perfect Man, the God-Man. *'A woman shall compass a man.'*"[581]

The "woman" [a woman clothed with the sun] of *Apocalypse,* as already stated in this work, is a figure-type of the Church, but the eternal Church is herself a type of Mary, who is "**the** woman" prophesied in *Genesis 3:15.* In explaining how *Apocalypse* Ch.12:1 pertains to Our Lady, St. John Eudes outlined the passage's meaning, of which the following is a brief synopsis.

• The woman appeared in Heaven, because she comes from Heaven; she is Heaven's masterpiece, its Empress, its joy and glory.[582]

• "She is clothed with the eternal sun of the Godhead and with all the perfections of the divine essence, which surround, fill and penetrate her to such an extent that she has become transformed, as it were, with the power, goodness, and holiness of God."

• "She has the moon under her feet to show that the entire world is beneath her." Save the Lord God Himself, none is above her.

• "She is crowned with twelve stars that represent the virtues which shine so brightly in her soul."

• "But why does the Holy Ghost call Mary 'a great sign'? It is simply to tell us that everything in her is wonderful, and that the marvels that fill her should be proclaimed to the entire world...Mary is truly admirable in all her perfections and in all her virtues. But what is most admirable in her is her virginal heart. The heart of the Mother of God is a world of marvels, an abyss of wonders, the source and principles of all the virtues which we admire in our Glorious Queen: *'All the glory of the king's daughter is within.'*"[583] That glory and secret is the hidden grace of Mary, the Immaculate Conception.

---

[581] Jer. 31:22.
[582] Eudes, op. cit., p. 4.
[583] Ibid., p. 5.

CHAPTER 20

The Immaculate Conception:
Mother of God, Mother of Men

"Hail, full of grace…"
−The angel Gabriel to the Virgin Mary, Lk. 1:28

Since the foundation of the world, God bound together Our Lady and her Divine Son. **The first mystery of Christ** is His Virgin Mother, she who is the Immaculate Conception. This dogma reminds us of St. Paul's teaching in regard to God's plan for the Redemption: "All things are done for your sakes"[584] to which St. John Eudes adds, "If He created the world, it was for us, if He became Man, it was *for us*. If He was born in a stable, it was for *our sake*…For *our sake*, He died on the Cross, ascended into Heaven, established Holy Church, confided the sacraments to her care and especially the most Holy Sacrament of the Altar where He resides for us…In a like manner, if He willed to have a Mother on earth, it was for *our sake*."[585] To the words of the saint must be added, "And if He created His Mother as the Immaculate One, it was for *our sake*."

The Divine Revelation that Mary is the Immaculate Conception remains the dogma which is most misinterpreted, misconstrued, and belittled. In treating of the confusion and resulting rejection of this most wondrous truth, an early 20th century Jesuit priest and author, Fr. P.J. Chandlery, S.J., recognized that "amongst the chief reasons why even 'learned and devout men,' outside the Church, do not understand the dogma of the Immaculate Conception is because they misunderstand the doctrine of Original Sin. **Not knowing the rule, they cannot realize the exception to the rule**; not recognizing the penalty, they cannot see the privilege. In other words, not appreciating what we mean by the stain and guilt of Original Sin, they do not and cannot know what is meant by exemption from it."[586]

"Great indeed was the injury entailed on Adam and all his posterity by his accursed sin," wrote St. Alphonsus de Liguori. [587] God had bestowed upon our

---

[584] 2 Cor. 4, 15.
[585] Eudes, St. John. *The Admirable Heart of Mary,* p. 80.
[586] Chandlery, S.J., P.J. *Mary's Praise on Every Tongue.* [London: Manresa Press, 1919]. Archived at [https://archive.org/details/maryspraise00chanuoft]
[587] de Liguori, St. Alphonsus. *The Glories of Mary,* p. 287.

first parents His sanctifying grace, "a gift to which, by nature, they had no claim. Through the sin of Adam, in which Eve bore her share, this gift was lost for all Adam's children." [588] In throwing away the gift that would have been his supernatural inheritance, Adam "also forfeited all the other precious gifts with which he had originally been enriched."[589]

When through his own fault, Adam lost Original Justice, Original Sin took its place, affecting both body and soul. **St. Thomas Aquinas** taught that while in the state of justice, "the whole body was held together in subjection to the soul" but, with the fall of Adam, all "the powers of the soul were left, as it were, destitute of their proper order, whereby they are naturally directed to virtue," and this "destitution is called a wounding of nature."[590]

Barred from the Tree of Life and wounded by the four chief effects of his sin (weakness, ignorance, malice and concupiscence), the first father Adam could bequeath to all of his descendants only his fallen human nature, sullied with the Original Sin.

The New Adam and the New Eve

"But from this general misfortune," wrote St. Alphonsus de Liguori, "God was pleased to exempt that Blessed Virgin whom He had destined to be the Mother of the second Adam—Jesus Christ—who was to repair the evil done by the first."[591]

A fundamental doctrinal theme of St. Paul's is that **Our Lord is Adam's archetype** by way of contrast, for Jesus came to undo the work of Adam and to open the gates of Heaven, long closed to the first man's posterity as a consequence of the Original Sin.[592] St. Paul speaks of "Adam, who is a figure of him who was to come...But not as the offense, so also the gift. For if by one man's offence, death reigned through one; much more they who receive abundance of grace, and of the gift, and of justice, shall reign in life through one, Jesus Christ."[593]

The Teaching of the Catholic Church explains, "A man led to our loss of the sanctifying grace of God; a Man gave us back the gift. Death reigned in the race of Adam; through one born of Adam's race, true Life was restored to men.

---

[588] Smith, D.D., Ph.D., Canon George D. *The Teaching of the Catholic Church: A Summary of Catholic Doctrine*, Vol. I. [New York: The MacMillan Co., 1959]: p. 526.
[589] de Liguori, loc. cit.
[590] Aquinas, St. Thomas. *The Summa Theologica*. Second and Revised Edition, 1920. First Part of the Second Part, Question 85.
[591] de Liguori, loc. cit.
[592] 1 Cor. 15: 44-49.
[593] Rom. 5:14, 17.

Death was the punishment decreed for our first father's sin; when the Redeemer died, death was found to be the one efficacious remedy for our loss."[594]

The corresponding doctrine that **the Blessed Virgin is the archetype of Eve** is the teaching of all antiquity, and it was for this reason that St. Ephrem wrote, "Those two innocents, those two simple ones, had been equal the one to the other, but afterward, one became the cause of our death, the other of our life." [595] Our Lady is "rightly called the second Eve in the same sense that her divine Son is rightly called the second Adam..."[596]

As Adam and Eve were created with sanctifying grace, so were the **New Adam and Eve**. Our Lord Jesus Christ, the second Adam and the Son of Mary, was always sinless in virtue of the hypostatic union of His sacred humanity with the Person of the Word. The hypostatic union is the mystery of the Incarnation of God; it is the reason for the mystery of the Immaculate Conception, the mystery of the perpetual virginity and sacred Motherhood of Mary, and the mystery of the redeeming Cross.

For the sake of the Incarnation and the Passion of Christ which would offer redemption to the human race, the Lord's Virgin Mother was conceived without sin, "redeemed in the highest way–*the way of prevention*–from the shipwreck that involved all the other children of Adam, all our race, in dire catastrophe."[597]

The Redemption of the Virgin

St. Alphonsus was careful to observe, "There are two means by which a person may be redeemed, as St. Augustine teaches us: *'the one by raising him up after having fallen, and the other by preventing him from falling,'* and this last means is doubtless the most honorable." [598]

The sanctified state of the first man and woman prefigure the Incarnation of Christ and the Immaculate Conception. God created Adam from the virginal earth and imbued him with sanctifying grace; He then created the virgin Eve from the virgin Adam. (Here it should be noted that by *virgin* is meant purity not only in the material sense of the body, but also of intellect, heart and soul.)

When Adam was in the state of original justice, the Lord God cast a deep sleep upon him and took one of his ribs to form the first woman, Eve. [599] From

---

[594] Smith, op. cit., p. 523.
[595] St. Ephrem. *Op. Syr., tom.ii*, p. 325. Cited by Canon Smith, op. cit., p. 531.
[596] Smith, op. cit., p. 524
[597] Ibid., p. 528. [Emphasis added]
[598] de Liguori, op. cit., p. 303.
[599] Gen. 2: 21-22.

the very moment of her existence, grace was imparted to the woman, granted by God through the stainless Adam.

In a similar fashion, the Virgin Mary (the New Eve) received at the very moment of her existence the gift of sanctifying grace, communicated from God through the virginal Jesus (the New Adam). **How was this done**, when Our Lady preceded her Divine Son in historical time?

The answer is found in the mystery of the Holy Trinity. God is present to all things that are, were or shall be. What He is and does, He is and does outside of time. To Him, creatures and events which succeed each other in time are ever present. In the great mystery of the Holy Trinity, which our limited human minds cannot fathom, the three Divine Persons applied to Our Lady the foreseen merits of Jesus, *the Word made Flesh.*[600]

To quote the illustrious words of St. Bernard of Clairvaux: "One man and one woman have wrought us exceeding harm; nevertheless, thanks to God, through one Man and one Woman all things are restored…and indeed Christ would have sufficed. Surely all of sufficiency is of Him, but it would not have been good for us that Man should be alone. Rather, it was fitting that both sexes should take part in our Reparation, for neither sex had been guiltless in our fall."[601]

"I have loved, O Lord, the beauty of thy house, and the place where thy glory dwelleth," [602] said King David, for the Holy Ghost inspired him to speak of his future daughter Mary, the living *Temple of God* and *Ark of the Covenant.* For the glory of His name, for the sake of the Incarnation of Christ, and for our sakes, the maiden Mary was prepared for her dignity and office as the Virgin Mother of God, both spiritually and physically, in her soul and in her body. Exempted and preserved from the sin which, as one of Adam's descendants, she otherwise would have inherited as the naturally generated child of St. Joachim and St. Anne, the Virgin Mary was conceived without sin.

The Immaculate Conception is "the woman," whose appearance in time commenced the fulfillment of the Lord's prophecy against the ancient serpent, the devil: *"I will put enmities between thee and **the woman**, and thy seed and her seed: she shall crush thy head and thou shalt lie in wait for her heel."*[603] Created by the Holy Trinity to be the ever-Immaculate Mother of God, Our

---

[600] Jn. 1:14.

[601] St. Bernard, *Sermo de Duodecim praerogativis B.V.M.,* I, 2. Cited by Smith, op. cit., p. 530.

[602] Ps. 25:8.

[603] Gen. 3:15.

Lady "was fittingly prepared for the virginal childbearing through which was crushed the serpent's head."[604]

"In the Christian religion," explained Cardinal Billot, "Mary is absolutely inseparable from Christ both before and after the Incarnation: Before the Incarnation in the hope and expectation of mankind; after the Incarnation in the worship and love of the Church. For, indeed, in the primeval prophecy [of *Genesis 3:15*] we were shown not only Christ, but also *the Woman* whose Child He is..."[605]

"The Immaculate Conception means the restoration of grace once more to the human race," [606] wrote Fr. H. O'Laverty, author of *The Mother of God and Her Glorious Feasts*. "The Immaculate Conception...was the long looked-for event in the history of the world, and from this we may really trace all the good things we have received through the sufferings and death of Christ."[607]

The Unbreakable Bond of the Woman and Her Seed

"A religion that separates Mary from Jesus–**the Woman from her Seed**–is neither the religion of the promises and prophecies as we read of in the Old Testament, nor the religion of their fulfillment as we see it in the New,"[608] explains *The Teaching of the Catholic Church*.

Christ is Our Divine Savior, and Mary is our holy Mother. Since the first days of the Church, there have always been those who try to separate Our Lord from His Mother. Just as many who forget that the entire human race was **not** condemned until Adam sinned are blindly inclined to point only to Eve as the reason for mankind's fall, conversely there are those who claim to admit Christ as Lord and Savior but contemptuously dismiss Our Lady's office in the Redemption. Just as the Lord God joined together the first Adam and Eve, whose fates were intertwined, so did He join together the new Adam and Eve in the *proto-evangelium* of *Genesis 3: 15*.

To further the points of **"figure-types"** previously made, the historical persons of Adam and Eve can always be positively compared or negatively contrasted to their perfect archetypes, the Lord Jesus and the Lady Mary. Gathered from the Fathers of the Church, the following syllabus clarifies God's binding of the first Adam and Eve and that of "the Woman and her seed":

---

[604] Smith, op. cit., p. 526.
[605] *De Verbo Incarnato*, p. 401 (Rome, 1912). Cited by Smith, op. cit., p. 530.
[606] O'Laverty, *The Mother of God and Her Glorious Feasts,* p. 4.
[607] Ibid.
[608] Smith, loc. cit.

• Adam was created before Eve; the Word in Eternity, the Second Person of the Holy Trinity Who said, *"Before Abraham came to be made, I am,"*[609] preceded His human but sinless mother.

• Adam was formed by God from the virginal earth; Jesus was conceived of the Holy Ghost and born of the Virgin Mary.

• Sanctifying grace was bestowed to Eve through Adam; Mary was conceived in grace through the foreseen merits of the new Adam.

• Eve sinned before Adam; Mary was born before Christ.

• Adam and Eve were created in Original Justice but fell from grace; Jesus and Mary were always full of grace.

• Adam and Eve were intended to be the lord and lady over all the earth; Our Lord Jesus Christ and Our Lady Mary possess dominion over all creation.

• Mary is the cause of our salvation, even as Eve was the cause of our ruin.

• "As Eve was seduced by an angel's word to shun God after having transgressed His Word, so Mary, also by an Angel's word, had the good tidings given her so that, after obeying His Word, she might bear God within her." (St. Irenaeus) [610]

• Adam, who sinned early in his life, sentenced the entire human race to death; Christ, Who died in the flower of His youth, redeemed us for eternal life.

• Both the Lady Eve and the Lady Mary became "the mother of all the living,"[611] Eve in the natural order, Mary in the order of grace—**for the Mother of God is also the Mother of men**.

In the third century, St. Proclus wrote of the Immaculate Conception, "Mary is the glory of virgins, the joy of mothers, the support of the faithful, the diadem of the Church, the express model of the true faith, the seat of piety, the robe of virtue, *the dwelling-place of the Holy Trinity.*"[612]

The Holy Scriptures relate that when the Virgin Mary, already full of grace, gave the angelic messenger her *Fiat*, "Behold the handmaid of the Lord; be it done to me according to thy word," [613] she was overshadowed by the Holy Ghost. The Lord of all was made Man, and "the woman" became *Theotokos* [614] (literally from the Greek, "God-bearer," or in a variable translation, "God's

---

[609] Jn. 8:58.

[610] Haer. V.19

[611] Gen. 3:20.

[612] St. Proclus, Patriarch of Constantinople (d. 446), *Orat. 6.* Cited by P.J. Chandlery, S.J., op. cit., Section IX.

[613] Lk. 1:38.

[614] The dogma that Mary is *Theotokos*, because Her Son Jesus is one Person but with two natures (divine and human; the hypostatic union), was formally defined at the Third Ecumenical Council of Ephesus in 431 A.D.

mother"). At the moment Our Lady became the Mother of God, she also became the spiritual Mother of all mankind. From that same instant, the new Adam and the new Eve together began the Redemption of mankind.

Those who truly adore Christ also honor the Perpetual Virgin who brought Him forth. In a similar manner, those who possess devotion "to Jesus through Mary" make their own the witness of St. Alphonsus: "The more we honor Mary, the more we shall honor God," for when Our Lord came to free us all, He did not disdain the humility of the Immaculate Virgin's womb.

"And she brought forth her first-born son, and wrapped him up in swaddling clothes, and laid Him in a manger; because there was no room for them in the inn."[615] Born in poverty and adored only by the humble Virgin, St. Joseph, and poor shepherds, the Christ Child would later be sought by wise men from the east, following a star.

"And entering the house, they found the child with Mary, his mother, and falling down they adored him."[616] So do all the faithful throughout time forever find Christ–always with Mary, His Mother and ours.

---

[615] Lk. 2:7.
[616] Matt. 2:11.

CHAPTER 21

The Star Before Dawn

"The two truths which stand out like mountain peaks in the chain of revelation concerning Our Blessed Lady, and around which cluster all other truths we hold about her, are her divine maternity and her fullness of grace, both of which are affirmed in the Gospels and in the Councils of the Church."

—Fr. Reginald Garrigou-Lagrange, The Mother of the Saviour

St. Bernardine of Siena once said that "to be the Mother of God is the miracle of miracles." Total consecration to Jesus through Mary paves a faster path for the three interior conversions. It is a shorter way, so to speak, to make the spiritual ascent of Mt. Carmel. At each modern-day apparition and in different ways, the Lady stressed this truth herself, especially the necessity of conversion. It also seems that the "character" of each successive visitation had much to do with the world's response or rejection of her previous message.

• **Mary, Conceived Without Sin:** With the first three apparitions of the Modern Age (Paris, 1830, known as Our Lady of the Miraculous Medal; again in Paris in 1840, through which the Church received the sacramental known as the Green "Scapular" Badge, and LaSalette, 1846, where the Virgin appeared weeping), the emerging theme is clear—*conversion* through the Immaculate Heart of Mary, who always brings us closer to her Divine Son, Jesus Christ.

She would also appear at Lourdes (1854), Pontmain (1871), Pellevoisin (1875), and Knock, Ireland (1879), revealing her divinely bestowed privilege as the Immaculate One and as Mediatrix with her Savior and Divine Son, Jesus Christ. At Lourdes, she directed a young girl to a hidden and miraculous spring. At Pontmain, she appeared just as the small village was on the verge of being raided, and there she silently directed attention to the Holy Cross of Jesus but also providing a discreet reference to her Immaculate Heart. At Pellevoisin, she frightened away a demon, cured the dying visionary, and gave the world another sacramental, the Sacred Heart Scapular. At Knock (the final Marian apparition before Fatima), her silent visage and the tableau in which she appeared leads us to the *Apocalypse*.

It is in our own age that the Secret of Mary is coming to fruition. "It was through Mary that the salvation of the world was begun," as we recall that which St. Louis Marie noted, "and it is through Mary that it must be consummated. Mary hardly appeared at all in the first coming of Jesus Christ, in order that men, as yet but little instructed and enlightened on the Person of her Son, should not remove themselves from Him in attaching themselves too strongly and too grossly to her…But in the Second Coming of Jesus Christ, Mary has to be made known and revealed by the Holy Ghost in order that through her Jesus Christ may be known, loved, and served. The reasons which moved the Holy Ghost to hide His spouse during her life, and to reveal her but very little since the preaching of the *Gospel*, subsist no longer."[617]

St. Montfort's inspired prophecy was written in the early 18th Century, in a Europe still reeling from the Protestant Revolt, in a Europe soon to experience the French Revolt against the altar of God and the Catholic throne. The "Catholic conscience of history" (as Belloc coined the term) sees from within; it then understands the series of conflicts were not spontaneous, random events but purposeful advancements of the Great Revolt against God, the Revolt which began in the 1500's and continues to this day.

Beginning in the 19th century to now, in which the Church Militant is desperately besieged by every heresy, the Holy Ghost is revealing Mary, according to the "general law of preparation," so that (as St. Louis de Montfort wrote), "through her, Jesus Christ may be known, loved and served."[618]

The Miraculous Medal:
"Medal of the Immaculate Conception"
"O Mary, conceived without sin, pray for us who have recourse to thee."
—Prayer of the "Miraculous Medal"

The Virgin Mary first came to Paris, formerly the very heart of the French Revolt where the forces of hell had struck at her heel. She appeared to a postulant of the Daughters of Charity on July 18, 1830, the eve of the Feast of St. Vincent de Paul, co-founder of the community. The Lady allowed the postulant, whom we now know as St. Catherine Labouré, to kneel before her and rest her clasped hands on her lap, just as a young girl would do with her mother. During the 2½ hour visit, the Virgin spoke of the evil times and foretold coming calamities which took place within the next 40 years, and her words proved true.

"But come to the foot of the altar," said the Virgin. "Here great graces will be poured out upon all who ask them with confidence and fervor. They will be bestowed upon the great and small."

---

[617] de Montfort, St. Louis. *True Devotion to Mary*, #49.
[618] Ibid.

"My eyes are ever upon you. I shall grant you many graces. Special graces will be given to all who ask them, but people must pray," were Our Lady's concluding words at the end of the first apparition.[619]

The message was clear: The Virgin turned the eyes of her children to the Blessed Sacrament, where God so patiently waits. All we have to do is turn to Him and ask Him for His help with "confidence and fervor" because He wants our love and trust. Furthermore, God is no respecter of persons; the graces distributed are not given according to social status, as the spirit of the world thinks. Finally, the Lady made clear that she herself watches and guards over us. As the Mediatrix of All Graces, she also promises graces but with a condition—"people must pray."

During her second visit to St. Catherine, in Paris where 40 years prior the godless revolutionaries replaced the Madonna's statue in the Notre Dame Cathedral with the shameless "Goddess of Reason," the Lady emphasized both a Marian doctrine, which would be defined as a dogma 24 years later, and her intercessory power before God. It was in Paris that she gave to the world the Medal of the Immaculate Conception (commonly known as the Miraculous Medal).

Our Lady appeared over the high altar, standing on a globe—her feet crushing a serpent, which immediately calls to mind the *proto-evangelium* of *Genesis 3:15: "I will put enmities between thee and the woman, and thy seed and her seed; she shall crush thy head and thou shalt lie in wait for her heel."*

The Virgin held a smaller globe with a small cross on top, which she held out as if offering it to God. The Lady explained to Catherine that the ball represented the world, adding, "I am praying for it and for everyone in the world."

Beautiful rays of many colors and lengths shone from what looked like gems on her fingers. The Virgin said, "The rays are the graces which I give to those who ask for them." The stones from which no rays came, she said, represented *the graces waiting to be bestowed **but for which no one asks**.*

This Vision then changed and an oval frame appeared around Our Lady. She lowered her arms and stretched out her hands, graces pouring in the form of light. Around the oval frame appeared words in gold, *"O Mary conceived without sin, pray for us who have recourse to thee."*

"Have a medal made according to this picture," the Virgin said to St. Catherine Labouré. "All those who wear it when it is blessed will receive many graces, especially if they wear it from their necks."

---

[619] Sharkey, *The Woman Shall Conquer,* pp.16-17.

Suddenly, the entire Vision seemed to revolve. On the back of the oval, which denoted the reverse side of the Miraculous Medal, St. Catherine saw the letter **"M,"** surmounted by a cross with a crossbar beneath it. Below the crossbar were two Hearts, one encircled by thorns and the other pierced by a sword. Surrounding the **"M"** were twelve stars within a golden frame.

The **symbolism of the two Hearts** emphasizes that the **Sacred Heart of Jesus** and the **Sorrowful** and **Immaculate Heart of Mary** are inseparable; the **"M"** underscores the truth that Mary is the cause of our salvation, for it was with her cooperation that **God became Man.** The **symbolism** also emphasizes the Marian doctrine that the Mother of God is the Co-Redemptrix of the human race. The **cross and crossbar** remind us of **the Passion**, while the **12 stars** within the golden frame symbolize the **12 Apostles** commanded by Christ to spread the *Gospel* and baptize all nations. The **12 stars** also symbolize the **12 virtues of Our Lady**, and they may also be a divine hint to *Apocalypse*, Ch. 12: 1, which begins, *"A great sign appeared in heaven; a woman clothed with the sun..."*

The Green "Scapular" Badge of the Immaculate Heart

"Immaculate Heart of Mary, pray for us now and at the hour of our death."
  —The inscription on the Badge of the Immaculate Heart

In 1840, the Virgin Mary appeared many times in Blangy, Paris, to another Sister of Charity, Sister Justine Bisqueyburu. Our Lady was clothed in a long white robe, over which hung a blue mantle. Her head was unadorned, her hair falling loosely over her shoulders. In her right hand, she held her Immaculate Heart surrounded by flames, with the top of the Heart issuing beautiful rays. In her left hand, she held a badge, a single piece of green cloth suspended from a string of the same color.

On one side of the badge was a miniature replica of the Blessed Virgin, as she revealed herself to Sister Justine. On the other side was a Heart pierced by a sword, surmounted by a cross, and surrounded by an oval inscription: *"Immaculate Heart of Mary, pray for us now and at the hour of our death."* Sister Justine described a "heart all ablaze with rays more dazzling than the sun and transparent as crystal"–amazing words which prefigure the description of Our Lady at the Fatima apparitions.

This "Badge of the Immaculate Heart," which became known as "the **Green Scapular**" (although it is not truly a scapular), was given to the Church as a new sacramental, and Our Lady said it was "for the conversion of those who had no faith and, above all, to procure for them a happy death."[620] The Blessed Virgin also directed that the badge must be properly blessed by a priest. It can be worn, or placed in the clothing, on the bed, or simply in the room of the person for whom we are asking the grace of conversion. The prayer on the badge should be offered daily, if not by the one wearing it, then by the one giving it. Graces would be given, she said, in proportion to the confidence in which the favors were asked—a very important matter to remember.

The Madonna Wept at LaSalette
"Well, my children, you will make this known to all my people."
   −Our Lady of LaSalette

Four years later, on **Saturday, September 19, 1846**−the eve of Our Lady of Sorrows−the Virgin Mary came to LaSalette, France, there to grant a one-time appearance to two shepherd children. The apparition occurred between **two and three in the afternoon**, a time of great significance because on this day and during this exact hour, the Divine Office prayers were being offered to the Virgin of Sorrows.[621]

Eleven-year old Maximin Giraud and fifteen-year old Melanie Mathieu were tending cows when there suddenly appeared a globe of dazzling light. The globe opened and they saw a woman seated on stones. The Lady's elbows rested on her knees, her face was buried in her hands, and **she was weeping**.

The Lady wore a crystal-white, floor-length gown, its long, broad, and straight sleeves reaching beyond her fingertips. A golden apron descended to the bottom of her dress. Over the gown, the Lady wore a white cape bordered with roses. On her feet were white shoes, encircled by roses. Her head-dress, too, was white, crowned by a royal diadem, wreathed with roses of many-colored hues. Around the Lady's neck hung a golden chain and golden crucifix, with a hammer on one side and a pair of pincers on the other, clearly emphasizing the Passion of Jesus.

Each sentence of the *known* LaSalette Message is intended for all of the Church's children, regardless of age, and for those outside of the Church, too. The Lady would privately give each child a secret, which they would not reveal

---

[620] Ibid., p. 25.

[621] The Seven Sorrows (Dolors) of Mary, once celebrated in the Church twice a year, are symbolized as seven mystical swords piercing the Immaculate Heart. In 1727, the feast day was added to the Roman Calendar on the Friday before Palm Sunday. It was also commemorated on the third Sunday of every September, until 1913 when Pope St. Pius X moved the feast to September 15, immediately following the Feast of the Holy Cross on September 14th, emphasizing the connection between Our Lord's Passion and Our Lady of Sorrows.

to anyone. Eventually they were asked if they would divulge it to the Pope, a suggestion to which both agreed. The two Secrets of LaSalette were entrusted to Pope Pius IX but he never publicly revealed them.

Unlike Sr. Lucia of Fatima, however, Melanie of the LaSalette apparition would later publicly release what she claimed was the secret given to her. While some insist that, after the apparition and after she learned to read and write, Melanie became extremely interested in apocalyptic literature which, they further claim, influenced what she revealed as her secret, one must wonder if the opposite is true—that is, if due to the secret given to her, Melanie became interested in apocalyptic writings. Be that as it may, the most startling part of Melanie's secret are the words allegedly uttered by the Virgin Mary: "Rome will lose the Faith and become the seat of anti-Christ."

If true, note that she did not say *the Church* herself will become anti-Christ's seat, because Christ promised He would always be with His Church, saying, "...behold I am with you all days, even to the consummation of the world." (Matt. 28:20) However, that promise does not mean that the visible Church will not endure many terrible things, that the city of Rome could not again be overtaken by evil powers, just as it was during the reigns of Caligula, Nero, and Diocletian, or that through the Church's entire history, particular men of the Roman Catholic hierarchy could not apostatize. To the contrary, the Church's human element is comprised of both saints and sinners. Like the Apostle Judas, among the hierarchy there will always be traitors, but such tragedies will never mean the Church herself ceases to exist. Furthermore, in the early days of the infant Church, Catholicism eventually overthrew pagan Rome, so it is to be expected that Satan, who will be the power behind the anti-Christ, wants to reclaim the ancient city that once was his, and which is now the central earthly city of Christ's Church.

Consider the evident lessons taught at LaSalette (although there are many more) in even a quick examination of Our Lady's opening words, reproduced below in exact order:

• **"Come near, my children, be not afraid; I am here to tell you great news."**

• *The Lesson*: Our Lady reveals her desire that we approach her in trust, as children approach their Mother.

• **"If my people will not submit, I shall be forced to let fall the arm of my Son. It is so strong, so heavy, that I can no longer withhold it."**

• *The Lesson*: When the Virgin spoke of "my people," she spoke as did the queens of old. At the same time she revealed her intercession as the Queen Mother before her Son, Whose arm is raised to punish. The Lady warns the people to submit—that is, to humbly give her Son the love and honor which He rightly deserves as Our Savior.

• **"For how long a time do I suffer for you! If I would not have my Son abandon you, I am compelled to pray to Him without ceasing; and as to you, you take not heed of it. However much you pray, however much you do, you will never recompense the pains I have taken for you."**

• *The Lesson*: Although the blessed in Heaven can no longer suffer, Our Lady uses these words to display the gravity of our sins in God's eyes. Again, she refers to her Son—implicitly revealing her own identity. Once more, she speaks of her prayerful intercession, for which we have been ungrateful. No mere human being can ever offer enough love and gratitude to her Son in His Passion, by which we were bought at a great price, or to His Mother, Our Lady of Sorrows.

• **"Six days I have given you to labor, the seventh I have kept for myself; and they will not give it to me. It is this which makes the arm of my Son so heavy."**

• *The Lesson*: Here is a great mystery, for Our Lady did **not** say, "The Lord our God gave you six days to labor;" rather, she spoke in the first person. Her words were a discreet reminder that she is the Perpetual Tabernacle of the Holy Trinity; God chooses to speak through her in these latter days. The Lady had referred to the Third Commandment, "Keep holy the Sabbath day," which means attending the Sacrifice of the Mass and receiving the Sacraments on Sundays and holy days. This commandment also forbids missing Mass through one's own fault, unnecessary servile work, public buying and selling, or court trials on the Sabbath.

• **"Those who drive the carts cannot swear without introducing the name of my Son. These are the two things which make the arm of my Son so heavy."**

• *The Lesson*: Our Lady warned of Our Lord's severe anger when people break the Second Commandment, "Thou shalt not take the name of the Lord thy God in vain." All should use reverence when speaking of God and holy things or matters, and keep oaths made in the name of God. Blasphemy, irreverent or disrespectful use of God's name, false oaths, and breaking of vows offend against this Commandment.

In essence, while the Virgin of LaSalette spoke of many other matters, she made clear that the only remedy is **conversion**—of which the true definition is almost lost in this age: *Christ must be the life of the soul.*

Once more, may we remember the Virgin's final words at LaSalette: "Well, my children, you will make this known to all my people."

CHAPTER 22

The Lady of Lourdes and St. Bernadette:
A Life of the Beatitudes

"Humility is the secret of God's glory."
−St. Bernadette Soubirous

In 1858, Our Lady came to Lourdes, France, appearing 18 times to a fourteen year old girl, who is solemnly canonized under her name in religion, St. Marie Bernard Soubirous, but who is commonly known as St. Bernadette. The Virgin's message for all was as simple as it was direct: "Pray for sinners" and "Penitence! Penitence! Penitence!" When asked her identity, she did not answer until March 25 (the Feast of the Annunciation, the day the Church joyously celebrates the Word incarnated as man in the Virgin's womb), saying, "I am the Immaculate Conception."

Only weeks before, the Mother of God had instructed the young girl to dig at a spot on the grotto floor. There came forth a spring, hidden until that time, which has bestowed graces of spiritual conversions and physical cures.

Due to the simplicity of the Lourdes message, it is all too easy to overlook it. The life of the chosen messenger, however, shows us the heroic degree to which God wishes us to seek sanctity. Unlike St. Catherine, whose identity as visionary of the Miraculous Medal was known only to her confessor but not by her Mother Superior until one year before the saint's death, St. Bernadette was the first visionary who was, during the apparitions, publicly known upon sight and constantly interrogated.

In her brief 36 years of life, Bernadette reached heroic heights of holiness (unlike Melanie and Maximum of LaSalette, who were always faithful Catholics but did not attain either St. Catherine's or St. Bernadette's heroic degree of virtue). Since she is the first visionary whose life was carefully scrutinized when she was still on earth, we will take a slight detour to briefly visit with the incorruptible maiden of Lourdes.

St. Bernadette: Little Maiden of Lourdes

In reading the lives of the saints, St. Bernadette once mused, "I think that they ought to point out the faults the Saints had and indicate the means they employed to correct them. That would be helpful to us. We would learn how to set about it. But all that is mentioned is their revelations or the wonders they performed. They cannot serve our advancement."[622]

However, her most famous biographer, Abbé Trochu, did not quite agree. "She failed to add that, even so, these imperfect authors are to be commended for raising the pre-eminent qualities of the Saints, and that she found in them examples to imitate. The Church in its infallible decisions was one day to adopt the well-founded verdict of a Superior General of Saint-Gildard: 'It is my own opinion that during her life Sister Marie-Bernarde [the saint's name in religious life] put into practice the virtues that constitute sanctity.'"[623]

What is sanctity? It is the "state of Christian perfection," which is the result of a "fervent surrender of one's self to God and the practice of virtue. It does not require extraordinary works. The Blessed Mother of God, the most holy of mortals, never performed any extraordinary works to excite worldly admiration. *'Love is fulfilling of the law.'"*[624]

A saint is a person who "fulfills all the demands of the law" (Rom. 13:10), which is accomplished by charity, the virtue by which we love God above all things for His own sake, and our neighbors as ourselves. Charity is considered the queen of all virtues, since it is the one virtue that will always exist in Heaven. In the Beatific Vision, souls will no longer possess any need for the other virtues. Charity, however, will remain, since it perfectly unites God and man, just as it perfectly unites man to man. [625] Those souls who are canonized as saints by the Catholic Church are those who were known to practice all of the virtues to a heroic degree—i.e., heroic virtue.

What is meant by heroic virtue? Pope Benedict XIV, "whose chapters on heroic virtue are classical," thus describes it: "In order to be heroic, a Christian virtue must enable its owner to perform virtuous actions with uncommon promptitude, ease, and pleasure, from supernatural motives and without human

---

[622] Trochu, Abbé Francois. *St. Bernadette Soubirous: 1844-1879.* [Rockford, IL: TAN Books and Publishers, 1985. Translated and adapted by John Joyce, S.J. First published in France under the same title by Librairier Catholique Emmanuel Vitte, Paris, 1954. English edition copyright 1957 by Longmans, Green and Co. Ltd., London. Published by TAN in arrangement with Longman Group Limited, London. Nihil Obstat and Imprimatur, June 21, 1957]: p. 346.
[623] Ibid.
[624] Morrow, *My Catholic Faith,* p. 85.
[625] Ibid., p.83.

reasoning, with self-abnegation and full control over his natural inclinations." The 1910 *Catholic Encyclopedia* comments, "A heroic virtue, then, is a habit of good conduct that has become a second nature, a new motive power [that is] stronger than all corresponding inborn inclinations, capable of rendering easy a series of acts each of which, for the ordinary man, would be beset with very great, if not insurmountable, difficulties."[626]

In reading the lives of the saints, time and prayer are needed to assess, study, and contemplate in them the supernatural virtues and the gifts and fruits of the Holy Ghost. In addition, it must be remembered that "the Holy Ghost also grants certain extraordinary gifts, which are given only on rare occasions and to selected persons. Such extraordinary graces are granted principally not only for the benefit of the recipient, but of others." Among these graces are included the gift of visions, of miracles, and of prophecy.

In St. Bernadette—handmaiden of the Lord's Handmaiden, the Blessed Virgin Mary—we will discover all of these things: the three theological virtues (faith, hope, and charity); the four cardinal virtues (prudence, justice, temperance, and fortitude); the seven Gifts of the Holy Ghost (wisdom, understanding, counsel, fortitude, knowledge, piety, and fear of the Lord), the twelve Fruits of the Holy Ghost (charity, joy, peace, patience, benignity, goodness, long-suffering, mildness, faith, modesty, continency, and chastity) and the extraordinary graces of visions, miracles, and prophecy. Of St. Bernadette's many virtues and gifts, only a few examples will be spotlighted—especially her fortitude and long-suffering.

The Saint's Early Years

Bernadette Soubirous, the firstborn of her parents, was born about two o'clock in the afternoon, as the bell was ringing for Vespers on Sunday, January 7, 1844 in Lourdes, France, a small market town near the Pyrenees in the country's southwest. Her parents had named her Bernarde Marie, but the priest who baptized her kept referring to her and registered the name as Marie Bernarde. Her father reminded the priest that the child's name was already registered at the Town Hall as Bernarde-Marie, but history shows that the priest

---

[626] BENEDICT XIV, De servorum Dei beatificatione et beatorum canonizatione, chs. xxxi-xxxviii, in Opera omnia, III (Prato, 1840); DEVINE, Manual of Mystical Theology (London, 1903); SLATER, A Manual of Moral Theology (London, 1908); WILHELM AND SCANNELL, Manual of Catholic Theology (London, 1906). Cited by Wilhelm, Joseph. "Heroic Virtue." *The Catholic Encyclopedia*, Vol. 7. [New York: Robert Appleton Company, 1910. [http://www.newadvent.org/cathen/07292c.htm]

never did change the register. Her family, however, considered her first name to be Bernarde, although she was called by the diminutive of Bernadette.

As for the parents, neither had ever gone to school but they were known to be good Catholics who faithfully carried out their religious duties and respectable people of irreproachable integrity. Of the nine children born of the marriage between Louise Castérot and Francois Soubirous, not all lived to adulthood.

In Bernadette's sixth year, she began to suffer from asthma, which afflicted her until the end of her life. She was small for her age but she was a happy and lovable child with a sweet smile. She easily took to caring for her younger siblings so her parents could work. She, like her parents, received no education. By her tenth year in 1854, the family was in serious financial straits. For various reasons, their mill was lacking customers and so the father sought odd jobs, as did her mother. Bernadette remained at home, taking care of her younger siblings. (On an important and related note, it was in this same year that Pope Pius IX defined as a dogma the Immaculate Conception.)

In the saint's 11th year of life, Bernadette became one of many children who were stricken by a cholera epidemic. Since cholera is usually fatal, her recovery truly must have been a miraculous one. In her 12th year, her godmother Aunt Bernarde took her home, where she was fed well but also became nurse-maid to her younger cousins. Once again, her education was neglected. Her aunt would later say that Bernadette knew the *Our Father*, the *Hail Mary*, and the *Credo*. However, she had never been taught to read, so her only "prayer book" was a small Rosary.

By the winter of 1856, Bernadette insisted on returning to her family. At this time, the Soubirous became so impoverished that they were forced to accept the free lodging of a cold, damp room known as *Le Cachot* (The Dungeon), once used to hold prisoners. Everyone in the town knew the family's situation, but this "was an age of scant help for the poor. For example, no conference of St. Vincent de Paul was established in Lourdes till 1874 (three years before Bernadette's death). It was a harsh age when too many of the wealthy, lacking pity because they lacked the *Gospel*, exploited the labour of the poor; and mothers of large families received only ten *sous* for a whole day's work!"[627]

Bernadette's father found work from day to day with the baker or the horse-and-coach service, while her mother worked in the fields, or gathered wood in the forest and later sold it to buy bread, or did the washing and housework for people in town. Previously, Bernadette and her sister Toinette

---

[627] Trochu, op cit., p. 17.

stayed at home, caring for the younger brothers. Now, however, Toinette at age ten was able to attend school with the Sisters of Charity of Nevers, who had come to Lourdes in 1834.

For her part, the 13 year old Bernadette would often say that books were not meant for her, that the Sisters did not know in which class to put her since she could not read and could hardly scratch out a few letters. There was also her asthma and the fact that she was needed at home. Her only real desire for herself was her First Holy Communion.

Little Shepherdess of Bartres

Louise Soubirous thought of what seemed to be a good solution. In June of 1857, Bernadette was sent to Bartres, to the household of Marie Lagües, who had been Bernadette's wet-nurse after Louise suffered an unfortunate accident with a candle. As a baby of 10 months of age, Bernadette was brought to live with the Lagües and there she stayed until her 20th month of life. Considering Marie's supposed affection for the child, as well as her home's proximity to church and school, Louise had thought it would be easier for Bernadette to attend school and catechism at Bartres. In reality, however, Bernadette again became a nursemaid, this time to her former "foster mother's" four young children. By August, she was also entrusted with the care of the family's lambs, and so she became a shepherdess. When school opened in September, she was not sent to class. Instead, she was given the additional care of the sheep.

What this meant was that the young girl worked from sunup to sundown, caring for children in the early morning and spending the rest of the day outside, in good weather or bad, with the sheep and lambs. At first, she was allowed to attend some catechism classes and the Sunday Masses and holy days. However, her inability to read and her legitimate exhaustion made it difficult for her to memorize the catechism. Bernadette was a responsible worker, she never complained, she asked for nothing, and she gratefully accepted whatever was given to her. This made it easy to treat her as an unpaid servant, working for her bed and board. The true purpose for which she was sent to her former wet-nurse was neglected. A priest, the brother-in-law of Mr. Lagües, did intervene on Bernadette's behalf, telling his sister's husband that he was not treating Bernadette as one of the family. The reproach had little effect. Rarely was she seen at catechism, and never was she seen in school.

It was during these solitary days as a shepherdess that Bernadette made a stone altar at the foot of an old chestnut tree, setting on top of it a picture of the Blessed Virgin Mary. There she would kneel, praying the Rosary with a gift given to her by her mother—a set of poor black beads, threaded on plain string. She would play with the flock of lambs and then, resting, her eyes would fall on the valley; her ears heard the rustling of the trees, the occasional bird song and the other sounds of nature. "God made all that," she would think to herself. She did not know she was in the very early stages of meditation or that God was already preparing her soul. She was to be another handmaiden of the Immaculate Mother of God.

In early January of 1858, Bernadette's 14th birthday found her still at the house of the Lagües. Circumstances continued as they had since August. She still helped with the children, she still retained the entire responsibility of the flock, and she still was not receiving any form of proper catechesis and education.

In humility, Bernadette did all that was asked of her, and she did it well, but eventually her ardent longing for her First Holy Communion began to manifest itself. At least three times, she asked to be brought home, through verbal messages given to her visiting Aunt Bernarde, a neighbor from Lourdes who was passing through the area, and the Lagües servant who one day took a trip to Lourdes. For the Soubirous, however, the situation was no better, so their daughter's entreaties fell on deaf ears. Finally, Bernadette took matters into her own hands.

On a Sunday near the end of January 1858, she requested permission to go to Lourdes. Although given consent, she was instructed by the Lagües to return the very next day. She came back three days later, humbly yet forthrightly explaining, "I must go home. The parish priest is going to have the children prepared for First Communion, and if I go back to Lourdes, I shall make mine." In this one example, one should easily recognize Bernadette's fortitude, that "moral virtue that ensures firmness in difficulties and constancy in the pursuit of the good. It strengthens the resolve to resist temptations and to overcome obstacles in the moral life. The virtue of fortitude enables one to conquer fear, even fear of death, and to face trials and persecutions. It disposes one even to renounce and sacrifice his life in defense of a just cause."[628]

Within two weeks upon Bernadette's return to Lourdes, the Queen of Heaven would appear to this poor, neglected, and uneducated child. As we have seen, she was obedient, meek, and conscientious. She had never insisted upon anything for herself—until now. Her only longing was a spiritual one, and that was to receive Our Lord in the Holy Eucharist. Bernadette was humble and

---

[628] "Divine Mysteries: The Four Cardinal Virtues: Prudence, Justice, Fortitude, and Temperance," *Legion of Mary* website.
[http://www.legionofmarytidewater.com/news/news07/may/divinemysteries.htm]

set her sight not on material riches but only those of the interior life. At the age of 14 years, her brief time on earth was already one of which Our Lord taught in the Beatitudes: "Blessed are the poor in spirit; for theirs is the kingdom of heaven."[629]

The Lourdes Apparitions Begin

"At fourteen, not knowing how to read or write, a complete stranger to the French language and ignorant of the Catechism, Bernadette looked upon herself as the most worthless child of her years." [630] On Thursday, January 28, 1858, the young Bernadette returned to her parents, joyfully exclaiming, "Now at least I shall be able to go to school and Catechism! That's why I've come back." [631]

Circumstances were no better for the Soubirous family, but her parents gave their promise. The next day, Bernadette was in school. Upon hearing the child's motive and determination, the Sisters enrolled her as a future communicant.

Coincidentally, on Thursday, February 11, 1858–exactly two weeks after her return because she greatly desired her First Holy Communion–the humble girl was graced to see a "most beautiful Lady." Bernadette would see this Lady a total of 18 times, the last vision occurring on July 16, 1858 (the Feast of Our Lady of Mt. Carmel).

That particular Thursday was a school holiday, so Bernadette was home with her family. Although a bitterly cold day, the air was still and there was no wind under the sunless sky. Shortly after 11 a.m., Bernadette set out on a necessary, tiresome task, accompanying her sister Toinette and a younger, impulsive classmate, Jeanne Abadie. The trio went in search of two things: fallen branches and twigs that they could rightfully take and use in the Soubirous' fireplace and old bones to sell to the rag-and-bone man. [632] Their expedition led them into a forest and then over a foot-bridge to the Lafitte family's property, which formed an island. One side was enclosed by a bend in the Gave River, the other by a canal which powered a saw-mill and flour-mill, called the Savy. The extreme point of the triangle was a tall, rocky formation known as "Massabielle" (Old Hump).

---

[629] Matt. 5:3.

[630] Trochu, op. cit., p. 36.

[631] Ibid.

[632] Bones were used "for knife handles, toys and ornaments and, when treated, for chemistry. The grease extracted from them was also useful for soap-making." Rag-and-bone man, *Wikipedia*. [http://en.wikipedia.org/wiki/Rag-and-bone_man]

Massabielle was "naturally shaped into an arch from which a cave ran backwards, and to the right, about fourteen feet up, there was a small niche where a wild rosebush was growing."[633] In the spring season, the bush was "ablaze with white blooms." This wild outgrowth of rock, with its little oval niche, was also called "the grotto." In the small space before the grotto, Bernadette was forced to wait, as her healthier companions decided to remove their shoes and stockings, cross the freezing cold stream, and continue their search for dead branches and discarded bones. They were already on the stream's other side when, anxious to help, Bernadette resolved to join them. She removed her shoes in anticipation of walking through the frigid water.

"I had hardly begun to take off my stocking when I heard the sound of wind, as in a storm."[634] (Two days later, Fr. Pomian, the assistant priest to Fr. Peyramele, the parish priest at Lourdes, was particularly struck by Bernadette's mention of the "sound of wind, as in a storm." It reminded him of *Acts 2:2*, when the Holy Ghost descended upon the Virgin and the Apostles: "And suddenly there came *a sound from heaven*, as of *a mighty wind coming*, and it filled the whole house where they were sitting.")

Although the trees across the way were not moving at all, Bernadette said, "I had half-noticed, but without paying any particular heed, that the branches and brambles were waving beside the grotto." She returned to removing her stockings when she again heard the same sound of wind, this time in front of her. She looked up and saw the branches and brambles "underneath the topmost opening in the grotto tossing and swaying to and fro, though nothing else stirred around."

The Beautiful Lady at the Grotto

It was within the oval niche that Bernadette saw a "golden cloud" and then a beautiful light, instantly followed by "a girl in white, no bigger than myself, who greeted me with a slight bow of the head; at the same time, she stretched out her arms slightly away from her body, opening her hands, as in pictures of Our Lady; over her arms hung a Rosary." Bernadette described that the Lady was "smiling at me most graciously and seemed to invite me to come nearer. But I was still afraid. It was not, however, a fear such as I have had at other times, for I would have stayed there forever looking at her; whereas, when you are afraid, you run away very quickly."

The Lady wore "a white dress reaching down to her feet, of which only the toes appeared. The dress was gathered very high at the neck by a hem from

---

[633] Foley, Donal Anthony. *Marian Apparitions, the Bible, and the Modern World.* [Herefordshire, England: Gracewing, 2002]: p. 159.
[634] Trochu, op. cit., p. 42.

which hung a white cord. A white veil covered her head and came down over her shoulders and arms almost to the bottom of her dress. On each foot, I saw a golden rose. The sash of the dress was blue and hung down below her knees. The chain of the Rosary was yellow; the beads white, big, and widely spaced. The girl was alive, very young, and surrounded with light."[635]

When asked for additional details, Bernadette would also describe the girl's face as oval in shape and of "an incomparable grace." The Lady's eyes were blue, and her voice, "Oh, so sweet!" The Rosary held by the Lady was not the usual length for the *Psalter* of all 15 decades but a five-decade Rosary. As Bernadette prayed the Rosary, the Lady let her own Rosary slip through her fingers, silently counting the beads with Bernadette. The Lady, however, did not pray the *Our Father* or the *Hail Mary*, but she did pray the *Glory Be.*

Abbé Trochu, St. Bernadette's foremost biographer, noted: "This last detail, which the little one in her ignorance could not have invented, reveals an accurate and deep theological truth. The *Gloria*, which is a hymn of praise to the Adorable Trinity, and is Heaven's Canticle, is indeed the only part of the Rosary suitable for her, whose name Bernadette would not learn for another month. The *Pater* is the prayer of needy mortals, tempted and sinful, on their journey to the Fatherland; as for the *Ave*, the Angel's greeting (to the Virgin Mary), this could be used only by the visionary, as the Apparition had no need to greet her own self."[636]

Note well that it was at Lourdes that the Queen of Heaven first offered to the people of the Modern Age a "concession," as it were, since she emphasized the *daily* Rosary, which is only *one-third* of Our Lady's Psalter.

Centuries before, Our Lady had said to St. Dominic, "Preach my Psalter." By these words, she meant the Angelic Psalter of 15 decades, with each decade—comprised of one *Our Father* and ten *Hail Mary's*—prayed while meditating on the 15 Mysteries from the Incarnation of Jesus Christ at the Annunciation of the Virgin to the Coronation of Our Lady, assumed into Heaven.

Why was there, at Lourdes, a silent emphasis on the Rosary of five decades, rather than the Psalter of fifteen? Was it a matter of great significance in Mariology (for St. Bernadette, although illiterate, prayed the Rosary every day)—or had the Merciful Mother of God made allowances for the spiritual sloth of the Modern Age? Perhaps both inquiries form the answer because, many decades later, **Sr. Lucia of Fatima** would reveal "...the Most Holy Virgin, in these last times in which we live, has given a new efficacy

---

[635] Loc. cit., pp. 42-43.
[636] Loc. cit., p. 44.

to the recitation of the Rosary…There is **no** problem, no matter how difficult it is, that we cannot resolve by the prayer of the Holy Rosary. **With the Holy Rosary**, we will **save** ourselves. We will **sanctify** ourselves. We will **console Our Lord** and **obtain the salvation of many souls**."[637]

In the first two apparitions, the Lady did not speak to Bernadette, although she greeted the girl with a noble, yet inviting, bow of the head. During the third apparition, the Lady spoke for the first time, asking Bernadette, "Will you do me the favour of coming here for a fortnight?"[638] Bernadette said, "After asking permission from my parents, I will come," to which the Lady replied, "I do not promise to make you happy in this world, but in the *other*" (a literal French-to-English translation).

As Bernadette would soon understand, the Lady did not state that she herself would always appear. Rather, the request applied only *to* Bernadette. A brief summary provided by the first inquiry of the ecclesiastical Commission which later investigated the Lourdes apparitions thus states: "Bernadette was faithful to her appointment: she went most punctually to the grotto for a fortnight. She always obtained the same favours there, except on two days when the Apparitions did not appear." It was from this time forward that the young Bernadette was "accompanied by an ever increasing crowd. When she had the happiness of seeing the Vision, she forgot everything: she no longer noticed what was taking place around her: she was entirely absorbed."[639]

This World and the *Other*

As for the Lady saying, "I do not promise you happiness in this world, only in the *other*," her words quickly became self-evident. From the first day of the Apparition and until the end of her brief life, Bernadette would suffer misunderstandings, humiliations, false accusations, open derision, and many other trying circumstances.

For example, when her mother, Louise, first heard the story from the younger sister, Toinette, she questioned Bernadette and then took a rod to discipline both girls. At school, a much younger student slapped Bernadette across the face, while some of the teaching sisters taunted her to learn her catechism from the Lady. For many hours, the secular authorities would discourteously treat her, not even offering her a chair while they interrogated her. Even Fr. Peyramele was, at the first, very gruff with Bernadette.

Throughout her life, Bernadette was many times cross-examined about the Apparitions. In fact, she "wrote and signed numerous accounts of her visions.

---

[637] Frère Michel, *TWTF,* Vol. III, pp. 507-508.
[638] A fortnight is 15 consecutive days.
[639] Trochu, op. cit., p. 63.

In addition, she underwent repeated interrogations by both ecclesial and civil authorities, during which her testimony was transcribed. In none of these accounts did she contradict herself; on the other hand, there is no one single version that includes every detail."[640]

What is consistent is Bernadette's fidelity to testifying to the Virgin's message and in living it. In the total of 18 apparitions, the Blessed Mother spoke perhaps a handful of times. Once, she delivered three secrets that were for Bernadette alone—"a commission which, on her deathbed, she [Bernadette] declared she had carried out." [641] For the public, however, the main message was one of penance, prayer for the conversion of sinners, and a request that the priests build a chapel and that processions come to the grotto. There was also the Lady's gift, through the hands of Bernadette, of a hidden spring of water where graces of spiritual and bodily healing are to this day bestowed.

When the fortnight ended, the Lady had still not identified herself. During that interim, Bernadette had, at Father Peyramale's insistence, requested two things of the heavenly visitor—her name, as well as a sign to confirm that the Apparition's request for a chapel was truly from God. On Thursday, February 25, 1858, the Lady had already instructed Bernadette, "Go and drink at the spring and wash yourself in it." It was on that day that the miraculous spring of Lourdes came forth. To the request for her name, however, the Lady only gave Bernadette a gentle smile.

After March 4, Bernadette felt no inner call to return to the grotto until March 25, the Feast of the Annunciation. When she arrived, she found the Lady was already waiting for her. On this day, Bernadette thrice implored the Lady for her name. Then came the final confirmation of Lourdes, for the Lady raised her eyes to Heaven as she joined her hands, brought them close to her heart, and said, "I am the Immaculate Conception." After the briefest moment, she then smiled at Bernadette and disappeared.

Life after Lourdes

The Holy Communion so ardently desired by Bernadette was received on the Feast of Corpus Christi. Then, on July 16, the Feast of Our Lady of Mt. Carmel, the Lady appeared to Bernadette one last and unexpected time. To deter pilgrims, civil authorities placed boards around the grotto, including the spring. Bernadette was by the Gave River when suddenly the Lady appeared: "I saw neither the boards nor the Gave. It seemed to me that I was in the grotto,

---

[640] McEachern, Ph.D., Patricia A. *A Holy Life: The Writings of St. Bernadette of Lourdes.* [San Francisco, CA: Ignatius Press, 2005. Kindle Edition]: Loc. 116.
[641] Foley, op. cit., p. 160.

no more at a distance than the other times. I saw only the Holy Virgin. I had never seen her so beautiful."[642]

Bernadette's actions during the apparitions emphasized both the Rosary and humiliating penance for sinners, but the Vision's requests also tested her humble piety, fortitude, spirit of penance, and perseverance. Thus her coming years were foreshadowed, for she would continue to practice and interiorly grow in these and many other virtues.

The future saint was well aware that the grace of seeing the Mother of God did not grant her automatic access to Heaven. She would later write in her spiritual diary: "Often remind yourself of this word that the Most Holy Virgin said to you: *Penance! Penance!* You should be the first to put it into practice. For this intention, suffer trials in silence so that Jesus and Mary may be glorified..."[643]

Bernadette learned to read, write, embroider, and sew. She became a Sister of Charity and Christian Instruction at Nevers, France, and was given the name of Sister Marie-Bernard. She worked in the infirmary as a nurse's aide, and was later given the lighter task of altar sacristan. In the convent, she lived a life of both interior and physical suffering. She was often ill and frequently misunderstood and humiliated by her superiors and, on occasion, her fellow sisters. Abbé Trochu noted that "for the space of eleven years—much as she was esteemed and loved by her companions—she had been subjected to an undeserved coldness by those in authority over her. She always refused to speak of her suffering, which was a mixture of bewilderment and pain. She put up submissively with being reprimanded in public and more frequently than was her share."[644]

Due to Bernadette's lack of higher education and her frequent illnesses, to cite just two examples, she was called a "good for nothing" and "a lazy lie-abed." Deeply hurt by such uncharitable comments, Bernadette never retaliated, although on occasion she might respond with a brief, appropriate remark. Once, when a passing superior flung a quick jest that the ailing Bernadette needed to arise and get about her business, the saint calmly replied, "It is my business to be ill."

St. Bernadette understood that hers was an apostolate of suffering. A brief glimpse into her diary reveals the concealed gem of her interior life: "My divine Spouse has made me desire a humble and hidden life. Jesus has often told me that I will not die until I have sacrificed all to Him. And to convince

[642] McEachern, op. cit., Loc. 2354.
[643] Ibid., Loc. 573.
[644] Trochu, op. cit., p. 284.

me, He has often told me that when it is over, He alone, Jesus crucified, will console me."[645]

At the young age of 35 years, on April 16, 1879, St. Bernadette died an agonizing death from tuberculosis of the bone. She was canonized by Pope Pius XI on December 8, 1933. Enclosed in a glass casket in the convent chapel in Nevers, France, her incorrupt body sleeps, as it awaits its reunion with her holy soul at the final Resurrection.

What was the secret of Bernadette? She tells us in her own words: "To love what God wills always, to will it always, to desire it always, to do it always: this is *the great secret of perfection*, the key to paradise, the foretaste of the peace of the saints!"[646]

---

[645] McEachern, op. cit., Loc. 330.
[646] Ibid., Loc. 542.

CHAPTER 23

Our Lady Mary,
The Evening Star at Pontmain

"But pray, my children. God will hear you in a short time.
My Son allows Himself to be touched."
—The Virgin of Pontmain

On the cold, snowy and clear starlit night of January 17, 1871, in the little village of Pontmain, the "Evening Star" appeared in France, just as the shadows of night literally and figuratively fell upon the country. What led to this beautiful event is a great lesson to the entire world.

France was suffering a horrendous conflict, the Franco-Prussian War. "The Third Empire of Napoleon III was no match for the Prussians under Bismarck. Paris was surrounded on September 18, 1870. On December 27, the siege began in earnest and the city was under daily bombardment. The Parisians were starving, desperate, and in deadly fear of being blown to bits. People in other parts of France lived in fear of invasion."[647]

By the New Year of 1871, the Germans occupied two-thirds of France. On January 15th, the Prussians were at the gates of Laval. The panic-stricken farmers hid their food and possessions, expecting further Prussian advances. In addition to the sufferings of war, the deadly diseases of typhoid and smallpox broke out. [648]

In these terrible hours of trial, the faithful gathered by the hundreds to beg the Virgin's intercession with her Divine Son, Our Lord and Savior, Jesus Christ. At Our Lady of Victories, at LaSalette, at Lourdes, in their parish churches and in their homes, the faithful prayed their Rosaries fervently, imploringly. Not far from Laval, the village priest of Pontmain, Curé Michel Guérin, who held a great devotion to Our Lady, led the weeping, disconsolate people to pray to the Virgin, under her title *Our Lady of Hope*. "Let us add penance to our prayers, and then we may take courage," the Curé urged his small flock. "God will have pity on us. His Mercy will surely come through the Virgin Mary."

---

[647] Sharkey, *The Woman Shall Conquer*, p. 57.
[648] "The Story of the Pilgrimage." *Sanctuary of Pontmain* website.
[http://sanctuaire-pontmain.com/en/1-01.html]

First Phase of the Apparition:
A "Grand, Beautiful Lady"
and a Triangle of Three Stars

On the evening of January 17, 1871, around 6 p.m. (the hour of the evening Angelus), Mr. Barbedette and his two younger sons, Eugène (12 years) and Joseph (10 years), were working in the barn. When a neighbor lady came to give them news of the war, Eugène walked to the barn door to observe the weather. [649]

Suddenly, the boy stood transfixed. About twenty or twenty-five feet above a neighbor's home, he beheld what he called a *"grande, belle Dame"* ("a grand, beautiful Lady").

The Lady appeared to be between 18-20 years old. Her face was small and beautiful. Her long gown was dark blue, much darker than the blue of the surrounding sky. It fell in loose folds; the sleeves were loose and hanging. She wore soft slippers fastened with golden ribbons. Over her head was a soft, black veil upon which rested a golden crown, which widened toward the top, and a red band wound around it. Her arms were at her sides and the palms of her hands were turned outward. The Lady was smiling at the child.

The father and the neighbor could not see anything, but ten-year old Joseph exclaimed, **"Oh, I see a beautiful Lady!"** and described her dress in detail. The mother, when summoned, also did not see the Lady but, at her suggestion, the family knelt and prayed five *Our Father's* and five *Hail Mary's*. Then they went into the house to eat supper. As soon as supper was finished, the boys rushed back to the barn and then fell to their knees. Three orphan girls from the village boarding school were brought without being told why. Two of them saw the Lady, but a third did not.

As events unfolded that night, it became clear that no adults would see the Vision. What the adults could see, however, were three bright stars forming a triangle, exactly where the children beheld the Lady. The children said the highest star was over the Lady's head, while the other two stars were near each of her elbows. Those three stars were seen by everyone that night—*but they were never seen again.*

Soon, about eighty people from the village had assembled at the barn door. The good Curé arrived, but he did not see the Lady. However, a little boy in ill health, Eugène Friteau, beheld the Vision. Due to his delicate condition, he could not stay long in the cold air. Two months later, he died.

---

[649] Sharkey, loc. cit. It will be noted that all direct quotes and pertinent facts about the Pontmain apparition are taken from the same work (pp. 57-63), with supplemental information from the *Sanctuary of Pontmain* website at [http://sanctuaire-pontmain.com/en/index.html]

A two year-old girl, the little daughter of Boitin, the shoemaker, clapped her hands as soon as she was at the front of the barn door. *"Le Jésus! Le Jésus,"* she happily exclaimed. These were the only words she knew to describe such a sight. Thus, the only visionaries out of the six who could later relate what they saw numbered four—the two Barbedette boys and the two girls from the Catholic orphanage.

Second Phase of the Apparition:
Symbols and a Message Written in Gold

With the arrival of the Curé, a small red cross appeared over Our Lady's Heart. Then the apparition became surrounded by an oval frame of a blue darker than the robe. Four candle holders were attached to the inside frame, two near the bottom sides and two near the top sides. Each holder held an unlighted candle.

The people talked amongst themselves as the children related these wonders. Suddenly, the children announced that the Lady had stopped smiling and was now looking sad. The Curé said, **"If the children only are privileged to behold the celestial vision, it is because they are more worthy than we are."** He then suggested that they pray. Everyone knelt down—some in the barn, some outside. No one seemed to mind the cold or the snow. When Sister Marie-Edouard, one of the sisters from the orphanage, led the Rosary and the people joined in prayer, the Lady smiled again.

As the Rosary prayers grew more fervent, the Vision began to grow larger. As the Lady grew taller, the blue frame extended in proportion, and the stars of the sky appeared to move aside, one by one rearranging themselves outside the frame but beneath her feet.

The children counted forty of these stars, stars visible only to them. Then other stars appeared at a distance from the apparition, coming to fasten themselves to the Lady's dress.

"Oh, there are so many stars the Lady will soon be gilt all over," one of the children cried with excited awe.

When the Rosary was completed, Sister Mary Edouard began the *Magnificat.* Before the first verse was sung, the children exclaimed, **"Something is happening!"**

A plain white band appeared and unrolled itself across the length of the house's roof. It was about a yard wide. Then a stroke of gold appeared. It was a letter of the alphabet.

"It's an *M*!" the children cried. **"And now there is another letter— it's an *A*!"**

The word *Mais* was formed. Other letters appeared. Before the *Magnificat* was concluded, the children read the words aloud: *Mais priez, mes enfants* ("But pray, my children").

At the exact moment the word *priez* ("pray") appeared, Joseph Babin, a villager returning from the neighboring town of Erneé and who had heard the singing, came to investigate, saying, "You do well to pray to the good God! The Prussians are at Laval!"

"If they were at the village entrance, we should have no fear now!" several villagers answered. When this man was told of the apparition, he went to his knees and joined the group in their prayers.

At the Curé's direction, the people now sang the Litany of Loreto. More letters appeared. The next part of the message read: *Dieu vous exaucera en peu de temps* ("God will hear you in a little while").

Next, the *Inviolata* was sung. At the words, 'O Mater alma Christi carissima,' a second line of letters appeared on the white banner. The children read aloud the new words they saw: *Mon fils* ("My son").

Upon hearing the children call out these two words, many began to weep. **"It really is the Blessed Virgin! Yes, yes, it really is she! It is Our Lady!"** the people exclaimed.

As the *Inviolata* ended, the people began to sing the *Salve Regina*. The rest of the sentence appeared and read: *Mon fils se laisse toucher* ("My Son allows Himself to be touched").

Completed now, the entire message read as follows: **"But pray, my children. God will hear you in a short time. My Son allows Himself to be touched."** Although she said not a word, Our Lady's appearance and her golden message, mysteriously written on the white banner, gave hope and consolation to her afflicted children in France.

Third and Fourth Phases of the Apparition:
A Mystical Harp, a Red Crucifix
and the Holy Name of Jesus

At the Curé's suggestion, the people sang the canticle, *Mère de l'Espérance* (Mother of Hope). The smiling Lady lifted her hands to shoulder-level, her fingers delicately moving in time to the hymn, as though she was playing an invisible instrument. At the canticle's end, the children related that the banner with its golden words faded away.

With the beginning of the next hymn, the Virgin's face suddenly became sad again. A red crucifix appeared near Our Lady. The Body of Jesus on the Cross, covered with blood, was clearly seen. As the people sang the words, *"Spare us, O Lord,"* Our Lady took the crucifix in her hands and slightly tilted it toward the children. At the top of the crucifix appeared the words, *Jésus Christ*, in red letters on a small white banner.

A small star gracefully rose from beneath the Virgin's feet, lighting the candle at the lower left of the frame and then the top one. Passing up and over Our Lady, it then lit the candles on the right side. The star moved outside the blue frame, only to rest over the Virgin's head.

Fifth Phase of the Apparition:
Two White Crosses and a Mysterious Veil

As the crowd sang another hymn–*Ave Maris Stella* (Hail, Star of the Sea)–the crucifix disappeared and the Vision again assumed the attitude of Our Lady on the Miraculous Medal, with one difference–on each of the Virgin's shoulders appeared a small white cross, both about eight inches high. When the hymn was finished, the Curé said, "Now let us all say our evening prayers."

When the people began the nightly *Examination of Conscience*, the children noted that a white, scroll-like veil began to rise from beneath the Lady's feet. Little by little, the Virgin was hidden from view, until she disappeared from sight.

It was a quarter past nine. The apparition had lasted more than three hours.[650] Ten days later, the armistice was signed.[651]

Meanings of the Apparition's Symbolism

Theologically-rich treatises could address each symbol and aspect permeating the Pontmain apparition, including but not limited to:

• The three stars (the Holy Trinity; the three theological virtues of faith, hope, and charity).

• The dark blue of Our Lady's dress (the color signifying fidelity to God).

• The forty stars at Our Lady's feet (recalling the Israelites' forty days in the desert, the Holy Family's forty days of seclusion before the Christ Child's

---

[650] A year later, on Candlemas (Feb. 2, 1872), the bishop of Laval confirmed the apparition as supernatural, also approving devotion to *Notre Dame d'Espérance de Pontmain* (Our Lady of Hope of Pontmain). As Sharkey further explains: "The Barbedette barn was converted into an oratory. A great twin-spired church rose on the spot of the apparition, and pilgrims went there in great numbers. As is usual in places where a true apparition from Heaven occurs, cures and conversions took place."

[651] The Prussians, only a few short miles away, never reached Pontmain. For inexplicable reasons, they turned back. The armistice, a prelude to a peace treaty, was signed on January 27, 1871, exactly ten days after the Pontmain apparition. Paris surrendered the next day, and eventually *The Treaty of Frankfurt* was signed May 19, 1871. France, under Napoleon III, initiated the war with Prussia (Germany) and lost it, paying a heavy indemnity, but the bloodshed was over.

Presentation in the Temple, Our Lord's forty days of fasting, the forty days of Lent).

• The four candles (the four marks of the true Church, which is one, holy, Catholic, and apostolic).

• The simple yet eloquent message written on a white banner in gold letters (the traditional liturgical colors of the Christmas season).

• The changes in the Virgin's countenance and in the apparition's development, in clear response to the people's attitudes, actions, and even to particular prayers and hymns.

• The red crucifix and the Holy Name of Jesus Christ, reminding the people of the priceless value of the Precious Blood of Our Savior.

While there is much more that could be said of each "sign," only one other facet will be explained in somewhat greater detail.

Our Lady's seeming play of an invisible instrument recalls the teaching of St. John Eudes, "The mysterious harp of King David…is another symbolic picture of the Holy Heart of Mary…The strings of this royal harp are the virtues of Mary's Heart." He further explained, "**Sacred Scripture tells us that King David employed his harp on four great occasions** and **we see Jesus, the Son of David, using His Mystical Harp [His Mother's Immaculate Heart] to accomplish** *four* **infinitely greater achievements.**"

• First, the mere sound of David's harp "put to flight the evil spirit which possessed Saul." Similarly, Christ uses the virtues of Mary's Heart to free the human race from the evil dominion of Satan.

• "Second, David used his harp to sing many psalms and canticles to the honor and glory of God." Likewise, the Immaculate Heart offers "five types of canticles to praise the most Blessed Trinity." These five canticles are: **1)** of love, "the strongest, purest, most perfect love that ever was or shall be," **2)** of praise and thanksgiving "for the benefits of Divine goodness on behalf of all creatures, for the Blessed Virgin Mary did not limit herself to thanking God for the infinite favors she received from His Hand, but she praised Him unceasingly for the graces He pours on all created things," **3)** of sorrow, anguish and bereavement at the sufferings and the death of her Son, **4)** of triumph for all the victories won by herself as general of the great King's armies over His enemies and, we may truly say, over Himself, having so often disarmed divine vengeance when it stood ready to destroy the world and punish it for its innumerable crimes," and **5)** of prophecy, "to announce the great designs of God for the future…"

• Third, King David used his harp to praise God with joy. "In like manner, Christ, the second David, not only attuned His holy Mother's Heart to praise and bless His divine majesty in every way, but He also induced Mary to seek her joy and bliss exclusively in His praises, and in all the acts she performed for His glory and in His Service."

• Fourth, King David's harp "attracted other men to the praise of God, with hearts full of joy and gladness like his own. So, too, Christ the King attracts innumerable souls to the love and praise of His heavenly Father by the sweet sound of His precious harp–that is, by means of the blessed Heart of His glorious Mother."[652]

The Evening Star, Our Lady of Hope, the Immaculate Heart–Mary chose to implicitly manifest these three titles at Pontmain. The Evening Star guides her children through the darkest nights, so they will not lose their way. Our Lady of Hope teaches us to approach her with confidence. And her Immaculate Heart, as she would later promise at Fatima, is our refuge and the path that leads us to God.

Of Our Lady Mary, the Evening Star, it can be truly said, *"May she be a light to you in dark places, when all other lights go out."*[653]

---

[652] Eudes, St. John. The Admirable Heart of Mary, pp. 73-74.

[653] Tolkien, J.R.R. *The Fellowship of the Ring.* [NY: Ballantine Books, 1982.]: 444. The author paraphrases a line uttered by the character of Lady Galadriel, the Mary-like figure who gave to Frodo a gift of the Evening Star's light, saying to him, *"May it be a light to you in dark places, when all other lights go out."*

CHAPTER 24

The Virgin of Pellevoisin:
Lady of Mercy, Lady of the Sacred Heart

"I choose the little ones and the weak for my glory."
—Our Lady of Pellevoisin

"God has willed that all things come to us through Mary," as St. Bernard of Clairvaux once wrote. That Our Lady always leads us to her Divine Son is proven repeatedly throughout history—in Tradition, in Scripture, and in true apparitions of the Modern Age. Five years after the Virgin came to Pontmain as the Evening Star and Mother of Hope, she again came to France—this time as the Lady of Mercy and of the Sacred Heart.

The story began in Paris when 32 year old Estelle Faguette, lady's maid to the Countess Arthur de La Rouchefoucauld, fell gravely ill in May, 1875. The diagnosis was pulmonary tuberculosis, acute peritonitis, and an abdominal tumor.[654] Estelle would later speak of her intense sufferings, not only of body but of the mind. During her long illness, she often made acts of resignation to God's Will, but then—when worrying about her parents and her orphan niece, of which she was the sole support—she would, as she said, falter in her heart.

"In the first days of September, after having begun alone several novenas, she made what she called her *last will*," notes a late 19th century book in which Estelle's memoirs are included. "A small grotto in honor of Our Lady of Lourdes had just been erected in the park at Poiriers. Estelle wrote a letter to the Blessed Virgin and, as she was unable to take the missive herself, she asked Mademoiselle Reiter to place it at the feet of Our Lady's statue, concealing it well under the stones."[655] Fifteen months later, this same letter would be found among the shrine's stones and brought to Estelle's employer, the countess.[656]

---

[654] *Mary of Nazareth* website. [http://www.mariedenazareth.com/] and [http://www.mariedenazareth.com/7955.0.html?&L=1]

[655] Faguette, Constance Estelle. *Mary All Merciful—Our Lady of Pellevoisin.* [Outremont near Montreal: Juvenate of the Clerics of St. Viateur, ca.1900; Imprimatur 1898]. Edited by the rector of Pellevoisin, Arthème A. Salmon. Contains also the statutes of the Archconfraternity of Our Lady of Pellevoisin and a Brief of Pope Leo XIII. Main page to access the scanned online book: *Early Canadiana Online.*

By December, the doctors had no hope for her. Her employers, carefully tending to her spiritual and physical needs, moved her to one of their homes in Pellevoisin. With a growing abdominal tumor and advanced consumption (tuberculosis), Estelle became so ill that even food and water caused her intense suffering. On February 10, 1876, the doctor said that she had only hours to live. She had already received the last sacraments. Although in great agony, Estelle was perfectly conscious and perfectly resigned.[657]

On Sunday evening, the 13th of February, Estelle requested that a candle be lit for her intentions at the local shrines of Our Lady of Victories and Our Lady of Lourdes. Her requests were honored the next day, Monday, February 14.

When Tuesday morning arrived, the still-suffering Estelle told the parish priest that the Blessed Virgin had come during the night. The priest, knowing that the patient was literally in her last agony, felt she might be hallucinating. On Wednesday, she said the Lady had again returned, this time promising her cure. The priest remained unconvinced. Estelle's anguish continued but, just as she said, it was on Saturday—Our Lady's Day—that she was miraculously cured.

"Fear Nothing; You are my Daughter"

On February 19, 1876, the very day after her health was completely restored, Estelle wrote of what happened to her in the early hours of February 14: "I was trying to rest when suddenly the devil appeared at the foot of my bed. He was horrible, and at once began to make grimaces at me. I had scarcely perceived him when Our Blessed Lady appeared on the other side, at the corner of my bed. She wore a pure white woolen veil, which fell in three folds. I can never describe how beautiful she was; her complexion white and rose-tint, rather pale. Her sweet gentle eyes reassured me somewhat but not completely, for the devil, seeing the Blessed Virgin, drew back, dragging the curtain and the iron rod of my bed. This increased my terror, which became unendurable. I crouched down in bed. [The demon] did not speak but turned his back on me."[658]

"The Blessed Virgin spoke to him sharply: 'What brings you here? Do you not see that she wears my livery and that of my Son?' He disappeared, gesticulating. Then she turned to me and said gently, 'Fear nothing; *you are my*

[http://www.canadiana.org/cgi-bin/ECO/mtq?doc=90956]: p. 6.
[656] Ibid., p. 57.
[657] Ibid., p. 7.
[658] Sharkey, *The Woman Shall Conquer*, p. 66.

daughter.' Then I remembered that from the age of fourteen, I had been a Child of Mary. I now felt less fear."

"Have courage; be patient," the Lady continued. "My Son will allow Himself to be prevailed upon. You will suffer five days longer in honor of the five wounds of my Son. On Saturday, you will either be dead or be cured. If my Son restores you to life, I wish you to publish my glory."

During the next night, the Blessed Mother came again, this time to tell Estelle she would be cured on Saturday "because of your resignation and your patience." However, Our Lady also reproved Estelle for the faults she had previously committed in this regard. They had seemed only small lapses or imperfections, but the grace of the Virgin's presence allowed the sick young woman to understand that any sin offends the good God. Of this revelation regarding her venial sins, Estelle wrote, "I would have longed to cry out for pardon but I could not; my grief overcame me…Oh, how sad I felt."

On the third evening since the first apparition, the Mother of Mercy appeared, again reassuring the mortally-ill Estelle, "By your resignation you have expiated your faults…Your good works and fervent prayers have touched my mother's heart, among others that little letter you wrote to me in September. What moved me were the words, *'See the sorrow of my parents. If I fail them, they are on the eve of begging bread. Remember, then, what you suffered when Your Son Jesus was stretched out upon the Cross.'*"[659] The fourth visitation was very similar to the third. During the fifth appearance of the Virgin Mary, Estelle asked if she should change her state in life.

"One can be saved in every state," the Lady answered. "Where you are, you can do a great deal of good." Then she spoke of what afflicts her most—"the want of respect shown by some people to my Divine Son in Holy Communion and the attitude taken for prayer, when at the same time the mind continues occupied with other things. I say this for people who pretend to be pious." With those words, the Mother of Mercy disappeared—and Estelle found herself cured.

Estelle's Prayer to Our Lady of Mercy

Not only did Estelle immediately write of what transpired in the five days before her wondrous restoration to perfect health, on the same day she also wrote a most beautiful prayer to the Virgin Mary, which we may make our own:

"O my good Mother, behold me in Thy hands. Look with pity on Thy poor servant. Do not permit the designs of Providence toward my unworthy self to

---

[659] Ibid., p. 67.

be frustrated by my infidelity to grace. May Thy Jesus, Who dwelt in Thy Heart, and Who has this day deigned to visit mine, be my salvation and my only support. May He subdue in me that pride which has so often nearly caused my ruin. May He root out of my heart every evil inclination and completely destroy everything that does not tend to His glory and Thine.

"Most Holy Virgin, Who hast shown Thy power by granting me health of body, heal also my soul, so often the slave of sin. O my powerful Protectress, Thou Who art, after God, my consolation, Thou Who didst soothe my pain, Thou Who art the light of my soul, having revealed all my iniquities to me; Thou Who art my treasure, my strength, my joy, the hope of my life and of my eternal salvation, Thou hast said to me: *You are my daughter*.

"Thou canst not then reject my prayers. Deign to grant them and to have compassion on me as beseems the Mother of my God, Who has shown such love and goodness to men. He is their Father; He has appointed Thee their Mother.

"Since Thou hast deigned to place me among Thy own privileged children, obtain for me all the grace necessary for the salvation of my soul. I promise Thee in return, O my good Mother, to do all in my power to become more worthy of Thy favors. Amen."

The Messages of Pellevoisin

Estelle would see the Virgin Mary ten more times before the year's end, with the last apparition occurring on December 8, the Feast of the Immaculate Conception. Though no other person beheld the apparitions, Estelle's ecstasies were witnessed by many credible individuals, from lay people of high station to those in religious life.

What is particularly striking about the 15 Pellevoisin apparitions is Our Lady's solicitude for Estelle's person in her trials of soul and body. While the Virgin gently reproved Estelle in regard to her faults, often with a motherly smile, she also impressed upon her daughter the particular virtues she needed to practice. The Lady would insist that Estelle remain calm, by which she meant holy indifference—that is, a total lack of self-interest—in order to instill in the visionary's soul a greater love and confidence in God. In setting before us the example of Estelle, whose long-suffering eventually led to true resignation and ultimately her marvelous cure, the Blessed Mother was again telling the world that Our Lord knows and loves each one of us, so very intimately.

In the first five visits granted to Estelle before her complete healing, Our Lady not only showed herself as the Mother of Mercy, but also as the terror of demons. As St. Alphonsus wrote in a prayer to the Blessed Mother, "I do not fear devils for thou art more powerful than the whole of hell."

At Pellevoisin, the Virgin Mary again revealed herself as Mediatrix of All Graces. It was in the last few apparitions that Estelle saw drops like rain falling from Our Lady's hands, in a manner similar to the 1830 visions of St. Catherine Labouré.

Above all, however, the Blessed Mother first pointed to Jesus Christ, for at the first apparition she spoke of "the Five Wounds of my Son," and by the last apparition, she would give the Church the sacramental known as the Sacred Heart Scapular.

Just as with any of Jesus' or Mary's expressions or actions as recorded in the Holy Scriptures, a series of sermons could be preached on every sentence uttered by the Virgin at Pellevoisin. Our Lady's words,[660] given below in the order in which she spoke them to Estelle Faguette, were also intended for all poor sinners whom the Immaculate leads to Jesus, Our Lord and Savior:

• "If my Son has allowed Himself to be prevailed upon, it is because of your resignation and patience."

• "I am all merciful and the Mistress [661] of my Son. Your good works and fervent prayers have touched my mother's heart."

• "If you want to serve me, be simple, and let your actions correspond to your words."

• "One can be saved in every state (of life). Where you are, you can do a great deal of good..."

• "What afflicts me most is the want of respect shown by some people to my Divine Son in Holy Communion and the attitude taken for prayer when at the same time the mind continues occupied with other things. *I say this for people who pretend to be pious.*"

• "They will treat you...as a fool, but pay no attention to that. Be faithful to me; I will assist you."

• "Be calm, my child, have patience. You will have sorrows, but I will be with you."

• "His Heart bears so much love for mine, that He cannot refuse me any requests. Through me, He will touch the most hardened hearts."

---

[660] Faguette, op. cit., pp. 22-51.

[661] Here the term "Mistress" is defined by its archaic form—i.e., as a courtesy title for a lady who is held in high esteem and possesses great authority. Our Lady was stating, in a simple manner, the great regard which Her Divine Son has for her.

• "Is not your cure the proof of my power?" she asked, smiling, and then she added, "I am come especially for the conversion of sinners."

• "For a long time, the treasures of my Son have been open; let them pray." Saying this, Our Lady lifted from her breast a white scapular, on which there was the Sacred Heart of Jesus, saying, "I love this devotion." She paused, and then she said, "It is here that I will be honored."

• "Let them pray: I show them the example."

• "I will remember the efforts you have made to be calm. It is not only for you that I ask this, but also for the Church and for France. In the Church, there is not the calm I desire. Let them pray and let them have confidence in me." Growing sad, the Lady then said, "And France, what have I not done for her? How many warnings, and yet she has refused to listen! I can no longer restrain my Son. France will suffer. " Then pausing once more, she said, "Courage and confidence. I have arranged all beforehand. So much the worse for those who may not be willing to believe you. Later on, they will recognize the truths of my words."

• "I choose the little ones and the weak for my glory."

• "You have not lost time today; you have worked for me." (Estelle had hand-made a Scapular of the Sacred Heart, duplicating it as it was shown to her during the visions.)

• "My child, remember my words. Repeat them often; may they strengthen and console you in your trials."

• Of the Sacred Heart Scapular, Our Lady said, "...nothing will be more acceptable to me than to see this livery on each of my children, and that they all must endeavor to repair the outrages received by my Son in the Sacrament of His Love. See the graces I will bestow on those who will wear it with confidence, and who will assist you in propagating it. These graces come from my Son; He can refuse me nothing."

As the Virgin spoke those last words, Estelle saw an abundance of raindrops fall from Our Lady's hands, and in each drop could be read such graces as *piety, salvation, confidence, conversion, health*, and many others.

"What more proper to excite in our hearts both the contrition of our sins and love of God, than the sight of this (Sacred Heart) Scapular with the crown of thorns, the cross, and the jet of blood and water! Pellevoisin is the complement of Paray-le-Monial [the 16th century apparitions of Jesus to St. Margaret Mary Alacoque, wherein Our Lord Himself asked for devotion to His Sacred Heart]...it is also the echo and resumé of the century in which Our Heavenly Queen came to request prayer and penance."[662]

---

[662] Faguette, op. cit., p. 60.

CHAPTER 25

Vision of Silence:

Our Lady of Knock

and the Apocalypse

"And when he had opened the seventh seal,
there was silence in heaven, as it were for half an hour."
−Apocalypse 8:1

When during a downpour of rain, the Virgin Mary, St. Joseph, and St. John the Evangelist appeared in the tiny hamlet of Knock, County Mayo, Ireland, the trio said not a word. The date was Thursday, August 21, 1879, the eve of the octave of the Assumption of the Virgin Mary. [663] Emanating a brilliant light that all could see, the one-time apparition took place outside, at the southern gable of a small church dedicated to St. John the Baptist. Any villagers who saw the light and came to the site beheld the vision, the symbolism of which appears to point to Chapter 8 of the *Apocalypse.*

The Knock events began at seven o'clock that August evening when a 15 year-old girl, Margaret Beirne, was sent to lock the church doors. Upon completing her task, she noticed a brightness over the building. Probably due to the inclement weather, she didn't investigate but hurried home. Mary McLoughlin, the priest's housekeeper, was on her way to visit Margaret's mother, the Widow Beirne, and passed within some distance from the church. Though the skies were grey, she noticed an unusual light by the south gable. In this radiance, she could see three figures of the Virgin, St. Joseph, and a bishop. Walking in the pouring rain to visit the Beirne family, she thought perhaps Fr. Cavanaugh had ordered new statues for the church. While at the Beirne home, she never thought to mention the event.

Between eight and a quarter after the hour, Miss McLoughlin concluded her visit. Mary Beirne, the older sister of the young doorkeeper, offered to walk with her. As they passed the church, Mary Beirne saw the light and the figures, and then asked Miss McLoughlin about the beautiful new statues. As both got closer to the church, Mary noticed the figures were moving and exclaimed, "They are not statues; they are moving. It's the Blessed Virgin!"

---

[663] August 21 is now also the eve of the Feast of the Immaculate Heart of Mary.

"Between the wall enclosing the church grounds and the church itself was an uncut meadow; three persons were seemingly standing on top of the small grass, about a foot or two from the snow-bright gable wall. They could not be statues, as their feet did not press down the meadow grass that supported them." [664] At the suggestion of the practical housekeeper, the awe-struck Mary Beirne immediately ran home to tell her family. Within the next hour, Miss McCloughlin left the apparition to inform Archdeacon Cavanaugh who, to his life-long remorse, did not that evening come to the church.

For his part, Archdeacon Cavanaugh, pastor of the church, was deeply devoted to the Immaculate Conception, and it is said he often referred to the Virgin as "the ever Immaculate Mother of God." [665] He also had a great devotion to the poor souls in Purgatory, for whom in May of that same year, he "commenced to offer one hundred Masses for them; this act of charity he completed on the very morning of the most memorable day Knock was ever to know." [666] Later that day, he visited parishioners in outlying districts, but a heavy drizzle began in the afternoon and by 7 p.m. became a downpour. Exhausted and drenched, Fr. Cavanaugh misunderstood his housekeeper. He would always regret it, but he later reflected, "If I had seen the apparition and if I had been the first to speak of it, many things would have been said that cannot now be advanced."[667]

What the People Saw at Knock

In the small village, word quickly spread, with the result that fourteen people, ranging in age from six to seventy-five, later testified before the Diocesan Commission that they had seen the apparition. Among the fourteen were three children (one girl and two boys), six women, two teenage boys, and three men. A fifteenth witness, Patrick Walsh, lived half a mile away from the church. He reported that about 9 p.m. that night, he saw from his field a great golden light by the church which he did not investigate. When he made inquiries the next day, he was told of the apparition. [668]

What those who did investigate saw that night were three dazzling figures, standing about two feet above the ground but a little distance from the gable. To the left and behind the figures was an altar with a large cross. On the altar, in front of the cross, a young lamb stood, its face toward the west. Around the

---

[664] Delaney, John J. *A Woman Clothed with the Sun.* [New York, NY: Image Book published by Doubleday, 1990]: p. 153.

[665] Ibid., p. 149.

[666] Ibid, p.150.

[667] Ibid., p. 161.

[668] Sharkey, *The Woman Shall Conquer*, p.78.

altar were hovering angels; their wings fluttered and their faces were at all times turned toward the altar and away from onlookers.

Speaking as an official witness, Mary Beirne stated, *"The altar was under the window, which is in the gable and a little to the west near the centre, or a little beyond it…The altar appeared to be like the altars in use in the Catholic Church, large and full-sized. It had no linens, no candles, nor any special ornamentations; it was only a plain altar."*[669]

All three figures were clothed in an indescribable silvery white and, as 14 year old witness Patrick Hill phrased it, "the figures were full round as if they had a body and life. They said nothing; but as we approached them, they seemed to go back a little toward the gable."[670]

"Our Lady's robe, strikingly white, was covered by a large white cloak that fastened at the throat and fell in ample folds to her ankles. On her head was a brilliant crown surmounted with glittering crosses and over the forehead where the crown fitted the brow was a beautiful rose. She held her hands extended apart and upward, in a position that none of the witnesses could have previously seen in any statue or picture, *'in the same position as a priest holds his hands when praying at holy Mass,'"* as one witness phrased it. [671] Her feet were bare, one was slightly poised ahead of the other. The Virgin's eyes were cast upward toward heaven; she seemed to be praying.

At Our Lady's right stood St. Joseph, his hair and beard slightly grey, his head respectfully inclined toward the Virgin. At her left was St. John the Evangelist, vested as a bishop and wearing a short mitre, similar to that of the eastern-rite patriarchs, instead of the taller bishop's mitre of the western Church. Standing at an angle to Our Lady, St. John was also at the *Gospel* side of the altar and the lamb. In fact, Mary Beirne said that "his right arm [was] inclined at an angle outwardly, towards the Blessed Virgin." [672] In his left hand, he held a book, while the index and middle fingers of his right hand were raised, in the manner of a Catholic priest giving a blessing or a speaker who is making a point.

Three of the witnesses (a boy, a young teen man, and a woman) dared to go inside the church wall and right up to the apparition. Young Patrick Hill drew extremely close to the three figures, later saying: "I distinctly beheld the Virgin Mary, life size, standing about two feet or so above the ground." After

---

[669] The Knock Shrine Official Website.
[http://www.knockshrine.ie/witnesses-accounts]
[670] Sharkey, loc. cit.
[671] Ibid.
[672] The Knock Shrine, Ibid.

describing her clothes and positioning, he said, "I saw her eyes, the balls, the pupils, and the iris of each." He moved closer to St. John and looked at the pages of the book, stating, "I saw lines and letters."[673] The written language he beheld was unknown to him.

During the apparition, none of the witnesses spoke to each other, but each responded to it in their own way. The 20 year-old sacristan Dominic Beirne, a brother of Mary's, was so moved that manly tears sprang from his eyes. An older woman, Bridget Trench, was so taken with the Virgin that she cast herself at the Lady's feet, trying to embrace them. But she felt nothing, for her arms seemed to grasp empty air. And so she remained there, on her knees before the Mother of God, praying the Rosary for over an hour.

During the entire time of the apparition, there was no let-up of the teeming rain. Everyone also noticed that the figures themselves and the grass beneath were not wet. Bridget Trench later confirmed she had carefully felt the ground under the Virgin but, despite the downpour and the wind blowing from the south, it was perfectly dry. In addition, unlike other true apparitions, this one did not disappear from sight. Instead, due to the weather and the late hour, the people began to leave, one by one, around 11 p.m. The last to leave was the elderly Bridget who, in her simple faith, did not want to go but believed that the heavenly figures would always remain there.

The Secret of Knock

At Knock, Our Lady appeared as both Queen and Mediatrix. Her hands, as previously mentioned, were raised in the exact manner of a priest saying the Holy Mass. A priest acts as intercessor for the people. At every Marian apparition of the Modern Age, the Virgin has in some way implied her power as Mediatrix. At Knock, so intent was her prayer of intercession, that she kept her eyes uplifted toward the God that she always sees; not once did she look down upon the people.

"The mission of Mary to Knock was not one of rebuke or complaint against the people...Neither was it a call to do penance...No, Mary's mission to her faithful Irish people that day was rather one of compassion and comfort, with an implied admonition, no doubt, of dangers ahead, and the imperative need of prayer," wrote the Very Rev. Jarlath Royanne, O.Cist.[674] But this implied warning was, as we shall see, not only for the good Catholics of Ireland.

"The two saints who appeared with Mary were the two people—next to Our Lord Himself—who were the most closely associated with her while she was in

---

[673] Sharkey, op. cit., p. 79.
[674] Ibid., p. 83.

this world."[675] St. Joseph, her most chaste husband, cared for her and protected her and Jesus. He is the head of the Holy Family, the model of husbands and fathers, protector of virgins, patron of a holy death, and Patron of the Universal Church.

St. John, the only apostle to stand with Our Lady at the Foot of the Cross, was the one to whom Jesus gave His last earthly command, "Behold thy mother."[676] On the day Our Lord died, St. John represented every disciple of Jesus. And so he took the Virgin Mary to his own. In the Church, St. John is known as the Virgin's son in the order of grace, the "beloved disciple," "the one whom Jesus loved," and the apostle of the Sacred Heart, for which cause St. Ambrose said of him, "It is not strange that St. John should have spoken better of the mystery of the Incarnation than the others did; he lived at the source of heavenly secrets."[677]

Recall that at Knock, "St. John was garbed as a bishop and reading from a Mass book. He stood next to the altar on which was the sacrificial lamb. St. John was Our Lady's priest. After the Resurrection, he celebrated Mass for her, renewing the sacrifice of Calvary, bringing her Son down upon the altar."[678] All of these points are imperative, but there is something more to be considered of St. John's role at Knock: In his entire manner, the saint seemed to be stressing a matter of great importance, as though he was reading aloud from the book in his hand.

Therefore, if one wishes to understand the message of Knock, one must read the *Apocalypse*. How is this known? The answer is the living lamb on the altar. Consider that in his *Gospel*, St. John twice records that Our Lord's precursor, St. John the Baptist (for whom the church was named), hailed Our Lord as "the Lamb of God."[679] However, 28 times in the *Apocalypse*, the Evangelist himself refers to the risen Savior as "lamb."[680]

The second hint is the silence of the Vision of Knock. Chapter 8 of the *Apocalypse* opens with this verse: "And when he had opened the seventh seal,

---

[675] Ibid., p. 84.

[676] Jn. 19:27.

[677] St. Ambrose, *De Institutione Virginia*, c. ix.

[678] Sharkey, loc. cit. The author believed the book held by St. John was a Missal, but none of the witnesses made that specific statement. They only said a book; in fact, one account said the letters were written in gold and in a language unknown to the witnesses. Therefore, it is also possible that the book held by St. John was the Holy Bible and that he was pointing to the Apocalypse, as the Apparition's symbolism strongly indicates.

[679] Jn. 1:29, 1:36.

[680] Apoc. 5:6; 5:8; 5:12; 5:13; 6:1; 6:16; 7:9; 7:10; 7:14; 7:17: 12:11; 13:8; 13:11; 14:1; 14:4; 14:10; 15:3; 17:14; 19:7; 19:9; 21:9; 21:14; 21:22; 21:23; 21:27: 22:1; 22:3; 22:14.

there was silence in heaven, as it were for half an hour." We recall that in the Scriptures, the word "heaven" denotes the kingdom of God on earth, the Church—i.e., there was silence *in the Church*, as it were for half an hour. *Haydock's Bible Commentary* (1859 edition) states [of the words] "*there was silence in heaven:* which is to represent as it were a general consternation, and an expectation of dreadful events at the opening of the seventh seal, and when seven Angels stood prepared to sound seven trumpets."

In writing of the *Apocalypse* and the silent message of Knock, the Rev. Fr. James, O.F.M., Professor of Philosophy at the University College of Cork, observed, "The artistry is that of Mary. She would have us see, in the apocalypse of Knock, the eternal issue of that struggle which is the crisis within every other crisis that takes place in time. There are many who do not even know in what that crisis consists; and that is part of the tragedy of the present situation. But it is nothing less than the eternal struggle of the archenemy of mankind for the possession, body and mind and spirit, of a humanity that belongs to Mary."

"To the people of that time, emerging out of a dark night when they had proved their fidelity to the Mass, the sacrifice of Redemption, it was given as a consolation and the poor old woman who expressed her gratitude was the voice of Ireland. But to the people of the present time, confronted with a new menace, the apparition at Knock is a challenge. It is no longer a question of offering the sacrifice of Redemption upon a bare rock, without the externals of religion, but of extending this very sacrifice of Redemption into lives that are fully and militantly Catholic. Catholic in the true balance of prayer and action, of contemplation and apostolate; Catholic in their social as well as their individual activities. To be worthy of the faith of our Fathers, and of the Queen of heaven who has come to us, Knock must become a school where we shall learn **the secret of true sanctity**; then we shall go forth from it in the secure and conscious protection of Mary who is Queen of the Church on earth as she is Queen of the Church in heaven."[681]

And so we return to Fatima, the crown of all Marian apparitions of the Modern Age, where Our Lady gave a Great Secret, of which Sr. Lucia said was in the *Gospel* and the *Apocalypse*, once specifically referring to *Apocalypse* chapters 8-13. If, as it seems, the silent message and symbols of Our Lady of Knock were also doing the same, the Mother of God was alerting us to the knowledge that the half-hour's silence in heaven (the Church) would soon

---

[681] James, OFM, Rev. Fr. James. "The Story of Knock. The Apparition at Knock, 21st August, 1879" in "Knock Shrine Annual," 1950.

begin. It was not until 1917, when the third stage of the Great Revolt against God arrived with the rise of the Bolshevik Revolution in Russia, that the Lord deigned to give the peoples of the world another incentive toward conversion when the Virgin came to Fatima.

Through the hands of Our Lady of the Rosary came the marvelous and unprecedented sign, the Great Miracle of the Sun. While the complete Fatima message, the Great Secret, and the Miracle reveal many dogmatic and doctrinal themes, Fatima's thesis is true devotion to the Immaculate Heart of Mary who, like her figure-type Queen Esther of old, wishes to save God's people from spiritual and physical annihilation. It is through this Immaculate Heart that countless souls in Russia and, later, other nations will be converted and saved. For the sake of our **own** ongoing conversions and that of our fellow sinners, may we heed Our Lady's many requests for prayer *and* sacrifice. As the modern-day battle for souls increases in intensity, it shall certainly be as Sr. Lucia once said, "…the triumph of the Immaculate Heart of Mary will arrive when a sufficient number of people have fulfilled the message."[682]

---

[682] Haffert, John M. *Russia will be Converted*. [Washington, NJ: AMI Press, the publishing arm of The Blue Army, 1956]

CHAPTER 26

The Dominion of the King and Queen

"It is certain that only Jesus Christ, God and Man, is King,
but Mary, as Mother of the King and associated to Him
in the work of divine redemption, participates in His royal dignity."
–Pope Pius XII, Radio Message to Fatima on May 13, 1946

Since veneration of Our Lady's Immaculate Heart honors Our Lord's Sacred Heart, it is probably no coincidence when at Fatima the Virgin Mary first chose to reveal her Immaculate Heart, cruelly pierced by a circle of thorns, during the second apparition in the month of June, the month of the Sacred Heart. With this singular symbolic imagery, the Queen's Immaculate Heart identified with that of her Son, Savior, and King. Pope Pius XII expressed the depths of these mysteries of the King and Queen in the following way: "**Jesus is king** of the Eternal Ages **by nature** and **by right of conquest**; *through* Him, *with* Him, and *subordinate* to Him, **Mary is Queen by grace, by divine relationship, by right of conquest** and **by singular election**. And her kingdom is as vast as that of her Son and God, since nothing is excluded from her dominion."[683]

Jesus, King of the Eternal Ages

"We lisp like children when we speak of things divine,"[684] especially when we speak of the very nature of God. Still, because our faith teaches that Divine Revelation is a world of mystery but not of contradiction, we believe all that God has revealed to us, including the truths about Himself. Jesus is King of the Eternal Ages because in His Divine Nature, He is God, the Second Person of the Holy Trinity, the Alpha and Omega. In the Old Testament, the mystery of the Blessed Trinity was not formally revealed but only foreshadowed, as this book earlier mentioned, in accordance with what St. Bonaventure called "the general law of preparation." This law refers to the way God provided Divine Revelation to make ready the human race for His "undoing of the awful consequences of Original Sin, taken in conjunction with man's response to

---

[683] Pope Pius XII, *Radio Message to Fatima*, May 13, 1946, *Bendito seia*, AAS 38.266. [Emphasis added.]
[684] Smith, *The Teaching of the Catholic Church*, Vol. 1, p. 41.

God's overtures."[685] This "law of preparation" applies to all the truths of Faith, including the Revelation of the Holy Trinity as well as the Lord's plan of Redemption.

The first implicit hint of the Old Testament's "law of preparation" for the revelation of the Triune God appeared in the history of creation when the Lord said, "Let *us* make man to *our* image and likeness."[686] St. Augustine noted similar utterances from God about His plurality: "Behold, Adam is become as one of *us*,"[687] and "Let *us* go down, and there confound their tongue."[688] The triple *Sanctus* of Isaias, "Holy, holy, holy, the Lord God of Hosts," and the triple blessing recorded in Numbers, [689] are also opaque heralds of the sublime mystery of the Holy Trinity, but there are many others.

The law of preparation was also heard in paradise lost, with the Lord's veiled promise of "the woman...and her seed."[690] In His curse upon the serpent, the Lord God uttered the prophecy known as the *proto-evangelium*, the first good news, recorded in *Genesis 3:15*: "I will put enmities between thee and the woman, and thy seed and her seed: *she shall crush thy head*, and thou shalt lie in wait for her heel."

Although our first parents could not know that four thousand years would pass before the fulfillment of the Lord's words, much less understand their full meaning, this first prophecy foretold the Virgin Mary ("the woman") and Jesus Christ ("her seed"). In the *proto-evangelium*, God bound together Mother and Son, the Mediatrix and the Redeemer.

Christ is King by Nature as God and Man

Before His Passion, Jesus made clear His *Divine* Nature when He said, "Before Abraham was made, *I am*."[691] The Second Person of the Holy Trinity, He is "the Word," the Eternally Begotten, consubstantial with the Father. St. John the beloved Evangelist phrased this mystery very simply: *"In the beginning, the Word was with God, and the Word was God."*[692]

---

[685] St. Bonaventure notes this law, which refers to the way God provided Divine Revelation to make ready the human race for His "undoing of the awful consequences of Original Sin, taken in conjunction with man's response to God's overtures." Also see Smith, D.D., Ph.D., Canon George D. *The Teaching of the Catholic Church: A Summary of Catholic Doctrine*, Vol. I [New York: The MacMillan Co., 1959]: p.115.

[686] Gen 1:26 [Emphasis added.]

[687] Gen. 3: 22 [Emphasis added.]

[688] Gen. 11:7 [Emphasis added.]

[689] Num. 7: 24-26.

[690] Gen. 3:15.

[691] Jn. 8:58 [Emphasis added]

[692] Jn. 1:1.

"It has long been a common custom to give to Christ the metaphorical title of 'King,' because of the high degree of perfection by which He excels all creatures,"[693] explained Pope Pius XII, affirming what the Church has always taught: "Christ–our Teacher, our Priest and Redeemer–is our King by reason of His eternal Divinity, but he is also King *as man*."[694] When Christ chose to assume a *human* nature, the Word Incarnate received from the Godhead the royal dignity as the rightful attribute of His humanity.[695]

As the Church also teaches in *Quas Primas*, Christ is King by right of nature as Man because He gave His Life to offer us Redemption. Accordingly, He has the right to rule in the hearts and the wills of men because He has purchased us "with a great price." It is "by His grace and inspiration He so subjects our free will as to incite us to the most noble endeavors."[696]

"He is the *King of hearts*, too, by reason of His 'charity which surpasseth all knowledge.' (Eph. 3:19)...But if we ponder this matter more deeply, we cannot but see that the title and power of King belongs to Christ as Man in the strict and proper sense, too. For it is only as Man that He may be said to have received from the Father *'power, and glory, and a kingdom'* (Dan. 7:14), since the Word of God [Jesus]...has all things in common with Him, and therefore has necessarily supreme and absolute dominion over all things created."[697]

Christ is King also by right of conquest: "But he is King of men by a special title, for we are His subjects by right of conquest. Under the domination of Satan, reduced to the servitude of sin from that fatal moment in which Adam sinned, involving us all in his ruin, we have been freed by Christ from captivity, and we are now justly subject to his salutary rule."[698]

"The Son of God, Who made us, was made one of us: and He rules us as Our King, because He is our Creator, Who made us," said St. Augustine. "As King, He fought for us, as Priest He offered Himself for us...In Him, let us rejoice."[699]

---

[693] Pope Pius XI, *Quas Primas* (On the Feast of Christ the King, December 11, 1925): #7.
[694] Smith, op. cit., p. 63. [Emphasis added.]
[695] Ibid. [Emphasis added.]
[696] Pius XI, loc. cit.
[697] Ibid. [Emphasis in the original.]
[698] Smith, op. cit., p. 64.
[699] St. Augustine's Commentary on Ps. CXLIX.

Christ's Kingdom, As It Should be on Earth

The Kingship of Christ is, above all, spiritual in character and, as Pope Leo XIII declared, it is exercised "by truth, by justice and, above all, charity."[700] Jesus said His kingdom is "not of this world" but it is both spiritual and temporal. On earth, His Kingdom is the Catholic Church, the One Supernatural, Supra-national Society. The Lord's Kingdom reigns within each of the Church's members who live in the state of sanctifying grace: *"For lo, the kingdom of God is within you."*[701]

Christ's Temporal Kingship is also intended to be shared by the rulers of natural governments, because God "wants order in the works of His hands. So the world is meant to mirror forth, however imperfectly, the unity of the Mystical Body in heaven, for the social life [of Heaven] of which we are meant to prepare here on earth," as explained by Fr. Fahey. "Accordingly, the history of the world…turns around the social acceptance and rejection of the Kingship of Christ, and thus the attitude of States to the one supernatural society and to the Indirect Power of the Catholic Church is the keystone of the arch of the world's social order."[702]

"We lost supernatural life by original sin and we need Divine Grace that we may live an ordered life," as Fr. Fahey reminds us, "yet this society proclaims that one can be a good man and true while utterly indifferent to the source of grace, Our Lord Jesus Christ and His Divinity."[703]

In giving our complete fidelity to Christ, we cooperate with His work because "… it is for Jesus Christ as King, in virtue of the work of Redemption which He must accomplish, to conquer His Kingdom and defend His faithful subjects against the enemies who strive to overthrow His reign here below."

Christ's authority in the temporal order "is not here a question of commanding and legislating in view of conducting human society to its common good in the natural order, which belongs to the civil power, but of opposing everything that could hinder **the progress of the supernatural life**

---

[700] Pope Leo XII, *Annum Sacrum,* cited by Canon George D. Smith in *The Teaching of the Catholic Church: A Summary of Catholic Doctrine,* Vol. 1. [New York: The MacMillan Company, 1959]: p. 64.

[701] Lk. 17:21.

[702] Fahey, Rev. Denis Fahey, C.S. SP., B.A., D. PH., D.D., *The Kingship of Christ: According to the Principles of St. Thomas Aquinas* [Palmdale, CA: Christian Book Club of America, 1990 republication. First published in 1931]: pp. 34-35.

[703] Ibid., p. 88.

and the social order consonant with it, and of obtaining from the rulers in the civil order the cooperation necessary therefore. This power forms part of the attributes of the Spiritual Kingship, for it is at its service and is, so to say, its instrument."[704]

His Spiritual Kingship is also "militant and the struggle against moral evil must go on as long as men remain here below exposed to suffering and death, to corruption and sin. Only in eternity shall the triumph be complete, by the victory of the good and the defeat of the wicked...[but] we must keep in mind the twofold aspect of Christ's Headship: the *negative* aspect of His combat against sin and His wearing down of evil, which belongs to His Kingship, and the *positive* one of uniting souls to God, which is the function of His Priesthood."[705]

Upon Christ, therefore, Who is Mediator, Prophet, Priest, Savior and King, all things converge. All creatures are subject to Him, and He offers His Sacred Humanity and Divinity as King and Priest to the Father. "All things are put upon Him," says St. Paul, "...and when all things shall be subdued unto Him, then the Son also Himself shall be subject unto Him that put all things under Him, that God may be all in all."[706]

Why Mary is Queen

Our Lord also gave to the Church and each individual soul His Mother, the Queen of Heaven and the Help of Christians. As Pope Pius XII stated, "Mary is Queen by *grace*, by *divine relationship*, by *right of conquest* and by *singular election*. And her kingdom is as vast as that of her Son and God, since nothing is excluded from her dominion."

• **Our Lady is Queen by grace** because, through the foreseen merits of her Son and Savior, she was preserved from Original Sin from the first moment of her existence. She is the Immaculate Conception, who never committed the slightest actual sin. Our Lady was not only conceived in sanctifying grace, but that grace grew abundantly as her life progressed; it is for this reason that the angel Gabriel saluted her, "Hail, *full of grace*."

• **She is Queen by divine relationship** because God chose her to be His Mother, the cause of salvation. The central and primary truth of Christianity is

---

[704] Ibid., pp. 22, 25.
[705] Ibid., p. 23.
[706] 1 Cor. 15: 28.

the fact that "the Word was made flesh and dwelt among us."[707] That God would become Man was the great secret, "hidden from ages and generations,"[708] until it was manifested at Bethlehem when the Christ Child was found "with Mary his Mother."[709]

Our Lady's relationship to each Person of the Holy Trinity explains her divine relationship. She is the first adoptive daughter of *God the Father*, Who created her highest in grace because she was to be the Virgin Mother of *God the Son*. She is the Virgin Bride of *God the Holy Ghost*, Who "infused into her soul the gifts of grace merited by the Son [Rom. 5:5] and miraculously brought about the conception of the Divine Word in her womb."[710]

• **She is Queen by right of conquest and by singular election** because Our Lady, the New Eve, gave free consent to her office in the mystery of the Incarnation and in the work of Redemption. The fulfillment of the *Genesis 3:15* prophecy of "the woman...and her seed" commenced with the Virgin's *Fiat*, "Be it done to me according to Thy Word."

Of the natural and supernatural unity between the Savior and His Mother, Pope Benedict XV wrote, "To such extent did Mary suffer, and almost die with her suffering and dying Son; to such extent did she surrender her maternal rights over her Son for man's salvation, and immolated Him– insofar as she could–in order to appease the justice of God, that we may rightly say she redeemed the human race together with Christ." [711] Pope Pius XI stated, "From the nature of His work, the Redeemer ought to have associated His Mother with His work. For this reason, We invoke her under the title of Co-Redemptrix. She gave us the Savior, she accompanied Him in the work of Redemption as far as the Cross itself, sharing with Him the sorrows of the agony and of the death in which Jesus consummated the Redemption of mankind."[712]

For all these reasons and more, Our Lady's Kingdom is as vast at that of her Son's. "She shares in His kingdom," says St. Albert the Great, "because

---

[707] Jn. 1:14.

[708] Matt. 2: 11.

[709] Lk 2:16.

[710] Duffner, O.P., Fr. Paul A. "The Queenship of Mary." The *Rosary Light & Life*, Vol. 45, No 4, July-Aug. 1992.[http://www.pacifier.com/rosary-center.org/ll45n4.htm]

[711] Apostolic Letter "Inter Sodalicia," cited by Father Paul A. Duffner in "The Queenship of Mary."

[712] Pope Pius XI, Allocution to Pilgrims from Vicenza assembled in Rome for the Jubilee of the Redemption, Nov. 30, 1933.

she shared in His suffering for the human race." Fr. Garrigou-Lagrange, O.P. echoes the same truth: "Mary was associated with Christ's victory over Satan, sin and death by her union with Him in His humiliations and sufferings. She is, therefore, really associated with Him in His Kingship."[713] Pope Pius XII declared: "It is certain that only Jesus Christ, God and Man, is King, but Mary as Mother of the King and associated to Him in the work of divine redemption participates in His royal dignity."[714]

The Immaculate Heart, Pattern of the Sacred Heart

It is in Our Lady's Immaculate Heart that Divine Love "gathers all the perfections of His divinity…and brings them together in the heart of the august Queen of all angels. It is fitting that, having chosen Mary to be His Mother and having become her Son, Our Lord should establish such a perfect resemblance between Mother and Son."[715]

As St. John Eudes taught, "In His infinite goodness, He also gave her to us to be our Queen, our Mother and our sure Refuge in all our needs. He therefore wishes us to honor her as He honors her and to love her as He loves her."[716]

Finally, there is another sublime consideration of Our Lady's Queenship: It was from the Immaculate Heart that the Sacred Heart drew its own Likeness. As St. John Eudes stated, "His divine love most perfectly draws its own image in His Mother's amiable heart."[717] What a beautiful truth upon which to contemplate—that **Christ traced His very Heart** after the Mother He created.

Since Jesus is King of All Hearts, it follows that Mary is Queen of All Hearts because They are united in all things. And since the Kingdom of Jesus Christ also belongs to Our Lady, it is the one and only Immaculate Heart who still says to us today, "Whatsoever He shall tell you, do ye."[718]

---

[713] Ibid.
[714] "The Queenship of Mary," TIME Magazine, November 8, 1954. [http://www.time.com/time/magazine/article/0,9171,857668,00.html]
[715] Eudes, St. John. *The Admirable Heart of Mary*, p. 107.
[716] Ibid., p. 106.
[717] Ibid., p. 3.
[718] Jn. 2:5.

CHAPTER 27

The Mystery
of the Sacred Heart Devotion

"Take up my yoke upon you, and learn of Me, because I am meek,
and humble of heart: and you shall find rest to your souls."
—Matt. 11:29

In the month of June, in which the Virgin showed the three children her Sorrowful and Immaculate Heart, the Church honors the Sacred Heart of Jesus, Who wishes us to return His love with our own. The most Holy Heart of Our Lord is so intimately connected with our last end, that He gives us many means "to make reparation to His Heart for the neglect of His love, to pay honour to His Heart, to place our trust in His Heart, to grow in our love for Our Father in heaven, to work to establish and extend the reign of His Heart, and to afford Him the occasion of pouring forth upon men the treasures of His Heart."[719] In all these things, the Lord once more demonstrates to us the mysteries of His Will—for God Himself usually chooses to act through mankind.

From whence comes the idea of devotion to the Sacred Heart of Jesus? "It is popularly believed that Devotion to the Sacred Heart of Jesus originated with the revelations which Our Blessed Lord granted to St. Margaret Mary Alacoque and that St. Claude de la Colombière, St. Margaret Mary's spiritual director, was the first to preach that devotion to the people. But this is not true.

"What is true, however, is that the enormous importance of the mission which St. Margaret Mary received from Our Lord Himself and the great zeal with which Father de la Colombière and many other priests of the Society of Jesus labored to fulfill the express desires of the Sacred Heart for spreading of this devotion to the universal Church have unduly obscured the role of St. John Eudes as the Father, Doctor and Apostle of this beautiful devotion."[720]

As St. Gregory the Great had said, "Just as the dove finds nourishment in hollow places, so the simple soul seeks in the wounds of Christ the food that

---

[719] Verheylezoon, S.J., Fr. Louis. *Devotion to the Sacred Heart: Object, Ends, Practice, Motives* [Rockford, IL: TAN Books and Publishers, 1978]: p. 52.

[720] Eudes, St. John. *The Sacred Heart of Jesus.* [New York, NY: P.J. Kenedy and Sons, 1946]: Introduction, xxi.

makes it strong."[721] Church history shows that saints like Bonaventure, Bernard, Francis of Assisi, Mechtilde (sometimes called Matilda), the Venerable Abbot Louis of Bloys, and Gertrude (of whom the latter strongly promoted religious piety to the Sacred Heart) held a special adoration and love toward Our Lord in His Passion. Their constancy was displayed with interior and exterior acts in veneration of His Five Holy Wounds or His Sacred Body pierced with a lance. In fact, "the faithful followers of Christ realized from very early times that the piercing of the sacred side of Jesus on the Cross by the lance of Longinus bore a deep and mysterious meaning, far beyond the mere physical act of a public executioner to assure himself that his victim is dead."[722]

"For a long time, however, the mystic significance of this event was associated only with the origin of the Church of Christ. Just as Eve, the spouse of Adam, had come forth from the side of her husband when God had cast a deep sleep upon him, so the Church, the Spouse of Christ, issued from His sacred wounded side when He had slept in death; for, from the sacred side of Jesus wounded by the lance there gushed forth blood and water, symbols of the origin of the Church of Christ and the fulness of redemption and grace which flowed from His Passion and death upon the souls of men ransomed by His Precious Blood and washed in the waters of Baptism. Thus too, the wounding of the heart referred to in the Song of Solomon–'*vulnerasti cormeum*' (Canticles 4:9)–was thought of in this context as the love of Jesus Christ for His Holy Spouse, the Church."[723]

In the life and mission of St. John Eudes, who studied upon the piety, practices, and doctrines expounded by previous saints, we once again see "the general law of preparation," in which God unveils His plan of redemption according to mankind's response. The truth is that, in a remarkable manner, St. John Eudes drew from Divine Revelation the sprouting seeds of this devotion, carefully tending to them so that, at the proper time willed by God, the flower of the Sacred Heart devotion bloomed.

This saint, who from his earliest years held an ardent devotion to what he called "the Admirable Heart of Mary," was led by the same Immaculate Heart to a closer love for the Sacred Heart of Jesus, Our Savior. This explains why in his writings the saint never separated the two Hearts, and in this he was right. The holy Mother of God always leads souls to her Divine Son. In the words of

---

[721] Migne, Comm. in Cant. Canticor, P.L .79:499.
[722] Ibid, p. xix.
[723] Ibid.

Cardinal Pie, the Devotion to the Sacred Heart of Jesus is "the very quintessence of Christianity and the substantial summary and compendium of all religion."[724]

Object and Acts of the Sacred Heart Devotion

"To designate this threefold *object* of the devotion to the Sacred Heart, St. John Eudes distinguished three Hearts in Jesus, namely, *His divine Heart* (indicating His uncreated love), *His spiritual Heart* (indicating the love of His soul, His human will and higher faculties), and His *corporeal Heart* (indicating the echo of love in the bodily organ which is its symbol and the seat of its emotional warmth). These expressions are no longer in use but they convey a doctrine which has not been altered with the ages. St. John Eudes hastens to add that these three Hearts are but one absolutely single Heart, filled with infinite love for the Holy Trinity and inconceivable charity for mankind; for, he says, the divine Heart of Jesus is the soul, the life and the heart of both His spiritual Heart and His corporeal Heart."[725]

St. John Eudes summed up four general headings of *acts* which constitute this devotion, as follows:

1) To adore the Sacred Heart of Jesus.

2) To praise, bless, glorify and thank Him for His love.

3) To ask pardon for our offenses against His great love and to make reparation for them.

4) To love Him in return for all His love and beg Him to establish within our hearts the reign of His holy love.

"When all this labor of love had been accomplished and the ground so well prepared for worldwide acceptance of this highly important devotion, Our Blessed Lord appeared to the holy Visitation nun, St. Margaret Mary Alacoque, and confided to her the desires of His most Sacred Heart. Jesus Christ Himself picked this saintly religious to be the divinely appointed instrument for the diffusion of devotion to His Sacred Heart throughout the length and breadth of Christendom..."[726]

"Behold this Heart, which has so loved men"

In a series of late 17th century apparitions, Our Lord spoke to St. Margaret Mary Alacoque. In the fourth apparition (also referred to as the "Great Apparition"), He showed to her His Heart, opening with these beautiful words, "Behold this Heart, which has so loved men." For her own part, St. Margaret

---

[724] Cardinal Pie, *Oeuvres Episcopales*, 3, 37.

[725] Eudes, op. cit., p. xxvii.

[726] Ibid., p. xxiii.

Mary wrote, "This Heart was shown me as on a throne of flames, more dazzling than the sun and transparent as crystal, with that adorable wound, and surrounded with a crown of thorns which signified the pricks caused by our sins. And above there was a cross, which signified that from the first moment of His Incarnation–that is to say as soon as this Heart was formed–the Cross was planted in It, and which His sacred humanity would have to suffer during His whole lifetime and His sacred Passion."[727]

In very human terms, the Sacred Heart of Jesus described to the saint His love for mankind, speaking of a love that makes His Heart glow, a Heart that feels grateful for love returned, a Heart that is "sensitive, suffering, compassionate" and a Heart which expresses other human sentiments, like joy, contentment, affliction, and grief.[728]

As a result, many view that the "Heart of Jesus, then, is to be considered under two aspects: both as glowing with love for men and cruelly offended by their ingratitude."[729]

Yet there is much more to this devotion, because it is not only for us that Christ died. The Heart of Our Savior teaches us how to love God the Father and God the Holy Ghost. He teaches us how to love the woman whom He chose to be His Virgin Mother. Finally, He teaches us how to love mankind and even ourselves. So often we hear that mankind is evil and that we were not worth Christ's sacrifice. That is true–we are undeserving. Of ourselves, we are nothing. Still, we are not totally worthless, because we were purchased at a great price.[730] We have no right to squander such a ransom.

Never should we forget our great worth is due only to God Himself, Who "so loved the world that He gave His only begotten Son; that whosoever believeth in Him, may not perish, but may have life everlasting."[731] Jesus is the Word made flesh. We should not forget that the Son's great love–for His Father and for mankind–caused Him to willingly choose to incarnate as God-made-Man and die in reparation for our sins.

No mere man could ever do what Jesus did, for only God could offer to God such a worthy recompense for the multitude of offenses made throughout all time, by all mankind, against the Lord our God. Jesus Christ–the Second Person of the Holy Trinity–chose to live a life of holy poverty and die a most cruel death for our offenses. By doing so, He offers all of us another chance at eternal life. God the Father lovingly allowed this; and so, He sent His Son into

---

[727] Ibid, pp. 2, 17.
[728] Ibid, p. 35.
[729] Verheylezoon, op. cit., p. 15.
[730] 1 Cor. 6:20.
[731] Jn. 3:16.

the world, He accepted His Son's sacrifice and glorified Him. As for us, we can never be grateful enough to the Divine Trinity. We, too, should want to glorify Him.

"Consequently, what we wish to honour in the devotion to the Heart of Jesus is not only His physical Heart but also His spiritual Heart. In other words, His physical Heart, the symbol of His love and of His whole inner life, does not make up the entire object of the devotion; this object also comprises His spiritual Heart, the principle and seat of His love and of His whole inner life."[732] However, as "the Person of Jesus is the general and ultimate object of the devotion, we may also say: it is devotion to Jesus, considered in His Heart, the symbol, principle, and seat of His love; or [in other words] it is devotion to Jesus, viewed in His love, produced and symbolized by His Heart."[733] This view is in accord with St. Thomas Aquinas' principle, which he stated as follows: "Honour is, properly speaking, rendered to the entire person. Even when we honour the foot or the hand of a person, we do not venerate these parts in themselves, but only by reason of the entire person to whom they belong."[734]

Constancy to the Sacred Heart
Needed More than Ever

"The most striking characteristic of the teaching of St. John Eudes on devotion to the Sacred Heart-as indeed of his whole teaching on the spiritual life-is that Christ is always its centre. Through Christ, with Christ, in Christ–*per Ipsum, cum Ipso et in Ipso*–all devotion and all piety achieves its end."[735]

Pope Pius XI, in his 1928 encyclical *Miserentissimus Redemptor* (On Reparation to the Sacred Heart), explained and reinforced the need for this devotion, but consider how much more, in these days, his insight applies: "Now, how great is the necessity of this expiation or reparation, more especially in this our age, will be manifest to everyone who, as we said at the outset, will examine the world, '*seated in wickedness*' (1 Jn. 5:19), with his eyes and with his mind. For from all sides the cry of the peoples who are mourning comes up to us, and their princes or rulers have indeed stood up and met together as one against the Lord and against His Church (Cf. Psalm 2: 2). Throughout those regions indeed, we see that all rights both human and Divine

---

[732] Ibid., p. 26.
[733] Ibid., p. 31.
[734] Aquinas, St. Thomas. *Summa Theologica*. Part III, q. 25, art. 1.
[735] Eudes, op. cit., p. xxix.

are confounded. Churches are thrown down and overturned, religious men and sacred virgins are torn from their homes and are afflicted with abuse, with barbarities, with hunger and imprisonment; bands of boys and girls are snatched from the bosom of their mother the Church, and are induced to renounce Christ, to blaspheme and to attempt the worst crimes of lust; the whole Christian people, sadly disheartened and disrupted, are continually in danger of falling away from the faith, or of suffering the most cruel death. These things in truth are so sad that you might say that such events foreshadow and portend the *'beginning of sorrows,'* that is to say of those that shall be brought by **the man of sin**, *'who is lifted up above all that is called God or is worshipped'* (2 Thess. 2: 4)."[736]

The Pope's words regarding all that the Church and mankind were already suffering by 1928 bear an uncanny resemblance to that which in 1917 the Virgin of Fatima foretold if her requests were not heeded: "[Russia] will spread her errors throughout the world, causing wars and persecutions of the Church. The good will be martyred, the Holy Father will have much to suffer, various nations will be annihilated."[737]

At Fatima, in June—the month of the Sacred Heart—the Virgin succinctly stated, "My Immaculate Heart will be your refuge and *the path that leads you to God*."[738] Once more, the Virgin Mother "stepped in" as Mediatrix between humanity and her Divine Son.

"If anyone love Me, he will keep My word, and My Father will love him, and We will come to him, and will make our abode with him." [739] The two Hearts are inseparable. While the central theme of Fatima is devotion to the Immaculate Heart, it still remains that the Virgin interceded, commanding as our Mother that people must cease offending God and also offer reparation to her Immaculate Heart. Not enough had harkened to the previous loving complaints of Our Lord, Who had kept in reserve for the people of the latter days devotion to His Sacred Heart. And though so many still do not listen, the words of Christ our Saviour will always apply: "If you love Me, keep My commandments."[740]

---

[736] Pope Pius XI, *Miserentissimus Redemptor* (On Reparation to the Sacred Heart, May 8 1928): para. 15.
[737] Ibid.
[738] Sr. Maria Lucia, *Memoirs,* 1976 edition, p. 163. [Emphasis added.]
[739] Jn. 14:23.
[740] Jn. 14:15.

CHAPTER 28
The Precious Blood of Jesus
and the Great Secret of Fatima

"God's goodness is at once the most public of all His attributes
and, at the same time, the most secret."
−Fr. Frederick Faber, The Precious Blood

"Devotion to the Precious Blood is as old as the world, and the devotion to this redemptive and Eucharistic Blood of Jesus is as old as the Church," wrote the Catholic priest, Fr. M. Waltz, in his early 20th century work on the Precious Blood.[741] At Fatima in 1917, Our Lady chose the month of July to give the Great Secret, in its three distinct parts, in the same month in which the Church commemorates the Precious Blood of Jesus. Is there a connection between each of the three parts of the Great Secret and July, the month of the Precious Blood?

The First Secret, which provides the means to save poor sinners of this era from hell, offers a spiritual remedy−i.e., worldwide devotion to the Immaculate Heart of Mary. The Second Secret tells the Pope and the rest of the Church *how to administer the remedy*. It includes two specific requests, conditional prophecies, and gives an infallible promise of robust spiritual health and vitality for the Church and the world when the remedy is given. The Third Secret, insofar as only the Vision is known but not Our Lady's words explaining it, describes what seems to be a particular historic era that will culminate in the Church's Way of the Cross. Where in all this is the Precious Blood of Jesus?

First, let us look again at the initial supernatural manifestations at Fatima, which began with the appearance of an angel. Three times through the spring and late summer of 1916, the angel appeared to three shepherd children, Lucia dos Santos (now Servant of God) and her two younger cousins, Blessed Francisco Marto and Blessed Jacinta Marto. On his first visit, he identified himself as the Angel of Peace, commanded the children to pray with him, and taught them a brief prayer.

On his second visit, the angel appeared suddenly, during the children's afternoon rest on an unbearably hot summer day, admonishing them, **"What**

---

[741] Walz, Rev. M. F. *Why is Thy Apparel Red? Or Glories of the Precious Blood,* [Collegeville, IN: St. Joseph's Printing Office, 1914]: Location 266.

are you doing? Pray! Pray very much! The Hearts of Jesus and Mary have designs of mercy on you. Offer prayers and sacrifices constantly to the Most High!"[742] Telling them that they could make everything they do as a sacrifice offered to God as an act of reparation for the sins by which He is offended, and in supplication for the conversion of sinners, the angel also revealed himself as the Angel Guardian of Portugal. As we have seen in Chapter I, he did not give his name but we can say with moral certainty that he was the great St. Michael the archangel, the Prince of the heavenly host who for 1,000 years has been invoked as Portugal's guardian. The wondrous St. Michael concluded his visit by saying **"Above all, accept and bear with submission the suffering which the Lord will send you."**[743]

Years later, Sr. Lucia wrote in her memoirs that on his third and last visit (which took place about a year before the Great Miracle of the Sun), the angel appeared "holding a chalice in his hands, with a host above it, from which some drops of blood were falling into the sacred vessel. Leaving the chalice and the host suspended in the air, the Angel prostrated on the ground and repeated this prayer three times:

'O Most Holy Trinity, Father, Son and Holy Spirit, I adore Thee profoundly. I offer Thee the Most Precious Body, Blood, Soul and Divinity of Our Lord Jesus Christ, present in all the tabernacles of the world, in reparation for the outrages, sacrileges and indifference by which He Himself is offended. And by the infinite merits of His Most Sacred Heart and those of the Immaculate Heart of Mary, I beg of Thee the conversion of all poor sinners.'

"Then, rising, he once more took the chalice and the host in his hands. He gave the host to me, and to Jacinta and Francisco he gave the contents of the chalice to drink, saying as he did so: **"Take and eat the Body and drink the Blood of Jesus Christ, horribly outraged by ungrateful men. Make reparation for their crimes and console your God."**[744]

Our Lady and the Precious Blood

From the beginning of the Fatima apparitions, focus began with the Holy Trinity, the True Presence of Jesus under the mere appearance of bread and wine, and reparatory prayer and sacrifice. The children were being prepared for lives of increasing atonement for sins, first with sacrifices made of their own accord and later with those which God sent them. This latter type of sacrifice is the kind from which so many people shy away, forgetting that "there is an

---

[742] Sr. Maria Lucia, op. cit., p.156.
[743] Ibid.
[744] Ibid. p. 157.

apostolate of suffering, as well as an apostolate of prayer and labor,"[745] as St. Paul reminds Christians: *For whom He foreknew, he also predestinated to be made conformable to the image of His Son.*[746]

The Holy Trinity prayer (offered three times in succession) is one that we, too, are meant to pray. It is the perfect prayer to offer when in the Presence of the Blessed Sacrament, before or after receiving absolution, when the Host is elevated as Mass, or when at Benediction, before or after our Rosary prayers, and most certainly in thanksgiving after receiving Holy Communion.

The True Presence of Our Lord is the same Jesus Who, in the hypostatic union of true God and true Man, assumed from His Immaculate Mother His own Flesh and Blood. "It is an article of faith that the Blessed Virgin gave to the Son of God that most pure and Precious Blood which the Holy Ghost drew from her virginal veins as from the original source of man's redemption. This body of the Mother of God, in order of nature, was purer than the rays of the sun and, in the order of grace, purer than the blessed Spirits" (the angels).[747]

The 19th century priest, Fr. Frederick Faber explained, "The Precious Blood was *assumed* directly to Our Blessed Lord's Divine Person from His Immaculate Mother. It was not taken merely to His Body, so that His body was directly assumed to the Person of the Word, and His Blood only indirectly or mediately (sic) as part of His Body. The Blood, which was the predetermined price of our redemption, rested directly and immediately on the Divine Person, and thus entered into the very highest and most unspeakable degree of the Hypostatic Union—if we may speak of degrees in such an adorably simple mystery. It was not merely a concomitant of the Flesh, an inseparable accident of the Body. The Blood itself as Blood, was assumed directly by the Second Person of the Holy Trinity."[748]

"It came also from Mary's blood. Mary's blood was the material out of which the Holy Ghost, the Third Person of the Most Holy Trinity, the artificer of the Sacred Humanity, fashioned the Blood of Jesus. Moreover," Fr. Faber continued, "there is some portion of the Precious Blood which once was Mary's blood, and which remains still in Our Blessed Lord…At this moment in heaven, He retains something which once was his Mother's…"[749] Already we receive glimpses of understanding why souls may attain salvation via devotion

---

[745] Walz, op. cit., Location 1490.
[746] Rom. 8:29.
[747] Walz, op. cit., Location 87.
[748] Faber, Fr. Frederick William. *The Precious Blood or the Price of Our Salvation.* [Baltimore, MD: John Murphy and Co., 1860 reprint, 10th American Edition]: Kindle location 470.
[749] Ibid.

to the Immaculate Heart, because "the Precious Blood is the fountain of the plenitude of all graces in Mary, but it is also the source of her power to help us."[750]

The Great Secret Revisited

As this book has already mentioned, the First Secret opened with Our Lady momentarily showing the children a terrifying apparition of hell. Then the Virgin said "so kindly and so sadly: You have seen hell where the souls of poor sinners go. To save them, God wishes to establish in the world to my Immaculate Heart."

"If what I say to you is done, many souls will be saved and there will be peace. The war is going to end; but if people do not cease offending God, a worse one will break out during the reign of Pius XI. When you see a night illumined by an unknown light, know that this is the great sign given you by God that He is about to punish the world for its crimes, by means of war, famine, and persecutions of the Church and of the Holy Father."[751]

Then begins the Second Secret, as Our Lady continued, "To prevent this, I shall come to ask for the consecration of Russia to my Immaculate Heart, and the Communion of Reparation on the First Saturdays. If my requests are heeded, Russia will be converted, and there will be peace. If not, she will spread her errors throughout the world, causing wars and persecutions of the Church. The good will be martyred, the Holy Father will have much to suffer, various nations will be annihilated. In the end, my Immaculate Heart will triumph. The Holy Father will consecrate Russia to me, and she will be converted, and a period of peace will be granted to the world."[752]

A Vision of the Church's Calvary

Like the First and Second Secrets, the Third Secret of Fatima is literal, not symbolic, and it also has two parts. As we have already seen, the Third Secret begins with the words written in Lucia's *Fourth Memoir*, "In Portugal, the dogma of the Faith will always be preserved, etc." At some point, the children saw another Vision (described below by Lucia), but the Church Militant and the world still await the publication of the Virgin's words that describe this mystifying Vision. Let us again look at Lucia's description of it, which indicates a modern-day Calvary for the Church.

"After the two parts which I have already explained, at the left of Our Lady and a little above, we saw an Angel with a flaming sword in his left hand;

---

[750] Waltz, op. cit., Location 109.
[751] Sr. Lucia, op. cit., p. 167.
[752] Ibid.

flashing, it gave out flames that looked as though they would set the world on fire; but they died out in contact with the splendour that Our Lady radiated towards him from her right hand: pointing to the earth with his right hand, the Angel cried out in a loud voice: '<u>Penance</u>, <u>Penance</u>, <u>Penance</u>!' And we saw in an immense light that is God: 'something similar to how people appear in a mirror when they pass in front of it' a Bishop dressed in White 'we had the impression that it was the Holy Father.' Other Bishops, Priests, men and women Religious going up a steep mountain, at the top of which there was a big Cross of rough-hewn trunks as of a cork-tree with the bark; before reaching there the Holy Father passed through a big city half in ruins and half trembling with halting step, afflicted with pain and sorrow, he prayed for the souls of the corpses he met on his way; having reached the top of the mountain, on his knees at the foot of the big Cross he was killed by a group of soldiers who fired bullets and arrows at him, and in the same way there died one after another the other Bishops, Priests, men and women Religious, and various lay people of different ranks and positions. Beneath the two arms of the Cross there were two Angels each with a crystal aspersorium in his hand, in which they gathered up the blood of the Martyrs and with it sprinkled the souls that were making their way to God."

Truly, the Third Secret Vision is a sobering one. It brings to mind what was said by Our Lord, appearing to St. Margaret Mary Alacoque with His Sacred Heart torn and His Body so grievously wounded: "Behold the state to which I am reduced by My chosen people that should have appeased My justice, and that instead persecute Me. If they amend not, I will chastise them severely. I will withdraw the just and the innocent, and immolate the rest in My just anger, inflamed against them by their sins." Christ's warning came to pass in the French Revolution and the 19th century's subsequent revolutions.

As St. Jean-Marie Vianney once said, "The good God asks not for the martyrdom of our body, but asks for the martyrdom of our hearts and wills."[753] Fr. Faber noted, "Each age is a stray sheep from God; and the Church has to seek it and fetch it back to Him…Each age needs persuading in a manner of its own," but as he also observed, "Works of mercy are not attractive to hearts untouched by love."[754]

Then, only a few years before the Fatima apparitions, Fr. Waltz of esteemed memory also remarked, "In our age of luxury and religious indifference, men do not want to be reminded of moral regeneration, of the necessity of struggling against the flesh, the world, and the devil; they do not

---

[753] Vianney, St. Jean Marie. Cited by Fr. Waltz, Location1486.
[754] Faber, op. cit., Location 914.

want to hear of their obligation to use the means of salvation and thus co-operate with God's grace."[755] Finally, St. Paul infallibly stated, "And almost all things, according to the law, are cleansed with blood: and without shedding of blood there is no remission."[756]

The Third Secret is a serious warning for the Church because the Church is the work of the Precious Blood. As Fr. Faber said, "The salvation of individual souls is dependent on the Church. Hence the building up of the Church is one of the grandest works of the Precious Blood. The conversion of nations, the history of doctrine, the holding of councils, the spread of the episcopate, the influence of the ecclesiastical upon the civil law, the freedom of the Holy See, the papal monarchy of ages past, the concordats of the present day, the filial subordination of Catholic governments—all these things alter the face of the spiritual world."[757]

For this particular era of history, the Mother of Mercy again intercedes with her Divine Son. She acts on our behalf to satisfy Divine Justice, save souls from hell, and convert millions to the Faith, so that God will grant the entire world an era of peace. Hidden in all of the Fatima Virgin's requests is the Precious Blood, the secret behind the Great Secret because, as Fr. Faber once wrote, "God's goodness is at once the most public of all His attributes and, at the same time, **the most secret**." The Virgin, fountain of the Precious Blood, is the rightful dispenser of the Precious Blood, the source of all the graces which the Savior channels through the hands of His Virgin Mother. And so it follows that whether for a nation or an individual, it always remains true that "belonging to Mary is a privileged means of belonging to Christ."[758]

---

[755] Waltz, Loc. 334.
[756] Heb. 9:9.
[757] Faber, op. cit., Location 1686, 1688.
[758] Murphy, John F. "The Immaculate Heart" in *Mariology*, Vol. III.

CHAPTER 29

The Exaltation of the Holy Cross:
The Sign That Shall Be Contradicted

"And Simeon blessed them, and said to Mary his mother: Behold this child is set for the fall, and for the resurrection of many in Israel, and for a sign which shall be contradicted; And thy own soul a sword shall pierce, that, out of many hearts, thoughts may be revealed."
–Luke 2:34-35

At Fatima, Our Lady promised that her Immaculate Heart shall be our refuge, and that path that leads us to God. Shortly before she appeared at Fatima, the Angel of Peace gave the children Holy Communion, saying to them: "Take and drink the Body and Blood of Jesus Christ, horribly outraged by ungrateful men! Make reparation for their crimes and console your God."

Two thousand years before, St. Simeon's prophesied "sign of contradiction" was the cross upon which Christ was crucified, sanctifying the very instrument of His torture and death, while piercing the soul of the Immaculate Virgin, so that the thoughts of many would be revealed. It is no coincidence, then, that Our Lady's appearance at Fatima on September 13, when the cloud thrice formed into a pillar that rose like incense, occurred on the eve of the Exaltation of the Holy Cross.

"*Through Thee the precious Cross is honored and worshiped throughout the world.*" Thus did Saint Cyril of Alexandria praise Our Lady on the morrow of that great day, which saw her Divine Maternity vindicated at Ephesus. Eternal Wisdom has willed that the Octave of Mary's Birth should be honored by the celebration of this Feast of the triumph of the Holy Cross. The Cross indeed is the standard of God's armies, whereof Mary is the Queen; it is by the Cross that she crushes the serpent's head, and wins so many victories over error, and over the enemies of the Christian name."[759] St. Cyril was speaking of a day honored since the second century and which should not be forgotten in ours: *The Exaltation of the Holy Cross* on September 14.

There exists a prevailing Catholic tradition that the aged St. Helene, mother of Emperor Constantine, experienced a dream about the Cross of Christ. As a

---

[759] "The Traditional Catholic Liturgy," adapted from *The Liturgical Year* by Abbot Gueranger, *Exaltation of the Holy Cross–September 14.*
[http://www.salvemariaregina.info/SalveMariaRegina/SMR-161/Exaltation.html]

result, the saint felt she was told it was her mission to find it. She then commenced a royal pilgrimage to Jerusalem and, along the way, the truly pious and charitable saint literally assisted many in need. Upon reaching Jerusalem, she was told by Bishop Macarius that all of the holy sites of Jesus had been covered by pagan Roman shrines almost 200 yrs. previously—i.e., the cave of the Nativity in Bethlehem sported an idol of Adonis; the spot on Calvary where Our Lord was crucified had a large marble bust of the idol goddess, Venus, and over the Holy Sepulcher was the idol Jupiter, the king of all the false Roman gods.

In the name of her son, the Emperor, St. Helene ordered the removal of these idols and had the sites prepared for the building of Catholic churches. The excavations led to the discovery of the True Cross on September 14, 326 A.D. The precious Relic was buried in a pit (also called a cistern), near Golgotha (the Place of the Skull), along with two other crosses and scattered crucifixion nails. With the crosses (but not attached to any of them) was also found the writing ordered by Pontius Pilate to be placed on Jesus' Cross. To discern which one of the three was Christ's Cross, the Bishop of Jerusalem "proposed a sure means of confirming which was the True One. They were taken to the bedside of a distinguished lady who was dangerously ill. As the bishop prayed for a revelation, the touch of the True Cross immediately cured her."[760]

The saint entrusted a portion of the True Cross to Bishop Macarius of Jerusalem, who every year thereafter exposed It for the veneration of the people. The second part of the Cross was sent to her son Constantine, who was in Constantinople, where it also was adored by the people. A third part was sent to Rome. Legend also says that at St. Helene's initiative, Constantine had built a most beautiful Church on the very spot in which the Cross was buried. In that particular edifice was placed the Relic entrusted to Bishop Macarius. This church is known as the Basilica of Calvary. Another building which St. Helene ensured was constructed is the Church of the Holy Sepulcher in Jerusalem. The solemn dedication of Constantine's basilica, which enclosed both Calvary and the Holy Sepulcher, took place on September 14, 335 A.D.[761]

Nearly three centuries later, Chosroes, King of Persia, captured the Holy Relic in 614 A.D. However, it was rescued by Heraclius, King of Judea, in 629 A.D. on the anniversary date of the Relic's discovery and the later

---

[760] Birley, A.R. "St Helena—Discoverer of the True Cross (250-330)."
[http://www.brown.edu/Research/Breaking_Ground/bios/St.%20Helena_Flavia%20Julia%20 Helena%20Augusta.pdf]
[761] There are, of course, variations in the legend and some historians today question every part of its veracity. Consistent in all of them is St. Helen's role in the discovery of the True Cross.

consecrations of the two Churches—September 14. According to an adaption of Fr. Gueranger's *The Liturgical Year*, it is stated, "and on his return to Jerusalem, Heraclius, with great pomp, bore It back on his own shoulders to the Mount whither Our Savior had carried It."

"This event was signalized by a remarkable miracle. Heraclius, attired as he was in robes adorned with gold and precious stones, was forced to stand still at the gate which led to Mount Calvary. The more he endeavored to advance, the more he seemed fixed to the spot. Heraclius himself and all the people were astounded; but Zacharias, the Bishop of Jerusalem, said: 'Consider, O Emperor, how little thou imitatest the poverty and humility of Jesus Christ, by carrying the Cross clad in triumphal robes.' Heraclius thereupon laid aside his magnificent apparel, and barefoot, clothed in poor attire, he easily completed the rest of the way, and replaced the Cross in the same place on Mount Calvary, whence It had been carried off by the Persians. From this event, the Feast of the Exaltation of the Holy Cross, which was celebrated yearly on this day, gained fresh luster, in memory of the Cross being replaced by Heraclius on the spot where it had first been set up for Our Savior."[762]

On a related note, Our Lord Jesus Christ instituted the Eucharist on "the eve of Passover, the 13th day of the moon of the month of Abib or Nisan, after the spring equinox, corresponding to our 6th of April; in the year A.D. 34."[763] This means that the Messiah was crucified on the 14th day of the moon, according to the Jewish calendar, yet His Holy Cross was found on the 14th day of the month, according to the Julian calendar.

Glorifying the Cross of Christ

Why, then, is September 14 called on the Church's liturgical calendar the *Exaltation* of the Holy Cross? "To exalt the Holy Cross is to glorify it. The word *exaltare* in Latin means to elevate, to raise to a high place, which is to glorify…It is to proclaim the glory of God in face of the attempt of His enemies to humiliate Him. Our attitude should smash the enemy's attempts to humiliate Our Lord."[764]

The Cross of Christ is and remains the "sign which shall be contradicted" foretold by the aged Simeon, who spoke to the Virgin Mary under the Holy Ghost's inspiration. The cross was the instrument of the most brutal

---

[762] "The Traditional Catholic Liturgy," Ibid.

[763] Meagher, Fr. James L. *How Christ Said the First Mass* [Rockford, IL: TAN Books and Publishers, Copyright 1906 by Christian Press Association Publishing Co., NY. Reprinted several times, beginning in 1975, by Marian Publications, South Bend, IN]: p. 317.

[764] de Oliveira, Prof. Plinio Corrêa. "The Exaltation of the Holy Cross." *Tradition in Action* website.
[http://www.traditioninaction.org/SOD/j194sd_ExaltationCross_9-14.html]

condemnation to death, reserved for the vilest of criminals among the slaves and conquered peoples of Rome. Crucifixion was considered so horrific that Roman law forbade such a death sentence to Roman citizens. However, the Son of God, the Word made flesh, allowed mere men to put Him to death in this way, to make an infinite act of reparation to God the Father, and to redeem us from our sins.

The manner of the Lord's death was foretold by the Old Testament prophets, especially Isaiah, but it was again foretold soon after His Holy Nativity. After Our Lady obeyed the ritual purification, according to the law of Moses, the Infant Jesus was brought to the Temple by the Virgin Mary and St. Joseph, there to be ransomed from the Lord, another Jewish ritual. The *Gospel of St Luke* records what happened:

"And behold there was a man in Jerusalem named Simeon, and this man was just and devout, waiting for the consolation of Israel; and the Holy Ghost was in him. And he had received an answer from the Holy Ghost, that he should not see death, before he had seen the Christ of the Lord. And he came by the Spirit into the temple."

"And when his parents brought in the child Jesus, to do for him according to the custom of the law, he also took him into his arms, and blessed God, and said: Now thou dost dismiss thy servant, O Lord, according to thy word in peace; Because my eyes have seen thy salvation, Which thou hast prepared before the face of all peoples: A light to the revelation of the Gentiles, and the glory of thy people Israel."

"And his father and mother were wondering at those things which were spoken concerning him. And Simeon blessed them, and said to Mary his mother: Behold this child is set for the fall, and for the resurrection of many in Israel, and *for a sign which shall be contradicted*; And thy own soul a sword shall pierce, that, out of many hearts, thoughts may be revealed."[765] The Holy *Bible* (Douay-Rheims translation) includes a footnote explaining the words "for the fall" as follows: "Christ came for the salvation of all men; but here Simeon prophesies what would come to pass, that many through their own wilful (sic) blindness and obstinacy would not believe in Christ, nor receive his doctrine, which therefore would be ruin to them: but to others a resurrection, by their believing in Him, and obeying his commandments."

As St. Andrew of Crete explained in a discourse on the Feast of the Holy Cross: "Had there been no cross, Christ could not have been crucified. Had there been no cross, Life itself could not have been nailed to the tree. And if Life had not been nailed to it, there would be no streams of immortality

---

[765] Lk. 2: 26-35.

pouring from Christ's side, blood and water for the world's cleansing. The legal bond of our sin would not be cancelled, we should not have attained our freedom, we should not have enjoyed the fruit of the tree of life and the gates of paradise would not stand open. Had there been no cross, death would not have been trodden underfoot, nor hell despoiled."

"Therefore, the Cross is something wonderfully great and honorable. It is great because through the Cross the many noble acts of Christ found their consummation—very many indeed, for both His miracles and His sufferings were fully rewarded with victory. The Cross is honourable because it is both the sign of God's suffering and the trophy of his victory. It stands for His suffering because on it He freely suffered unto death. But it is also His trophy because it was the means by which the devil was wounded and death conquered; the barred gates of hell were smashed, and the Cross became the one common salvation of the whole world."

"The Cross is called Christ's glory; it is saluted as His triumph. We recognize it as the cup He longed to drink and the climax of the sufferings He endured for our sake. As to the Cross being Christ's glory, listen to His words: '*Now is the Son of Man glorified, and in him God is glorified, and God will glorify him at once.*' And again: '*Father, glorify me with the glory I had with you before the world came to be.*' And once more: '*Father, glorify Thy name.*' *Then a voice came from heaven: 'I have glorified it and will glorify it again.*' Here He speaks of the glory that would accrue to Him through the Cross. And if you would understand that the Cross is Christ's triumph, hear what He Himself also said: "*When I am lifted up, then I will draw all men to myself.*" Now you can see that the Cross is Christ's glory and triumph."[766]

From His holy Infancy to the choosing and teaching of His Apostles, the whole of Our Lord's earthly life was in anticipation of the Cross and the birth of His Church, His own kingdom on earth. "Why did the Lord spend His public life wandering from place to place? He wanted to train his Apostles like soldiers, accustom them to hardships, drill them by a severe novitiate, harden

---

766 St. Andrew of Crete. "Triumph and Exaltation of the Holy Cross." Crossroads Initiative website.
[http://www.crossroadsinitiative.com/library_article/237/Triumph_and_Exaltation_of_the_H oly_Cross__Andrew_of_Crete.html] The webpage states: "St. Andrew of Crete shows that the feast of the victory and exaltation of the holy cross of our Lord and Savior Jesus Christ was celebrated even in the era of the Early Church Fathers. This excerpt from one of St. Andrew's discourses (Oratio 10 in Exaltatione sanctae crucis: PG 97, 1018-1019, 1022-23) is used in the Roman Catholic Office of Readings on September 14, the Feast of the Exaltation of the Holy Cross. The corresponding biblical reading is taken from St. Paul's Letter to the Galatians (Gal 2:19-3:7-14 and 6:14-16)."

their muscles, strengthen their wills, that they might be prepared later to travel through the nations while preaching His *Gospel*, and to enable them to stand all kinds of trials and hardships, even martyrdom destined for them all, except St. John."[767] Such is the lot of Christ's true Apostles and true disciples.

To perpetually remind us of the True Cross, which the world considers "*a sign which shall be contradicted*," **St. John Chrysostom** said: "Do not ever go out of your house without making the Sign of the Cross. It will be for you a shield, a weapon, an inexpugnable tower. Neither man nor demon will ever dare to attack you, if they see you clothed with this armor." **Origen** declared: "The Sign of the Cross is the invisible armor of Christians. Soldier of Christ that you are, wear this Armor always during the day, and during the night, and everywhere. Without It, do not undertake any task, whether it be sleeping or traveling, resting or working, eating or drinking, be always clothed with this Protective Armor. Adorn and protect every single one of your members with this Victorious Sign. At the sight of this Sign the infernal powers flee scared and stupefied." As **St. Augustine** taught the catechumens: "We must confront the enemy with the Symbol and Sign of the Cross; so that the Christian vested with these weapons may easily triumph over the ancient and prideful tyrant." **St. Athanasius** said: "By means of the Sign of the Cross the works of magic are made impotent; all the enchantments lose their efficacy. By means of It, the impetus of the most brutal will is moderated and pacified."768

Finally, may we always remember: "We make the Sign of the Cross to express two important mysteries of the Christian religion, the Blessed Trinity and the Redemption…By means of the Sign of the Cross, we obtain *God's blessing* and protection from dangers both spiritual and physical…Since it is a sign of God and His crucified Son, the devil fears it, and it is a shield against temptation. The saints used to make the Sign of the Cross when evil thoughts assailed them; many Catholics today follow their example, and we should do the same. In doing so, we put a seal on our foreheads that proclaims: **'I belong to Christ, the King of all.'**"[769]

We adore You, O Christ, and we bless You, because by Your Holy Cross You have redeemed the world.[770]

---

[767] Meagher, op. cit., p. 252.
[768] "The Sign of the Cross—III." *Traditional Catholicism* website.
[http://traditionalcatholicism83.blogspot.com/2007/05/sign-of-cross-iii.html]
[769] Morrow, Bishop. *My Catholic Faith,* p. 377. [Emphasis in the original]
[770] Prayer from the traditional Stations of the Cross.

CHAPTER 30

The Greatest Secret:
Our Imitation of Christ

"Love God, serve God; everything is in that."
−St. Clare of Assisi

At Fatima, the Angel of Peace taught the children this prayer: **"O my God, I believe, I adore, I trust and I love Thee! I ask pardon of Thee for those who do not believe, do not adore, do not trust and do not love Thee."** As members of the Catholic City, how often do we consider the great privileges granted us by Christ our King? At the very moment we became citizens of His Kingdom by baptism, we also became His adopted children. As His children, we received the right and the duty to enter the Christian school of perfection, in which we learn how to pray, study, and act. If we are loving children, we become willing students who learn how to "school our own character to a consistent and persevering practice" [771] after that of our King's, who gave Himself to be our Divine Teacher and Model. Our imitation of Christ in His Life, Passion, Death and Resurrection is the greatest secret of the Catholic City.

The Saints and Their Love of Christ Crucified

"Look at the life of any Saint you like, and you will find an extraordinary devotion to the Passion. It was the distinguishing mark of the Saints; they would not have been Saints without it."[772] This statement is affirmed by the saints themselves, from whom the following quotes offer only a small collection of their testimony:

• St. Alphonsus di Liguori noted that all the Saints cherished a tender devotion towards Jesus Christ in His Passion, emphasizing that it was the only means by which they sanctified themselves.[773]

---

[771] Walsh, O.P., Rev. Reginald, Editor. *Meditation on the Passion.* [Westminster, MD: The Newman Press. Reprinted February, 1963. Compiled from various sources associated with the nuns of the Institute of the Blessed Virgin Mary, with Introduction by Rev. Walsh, O.P. Feb. 23, 1922]: p. 3.

[772] Ibid., p. 6.

[773] Ibid., p. 1.

• St. Augustine proclaimed, "There is nothing more advantageous, nothing better adapted to ensure our eternal salvation, than daily to contemplate the sufferings which Jesus Christ bore for our sake."[774]

• St. Paul wrote, "I judged not myself to know anything among you but Jesus Christ and Him crucified"[775] meaning he meditated on "the love that Our Lord has shown us on the Cross."[776]

• "He who desires to advance from virtue to virtue, from grace to grace, should meditate continually on the Passion of Jesus," said St. Bonaventure.[777]

• At another time, St. Bonaventure showed the Angelic Doctor an image of the Crucified Lord, explaining, "This is my book, whence I receive everything I write, and it has taught me whatever little I know."[778]

• "I found more wisdom in prayer at the feet of the Crucified than in all the books I ever read," wrote St. Thomas as he penned his famous meditation, "The Crucifix: The Book of Life."[779]

• St. Francis of Assisi simply stated, "My book is Jesus Crucified," and often encouraged his brethren to think of the Passion of Jesus.[780]

• St. Terese of Avila said that souls in every state of prayer should think of the Passion. "Life is long and full of crosses and we have need to look on Christ, our pattern, to see how He bore His trials, and even to take example by His Apostles and saints if we would bear our own trials perfectly. Our good Jesus and His most Blessed Mother are too good company to be left [alone]…"[781]

Why the Passion of Christ?

Why did Our Lord choose to suffer so intensely in soul and body? After all, God was under no obligation to assume our nature and to save us. For three principle reasons, the Son of God became Man of His own free will: **1)** to make full reparation to the love and justice of His Father, so deeply offended by mankind's sinfulness and ingratitude; **2)** to redeem us from all iniquity, and **3)**

---

[774] Ibid., p. v, *Introduction.*

[775] 1 Cor. 2:2.

[776] Walsh, op. cit., p. 5.

[777] Ibid., p. 4.

[778] Ibid, p. 5.

[779] Ibid, p.6.

[780] de Liguori, St. Alphonsus. *The 12 Steps to Holiness and Salvation.* Subtitled *From the Works of St. Alphonsus Liguori.* [Adapted from the German of Rev. Paul Leick by Rev. Cornelius J. Warren, C.SS.R. Boston, MA: Mission Church Press under the title *The School of Christian Perfection.* Re-typeset and published under new title in Rockford, IL: TAN Books and Publishers, 1986]: p. 58.

[781] St. Terese of Avila. *The Interior Castle.* [http://www.sacredtexts.com/chr/tic/tic24.htm]: p. 226.

to show mankind the terrible consequences of sin. It is for these three reasons that the earthly life of Christ, from its humble beginnings to its cruel closing, presented Him with a continual martyrdom. His Divine Heart was ever "mourning within Him, its sorrow above all human sorrow."[782]

The saints explain that *suffering gives a certain intensity to acts of the will, which nothing else can give.* An act of the will or of the heart may be strong—but how much stronger it must be in the face of suffering. Human nature shrinks from suffering and dreads it, but not one of the sons of men was ever so sensitive as Our Lord, Jesus Christ, or endured sufferings in any way comparable to His. Our Lord chose the greatest intensity of suffering to prove the reality and depth of His love for us—a love of which we are capable of returning as we learn to subdue **Self**.

All of us experience moments of spiritual solace, in which we feel the sweetness and joy of belonging to Him. Without realizing it, these consolations become "the only delight we crave."[783] God then begins to wean us from them, for we must learn to love the God of consolations rather than the consolations of God.

"We would like to serve the Lord, but in our own way, and not as He desires," as St. Alphonsus notes.[784] To overcome the inclinations of Self, we must pray, study and act on the Passion of Christ. As God weans us with great or small trials, to whatever degree, we soon discover that Self is still strong, with all its subtlety, self-centeredness and weakness—"**Self**, which stands importunate beside us, protesting, crying, wailing, resisting."[785]

Then one of two things happens: either we give into that hurt and smarting Self, which complains, grows bitter, and resists fidelity to God **or** we turn to God in our interior and exterior sufferings. Should we succumb to Self, we deeply hurt Jesus, for as St. Therese the Little Flower said, "What offends Jesus, what wounds Him to the Heart, is want of confidence."[786]

When we take the right course by choosing to turn to God, we "seize the pain or trouble or bitterness, and offer it, turning it into fuel to feed the flame of our hearts, and so we intensify the act of our union and love…"[787] It is when we are suffering that Christ is very near to us. "We always find that those who

---

[782] Jer. 8:18.

[783] Walsh, op. cit., p. 1.

[784] Liguori, op. cit., p. 193.

[785] Walsh, op. cit., p. 2.

[786] *Thoughts of Saint Therese: The Little Flower of Jesus, Carmelite of the Monastery of Lisieux.* [New York: P.J. Kennedy and Sons, 1915. Re-typeset in Rockford, IL: TAN Books and Publishers]:p. 82.

[787] Ibid.

walked closest to Christ were those who had to bear the greatest trials," avowed St. Teresa of Avila.

With our free will, we make the choice whether or not we shall follow in Christ's footsteps with *His* grace or with *our own* grumbling bitterness. Whether we like it or not, carry the Cross we must. **Like the two thieves crucified with Christ**, what makes the difference between our salvation or our perdition is our disposition and inclination to accept grace.

The contrast between the two thieves explains why St. Ignatius advises us, when we even glance at a Crucifix, to ask for a true compassion of the will. This true compassion is **not** only of heart, eyes, feelings or tears, which can mislead us – but consists of a higher, *effective* compassion in which the will is determinedly resigned to whatever God wills or allows. Such a resolve was St. Paul's intention when he wrote, "I...fill up those things that are wanting of the sufferings of Christ, in my flesh, for His body, which is the Church."[788] As the *Douay-Rheims* footnote explains: "There is no want in the sufferings of Christ in Himself as Head: but many sufferings are still wanting, or are still to come, in His Body the Church, and his members the faithful."

"The perfection of religion is to imitate whom you adore."[789] That is why, in bearing the pain of our own crosses, our wills can turn to Jesus Crucified and offer Him all that we are enduring. St. Alphonsus wrote, "The best prayer you can say is to resign yourself to the will of God in the midst of your sufferings, uniting your pains to the pains of Jesus Christ and offering them as a sacrifice to God."[790] If we can make that offering, which is truly an act of the will and not of "feelings," in the face of all kinds of suffering–grief, abandonment, humiliation, mockery, unjust treatment, illness or infirmity–then never is our love for God so true and meritorious.

Charity: The Height of Virtue, the Perfection of Sanctity

In faithfully making the Morning Offering, we also make our first meditation on the Passion because we immediately offer to God, in union with the Immaculate Heart of Mary, the Most Precious Body, Blood, Soul and Divinity of Our Lord Jesus Christ. To this offering, we then unite our every thought, word, and action of the day.

No matter our state in life, meditation on the Passion of Our Lord is good for all persons. The Passion has power to rouse sorrow and penance in sinners, just as "it gives strength and a most powerful example of virtue to those who

---

[788] Col 1: 24.
[789] Pope Pius XII, *Mediator Dei* [November 20, 1946]: para.146.
[790] Liguori, op. cit., p. 193.

are making progress, and it is the most forcible incentive to love for the perfect."[791]

In the school of Christian perfection, the Passion of Our Lord contains all that is highest and most complete in excellence. All of His virtues, all His instructions, all His doctrine, and all His counsels are preached in His Passion. "All the depth of suffering that anyone can undergo, all the extremities of misery to which anyone may be brought–all are in the Passion: all deliverance from illusion and all learning of the truth are in the Passion; all knowledge, understanding, and heavenly wisdom are to be found in the Passion…"[792]

"O my adorable Master," says Dom Chautaurd in *The Soul of the Apostolate*, "there are three sentiments which hold sway in Your Sacred Heart: complete *dependence* upon Your Father, and therefore *perfect humility*; then secondly, *a burning and universal love for men*; and finally, *the spirit of sacrifice*."[793]

"All that I can do I will do for them" was Christ's motto through life. When the hour had come, He did not what benefited Him but what would help us most. Like us in all things except sin, He would meet suffering and death. To be like us in all things, this was His rule from first to last: that **having shown Himself *like us*, He might win us to be *like Him*,** ready to say in the hour of trial, "Father, if thou wilt, remove this chalice from Me; but yet not My will, but Thine be done."[794]

"My soul is sorrowful unto death,"[795] Our Lord so piteously mourned. **And what was the relief?** It was **prayer**, just as He had admonished the Apostles: "Watch ye, and pray that ye enter not into temptation. The spirit indeed is willing, but the flesh weak."[796] The secret of Our Lord's desire to suffer was His Love, but it was not the suffering itself for which Christ longed. No, it was the **result** of that suffering–for that joy that was set before Him–for which He willingly endured the Cross.

Like Him, when we suffer, we suffer for a reason but, unlike Him, we may not know why. Still, like the Angel who comforted Christ in the Garden of Gethsemane, He comforts us: "So also you now indeed have sorrow; but I will see you again, and your heart shall rejoice; and your joy no man shall take from you."[797]

---

[791] Walsh, op. cit., p. 2.

[792] Ibid., p. 3.

[793] Chautard, *The Soul of the Apostolate*, p. 228. [Emphasis in the original]

[794] Lk. 22: 42.

[795] Matt 26: 38.

[796] Matt 26:41.

[797] Jn. 16: 22.

The Holiest of Schools

"It is an excellent and holy practice to call to mind and meditate on Our Lord's Passion, since it is by this path that we shall arrive at union with God. In this, the holiest of all schools, true wisdom is learned, for it was there that all the saints became wise," said St. Paul of the Cross.[798]

How strongly and eloquently the Passion defines charity in all its branches: *"This is My commandment, that you love one another as I have loved you. Abide in my love...You are My friends, if you do the things that I command you."*[799]

Our Lord Himself said, "Greater love than this no man hath, that a man lay down his life for his friends."[800] True Christians have no excuse in forgetting this magnificent lesson of charity, since the loving Jesus set the path before us. The Passion of Christ is the culmination of sanctity, the highest exercise of virtue, and the greatest cause of merit. It is in His Sacred Passion that He specially desires to be remembered by us.[801]

"He that loveth not," says St. John, *"knoweth not God, for God is charity.* By this hath the charity of God appeared towards us, because God hath sent his only begotten Son into the world, that we may live by him. In this is charity: not as though we had loved God, but because he hath first loved us, and sent his Son to be a propitiation for our sins."[802]

God loved us *first*. Charity, the highest of all virtues by which we love God and then our neighbors for love of God, is what moved Jesus Christ to be "conceived by the Holy Ghost, born of the Virgin Mary" and become Man. It is because of Christ's charity that we can truly say, as in Gal. 2:20: "I live in the faith of the Son of God, who loved me and delivered Himself for me."

I Love You *More...*

"The charity of Christ presses us" meaning Jesus' sacrificial love naturally inspires reciprocation, not to mention gratitude. It is not enough to say we love God because love is proven by deeds **and** by a pure intention.

"Forget not the kindness of thy Surety, for He hath given His life for thee, teaches the Holy Ghost in *Galatians 2:20.* St. Alphonsus posed this same truth in the form of a question, one we should ask ourselves, especially when we

---

[798] "Paul of the Cross." (January 3, 1694–October 18, 1775) Taken from a letter written by St. Paul of the Cross. *Wikipedia.*
[http://en.wikipedia.org/wiki/Saint_Paul_of_the_Cross#An_excerpt_from_a_letter_from_Saint_Paul_of_the_Cross]
[799] Jn. 15:12,14.
[800] Jn. 15:1.
[801] Walsh, op. cit., p. v, *Introduction.*
[802] 1 Jn. 4: 8-10.

think of the Passion of Christ: *"And you, Christian soul, what have you done for your Divine Redeemer? What proof of your love have you given Him?"*[803]

Perhaps the best answer to these two questions was given by St. Robert Southwell: "God gave Himself to you; now give yourself to God." By cooperating with grace, by thinking upon the Passion of Jesus, by striving against our natural inclinations, in subduing Self and in returning Christ's love, we say to Jesus, "**I love You** *more...*"–*more* than this consolation, *more* than my self-interest, *more* than my anxiety, *more* than my grief, or *more* than this moment of gratification. To pray, to study and to act upon the Passion of Christ means to cultivate charity within our souls.

In our day and age, we often forget **the true meaning of charity**–that divinely infused virtue by which we prefer God as the sovereign good before all else. It is with charity alone that we can do God's Will and with charity alone that we are united to Him. Charity is called the "queen of virtues," because it will rule forever in Heaven– but before we can hope to attain that Heaven, *charity must first become queen of our hearts.*

---

[803] Liguori, op. cit., p. 54.

CHAPTER 31

Our Lord's Escorts
on the Way of the Cross

"The crosses with which our path through life is strewn
associate us with Jesus in the mystery of His crucifixion."
–St. John Eudes

At Fatima, St. Michael the archangel said, **"Make of everything you can a sacrifice, and offer it to God as an act of reparation for the sins by which He is offended, and in supplication for the conversion of sinners...Above all, accept and bear with submission, the suffering which the Lord will send you."** And to whom should we look for the perfect examples of such charity, other than Our Lord and His Virgin Mother?

Three times had Pontius Pilate attempted to save Jesus' life but, in the end, he delivered Our Lord to the will of those demanding His crucifixion.[804] "And in bearing His own Cross, He went to that place which is called Calvary, but in Hebrew Golgotha."[805]

Along the Via Dolorosa (the Way of Sorrows), Our Lord was accompanied by a great escort of people from all walks of life, each playing a part in Our Lord's Passion. Distinguished from this company are three divisions: **1)** Those who load the Savior with the Cross, **2)** Those who literally carry the Cross with Him, and **3)** Those who spiritually participate with Jesus in bearing the Cross.[806]

• Within the first group are those who lay the cross upon Our Lord. Foremost among this assembly were those responsible for His unjust trial, the tortures that accompanied it, and the death sentence proclaimed against Him. These men, the leaders of the first ecclesia, heard Jesus' holy doctrine, witnessed many of His miracles and signs, and yet refused to acknowledge Him as the Messiah, the Son of God.

On the first Palm Sunday, Christ entered Jerusalem as the city prepared for the Jewish Passover, and all that happened concerning Jesus filled the chief priests and scribes with fury. They were scandalized by the honor shown to

---

[804] Lk. 23: 1-15.
[805] Jn. 19:17.
[806] Walsh, *Meditation on the Passion,* p. 228.

Jesus by the multitude, who strewed both their garments and tree boughs before Him and who praised Him, "Hosanna to the Son of David! Blessed is He who comes in the name of the Lord: Hosanna in the highest."[807]

After Jesus threw the moneychangers from the temple, the lame and blind went to Him and He healed them. "And the chief priests and scribes, seeing the wonderful things that He did, and the children crying in the temple, and saying: Hosanna to the son of David; were moved with indignation."[808]

The Pharisees and the Sadducees would not leave Christ alone. They demanded explanations from Our Lord. Then they devised various tests for Him, and they asked from whence came His authority. He in turn tested them with His question about the source of John the Baptist's authority to baptize. To the ongoing exchanges, Jesus added two parables, which further angered them, for they knew He spoke of them.[809] Finally, they tried one last tactic by feigning goodwill toward His mission, while publicly asking Him cunning questions to ensnare Him before all the people, who "were in admiration of His doctrine."[810]

In their last attempt to trick Him and justify themselves before the people, Jesus severely rebuked them. From that day, as the *Gospel of St. Matthew* records, no man dared ask Him any more questions.[811]

It was on the latter occasion that Our Lord eight times openly described these men and their disciples (the Herodians) as "hypocrites." [812] In the same discourse, He also called them "blind guides,"[813] "foolish and blind,"[814] "whited sepulchers, which outwardly appear to men beautiful, but are full of dead men's bones and all filthiness,"[815] "full of hypocrisy and iniquity," [816] "sons of them that kill the prophets. Fill ye up then the measure of thy fathers,"[817] and addressed them as "you serpents, generation of vipers, how will you flee from the judgment of hell?"[818]

In their sanctimonious rage, they remained silent–but they chose to act quickly and furtively. Soon "were gathered together the chief priests and

---

[807] Matt. 21: 8-10.
[808] Matt. 21: 15. [Emphasis added.]
[809] Matt. 21: 28-46.
[810] Matt. 22:33.
[811] Matt. 22: 46.
[812] Matt. 22:18. See also Matt. 23: 13-15, 23, 25, 27, 29.
[813] Matt. 23: 16, 24.
[814] Matt. 23: 17.
[815] Matt. 23: 27.
[816] Matt. 23: 28.
[817] Matt. 23: 31-32.
[818] Matt. 23: 33.

ancients of the people into the court of the high priest, who was called Caiphas. And they consulted together, that by subtlety they might apprehend Jesus, and put him to death. But they said: Not on the festival day, lest perhaps there should be a tumult among the people."[819]

Those *Gospel* sentences reveal both their craftiness in plotting Christ's death and their over-riding desire for human respect—for it was not God they feared, but the people! It was they, the elders of God's first chosen ones, who plotted and carried out the stealthy and illegal arrest of Our Lord, twisting His words to suit their own purposes, allowing servants to spit in His face and strike Him, accusing the Lord Himself of blasphemy, and stirring up the multitude to a murderous frenzy, demanding Christ's death! Yet, even when they had attained Jesus' sentence of death by crucifixion, they were still not satisfied. These instigators chose to follow Christ to Golgotha, so as to relish and gloat over every moment of His suffering.

Also among this first group were the soldiers and executioners of Rome. They were not down-trodden servants of the empire, forced to comply with an appalling command against one whom even Pilate, their governor, declared a "just man."[820] Rather, these were debased men of the world, their interests malicious and sadistic. They delighted in scourging Our Lord almost to the point of death. Then, by their own volition, they clothed Him in purple, crowned Him with thorns, struck His Holy Face with a reed, spat on Him, insolently knelt before Him and contemptuously adored Him, and eagerly led Him out to crucify Him.

In imitating the men described above, those who lay the Cross upon Our Lord only follow the Way of the Cross because they take a malicious delight in abusing Jesus. Accordingly, such people "are all guilty of His Passion, and increase it by their cruelty and mockery."[821]

They, too, carry a cross, but it is not a cross of faith and virtue. Rather, it is a cross of their own making, formed by their obstinate rejection of grace and loaded with their own sins. They are driven by any one, or more, of the seven deadly sins: pride, anger, envy, greed, gluttony, lust, and sloth. Through their own free will, they become the agents of Satan, "and it is his yoke that they drag along. This is an inglorious cross—a fatal cross, which leads not to redemption, but to eternal death. Whoever does not embrace the Cross of Jesus must bear that of Satan."[822]

---

[819] Matt. 26: 3-5.
[820] Matt. 27: 24.
[821] Walsh, loc. cit.
[822] Ibid.

• In the second group are those who literally carry the Cross with Jesus. "And as they led him away, they laid hold of one Simon of Cyrene, coming from the country; and they laid the cross on him to carry after Jesus."[823] In this escort were also the two thieves who were to be crucified beside Our Lord.

These three men are historical figure-types of souls who initially carry crosses only because exterior forces compel them. The internal reactions of free will to the events on the Way of the Cross determine their individual and eternal fates.

In the case of Simon the Cyrene: This man was returning from the country and had just entered the city gate when the soldiers forced him to take up Our Lord's Cross. The soldiers did not act from a motivation of mercy, but because Jesus' weakness and exhaustion was so great that they feared He would die before He was crucified.

Simon had his own plans for the day, not knowing "that grace was lying in wait for him on the road to Calvary—that hidden in the cross of pain and shame was laid up for him the highest honor and never-ending joy."[824] So, too, we "rise in the morning and make our plans for the day. [But] God has made His for us. Turning a corner, we find the Cross of Christ awaiting us, and with it the grace that, with a little effort on our part, will enable us to bear it bravely after our Master."[825]

So we understand, "It is for Simon's sake much more than for His own that Our Lord shared His Cross with him. The virtue that came from its contact with the Son of God went out to him who followed in His footsteps. Quickly Simon learned his lesson. From bearing the Cross reluctantly, he came to bear it patiently, willingly, joyfully, reaching thus the highest perfection of which love is capable on earth."[826]

As for the two thieves, individuals who spiritually belong to their entourage will interiorly select one of two choices, for there are no others. They will either trace the final steps of the man traditionally known as "Dismas, the Good Thief," thus saving their souls—or they will stumble after the unrepentant thief, cursing fate and mocking Jesus to their last breaths, and thus die in their sins.

In their final choices, both thieves illustrated the final results of grace received or grace rejected. On the bitter Way of the Cross, both Dismas and the Unrepentant Thief saw Jesus fall three times, watched as Veronica

---

[823] Lk. 23: 26.
[824] Walsh., op. cit., p. 231.
[825] Ibid.
[826] Ibid., p. 230.

courageously wiped Our Lord's face, heard Him console the weeping women, and witnessed Christ's meeting with His Mother, the Virgin Mary.

Both were crucified with Jesus—"And they that were crucified with Him reviled Him."[827] Still, the last hours of trial and grace were not yet over for them, and how each interiorly met his final moments were quite different.

As the *Gospel of St. Luke* briefly testifies, the Good Thief's fellow robber blasphemed Jesus, after all three were crucified: "If thou be Christ, save thyself and us."[828]

To the Unrepentant Thief, Our Lord did not respond. Jesus, being God, knew this man resisted His grace. Accordingly, this thief possessed neither compunction of heart nor any faith in Him. Yet the mystery of grace was at work, and the Savior waited—but for what? Christ on the Cross, whose very Presence is grace, awaited the free will reaction from "the other"—Dismas, the Good Thief—whose soul was now stirred to perfect contrition.

"But the other answering, rebuked him, saying: Neither dost thou fear God, seeing thou art condemned under the same condemnation? And we indeed justly, for we receive the due reward of our deeds; but this man hath done no evil. And he said to Jesus: Lord, remember me when thou shalt come into thy kingdom. And Jesus said to him: Amen I say to thee, this day thou shalt be with me in paradise."[829]

In those few sentences, so painfully uttered from his own cross, the Good Thief first reproached the other robber for scorning God and for his lack of pious fear of the Lord, even when death was approaching. With charity and honesty, Dismas included himself when he confessed their sentences as just punishment for their crimes. In doing so, the Good Thief showed his resignation and acceptance of his own cruel end as his penance. He not only defended Jesus as innocent, but he acknowledged Him as the Messiah and called Him "Lord." Finally, he expressed his hope in Jesus, with his humble request of only Christ's remembrance when He came into His Kingdom. And then came the Savior's promise: "Amen, I say to you, this day thou shall be with Me in Paradise."[830]

But what of the Unrepentant Thief? When rebuked by the Good Thief, the unrepentant one had no more words to hurl against Our Lord. He had no defense at all. Rather than follow the just example of the Good Thief, he instead chose to sink into final despair.

---

[827] Mk. 15:32.

[828] Lk. 23:39.

[829] Lk. 23:40-43, [Emphasis added]

[830] Lk. 23:43. [Emphasis added]

Like the Good Thief, he could have repented and confessed his sins. Like the Good Thief, he could have offered his sufferings as reparation for his crimes. Like the Good Thief, his own cross could have become a source of merit—if only he had accepted God's grace. But he did not. In his soul, he turned away from the Lord, and the final grace offered him was lost.

Two sinners, both given the same grace to die alongside Our Lord, to repent and to confess their sins, to seek pardon, to offer their deaths in reparation for their sins, to receive God's forgiveness after confession, to ask the Lord to remember them, to accept the fruits of the Redemption, and to merit eternal salvation. But only one—Dismas, the Good Thief—earned the Savior's promise of salvation.

• Finally, there is the third escort: Those who participate in spirit on Our Lord's Way of the Cross. "And there followed him a great multitude of people, and of women, who bewailed and lamented him."[831]

In the first part of this division, an immense number felt sympathy for Our Lord's fate, and the women openly mourned Him. "This expression of their grief was right, and required great courage, since it was made in the presence and the hearing of Our Lord's triumphant foes. What was imperfect about it was that they regarded Our Lord's Passion as pure misfortune, and bewailed it as such."[832]

Of this assembly, the majority are a type of the souls who feel pity for the sufferings of Jesus, but who lack an *effective* compassion—that is, good deeds. Still, Our Lord receives such tokens of grief and rewards it in His own way, as He did when offering His pity to the women and their children in His prophecy of Jerusalem.[833]

According to Tradition, out of this throng was a woman named Veronica. Of a rare and different type, she displayed her compassion in a small but practical, noble and courageous act. Despite the threatening presence of the first escort, she offered Christ her veil to wipe His beaten and bloody Face. This one service was her confession of faith and fidelity in Jesus, and He rewarded her by miraculously imprinting His Holy Face on the cloth.

Another minority within this group were "all his acquaintance, and the women that had followed him from Galilee, stood afar off, beholding these things." Among them were Joseph of Arimethea, who would beg Pilate for the body of Jesus and laid Him in an untouched sepulchre, and the women who

---

[831] Lk. 23:27.
[832] Walsh, op. cit., p. 231.
[833] Lk. 23: 28-31.

could only show their love for Him in their plans to return to His tomb with spices and ointments.[834]

Finally, we find in this multitude one who stands apart, the holiest of all women–the Virgin Mary, of whom Tradition relates awaited Her Divine Son on the Way of the Cross. "The Son and the Mother meet; but it is as the Redeemer and Co-Redemptrix of the world. The sacrifice that their mutual love increases occupies them entirely…and now His hour has come, the hour of which He had so often spoken to her at Nazareth, the hour that was the subject of such earnest prayer put up together; the hour for which He had promised to strengthen her that, first in privilege as in dignity, she might drink deeper than any other of His chalice."[835]

What, then, do we learn from these escorts on the Way of the Cross? "All of us have a cross to bear, [be it] the cross of sin and passion, the cross of misfortunes permitted by God, or the cross of penance and of love…Whoever we are, willing or unwillingly, we must form part of the escort of our Cross-bearing Savior."[836]

All we have to do is choose the escort to which we wish to belong.

---

[834] Lk. 23: 50-56.
[835] Walsh, loc. cit.
[836] Ibid.

CHAPTER 32

Purgatory: The Doctrine
of God's Mercy and Justice

"Out of the depths have I cried to thee O Lord; Lord, hear my voice. Let Thine ears be attentive to the voice of my supplication. If Thou, O Lord, shall observe iniquities; Lord, who shall endure it? For with Thee there is merciful forgiveness; and by reason of Thy law, I have waited for Thee, O Lord. My soul hath relied on his word; my soul hath hoped in the Lord. From the morning watch even until night, let Israel hope in the Lord. For with the Lord there is merciful forgiveness and with Him plentiful redemption. And He shall redeem Israel from all his iniquities."
—De Profundis, prayer from Psalm 129

In the immediately preceding sections, the topics addressed included the life of ongoing conversion, why there is a need for devotion to the Sacred Heart of Jesus, the Precious Blood, our exaltation of the Holy Cross, our imitation of Christ, and the various escorts of Our Lord during His Passion. Inherent is all this are the four last things: death, judgment, heaven or hell. For the sake of souls living in an age permeated by the modernist heresy, it is not by chance that, at Fatima, Heaven highlighted the Church's doctrines and dogmas so frequently undermined. Perhaps foremost among these ignored truths is Purgatory, a doctrine pertaining to the interior life of the soul and the mercy and the justice of God.

The term, Purgatory, comes from the Latin *purgare*, which means "to purify" or "to cleanse." "The word Purgatory is sometimes taken to mean a place, sometimes as an intermediate state between Hell and Heaven," explains Fr. Schouppe, S.J., author of *Purgatory Explained by the Lives and the Legends of the Saints*.[837]

"It is, properly speaking, the condition of souls which, at the moment of death, are in the state of grace, but which have not completely expiated their faults, nor attained the degree of purity necessary to enjoy the Vision of God."[838] Fr. Schouppe continues, "Purgatory is a transitory state which

---

[837] Schouppe, S.J., Fr. F.X. *Purgatory Explained by the Lives and Legends of the Saints* [Rockford, IL: TAN Books and Publishers, 1986. Republished from the original 1893 edition]: p. 6.

[838] Ibid., p. 7. [Emphasis in the original]

terminates in a life of everlasting happiness. It is not a trial by which merit may be gained or lost, but a state of atonement and expiation."[839]

The dogma of Purgatory reinforces the necessity of the three conversions of the interior life, for "it forms one of the principal parts of the work of Jesus Christ, and plays an essential role in the economy of the salvation of man."[840] We may think otherwise, but sanctity is not impossible, for Jesus Himself encourages and instructs us, "Be you therefore perfect, as also your Heavenly Father is perfect."[841] Neither can we reach spiritual perfection by our own efforts, but "*with* God, all things are possible."[842] For the living, each day of earthly life is "a time of trial, a time of merit for the soul,"[843] and at the very moment life ends, the immortal soul remains in the state in which death claimed it. **While we hope that our merits will gain us heaven, we must also remember that what we deem as only trivial faults are not small in God's eyes**. In considering Purgatory, our frail human nature frequently tends to think only of God's mercy, simultaneously preferring to forget His Justice. Regardless of our personal opinions, God has revealed that His two attributes of Mercy and Justice are never separated.

Like the slightest shadow which must disappear before the sun's bright light, "no shadow of sin can endure before His Face."[844] Souls who depart this life in a state of sanctifying grace are saved and will attain Heaven, but if there is any debt still remaining for absolved sins, any slight lack of perfect charity in love for God or neighbor, then God's Mercy and Justice allows the saved soul to expiate its sins in Purgatory.

Purgatory: A Teaching from Antiquity

From the ancient tradition of the Jews, to the time of Christ and from the earliest days of His one, holy, Catholic, and apostolic Church, "the people of God had no hesitation in asserting the efficacy of prayers offered for the dead in order that those who had departed this life might find pardon for their sins and the hope of eternal resurrection."[845]

With infallible examples from the Holy Scriptures and Tradition, the witness of the early Church, the Holy Ghost makes clear that forgiven sins can and will be atoned, either in this life or in the next:

---

[839] Ibid.

[840] Ibid., p. 3.

[841] Matt. 5:48

[842] Matt 19: 26.

[843] Ibid.

[844] Schouppe, op. cit., p. 4.

[845] Hanna, Edward. "Purgatory." *The Catholic Encyclopedia*, Vol. 12. [New York: Robert Appleton Company, 1911]

• The Old Testament clearly states in *Macabees*, "It is therefore a holy and wholesome thought to pray for the dead, that they may be loosed from sins."[846] This passage tells of an offering of silver "to Jerusalem for sacrifices to be offered for the sins of the dead, thinking well and religiously concerning the resurrection. For if he (Judas of the Macabees) had not hoped that they that were slain should rise again, it would have seemed superfluous and vain to pray for the dead."[847]

• In *Zacharias*, the Holy Ghost speaks of the purification of souls in the next life, "I will refine them as silver refined, and I will try them as gold is tried."[848] Gold and silver are burned in the fire to be freed from dross; similarly, souls are tried and purified in fire by the Lord.[849]

• Our Lord Himself affirms that there is a place of expiation after death, likening it to a prison: "I say to thee, thou shalt not go out from thence till thou repay the last farthing." [850] Jesus refers not to hell, which is eternal, but teaches "distinctly of a temporary place…of purification, where the souls of the just can be freed…and purified for their entrance into heaven."[851]

• Our Divine Savior also reveals: "And whosoever shall speak a word against the Son of Man, it shall be forgiven him: but he that shall speak against the Holy Ghost, it shall not be forgiven him, neither in this world, nor in the world to come."[852]

Repented sins can be forgiven, and expiated in this world or the next, but the sin against the Holy Ghost is the terrible exception of which Christ warned the peoples of all ages–"*persistent impenitence*, the sin of one who rejects conversion and dies in mortal sin. One guilty of this sin can never obtain forgiveness of God, because at the hour of death he continues to thrust God away from him."[853] Let us hear it again: The reason this sin is not forgiven in this world or the next is only because the *individual person* continues to reject God, even at death! Is it any wonder why **Our Lady of Fatima** so often stressed sacrifice for the conversion of our fellow sinners?

---

846 2 Mach. 12:46.
847 2 Mach. 12:43-45.
848 Zach. 13:9.
849 "Sermons for the Feast Days of the Year." *The Sermons of the Curé of Ars* [Long Prairie, MN: The Neumann Press. Republished from the original 1901 edition, 1991]: Part II, p. 10.
850 Matt. 5: 26.
851 "Sermons for the Feast Days of the Year," op. cit., Part II: p. 11.
852 Matt. 12: 32.
853 Morrow, *My Catholic Faith*, p. 151.

• **St. Paul** speaks of the exact way by which souls are freed from repented sins not yet atoned: "For other foundation (sic) no man can lay, but that which is laid; which is Christ Jesus...Every man's work shall be manifest: for the day of the Lord shall declare it, because it shall be revealed *in fire*, and the fire shall try every man's work, of what sort it is. If any man's work abide, which he hath built thereupon, he shall receive a reward. If any man's work burn, he shall suffer loss: but he himself shall be saved, yet so as *by fire*."[854]

The Catholic Encyclopedia (1911 entry on "Purgatory") explains, "While this passage presents considerable difficulty, it is regarded by many of the Fathers and theologians as evidence for the existence of an intermediate state in which the dross of lighter transgressions will be burnt away, and the soul thus purified will be saved."

• **St. John the beloved disciple**, in offering hope and consolation to those who live in the valley of tears and faithfully endure all of life's trials and tribulations, reveals: "And God shall wipe away all tears from their eyes, and death shall be no more; nor mourning, nor crying, nor sorrow shall be any more."[855] In speaking of Heaven, however, St. John also reminds the elect, "There shall not enter into it anything defiled." [856]

• **St. Augustine of Hippo** teaches, "That there should be some fire even after this life is not incredible, and it can be inquired into and either be discovered or left hidden whether some of the faithful may be saved, some more slowly and some more quickly, in the greater or less degree in which they loved the good things that perish—through a certain purgatorial fire."[857]

• Because the doctrine of Purgatory has been held throughout the ages, the **Council of Trent** declared: "Since the Catholic Church, instructed by the Holy Ghost has, following the sacred writings and the ancient tradition of the Fathers, taught in sacred councils and very recently in this ecumenical council, that **there is a Purgatory**, and that the souls there detained are aided by the suffrages of the faithful and chiefly by the Acceptable Sacrifice of the Altar, **the Holy Council commands the bishops that they strive diligently to the end that the sound doctrine of Purgatory**, transmitted by the Fathers and the sacred councils, be believed and maintained by the faithful of Christ, and **be everywhere taught and preached**."[858]

---

[854] 1 Cor. 3: 11-15. [Emphasis added.]

[855] Apoc. 21:4.

[856] Apoc. 21: 27.

[857] St. Augustine of Hippo, cited by William A. Jurgens, *The Faith of the Early Fathers*, Vol. 3. [Collegeville, MN: The Liturgical Press, 1979]: p. 149.

[858] "Decree Concerning Purgatory." The Council of Trent, Session XXV (December 4, 1563). Also see Denzinger, "Enchiridon", #983.

The Fate of Two Souls Revealed

Finally, in recent times, Our Lady Herself referred to Purgatory when, at the first Fatima apparition in May 1917, she was asked by the child Lucia about the souls of two young village ladies who had recently died. The Virgin answered that the first girl, Maria das Nevas, who died when about 16 years of age, was **in Heaven**. But of Amelia, a young woman of 18 years at her death, Our Lady said, "She will be in Purgatory until the end of the world."[859]

The latter disclosure about Amelia's prolonged period of expiation never fails to shock and trouble those who first hear of it. While mere curiosity should not instigate the inquiry, it appears there is one immediate and common question about this revelation:

What did Amelia do? That is, what confessed and forgiven sin(s) committed by a young person (a "teenager" by today's standards), who lived in a remote village without any modern conveniences or amusements, could lead to a Purgatory of such time and duration?

The only answer upon which we can assuredly rely comes from Sr. Lucia when, years later, she was asked by Fr. Thomas McGlynn, O.P, about certain details regarding Amelia. Sr. Lucia's charitable, prudent, and brief response was befitting of a Servant of God: "Amelia was eighteen years old, Father, and, after all, for **one mortal sin** a soul may be in Hell forever."[860]

"Just" **one** mortal sin! Was Lucia's response a delicate hint that it was one mortal sin—obviously repented, confessed, and absolved—for which Amelia would endure a Purgatory incomprehensible to our minds? Did Our Lady make this known to Lucia? If such is the case, it still remains that we do not know the details of Amelia's solitary mortal sin—but neither do we need to know.

Instead, we should consider the reasons why Our Lady allowed to be made public the state of two souls, one who was already in Heaven (a revelation which many overlook) and one who would be in Purgatory until the end of time.

"What is certain is that Our Lady wanted us to know this for our instruction, and it would be foolish presumption to pretend to dispute the judgments of God," observes Fatima historian, Frère Michel de la Sainte Trinité. "He alone, Who intimately knows each soul, the abundance of graces He has given to it, the degree of knowledge it had of its fault and the quality of its repentance, is the judge of the gravity of sin."[861]

---

[859] Sr. Mary Lucia, *Memoirs*, 1976 edition, p. 161.
[860] Delaney, John J. (Editor). *A Woman Clothed with the Sun* [New York: Image Edition, published by Doubleday, 1990]: p. 184. [Emphasis added.]
[861] Frère Michel, *TWTF*, Vol. I, p. 128.

Frère Michel also wisely notes that we may rarely think about Maria das Nevas, the young soul of whom Our Lady said so simply, "She is in heaven." No, we are not inclined to ponder much about Maria, for today we are misled to believe that Heaven is our supernatural "right." Perhaps, too, we make light-hearted jokes like, "Well, at least in Purgatory, I'll be with friends." Yet the sufferings of Purgatory are not objects of jest, for God is offended by sin, and even confessed and absolved sins must be atoned in this world or the next. The agonies of Purgatory are no joke, especially because the straight and sure path to Heaven is made known to us by Christ: "*Pick up your cross daily and follow Me.*"[862]

Should we not first contemplate the teenaged Maria, if only for a few moments, and wonder: How did she fulfill God's Commandments? What heroic virtues did she practice? Did she endure Purgatory at all, or was her soul taken straight to Heaven? Were inquiries ever made about the details of her life or death? Is there anything really known about this young lady, other than her name and age? **Or did her hidden and humble interior life**—in which (as it seems) no one showed interest, even when her glorious state in Heaven became known—**serve as a lesson in itself?** Since it appears no questions about Maria were ever asked, we have no details. What we do have, however, is Our Lady's word that Maria is in Heaven, and that is enough to tell us two simple and beautiful things about Maria—"she was a good girl and a good Christian." [863]

Out of the Depths I Have Cried to Thee, O Lord...
But we do not forget Amelia, who died in the state of grace and is saved, nor should we forget her. It is, after all, our "sacred duty to pray for and make sacrifices on behalf of the Poor Souls in Purgatory."[864]

We call these souls **"poor"** because they can do nothing for themselves, relying always on our charity offered on their behalf; we call them **"holy"** because there is no question that they are among the saved. Cherished by God and assured of their salvation, they can and do intercede for us with their prayers. However, while the poor souls can pray for us, they can no longer gain merit for themselves, and since the saints in Heaven pray for them but cannot acquire any indulgences for them, those who languish in Purgatory rely on the charity of the living on earth.

This is the beautiful "secret" regarding Purgatory, as St. John Chrysostom reminds us, "Not by weeping, but by prayer and almsgiving are the dead

---

[862] Lk. 9:23, Matt. 16:24, Mk. 8:34. (paraphrased)
[863] Frère Michel, op. cit., p. 129.
[864] Schouppe, op. cit., Publisher's Preface, p. xxviii. [Emphasis in the original]

relieved."[865] **It is only we**, the Church Militant, who can obtain many indulgences (plenary and partial) for the faithful departed.[866]

We have **three central means** at our disposal to offer them relief and deliverance: The Holy Mass, the Holy Rosary, and almsgiving (fasts, penances, and sacrifices). For the benefit of our own souls and those in Purgatory, there exist many other highly indulgenced prayers and practices, including but not limited to:

The Brown Scapular of Mt. Carmel: To those who wear this Scapular with devotion, Our Lady promises, "Whosoever dies wearing this Scapular shall not suffer eternal fire." Too, a pious kiss given to the Brown Scapular offers 500 days' indulgence, which we can offer for the Poor Souls.

The Sabbatine (Saturday) Privilege, also granted to those who wear the Brown Scapular: "I, the Mother of Grace, shall descend on the Saturday after their death and whosoever I shall find in Purgatory, I shall free, so that I may lead them unto the holy mountain of life everlasting."

A Thousand Souls (the Prayer of St. Gertrude), by which Christ revealed He would release 1,000 souls from Purgatory, each time the prayer is offered: "Eternal Father, I offer thee the Most Precious Blood of Thy Divine Son, Jesus, in union with all of the Masses said throughout the world today—for all the holy souls in Purgatory, for sinners everywhere, for sinners in the universal Church, for those within my own home and within my own family. Amen." [867]

Since God's generosity can never be out-done, He not only allows all of our offerings to help the souls in Purgatory, but He also grants that these same actions "gain us merit, an increase in sanctifying grace, a higher degree of charity, closer union with God, and thus a higher degree of glory in Heaven for all eternity."[868] There is much more that Our God has revealed about Purgatory, but what is most important is to follow the charitable advice of the eternal Church, and which is so beautifully summarized by St. Augustine: "Forget not the dead and *hasten* to pray for them!"[869]

---

[865] Morrow, op. cit. p. 159.

[866] An indulgence is the remission before God of the temporal punishment due to sins whose guilt has already been forgiven. A plenary indulgence remits all punishment; a partial indulgence remits some part of it. That the Church has the power and authority to grant indulgences is a matter of faith, defined at the Council of Trent, Session XXV, December 4, 1563.

[867] Approved and recommended by M. Cardinal Pahiarca at Lisbon, Portugal, March 4, 1936.

[868] Schouppe, op. cit., Publisher's Preface, p. xxix.

[869] "Sermons for the Feast Days of the Year," op. cit., Part II, p. 13. [Emphasis in the original.]

Secrets of the Devotion
to the Immaculate Heart

"To whoever embraces this devotion, I promise salvation; those souls will be cherished by God, as flowers placed by me to adorn His throne."
—Our Lady of Fatima

"You have seen hell, where the souls of poor sinners go. To save them, God wishes to establish in the world devotion to my Immaculate Heart."[870] Such were the opening words of the Virgin Mother of God when, in July 1917, she revealed to three shepherd children a secret in three distinct parts, known as "The Great Secret of Fatima."

"If what I say to you is done," the Lady continued, "many souls will be saved and there will be peace. The war is going to end, but *if people do not cease offending God*, a worse one will break out during the reign of Pius XI. When you see a night illumined by an unknown light, know that this is the great sign given you by God that He is about to punish the world for its crimes, by means of war, famine, and persecutions of the Church and of the Holy Father."

"To prevent this, *I shall come to ask for the consecration of Russia to my Immaculate Heart, and the Communion of Reparation on the First Saturdays.* If my requests are heeded, Russia will be converted, and there will be peace; if not, she will spread her errors throughout the world, causing wars and persecutions of the Church. The good will be martyred, the Holy Father will have much to suffer, various nations will be annihilated."

"In the end, my Immaculate Heart will triumph. The Holy Father will consecrate Russia to me, and she will be converted, and a certain period [era] of peace will be granted to the world. In Portugal, the dogma of the Faith will always be preserved; *etc.* " (sic)

To this day, Our Lady's requests at Fatima are still not heeded throughout the Church. Instead, it is wrongly insisted that what was prophesied at Fatima is in the past and all that remains of the Virgin's words is a heavily-diluted message: "Pray the Rosary for world peace." Rare are the parish priests who

---

[870] Frère Michel, *TWTF,* Vol. I, pp. 182-183.

advocate the *daily* Rosary or promote the Five First Saturdays of Reparation for the five major blasphemies against the Blessed Virgin (all of which are sins against faith).

The hierarchy of the Church has not, as one collegial body, universally propagated filial devotion to the Mother of God. To eradicate even greater errors (heresies and mortal sins) that would soon spread throughout the world, Our Lady also asked that the Pope and bishops spiritually unite together, on one day, to solemnly consecrate Russia to her Immaculate Heart–but that, too, has not been done. Nor is much attention paid to Our Lady's revelation of what she wanted, made on the very day of the Miracle of the Sun on October 13, 1917: *"Do not offend the Lord our God any longer. He is already deeply offended."*[871]

Centuries ago, Our Lady revealed, *"One day, through the Rosary and the Scapular, I shall save the world."* One ponders why the Virgin made no mention of the Holy Sacrifice, which leads one to further wonder if or when the Mass will one day completely disappear. One can only consider how close is that day when the Virgin Mary, Mother of the Church, shall save the world through the Rosary and the Scapular. Awash with confusion, Her Divine Son's only Church is besieged by the world, where Our Lord is rarely adored in the Holy Tabernacle (if He can be found at all), where the light of Faith is eclipsed, where the faithful cannot easily avail themselves of the Sacraments, where the very words of the infallible Scriptures are revised and updated, where contemporary catechesis is permeated with modernist thought, where mortal sin is rampant, and where heinous crimes are reported daily.

In this insanely inverted world, anything that is even lightly scented as "traditional Catholicism" is odiously distasteful to the olfactory senses of the rationalist, whether it be articles of faith, dogmas, doctrines, sacraments, sacramentals, and other long-standing beliefs, prayers, and practices of the Church. All this is only a part of the Church's persecutions, which the Virgin foretold at Fatima. History proves that, with the exception of the annihilation of nations and the Third Secret (which may yet be fulfilled), all which Our Lady of Fatima prophesied came to pass.

In different degrees, the Church is everywhere persecuted. Good people are still being martyred, but we do not hear of that in mainstream news. In the more "fortunate" countries, the persecution comes in different forms. Catechesis for the laity and the training of priests, nuns, and other religious has

---

[871] Our Lady of the Rosary at Fatima, October 13, 1917, as recorded by the visionary Sr. Mary Lucia, *Memoirs*, 1976 edition, p. 173.

long been doctrinally diluted, with disastrous results. While parishes are closing, bishops and pastors "circle the wagons" against the Tridentine Rite of Liturgy, feigning obedience to the Pope whilst simultaneously seeking loopholes in *Summorum Pontificum*, Pope Benedict XVI's *Motu Propio*, dated July 7, 2007.

An increasing number of Catholics attend Mass for the "fellowship," but they do not believe in Transubstantiation—i.e., that Christ is truly present (Body, Blood, Soul, and Divinity) in the Holy Eucharist. Those who do believe in the efficacy of the Sacraments are forced into the uncomfortable position of examining the form, matter, and priestly intent. Many Catholics wrongly disregard their absolute need for the Sacraments of Confession and Holy Communion. On the other side of the same coin, many priests fail to acquiesce to requests for Extreme Unction or the baptism of newborn babies in danger of death [872]—and the list goes on and on.

Attending the Holy Sacrifice of the Mass on Sundays and Holy Days of Obligation are for "those *really* Catholic" people. Those who do wish to avail themselves of Confession and seek pardon and absolution frequently find the sacrament is available only once a week (and usually allotted to a total of 30 minutes for one priest to hear all those waiting in the confessional line). Catholics who confess on a weekly or bi-weekly schedule may find themselves harshly dismissed by the priest in the confessional and told that their habitual practice of Confession reveals that the said penitent does not trust the Lord. Pedophile or otherwise lascivious "priests" are protected but "tradition-friendly" priests, while sought out by the laity, either learn to hide their "leanings" or are inevitably assigned to the most dangerous parts of cities or booted to the boondocks by their bishops.

From the pulpit, the souls of Catholics who receive Our Lord on the tongue are publicly, unjustly and artfully shamed by their own priests who falsely accuse them of possessing "reserved hearts that are closed to others." Convicted of lacking in charity towards their neighbor (based solely on the reverent position of their hands while receiving Holy Communion), those who physically display a proper attitude of reverence are admonished that they are only concerned about their own relationship with Christ (the accuser conveniently ignoring the first Great Commandment which declares that

---

[872] In an emergency, lay people (Catholic or not) may baptize another with regular water (if holy water is not available), as long as the one baptizing shares the Church's intent to baptize. The water (holy or plain) is poured over the recipient's forehead, and the proper words are said as the water is administered, "I baptize thee in the name of the Father, and of the Son, and of the Holy Ghost."

charity is first aimed toward God and secondly, that God has always taught our first obligation is to save our own souls). Meanwhile, those who receive the consecrated Host in outstretched hands (regardless of the fact that many actually chew the Body of Christ like a piece of gum that must be hastily swallowed) are praised for having "hearts that are open to others." (And lest we forget, those who kneel for Holy Communion are often maliciously treated by the officiating priest, forced to stand—or otherwise denied the Body of Christ.)

Daily prayer and sacrifice are incorrectly perceived as practices for the overly-pious. Praying the daily Rosary is wrongly considered to be either much too difficult or appeals only to religious fanatics (often called "fundamentalists"). Again, in mainstream Catholic parishes, the First Friday and First Saturday devotions are rarely found. As for wearing the Brown Scapular of Mt. Carmel, the Miraculous Medal, or other Church-approved sacramentals, the faithful are too often and wrongfully told that they are not necessary and/or that those "old-fashioned things" are worn by people who either think they are "holier-than-thou" or are judged by others to be "off the deep end."

Tragically, many a poor soul succumbs to these and other erroneous notions, conned by a false conception of holy obedience or humiliated into compliance by fear of human respect. Some flee the Church and never return. Others, through some mysterious grace of Faith, endure. Among the latter, God will lead them to learn that everything previously mentioned (traditional catechesis, the Tridentine Rite of Liturgy, prayer, sacrifice, regular reception of the Sacraments, respectful posture and gestures when receiving Christ in the Eucharist, the right use of sacramentals like blessed medals, scapulars, and holy water, the habitual practice of the virtue of charity—first to God, secondly to neighbor—and standing patiently firm against the temptation to conform to the onslaughts of the misinformed or the spiteful) constitutes their fidelity to their daily duty *as Catholics*.

Is it any wonder, then, that Jesus Christ spoke of "daily duty" to Sr. Lucia, of which she wrote, "He (Our Lord) wishes that it be made clear to souls that the true penance He wants and requires consists first of all in the sacrifice that each one must make to fulfill his own religious and temporal duties"?[873] In other words, Our Lord made it clear that our "true penance" would be the faithful fulfillment of our loving obligations *to* Him and *in* our states in life. In this day, to accomplish our daily duty *as Catholics* means practice of all the virtues to a heroic degree.

---

[873] Frère Michel, *TWTF*, Vol. III, pp. 20-21.

Why Devotion to the Immaculate Heart?

What is the cure to these ongoing disasters? Why does the Lord God wish to save poor sinners from eternal perdition by establishing world devotion to the Immaculate Heart of Mary? Our Lady herself gave the answer when she said to the three children (and through them, to each one of us), "*Are you suffering a great deal? I will never abandon you. My Immaculate Heart will be your refuge and the path that leads you to God.*"[874]

Mary, the Mother of God, is also the true Mother of all men and Queen of all Hearts. We have already seen that Pope Pius XII expressed the depths of these mysteries of the King and Queen in the following way: "Jesus is King of the Eternal Ages by nature and by right of conquest; *through* Him, *with* Him, and *subordinate* to Him, Mary is Queen by grace, by divine relationship, by right of conquest, and by singular election. And her kingdom is as vast as that of Her Son and God, *since nothing is excluded from Her dominion.*"[875]

Our Lady Mother and Queen promises each one of us that her Immaculate Heart will be our *refuge*–i.e., our sanctuary, our safe haven, our place of shelter and retreat. She further promises that this same sanctuary is "the path that leads you to God." Like the secret that God would become Man was "hidden from ages and generations"[876] until it was publicly manifested at Bethlehem when the Christ Child was found "with Mary his Mother,"[877] the devotion to the Immaculate Heart of Mary is found in the Deposit of Faith. It, too, falls under what St. Bonaventure called "the general law of preparation."

It has been heretofore mentioned that this law refers to the way God provided Divine Revelation to make ready the human race for His "undoing of the awful consequences of Original sin taken in conjunction with *man's response to God's overtures.*"[878] With those last five words, we are given an important reminder about **free will**, which is the faculty of choice.

At Fatima, Our Lady emphasized that *people* must stop offending the Lord God. She did not mark any office or class as that which most offends the Holy Trinity; she neither placed all the blame on the hierarchy nor on the laity. She simply said "people." May we always remember that and do as she asks.

---

[874] Sr. Mary Lucia, op. cit., p. 163.

[875] Pope Pius XII, *Radio Message to Fatima*, May 13, 1946, *Bendito seia*, AAS 38.266. [Emphasis added.]

[876] Matt. 2:11.

[877] Lk. 2:16.

[878] St. Bonaventure. Cited by Smith, D.D., Ph.D., Canon George D. *The Teaching of the Catholic Church: A Summary of Catholic Doctrine*, Vol. I. [New York: The MacMillan Co., 1959]: p. 115.

CHAPTER 34

A Mystery of Mercy:
The Virgin Mary as Mother

"Mary was raised to the dignity of Mother of God
rather for sinners than for the just, since Jesus Christ declares
that He came to call not the just, but sinners."
—St. Anselm

When on a great scale mankind abandons God and tempts Him to turn His face from us, Our Lady's continual intercession is the last means to save souls: that is the reason why God wishes to establish devotion to the Immaculate Heart. The origins and development of devotion to the Immaculate Heart of Mary are found in the Deposit of Faith (otherwise known as Divine Revelation, which issues from Tradition and Scripture). It, too, falls under what is coined as "the general law of preparation." This law, so often mentioned because it is so essential in understanding the Deposit of Faith, refers to the way God provided Divine Revelation to make ready the human race for His "undoing of the awful consequences of Original Sin taken in conjunction with *man's response to God's overtures.*"[879]

Throughout the Church's history, "we find that God in His wisdom and goodness has inspired and directed the minds of men to the clarification of various points of revelation. One after another in a pattern fully understood only by God, these treasures have been brought to the fore by saint and scholar, considered profoundly, and submitted to the infallible magisterium of the Church. Under the guidance of the Holy Spirit, the Church has investigated and explained century after century the many secrets of the Godhead hidden in the depths of Christian revelation. Through this unfolding of the ineffable truths of revelations, souls are drawn to God, the source of every good."[880] Since our faith teaches that Divine Revelation is a world of mystery but not of contradiction, we believe all that God has revealed to us.[881]

---

[879] St. Bonaventure, loc. cit.
[880] Murphy, John F. *Mary's Immaculate Heart–The Meaning of the Devotion to the Immaculate Heart of Mary.* [Milwaukee: The Bruce Publishing Co., 1951]: p. 1.
[881] Herbermann, Charles George. *The Catholic Encyclopedia, an International Work of Reference* [Universal Knowledge Foundation, 1913. Original from the New York Public Library, digitized August 15, 2006]: p. 219.

We see the "general law of preparation" in the Old Testament's opaque revelation of the mystery of the Holy Trinity. As already discussed, the first implicit hint of the Old Testament's "general law of preparation" for the revelation of the Triune God appeared in the history of creation when the Lord said, "Let *us* make man to our image and likeness." St. Augustine noted similar utterances from God about His plurality: "Behold, Adam is become as one of *us*,"[882] and "Let *us* go down, and there confound their tongue."[883] The triple Sanctus of *Isaias*, "Holy, holy, holy, the Lord God of Hosts," [884] and the triple blessing recorded in *Numbers*[885] are also opaque heralds of the sublime mystery of the Holy Trinity. There are, however, many others.

Scriptural prophecies of the coming Savior and His Mother are found throughout the Old Testament. As previously mentioned, the first prophecy of this was declared by the Holy Trinity in *Genesis 3:15* and is known to us as the *proto-evangelium* (the "first Good News"). From the beginning, then, we see that the Lord God Himself formed an irrevocable union between Jesus Christ and his Mother, full of grace.

Divine Revelation closed with the passing of the last Apostle, St. John the Evangelist, one of the two Apostles whom Jesus, in Mk. 3:17, called the sons of thunder, in order "to express the strength and activity of their faith in publishing the law of God, without fearing the power of man." Lest we forget, St. John is called the *Apostle of the Sacred Heart*, to which the Immaculate Heart is so intimately connected. [886]

St. John the Evangelist is also known as "the disciple whom Jesus loved,"[887] which is not to say that Our Lord did not love the other Apostles. Rather, St. John is the beloved disciple because he was the Apostle most like Our Lord (and we may also truly say, like Our Lady)–a virgin in mind, body, and soul, a virgin great in charity towards God and man, a virgin strong in faith and hope and yet humble of heart. Due to this Apostle's great love for Our Lord and His Virgin Mother, St. John was the only member of the newly-established Church hierarchy to stand with Our Lady at the Foot of the Cross. In overcoming his own fears of persecution and possible death, St. John chose to follow Jesus during His Passion and assist Our Lady in her greatest sorrow.

---

[882] Gen. 1:26 [Emphasis added.]
[883] Gen. 3:22 [Emphasis added.]
[884] Gen. 11:17 [Emphasis added.]
[885] Num. 6: 24-26.
[886] Butler, Rev. Alban. "December 27, St. John the Apostle and Evangelist." *The Lives of the Saints, Vol. XII: December.* Published in 1866. Digitized at Bartleby.com, Great Books Online [http://www.bartleby.com/210/12/271.html]
[887] Jn. 13: 23; Jn. 19:26: Jn. 20:2; Jn. 21:7: Jn. 21: 20.

In his *Gospel*, St. John recorded that Our Lord, looking down at His Mother and the disciple (himself), said: "Woman, behold thy son. After that, he saith to the disciple: Behold thy mother."[888] St. John continued: "And from that hour, *the disciple took her to his own*. Afterwards, Jesus *knowing that all things were now accomplished*, that the scripture might be fulfilled, said: I thirst."[889]

Let us take special care to note that it was only *after* Jesus addressed His Mother as "Woman," and *after* St. John "took her to his own" that Christ knew "all things were now accomplished, that the scripture might be fulfilled." In his *Gospel*, St. John revealed that Jesus first spoke to Mary, His Mother, rather than to him (an Apostle). This is highly relevant because first, Our Lady's office is even higher than that of the Apostles and, second, because Our Lord's brief words to the Virgin and St. John are not a matter of only asking the Apostle to take physical care of Mary.

In speaking of Scriptural fulfillment, St. John recognized the unfolding of "the general law of preparation" found throughout the Old Testament. "For this purpose, the Son of God appeared, that he might destroy the works of the devil," as St. John would later write. He further grasped the prophecy of *Genesis 3:15* about *the woman and her seed*. Jesus is the Messiah, the promised Savior, and Mary is "the Woman" prophesied–the "Woman" who is to be accepted and honored as Mother. Christ is the only-begotten of the Ages but He is also truly the Son of Mary. The faithful who follow Him also become the "seed" of the "Woman," Mary. For if Christ is First-born and "Brother," then Mary is, indeed, Mother. To emphasize this truth, Our Lord stated simply to St. John: "Behold thy Mother."

As for St. John, who became the living figure-type for all of the elect until this world ends, he took Our Lady "to" (not "for") his own. St. John heard, believed, and immediately acted upon Christ's three simple words to him: "Behold thy mother." He did not hesitate, he did not question, and he did not wrangle with sophistries. Although his own mother lived, he was to accept Mary as Mother, too.

Fully understanding Our Lord's revelation that Mary is also our *Mother* in the order of grace, it was "from that hour that the disciple took her *to* his own." This fact again points to "the general law of preparation," the mystery unveiled by Christ on the Cross. Mary is mother to "the disciple whom Jesus loved," which means she is Mother to all Christians.

---

[888] Jn. 19: 26-27.
[889] Jn. 19:27-28. [Emphasis added.]

Quoting a celebrated writer, St. Alphonsus wrote in *The Glories of Mary* "'that it was, properly speaking, on Mount Calvary that Jesus formed His Church;' and then it is evident that the Blessed Virgin cooperated in a most excellent and especial manner in the accomplishment of this work. And in the same way it can be said, that though she brought forth the Head of the Church, Jesus Christ, without pain, she did not bring forth the body of this Head without very great suffering, and so it was on Mount Calvary that Mary began, in an especial manner, to be the Mother of the whole Church."

The saint continued, "To say all in a few words, Almighty God, in order to glorify the mother of the Redeemer, has ordained that her great charity should intercede for all those for whom her Divine Son offered and paid the super-abundant ransom of His Precious Blood, in which alone is our salvation, life, and resurrection."[890]

The Immaculate Heart: A Secret of God

"Secret things to the Lord our God: things that are manifest, to us and to our children forever, that we may do all the words of this law."[891] Found in the Old Testament's *Book of Deuteronomy*, the verse is briefly explained in a footnote of the Douay-Rheims translation of the *Holy Bible,* as follows: "As much as to say, secret things belong to, and are known to, God alone; our business must be to observe what He has revealed and manifested to us, and to direct our lives accordingly."

When we look to the *Holy Bible* (from *Genesis* through the *Apocalypse*), we know we shall find both opaque "secrets" about Our Lord, Our Lady, and the future of the Church. Tradition cannot be forgotten, either, since St. Paul is clear that we must hold fast to Tradition and Scripture, the two pillars of Divine Revelation.[892]

Throughout the long centuries since Christ's Resurrection and Ascension into Heaven, the Lord God has been ever-so-slowly manifesting the Virgin Mary's office in His plan of Redemption. Four thousand years before Advent, the Woman (Mary) and Her seed (Jesus, the God-Man and Savior, and those who follow Him, who are her children in the order of grace) were prophesied by God Himself. In a similar manner, the doctrine of devotion to the Immaculate Heart of Mary as necessary for salvation is brought to the world when God deems that it is most needed.

---

[890] de Liguori, St. Alphonsus. *The Glories of Mary*, pp. 25-26.
[891] Deut. 29:29.
[892] Thess. 2:2:14.

"It was through Mary that the salvation of the world was begun," wrote St. Louis-Marie de Montfort, "and it is through Mary that it must be consummated. **Mary hardly appeared at all in the first coming of Jesus Christ**, in order that men, as yet but little instructed and enlightened on the Person of her Son, should not remove themselves from Him in attaching themselves too strongly and too grossly to her... But in the Second Coming of Jesus Christ, Mary has to be made known and revealed by the Holy Ghost in order that through her Jesus Christ may be known, loved, and served. The reasons which moved the Holy Ghost to hide His spouse during her life, and to reveal her but very little since the preaching of the *Gospel*, subsist no longer."[893]

In his own way, St. Louis-Marie was referring to "the general law of preparation." The saint specifically mentioned that further knowledge and revelation of Mary (by the Holy Ghost) is the prerequisite to the *Parousia*–i.e., the Second Coming of Jesus. When we further consider that, in 1917, Our Lady clearly stated, "God wishes to establish throughout the world devotion to my Immaculate Heart," there is certainly ample reason to pause and consider how late must be the days of this world. However, like St. John the Apostle, we should not hesitate but simply take Mary "to" our own.

In the *Gospel of St. Mark*, Our Lord forewarned of a time when there would arise false Christs and false prophets, who will show great signs and wonders, "to seduce (if it were possible) even the elect."[894] St. Matthew's record of Christ's words is almost identical to St. Mark's. However, instead of saying "to seduce," St. Matthew states "insomuch as to *deceive* (if possible) even the elect."[895]

In the Modern Age, wherein every Church dogma, doctrine and article of faith is under attack, wherein Our Lord and His saints–especially Mary, the Virgin Mother of God–are blasphemed, the faithful would do well to not only act by practicing devotion to the Immaculate Heart of Mary, but also to study its history. As St. Paul admonished the Ephesians: *"Put you on the armor of God, that you may be able to stand against the deceits of the devil."*[896]

---

[893] de Montfort, *St. Louis*. True Devotion to Mary. #49.
[894] Mk. 13: 22.
[895] Matt. 24:24. [Emphasis added]
[896] Eph. 6:11. [Emphasis added]

CHAPTER 35

The Remedy:

An Immense Devotion

"The Virgin received Salvation
so that she may give it back to the centuries."
—St. Peter Chrysologus, Sermon 140

In the years since the Fatima apparitions, in which Our Lady clearly stated that *"God wishes to establish throughout the world devotion to my Immaculate Heart,"* the truth remains that *"...*Mary is not half enough preached. Devotion to her is low and thin and poor. It is frightened out of its wits by the sneers of heresy. It is always invoking human respect and carnal prudence, wishing to make Mary so little of a Mary that Protestants may feel at ease about her. Its ignorance of theology makes it unsubstantial and unworthy. It is not the prominent characteristic of our religion which it ought to be. It has no faith in itself. Hence it is that Jesus is not loved, that heretics are not converted, that the Church is not exalted; that souls, which might be saints, wither and dwindle; that the Sacraments are not rightly frequented, or souls enthusiastically evangelized."[897]

The quote above was written over 150 years ago, by Fr. Frederick William Faber in his *Translator's Preface* to St. Louis Marie de Montfort's *A Treatise on True Devotion to the Blessed Virgin Mary with Preparation for Total Consecration.*[898] In the same preface, with words that still apply to the plight of the faithful, Fr. Faber had previously penned:

"All those who are likely to read this book love God, and lament that they do not love Him more; all desire something for his glory—the spread of some good work, the success of some devotion, the coming of some good time. One man has been striving for years to overcome a particular fault, and has not succeeded. Another mourns, and almost wonders why he mourns, that so few of his relations and friends have been converted to the faith. One grieves that he has not devotion enough; another that he has a cross to carry, which is a particularly impossible cross to him; while a third has domestic troubles and

---

[897] "Father Faber's Preface" in *True Devotion to Mary*, pp. xix-xxiii.

[898] On May 12, 1854, Rome decreed that the writings of St. Louis de Montfort were free from all error which could bar his canonization so that, by 1862, Fr. Faber first translated *True Devotion* from the original French into English.

family unhappinesses, which feel almost incompatible with his salvation; and for all these things, prayer appears to bring so little remedy."

"But what is the remedy that is wanted? What is the remedy indicated by God Himself?" Fr. Faber understandably asked. "If we may rely on the disclosures of the Saints, it is an immense increase of devotion to Our Blessed Lady; but, remember, nothing short of an *immense* one."[899]

A Glimpse at the Devotion's History

The necessary devotion to Our Lady, especially to her Immaculate Heart, is not a spontaneous development in the Church. Like other Marian doctrines in the Deposit of Faith, which closed with the death of St. John the Evangelist, this elevated piety to Mary's Heart is like the tiny bud of a rose, slowly blossoming throughout the centuries. In taking a very brief look at this devotion's history, we must remember the three following things:

• First, the Church and her children will always rely on Divine Revelation, which issues from either long-standing Tradition or Scripture or both;

• Second, we remember that Divine Revelation, given only to the Church founded by Christ and interpreted correctly only by this same Church through the Magisterium (Ordinary and Extraordinary), continues to ensue until the last day of this world's existence;

• Third, we recall "the general law of preparation," which refers to the way God provided Divine Revelation to make ready the human race of His "undoing of the awful consequences of Original Sin, taken in conjunction with man's response to God's overtures."[900] This law spans throughout all of Divine Revelation which, of course, includes the past, the present, and the future.

The question of the proofs of this doctrine (devotion to the Immaculate Heart) are somewhat akin (but not identical) to those which led to the solemn dogmatic definition of the Assumption of Mary. That particular doctrine, as Fr. Garrigou-LaGrange wrote, was "not possible to prove *directly* from Sacred Scripture nor from primitive documents…it can be proved *indirectly* from later documents that there was at least an implicit revelation [to the Apostles or at least to one of them] since there are certain facts" that are "explicable in no other way."[901]

---

[899] Faber, Ibid. [Emphasis in the original.]
[900] St. Bonaventure. Cited by Smith, D.D., Ph.D., Canon George D. *The Teaching of the Catholic Church: A Summary of Catholic Doctrine*, Vol. I [New York: The MacMillan Co., 1959]: p. 115.
[901] Garrigou-Lagrange, O.P., Fr. R. *The Mother of the Savior and our Interior Life* [Charlotte, NC: TAN Books, 1993. Reprinted from 1948 edition by B. Herder Book Company, St. Louis, Missouri]: pp. 130-131.

Conversely, the doctrine of devotion to the Immaculate Heart of Mary can be indirectly proved from both Holy Scripture and Tradition, which includes commentaries on the *Canticles* from Church Fathers like St. Hippolytus of Rome (170-235 A.D.), St. Ephrem (306-373 A.D.), St. Ambrose (340-397 A.D), St. Gregory of Nyssa (335-395 A.D.), St. Peter Chrysologus (560-636 A.D.), and St. John Damascene (676-749 A.D.).

In recent times, Pope Pius XII alluded to the historical fact that "remote vestiges of the devotion to the Immaculate Heart of Our Blessed Mother are to be found in the commentaries of the Fathers on the *Sponsa* [Spouse] of the *Canticle of Canticles*...for the bride of the *Canticle*, adorned with the beauty of spotless purity and deep affection for her spouse, is a figure [type] most appropriate to the Mother of God."[902] In addition, there are "innumerable passages in the *Canticle of Canticles* which the Fathers apply to the *Singula Anima Fidelus*, or adoring soul," which certainly applies to the Virgin Mary, the "most perfect of all souls and the most worthy to be called the spouse of the Bridegroom."[903]

Even further, the *Canticle* includes two verses which mention the Heart of the Beloved, as follows: *"I sleep, and my heart watcheth: the voice of my beloved knocking: Open to me, my sister, my love, my undefiled"* (Cant. 5:2). Of this verse, St. Isidore of Seville (560-636 A.D.) said it means, "Open to me, that is, reveal to me thy heart, my sister, my undefiled, *because you alone are worthy of my sight."*[904] Alain de l'Isle (1128-1203 A.D.) understood the same verse as referring to the Blessed Virgin before the Incarnation of Christ, believing that *"I sleep"* referred to Our Lady's complete freedom from motherly anxieties and concerns, while the words *"and my heart watcheth"* refers to her constant contemplation of the Divine.[905]

"Put me as a seal upon thy heart, as a seal upon thy arm" (Cant. 8:6). The afore-mentioned Alain de l'Isle's commentary on this verse states the Virgin Mary so carried Christ as a seal upon her Heart that through imitation of Him, she came more and more to resemble Him. [906] Of the words *"...he set in order*

---

[902] Pius XII, "Urbis et Orbis," AAS, XXXVII, 1945, p. 50.

[903] St. Ambrose, *Commentarius in Cantica Cantic.* (PL, 15, 1919); see also St. Gregory the Great, *Super Cantica Canticorum Expositio* (PL, 79, 517 and 541). Cited by John Murphy, *Mary's Immaculate Heart—The Meaning of the Devotion to the Immaculate Heart of Mary* [Milwaukee, WI: The Bruce Publishing Co., 1951]: p. 3.

[904] St. Isidore of Seville, Appendix VI, *Exposito in Canticum Canticorum* (PL, 83, 1125).

[905] Alanus de Insulis (Alain de l'Isle). Op. čit. (PL, 210, 85). [Emphasis added.]

[906] Ibid. (PL, 210, 105).

charity in me" (Cant. 2:4), he wrote, "In whom was charity formed, if not in the Virgin Mary; who loved Christ from the depths of her heart..."[907]

We know that almost every page of the Old Testament includes prophecy, figure-types, and attributes applicable to the Holy Mother of God. In the *Psalms*, she appears as the Sanctuary and in the *Book of Wisdom*, she is the "first-born daughter of God" and the "heavenly Queen of the world," but there are many other examples. When we look to the *New Testament*, however, we find a few explicit references to her which possess deep and precious meaning. Specifically, in the *Gospel of St. Luke,* it is found that, three times, the word "heart" is used in connotation to Mary.

• At the Nativity, upon hearing the shepherds reveal how angels directed them to find the Christ Child: *"...all who heard marveled at the things told them by the shepherds. But Mary kept all these words, pondering them in her heart."* (Luke 2:19)

• At the Presentation of the Divine Infant in the Temple, Simeon the Prophet said to the Virgin Mary: *"Behold this Child is set for the fall and for the resurrection of many in Israel and for a sign which shall be contradicted. And thy own soul a sword shall pierce, that out of many hearts thoughts may be revealed."* (Luke 2:35)

• After the three day disappearance of the Christ Child, and the mysterious words He spoke to Our Lady: *"And he went down with them and came to Nazareth and was subject to them. And his mother kept all these words in her heart."* (Luke 2:51)

Hence, we see that twice do the Scriptures declare that Mary "kept" these words in her Heart, while once the Holy Ghost inspired St. Simeon to speak to Our Lady, prophesying that the *thoughts* of many hearts shall be revealed by the piercing of her own *soul*. In this one heavenly-inspired announcement, Christ is proclaimed to Israel by the Holy Ghost—and so is Mary's office in the Redemption, for otherwise why should the piercing of her soul possess any power to reveal the thoughts "out of many hearts"?

We know Simeon's words are not literal in every aspect, because neither Scripture nor Tradition subsequently teach that a sword ever touched Mary's body; the prophecy specifically speaks of her *soul*, not her Heart. How, then, should these mysterious allusions to Mary's Heart and soul be properly understood? The astounding answer is given by the Church Fathers, who

---

[907] Ibid. (PL, 210, 65).

"depict Mary's Heart as the receptacle or *tabernacle for the divine mysteries and augments of faith*." [908]

Furthermore, in describing the eight meanings of the word "heart" in Sacred Scripture, St. John Eudes explained, "We must understand by the word 'heart' that highest part of the **soul** which theologians call the *point of the spirit*. It is the seat of contemplation, which consists in turning the mind directly toward God and viewing Him in all simplicity, without discursive reasoning or multiplicity of thoughts. The Fathers of the Church apply to this power of the soul those words which the Holy Ghost puts in the mouth of the Blessed Virgin Mary: 'I sleep, and my *heart* watcheth.' According to St. Bernadine of Siena and several other writers, sleep and rest of the body did not prevent Mary's holy heart—that is, the highest part of her mind—from being always united to God in sublime contemplation." [909]

The Slowly-Germinating Seeds

Like the blue spruce tree, with its very slow growth rate but which, upon reaching its full maturity, will live and stand magnificently for centuries, the same fact of slow maturation applies to devotion to the Immaculate Heart of Mary. In the time-span between the Patristic era and the twelfth century, wherein the greatest saints of the Church began to arise, there are scant references to Mary's Heart. The seeds of the devotion to Mary's Immaculate Heart are found in the Scriptures, but the first signs of their germination are found in Tradition.

Not long before St. Bernard's time, there exist a few references to the joys and sorrows of Mary's Heart; St. Anselm links the Immaculate Heart of Mary with her role as Co-Redemptrix, but it is St. Bernard, in his sermon *Dominica Infra Octavam Assumptionius B. V. Mariae*, who left a historical record of particular devotion to the Heart of Mary. Then came St. Bernadine of Siena and later, St. John Eudes and St. Alphonsus di Liguori, who strikingly stand out in their propagation of profound piety to the *Heart* of Mary or the glories of Mary. Church history proves that devotion to Our Lady reached its peak in the Middle Ages. It would seem, then, to be no coincidence that, as devotion to Our Lady's Heart grew, so did the number of saints.

---

[908] St. Ambrose, *Expositionis in Lucam*, Lib. II (PL, 15, 1654): "Discamus sanctae Virginis in omnibus castittem, quae, non minus ore pudica quam corpore, arguments fidei conferebat in corde." St. Gregory Thaumaturgic (Dubius), *Hom. 2 In Annntiat. Virgin Mariae* (PG, 10, 1169-70): "Sancticssima porro Dei Genetrix conservabat Omnia verba haec, conferens in corde suo; velut quae omnium mysteriorum vas ac receptaculum esset." Cited by John Murphy, op. cit.: p. 8. [Emphasis added.]

[909] Eudes, St. John. *The Admirable Heart of Mary*, p. 9.

Tragically, this devotion began to wane, due in great part to the Protestant and French Revolts—and the terrible effects are not only still with us, but they have grown stronger and are increasingly widespread. Don Sharkey, author of *The Woman Shall Conquer*, noted, "The leaders of the Protestant Revolt, in their hatred for everything Catholic, struck especially at Our Lord in the Blessed Sacrament and at devotion to the Blessed Virgin. These, ironically, are the very things we need most in our struggle for salvation."[910]

Countless are the number of Catholics who knew these truths and were martyred, simply because they resisted Martin Luther, the Catholic priest who, after Judas, may be the world's most infamous apostate. They also resisted the princes who were rather delighted with Luther's blasphemous and boorish tirades. The faithful Catholics of England resisted King Henry VIII, the once-Catholic king who, due to his unbridled lust and pride, became an adulterer, a heretic, and a mass-murderer of his wives and his subjects. The Catholics who did not acquiesce to the king's demands (or those of his illegitimate daughter, Elizabeth, when she became queen) were martyred.

Next on the historical scene came the "progressivists" of the so-called Enlightenment, with their insane ideas of a "Man" with a "new order," a "new paradigm," and a "new era," a "Man" who does not need God. These prideful ideas were inevitably followed by the French Revolt, with its outright, wholesale denial of God, His Church, and Divine Revelation, all of which led to the vicious persecutions and martyrdoms of the royal Catholic family of France and the faithful from all walks of life.

There is much more history that could be mentioned, but may it suffice to say this: For almost five centuries now, the Catholic Faith, which is what made Europe and made "Western Civilization," is suffering from the most insidious forms of heretical attacks. With the Church, the whole world suffers for, as the old maxim declares, "As Rome goes, so goes the world." And so we return to the question, asked by Fr. Faber only 150 years ago:

"But what is the remedy that is wanted? What is the remedy indicated by God Himself? If we may rely on the disclosures of the Saints, it is an immense increase of devotion to Our Blessed Lady; but, remember, nothing short of an *immense* one."[911]

---

[910] Sharkey, *The Woman Shall Conquer*, pp. 7-8.
[911] Faber, loc. cit. [Emphasis in the original.]

CHAPTER 36

The Synthesis of All Devotions

"If I have found favor in thy sight, oh king,
give me my people for which I request."
–Book of Esther 7:23

Most of us understand that when we say of another, "She has a good heart," we are referring to the interior goodness of the person, a moral integrity perceived by an individual's words and actions. It follows that when we speak of Mary's Immaculate Heart, we are truly speaking of her whole *person*. Therefore, devotion to the Immaculate Heart means a filial devotion to the *person* of the Virgin Mary, the Mother of God who is assumed body and soul into Heaven. The synthesis of all devotions to the Virgin Mary is found in devotion to her Immaculate Heart, which includes (but is not limited to) the praying of the Holy Rosary.

"The Church says of her person that Mary is 'the temple of the Lord, the sanctuary of the Holy Ghost,'" as St. John Eudes wrote, "and we can apply these words with still better reason to her Admirable Heart, having seen that it is the source of all the qualities and excellences with which she is adorned."[912] What St. John Eudes called "the Admirable Heart of Mary" is the Immaculate Heart of Mary, "the receptacle or *tabernacle for the divine mysteries and augments of faith*."[913]

St. Louis de Montfort taught, "Mary is the sanctuary and the repose of the Holy Trinity, where God dwells more magnificently and more divinely than in any other place in the universe...**Neither is it allowed to any creature**, no matter how pure, to enter into that sanctuary **without a great and special privilege**."[914] At Fatima, however, Our Lady expressly said that God wills the universal devotion to her Immaculate Heart. Since this same Heart is the tabernacle of God, can we even begin to understand the "great and special privilege" that is offered to us when Our Lady invites us to take refuge in her Immaculate Heart?

---

[912] Eudes, St. John. *The Admirable Heart of Mary,* p. 82.
[913] St. Ambrose, loc. cit.
[914] de Montfort, St. Louis. *True Devotion to Mary,* #6.

"Then rose up her children."[915] Richard of St. Laurence, commenting on *Proverbs*, remarked that one cannot be a child of Mary who does not first rise from the iniquity into which he has fallen. To this he added, "The sons of Mary are her imitators in chastity, humility, meekness, mercy." As the ultimate tonic to eradicate the rising errors of the modernist heresy and those of atheistic Russia, Our Lady came to Fatima, there to implore her children to rise up, amend their lives, and cease offending God, Who is already much offended.

Why the Virgin Mary Draws Our Attention

"In the person of Mary, a daughter of Adam like ourselves, God sets before us an accomplished model, but one more adapted to our weakness."[916] What is it in the Virgin Mary that appeals to our human weaknesses? She attracts us because she is a mother, the embodiment of all that is loving, self-sacrificing, compassionate, understanding, graceful and strong, interceding and protecting. She draws us because, like us, she is fully human, and yet she alone is "the most perfect master-piece which nature and grace combined have ever formed of a simple creature."[917]

Grace and mercy are what we inherently perceive in the Virgin Mary. "Wherefore St. Anselm well remarks that when we implore the Holy Virgin to obtain graces for us, it is not that we distrust the divine mercy, but rather that we distrust our own unworthiness, and commend ourselves to Mary that her merits may compensate for our unworthiness," as St. Alphonsus de Liguori wrote.[918] Centuries later, Fr. Garrigou-Lagrange[919] stated, "Theologians note that she does not seem to share in any special way in the royal judicial power of inflicting punishment for sin, for Tradition calls her not the Mother of Justice but the *Mother of Mercy*, a title which is hers in virtue of her mediation of all graces.[920] Jesus seems to have kept to Himself the reign of justice[921] as is becoming [of] Him who is the *'judge of the living and the dead.'*"[922]

"The Church, in devotion to the Immaculate Heart, does not exclude Mary's extraordinary love for God in celebrating in a special way her maternal love for men; thus we might summarize the spiritual element in our devotion as

---

[915] Prov.31:28; Richard of St. Laurence commentary appears to be a paraphrase of this passage.

[916] "Devotion to the Immaculate Heart of Mary." *Messenger of the Sacred Heart of Jesus* (1876).

[917] Ibid.

[918] St. Anselm. Cited in St. Alphonsus, *The Glories of Mary*, Location 1587.

[919] Garrigou-Lagrange, *Mother of the Savior and Our Interior Life*, p. 229.

[920] *Mariale*, q. 43, 2. Cited by Fr. Garrigou-Lagrange, Ibid.

[921] Jn. 5:22-27. Cited by Fr. Garrigou-Lagrange, Ibid.

[922] Acts 10:42; cf. IIIa., q. 59, a.1. Cited by Fr. Garrigou-Lagrange, Ibid. [Emphasis added.]

the charity of Mary toward God, her love for Christ, and especially her love for us as her spiritual children."[923] As the Virgin full of grace who is also Mother Most Merciful, Our Lady Mary is the flawless human image of her Creator. Her Immaculate Heart reflects the glory and virtues of Christ's Sacred Heart. In all these truths are glimpsed the mysteries of salvation for, prior to His Incarnation, the Word created His own Mother. He created her Immaculate, not only free from Original Sin but also full of grace.

Jesus Christ had no human father, so it is from the Virgin Mother that He formed His Body. From her beautiful countenance came the masculine form of His Holy Face. Her blood is the source of Our Lord's Precious Blood, by which all mankind is offered redemption. Her Immaculate Heart was the pattern from which Our Lord traced His Sacred Heart. Jesus is the source of our salvation, but the sinless Virgin Mary is the cause due to the *Fiat* ("Let it be done") of her own free will. It is for these reasons that St. Bonaventure wrote in such simple and beautiful words, "All salvation springs from Mary's Heart."[924]

Secrets in the Order of Grace

De Maria nunquam satis! (Of Mary, there is never enough!) St. John Eudes asks: "How much more, then, should we not honor and magnify Our Savior in the Heart of His Blessed Mother?"[925]

"To be devout to you, O holy Virgin," says St. John Damascene, "is an arm of salvation which God gives to those whom he wishes to save."[926] St. Alphonsus boldly declared that "the intercession of Mary is necessary to salvation." In a similar manner, St. Louis de Montfort taught, "Our Blessed Lady is the means Our Lord made use of to come to us. She is also the means which we must make use of to go to Him."[927] Fr. Garrigou-Lagrange, writing on Mary's role in the Redemption, the Church, and the interior life of the soul, stated: "God has continued to make use of Mary for the sanctification of souls."[928]

"We must choose, therefore, among all the devotions to the Blessed Virgin, the one which draws us more towards death to ourselves, inasmuch as it will be the best and the most sanctifying," concluded St. Louis de Montfort, the apostle of *True Devotion to Jesus through Mary*. "As there are secrets of nature to do in a short time, at little cost and with facility, natural operations, so also in like

---

[923] Murphy, John. *Mary's Immaculate Heart,* p. 83.

[924] *In. Psalt. B. Virgin*, p. 79. Cited by St. John Eudes, op. cit., p. 43.

[925] Eudes, op. cit., p. 81. [Emphasis in the original.]

[926] Damascene, St. John. Cited by St. Louis-Marie Grignon de Montfort, op. cit., Location 614.

[927] de Montfort, op. cit., #76

[928] Garrigou-Lagrange, op. cit., p. 245.

manner *there are secrets in the order of grace* to do in a short time, with sweetness and facility, supernatural operations, such as emptying ourselves of self, filling ourselves with God, and becoming perfect."[929]

These "secrets in the order of grace" are discovered in devotion to the Immaculate Heart of Mary, the synthesis of all devotions "to Jesus through Mary." In a succinct manner, Our Lady herself said the same at Fatima: "My Immaculate Heart will be your refuge, and the path that will lead you to God." Fr. Garrigou-Lagrange explains the reasons for this devotion, "The cult[930] offered to Mary in the Church confirms in a general way the foundations of our faith since it derives from the Redemptive Incarnation. Thereby it destroys heresies: '*Cunctas haereses interesmist in universe mundo*.' The same cult leads to holiness by suggesting the imitation of Mary's virtues, and it glorifies the Son by honoring the Mother." [931]

This devotion is an "interior and perfect practice," as St. Louis de Montfort describes, meaning any external practices are intended for the life of the soul. Fr. Garrigou-Lagrange offers a summation of the saint's teaching on personal consecration to Mary: "Like the other Christian virtues, true devotion grows in us with charity, advancing from the stage of the beginner to that of the more proficient, and continuing up to the stage of the perfect." [932]

In speaking of personal consecration to Our Lady, which St. de Montfort taught is the third degree of Marian devotion, Fr. Lagrange added that it is "a practical form of recognition of her universal mediation and a guarantee of her special protection…In the practice of this complete dependence on Mary, there may be included the resignation into Mary's hands of everything in our good works that is communicable to other souls, so that she may make use of it in accordance with the will of her Divine Son and for His glory." [933]

At every Fatima apparition, the Blessed Virgin asked for the daily Rosary, which is itself is a synthesis of the Redemption history and of prayers taught by

---

[929] de Montfort, op. cit., #82.3. [Emphasis added.]

[930] "Cult in general means honor paid in a spirit of submission and dependence to a superior because of his excellence…Created persons who have a certain excellence are entitled to the cult called *dulia*: a cult of respect. Thus, in the natural order respect is due to parents, kings, teachers; in the super natural order it is due to the saints, the heroicity of whose virtues has been recognized. The latter cult paid to God's servants honors God Himself who is revealed to the world in the saints and draws us by them to Himself. It is commonly taught in the Church that the Blessed Virgin is entitled to a cult of *hyperdulia*, or supreme dulia, because of her eminent dignity as Mother of God." Fr. Garrigou-Lagrange, op. cit., pp. 240-241. [Second emphasis in this definition added.]

[931] Garrigou-Lagrange, Ibid., pp. 243-244.

[932] Ibid., p. 251.

[933] Ibid., p. 252.

Jesus (the *Our Father*), St. Gabriel and, with him, the Church (the *Hail Mary*). Unchanged for centuries, Our Lady herself made one seemingly small but imperative addition with the "O my Jesus prayer." [934] Thus, the Rosary is the foundation of devotion to the Immaculate Heart. We gain through the Rosary that which we spiritually need because, as St. Robert Bellarmine noted, "that which is daily required must be asked for every day." [935] Without prayer, we lose final perseverance, which we cannot merit but only gain by daily *asking* for it as a gift from God.

The Rosary helps us practice the virtues of Jesus and Mary. Fr. Garrigou-Lagrange said of the Psalter: "The fifteen mysteries of the Rosary thus divided into three groups are but different aspects of the three great mysteries of our salvation: The Incarnation, the Redemption, Eternal Life…Thus, the Rosary is a *Credo*…It is the whole of Christian dogma in all its splendor and elevation…The joyful mysteries lead to the Passion, and the Passion to the door of Heaven…The Rosary, well understood is, therefore, a very elevated form of prayer which makes the whole of dogma available to all." [936]

Moreover, the eminent theologian compared the Rosary to the four ends of the Liturgy of the Mass when he wrote, "The Rosary is more than **a prayer of petition**. It is **a prayer of adoration** inspired by the thought of the Incarnate God, **a prayer of reparation** in memory of the Passion of Our Savior, **a prayer of thanksgiving** that the glorious mysteries continue to reproduce themselves in the uninterrupted entry of the elect into glory." [937]

Willed by God and revealed by Him, devotion to the Immaculate Heart of Mary is intended for these days, which are the latter days. St. Louis de Montfort foresaw that this devotion "**would come to pass particularly at the end of the world**, and indeed presently [as in "soon"] because the Most High with His holy Mother has to form for Himself great saints, who shall surpass most of the other Saints in sanctity…" [938]

To fully eradicate modernism, which is a synthesis of all spiritual evils, the Virgin Mary came to Fatima. There she requested a spiritual solution, a mystery of salvation that overcomes the mystery of iniquity. Willed by God, the offered remedy is a "synthesis of all devotions"–the universal devotion to Mary's Immaculate Heart.

---

[934] *"O my Jesus, forgive us our sins. Save us from the fires of hell. Lead all souls to heaven, especially those with the greatest need of Thy mercy."* This is the prayer which Our Lady of Fatima instructed to add after every Rosary decade.

[935] Bellarmine, St. Robert. Cited in St. Alphonsus, *The Glories of Mary*, p. 88.

[936] Garrigou-Lagrange, loc. cit. pp. 246-247.

[937] Ibid., pp. 247-248.

[938] de Montfort, op. cit., #47, 48.

CHAPTER 37

The Ultimate Reason for Fatima:
The One Thing Necessary

"In the end, my Immaculate Heart will triumph.
The Holy Father will consecrate Russia to me, and she will be
converted, and an era of peace will be granted to the world."
—*Our Lady of Fatima, July 13, 1917*

July 13 marks an important date in salvation history. It is the date when, in 1917, Our Lady addressed essential matters of Divine Revelation in a way never before known in the Church's chronicles. With the third stage of the Great Revolt against God already commencing, the Virgin Mary came to Fatima to remind each person throughout the world of the one thing necessary: *The salvation of our individual souls through devotion to her Immaculate Heart.* That is truly the center of the Great Secret because in June, she had already showed her Heart to the children, saying specifically to Lucia: *"Jesus wishes to make use of you to make me known and loved. He wants to establish in the world devotion to my Immaculate Heart."*

The Promises and the Prophecies:
A Pattern of Three's

"In the whole cycle of the apparitions, that of July 13 is unquestionably the most important," wrote Fatima historian Frère Michel. "It is the central apparition which the two previous ones prepared for and the three subsequent ones were to confirm."[939] He continued, "The history and the content of this extraordinary message is unprecedented in all the history of the Church..."[940] It is also the apparition in which we see **a pattern of three's**, possibly to implicitly remind us of the Holy Trinity, Who is one God in Three Divine Persons—the Father, the Son, and the Holy Ghost.

Our Lady chose the *third* apparition in July—the month in which the Church especially honors the Most Precious Blood of Jesus shed for our redemption—to disclose *four* matters of import: **1)** a **three-fold** promise for October, including a miracle which, when fulfilled, occurred in **three** stages, **2)** the prophecies of the Great Secret, comprised of **three** distinct parts, **3)** a

---

[939] Frère Michel. *TWTF*, Vol. I, pp. 185-186.
[940] Ibid., p. 187.

prayer of sacrifice, with **three** pleas to Jesus, and **4)** an addition after each Rosary decade, a prayer of **three** entreaties to Our Savior.

The Three-fold Promise: "In October, *I will tell you who I am and what I want, and I will perform a miracle for all to see and believe*." [941] The Lady made this promise a mere moment before revealing the Great Secret.

The Miracle, as Frère Michel notes, "would guarantee the divine origin of the secret, as well as the fulfillment of this prophetic secret. Thus the great miracle of October 13 was closely associated, by the Blessed Virgin herself, not only with the whole of her message, but especially with the prophetic text of July 13."[942]

The Sacrifice Prayer with three intentions: The Lady, who from the beginning of the apparitions displayed consistent concern for sinners, said: "Sacrifice yourselves for sinners, and say many times, especially whenever you make some sacrifice: *O Jesus, it is for love of You, for the conversion of sinners, and in reparation for the sins committed against the Immaculate Heart of Mary*." [943] In this brief offering, we recognize *three* points: A prayer addressed to Jesus which speaks of love for Him, offers sacrifice for the souls of others, and makes an act of reparation for sins.

Although this book has previously shared what is known of the Great Secret's contents, it is efficacious for our souls to read it again, meditate upon Our Lady's words, and consider why Heaven gave this Great Secret in three distinct parts:

The First Part of the Great Secret: Hell is Real. In speaking those last words, Our Lady opened her hands...from which "rays of light seemed to penetrate the earth, and we saw as it were a sea of fire," Sr. Lucia wrote. "Plunged in this fire were demons and souls in human form, like transparent burning embers, all blackened or burnished bronze, floating about in the conflagration, now raised into the air by the flames that issued from within themselves together with great clouds of smoke, now falling back on every side like sparks in huge fires, without weight or equilibrium, amid shrieks and groans of pain and despair, which horrified us and made us tremble with fear. The demons could be distinguished by their terrifying and repellant likeness to frightful and unknown animals, black and transparent, like burning coals. Terrified and as if to plead for succor, we looked up at Our Lady..."[944]

---

[941] Ibid., p.181.
[942] Ibid., p.187.
[943] Sr. Mary Lucia, *Memoirs*, 1976 edition, p.165.
[944] Ibid., p. 167.

Unexpectedly, the very first part of the Great Secret, given to three young children, was this momentary but soul-searing glimpse of hell. Terrifying as it was, the Vision of Hell was truly one of Heaven's last recourses of mercy to a world already steeped in sin. This frightening vision further transformed the increasingly holy interior lives of the three Fatima children, who would valiantly fulfill their roles as faithful witnesses and selfless victims of reparation. The children's unswerving fidelity to the Lady and the entire Message of Fatima, and their great sacrifices for the sake of others, testify to the reality of eternal hell—a reality which Heaven saw fit to reveal to them in the First Part of the Great Secret.

The Second Part of the Great Secret: "If What I Say to You is Done..." Our Lady then gave the Second Secret, "You have seen hell, where the souls of poor sinners go. To save them [poor sinners], God wishes to establish in the world devotion to my Immaculate Heart. If what I say to you is done, many souls will be saved and there will be peace."

"The war [WWI] is going to end; but if people do not cease offending God, a worse one will break out during the reign of Pius XI. When you see a night illumined by an unknown light, know that this is the great sign given you by God that He is about to punish the world for its crimes, by means of war, famine and persecutions of the Church and of the Holy Father."[945]

"To prevent this, I shall come to ask for the consecration of Russia to my Immaculate Heart and the Communion of Reparation on the First Saturdays. If my requests are heeded, Russia will be converted and there will be peace. If not, she will spread her errors throughout the world, causing wars and persecutions of the Church. The good will be martyred, the Holy Father will have much to suffer, various nations will be annihilated."

The following sentence which, as far as we now know, concludes the Second Secret, also follows **the pattern of threes**: "In the end, my Immaculate Heart will triumph. The Holy Father will consecrate Russia to me, and she will be converted, and an era of peace will be granted to the world."[946]

The Third Secret begins with the words, "In Portugal, the dogma of the Faith will always be preserved, *etc.*"[947] All that is currently known is the Third Secret *Vision*, which Lucia described as follows:

"After the two parts which I have already explained, at the left of Our Lady and a little above, we saw an Angel with a flaming sword in his left hand;

---

[945] "This was the aurora borealis on the night of January 25-26, 1938, which was unusual, and always regarded by Lucia as the God-given sign which had been promised." Cited in Sr. Mary Lucia, *Memoirs* by editor Fr. Kondor, SVD, p. 190.

[946] Sr. Mary Lucia, loc. cit.

[947] Ibid.

flashing, it gave out flames that looked as though they would set the world on fire; but they died out in contact with the splendour that Our Lady radiated towards him from her right hand: pointing to the earth with his right hand, the Angel cried out in a loud voice: 'Penance, Penance, Penance!'"

"And we saw in an immense light that is God: 'something similar to how people appear in a mirror when they pass in front of it;' a Bishop dressed in White 'we had the impression that it was the Holy Father.' Other Bishops, Priests, men and women Religious going up a steep mountain, at the top of which there was a big Cross of rough-hewn trunks as of a cork-tree with the bark; before reaching there the Holy Father passed through a big city half in ruins and half trembling with halting step, afflicted with pain and sorrow, he prayed for the souls of the corpses he met on his way; having reached the top of the mountain, on his knees at the foot of the big Cross he was killed by a group of soldiers who fired bullets and arrows at him, and in the same way there died one after another the other Bishops, Priests, men and women Religious, and various lay people of different ranks and positions. Beneath the two arms of the Cross there were two Angels each with a crystal aspersorium in his hand, in which they gathered up the blood of the Martyrs and with it sprinkled the souls that were making their way to God."[948]

While at least a part of the Third Secret *Vision* is now known, the Virgin's Message relating to it remains yet concealed. Bishop Emeritus Benedict XVI, however, knows *the remaining words* Our Lady spoke in the "Third Secret" of Fatima, for he read them when he was still a Cardinal of the Church.

It shall be mentioned once more that in 1984, after admitting he [Cardinal Ratzinger] had read the Third Secret, he was asked why it was still not released. His response revealed that the Third Secret possesses the following "six themes" (mysteriously correlating with the same number of times Our Lady appeared at Fatima): **1)** It is in accord with Divine Revelation, **2)** It demands a radical call to conversion and penance, **3)** It refers to the absolute importance of history, **4)** It alerts the Church and the world to the dangers threatening the faith, the life of the Christian and therefore the world, **5)** It is integral to the importance of the last times, and **6)** Although it could be mistaken for sensationalism, it is nevertheless a religious prophesy corresponding to Scripture and confirmed by many other Marian apparitions.

And so it is asked again: Could these six themes of the Third Secret direct our attention to one or more of the "six signs"[949] of the last times, given by

---

[948] *The Message of Fatima.*
[949] Lk. 21: 10-11; Matt. 7: 7, 11, 14.

Christ Himself? They, too, fall within the realm of "the absolute importance of history," for salvation history centers on two things: The Incarnation of Christ, when Our Lord came to offer Redemption and Mercy, and His Second Coming, when He will come as Just Judge.

The Rosary Decade Prayer, with three intentions: To return to the sequence of events during the July apparition, Our Lady said, "When you pray the Rosary, say after each mystery: *O my Jesus, forgive us our sins, save us from the fires of hell. Lead all souls to Heaven, especially those with the greatest need of Thy Mercy.*"[950]

Of the latter part of this prayer–"especially those with the greatest need of Thy Mercy"–Sr. Lucia would years later humbly explain "that Our Lady was referring to the souls in the greatest danger of damnation."[951]

In October, the Lady kept all three of her promises. With her first sentence, she revealed two of three things she wanted, as well as her title: "I want to tell you that a chapel is to be built here in my honor, for I am the Lady of the Rosary. Continue always to pray the Rosary every day."[952]

Those unadorned words verify the Virgin's statement in June that her Immaculate Heart leads us to God–for every Catholic chapel contains the Hidden Presence of Jesus. By praying the Rosary every day, we cultivate the practice of prayer and meditation on the lives of Christ and His Virgin Mother, we gain all 15 promises Our Lady gave to those faithful to her Rosary, we grow further confident in Jesus and Mary, and we may gain a daily plenary indulgence (under the proper conditions).

The final desire of Our Lady of the Rosary–given just before opening her hands to initiate the Great Miracle of the Sun–was made known in the form of a most solemn and grieved command: "People must amend their lives and ask pardon for their sins. They must not offend Our Lord any more, for He is already too much offended."[953]

A Mystical Doctrine

"Fatima is indeed a mystical doctrine or, so to speak, a devotion completely centered on the Immaculate Heart of Mary, and the consecration and reparation due it. It is also the fully traditional conception of religion and theology, completely oriented toward the last ends without any compromise with the world, or the idle dreams of Christian progressivism…it is a politics of Christendom which invites the Church to stand up resolutely to the gravest

---

[950] Sr. Mary Lucia, op. cit., pp. 167-168.
[951] Frère Michel, op. cit., end note 29: p. 212.
[952] Sr. Mary Lucia, op. cit., p. 172.
[953] Frère Michel, op. cit., p. 291.

peril of the hour..."[954] The whole Message of Fatima, including the Great Secret and the Great Miracle of the Sun, plumbs oceanic depths of the Faith which this volume can merely outline and urgently repeat:

• The Lady's gentle but insistent command to the Pope to consecrate Russia, in union with the world's bishops, to her Immaculate Heart is intended to save the Church's human element, convert sinners, and remind the Vicar of the dignity, the authority, and the duties of his high office. As reigning Steward of the Catholic City, the Pope's role, which safeguards the Deposit of Faith, is intended for the salvation of souls.

• The Virgin Mother of God also wishes the Vicar of Christ to universally promulgate the Five First Saturdays of Reparation for the blasphemies made against her Most Amiable Heart. With her specific requests to the Pope, Our Lady desires that the Vicar of her Divine Son's Church recalls his solemn obligation to preserve the Faith, whole and intact, in "restoring all things in Christ."[955] As Steward, he is guardian of the Church. As such, it is the Pope's honor and duty to obey the Queen of the Catholic City, just as He must obey the King, Our Lord Jesus Christ.

• The Virgin's insistence that the bishops must join the Holy Father in the Collegial Consecration reminds the princes of the Church that their offices, while elevated, remain subordinate to the Holy Father; they, too, must obey his lawful commands. With the Pope—whose responsibility is even greater than theirs—they are accountable to God for the souls placed under their care.

• The Blessed Mother stated succinctly, "God wishes to establish in the world devotion to my Immaculate Heart"—a devotion to the Mediatrix of all Graces, the final recourse to save "poor sinners" from hell. Decades have passed since the Virgin Mary uttered those words, and still we do not see this devotion universally practiced, much less promulgated by the Church's pastors.

While we cannot be certain which will come first—the Collegial Consecration of Russia or the worldwide devotion to Our Lady's Heart—we do know that we should follow Our Lady's five requests for all of the faithful, addressed to each and every one of us, from the Pope in Rome to the least of God's little ones.

Finally, we should also remember that the five things of which the Lady of the Rosary asked of us are as straightforward as they are profound. Intended to sanctify us and keep us on the path of ongoing conversion (the secret of the interior life), these five practices must be well-memorized, shared with others and, above all, practiced. They are as follows: **1)** The daily Rosary, **2)** Faithful

---

[954] Frère Michel, *TWTF,* Vol. II, pp. 770.
[955] Ephes. 1:10.

accomplishment of daily duty (as Catholics and also in our states in life), **3)** Sacrifices for the conversion of sinners, **4)** The wearing of the Brown Scapular of Our Lady of Mt. Carmel, and **5)** Our practice of devotion via the Five First Saturdays of Reparation.

In heeding these five requests of the Mother of God, we shall deepen devotion to the Immaculate Heart in our own lives and that of our families, hopefully make further steps in the three conversions of the interior life, assist God (Who usually acts through people) in the conversion of our fellow sinners, and attain salvation.

The "Business" of Salvation

In its entirety, then, the Fatima Message is given for the sake of all who must battle for their souls in the most dangerous of times—the age of the great apostasy. The Message, Miracle and Secret rest on a central theme of salvation in three parts. "First is the salvation of souls; second is the salvation of the nations and of Christendom, the peace of the world; and third is the preservation of the Catholic Faith and the salvation of the Church."[956]

"Truly, it is the greatest of errors to neglect the business of eternal salvation," said St. Eucherius, a truth upon which St. Alphonsus de Liguori further elaborated by saying "it is an error that exceeds all others, for to lose the soul is a mistake without a remedy."[957]

"One thing is necessary," wrote St. Alphonsus as he emphatically quoted the *Gospel of St. Luke*, "the salvation of our souls...For this God has placed us here: not to acquire honors, riches, or pleasures, but to acquire by our good works the eternal kingdom that is prepared for those who, during this present life, fight against and overcome the enemies of their eternal salvation." [958]

With this truth in mind, as we pray and sacrifice for the triumph of the Most Pure Heart of Mary, may we always keep confidence in the Virgin's words at Fatima: "Don't lose heart. I will never forsake you. My Immaculate Heart will be your refuge, and the path that will lead you to God." [959]

---

[956] Frère Michel, op. cit., pp. 9-10.
[957] de Liguori, St. Alphonsus. *The Way of Salvation and Perfection.* [Brooklyn, NY: Redemptorist Fathers, 1926]: p. 254.
[958] Ibid., p. 42.
[959] Sr. Mary Lucia, op. cit., p. 163.

CHAPTER 38
Five Simple Steps to Sanctity

"The world must conform to Our Lord, not He to it."
—Fr Denis Fahey

"We must pray a great deal and beg God not to chastise us and **save us in time** and **for eternity**," Sr. Lucia once urged in carefully guarded yet revealing terms, as she spoke about the third part of Fatima's Great Secret.[960] Compare those words of the Servant of God to the novel and empty mottos of our own times. In response to the senseless rhetoric and in hopes of restoring the social order of Christ the King, Catholics of good will are asking their fellows to make some changes of their own. Whatever changes must be made, however, must be in accord with God's Will. In fact, it is past time for a universal epiphany amongst all true Catholics: In our homes, parishes, and Catholic apostolates, our common cause must be the public and solemn Collegial Consecration of Russia and devotion to the Immaculate Heart of Mary.

Right and just is the recent clarion call from Catholics asking other members of the Mystical Body of Christ to work together to "restore all things in Christ"[961] for the eternal Church, upholding the teaching of St. Thomas Aquinas, maintains: "Each one is under obligation to show forth his faith, either to instruct and encourage others of the faithful, or to repel the attacks of unbelievers." [962] As the Angelic Doctor also explained, "In all ages, men have been divinely instructed in matters expedient for the salvation of the elect...and in all ages there have been persons possessed of the spirit of prophesy, not for the purpose of announcing new doctrines, but to direct human actions."[963] Such was the purpose of the Fatima revelations.

The Five Point Defense of the Catholic City
In praying and working for the Restoration of the Social Reign of Christ the King, all our actions as the Church Militant should be placed under the supreme battle plan given by Our Lady of Fatima, She who "cometh forth as the morning rising, fair as the moon, bright as the sun, terrible as an army set in

---

[960] Frère Michel, *TWTF*, Vol. III, p. 509.
[961] Pope St. Pius X (Our Apostolic Mandate, August 25, 1910): para. 11
[962] Pope Leo XIII, *Sapientiae Christianae* (On Christians as Citizens, January 10, 1890): para. 14.
[963] Aquinas, St. Thomas. *Summa*: 2:2:174: Res. et ad 3.

array." [964] Her battle plan is intended for each one of us, on an individual basis as a beloved child of God, a dutiful citizen of the Catholic City, and a stalwart soldier of Christ.

As children of God, we should approach Our Lord and Our Lady as little ones approach their parents on earth, full of love, confidence and hope.

As citizens of the Catholic City, we follow the Royal Road because it was first trod by Christ the King and His Virgin Mother, for as Our Lord taught, **"If any man will come after Me, let him deny himself, and take up his cross daily, and follow Me."** [965]

As soldiers of Christ, our best defense is a good offense. The victorious "peaceful battle strategy" to "save us in time and for eternity," as Sr. Lucia phrased it, has been given to every single member of the Church Militant at Fatima by Our Mother and Mediatrix, Conqueror of Heresies. So important are they that once more shall they be repeated:

1) The daily Rosary,

2) Faithful accomplishment of daily duty (as Catholics and in our states in life),

3) sacrifice for the conversion of sinners,

4) The Brown Scapular of Our Lady of Mt. Carmel,

5) The Five First Saturdays of Reparation.

6) Specific to the Pope, Steward of the Catholic City, Our Lady requested the Consecration of Russia to her Immaculate Heart in union with all the bishops of the world.

May God Save Us in Time and in Eternity

Lest we think the term "peaceful battle" an oxymoron, let us also recall the Church's counsel as explained by Pope Pius XI, "Certainly there is the greatest need now of such **valiant soldiers of Christ** who will work with all their strength to keep the human family safe from the dire ruin into which it would be plunged were the teachings of the *Gospel* to be flouted, and that order of things permitted to prevail which tramples underfoot no less the laws of nature than those of God. The Church of Christ, built upon an unshakable rock, has nothing to fear for herself, as she knows for a certainty that the gates of hell shall never prevail against her…"

"Venerable Brethren and Beloved Sons, let us not permit the children of this world to appear wiser in their generation than we who by the Divine Goodness are the children of the light. We find them, indeed, selecting and training with the greatest shrewdness alert and resolute devotees who spread

---

[964] Cant. 6:9.

[965] Lk. 9:23.

their errors ever wider day by day through all classes of men and in every part of the world. And whenever they undertake to attack the Church of Christ more violently, We see them put aside their internal quarrels, assembling in fully harmony in a single battle line with a completely united effort, and work to achieve their common purpose."

"Surely there is not one that does not know how many and how great are the works that the tireless zeal of Catholics is striving everywhere to carry out, both for social and economic welfare as well as in the fields of education and religion. **But this admirable and unremitting activity not infrequently shows less effectiveness because of the dispersion of its energies in too many different directions. Therefore, let all men of good will stand united, all who under the Shepherds of the Church wish to fight this good and peaceful battle of Christ; and under the leadership and teaching guidance of the Church let all strive according to the talent, powers, and position of each to contribute something to the Christian reconstruction of human society** ...seeking not themselves and their own interests, but those of Jesus Christ, **not trying to press at all costs their own counsels, but ready to sacrifice them, however excellent, if the greater common good should seem to require it, so that in all and above all Christ may reign, Christ may command** to Whom be *'honor and glory and dominion forever and ever.* "[966]

In heeding the Fatima Virgin's gentle commands, we can do more than imitate "the children of this world" who "put aside their internal quarrels, assembling in fully harmony in a single battle line with a completely united effort, and work to achieve their common purpose." In our own private lives, in our homes, and in our various Catholic apostolates, we are already united because we are members of the Mystical Body of Christ. For what other common purpose should we spiritually join forces other than to accomplish what Our Lady of Fatima asked, by praying the daily Rosary and sacrificing for the conversion of sinners, and asking always for the collegial consecration of Russia to the one and only Immaculate Heart?

Our Lady and Catholic Action

We can take other important *Catholic* steps, from homeschooling our children to participating in various volunteer efforts, subscribing to tried-and-true traditional Catholic papers, and much more. At the same time, we must realize that these worthy efforts, which can save individuals and perhaps whole families for eternity, will not bring forth *worldwide* conversion—which in turn will save hundreds of millions of souls. Our actions alone can neither destroy

---

[966] Pope Pius XI, *Quadragesimo Anno* (Reconstruction of the Social Order, May 15, 1931): para. 144, 146-147.

modernism (the synthesis of all heresies), nor effect the conversion of Russia nor grant an era of peace to mankind. Those are miracles reserved by God for Our Lady, who revealed at Fatima that only she can help us and who also said at Akita, "Those who place their confidence in me will be saved."

"But seek ye first the Kingdom of God and His justice, and all these things shall be added unto you,"[967] as Christ Our Lord taught. "My Immaculate Heart will be your refuge and the path that will lead you to God," said Our Lady at Fatima. These words of Christ and His Virgin Mother complement each other, for as St. Bernadine of Siena explained, "Every grace that is communicated to this world has a threefold course. For by excellent order, it is dispensed from God to Christ, from Christ to the Virgin, from the Virgin to us."

The Virgin and a Mystery of the Holy Trinity

The Rosary is the storehouse of blessings, wrote Blessed Alan de La Roche. Today, as Sr. Lucia revealed "... the Most Holy Virgin in these last times in which we live has given a new efficacy to the recitation of the Rosary...**There is no problem,** no matter how difficult it is, that **we cannot resolve by the prayer of the Holy Rosary.** With the Holy Rosary, we will save ourselves. We will sanctify ourselves. We will console Our Lord and obtain the salvation of many souls."[968]

In the following excerpts from Sr. Lucia's private letters, we may gain beautiful insights about the Rosary: [969]

"Our Lady requested and recommended that the Rosary be prayed every day, having repeated this [request] in all the Apparitions, as if forewarning us that in these times of *diabolical disorientation*, we must not let ourselves be deceived by false doctrines that diminish the elevation of our soul to God by means of prayer."

"For certain, it is not necessary that during the celebration of the Holy Sacrifice of the Mass that one pray the Holy Rosary, [for] besides time set aside for the Holy Mass, we must also put aside time for praying the Holy Rosary. We can and should take part in the one without forsaking the other."

"The Rosary is, for the majority of souls who live in the world, their daily spiritual bread; and to deprive them or draw them away from this prayer is to

---

[967] Lk. 12:31.

[968] Frère Michel, *op. cit.*: pp. 507-508.

[969] Quotes from Sr. Lucia come *from A Little Treatise by the Seer on the Nature and Recitation of the Rosary*, a collection of excerpts from Sr. Lucia's letters written between 1969-1971. It was originally published in *Uma vida ao service de Fatima* with an Imprimatur from the Bishop of Leiria, Fatima, Dom Joae Venancio, May 13, 1971.

decrease in their minds the appreciation and good faith with which they pray…"

"All the prayers that we say in the Rosary are prayers that form part of the Sacred Liturgy. More than a prayer directed to Our Lady, it is a prayer directed to God:

• "The *Our Father* was taught to us by Jesus Christ, Who said, 'Pray thus, *Our Father Who art in heaven…*' "

• "*Glory be to the Father, and to the Son, and to the Holy Ghost* is the hymn sung by the Angels who were sent by God to announce the birth of His Word, God-made Man."

• "The *Hail Mary*, when well understood, is nothing less than a prayer directed to God: '*Hail Mary, full of grace, the Lord is with Thee.*' I hail Thee, Mary, because the Lord is with Thee! These words were most certainly dictated by the Father in heaven to the Angel when He sent him to earth, in order that with these words he (the angel) should greet Mary."

"So this salutation [Hail Mary] is an act of praise addressed to God: Blessed art Thou amongst women because Blessed (sic) is the fruit of Thy womb; and because Thou are the Mother of God-made Man. In Thee, we adore God as in **the first Tabernacle** in which the Father enclosed His Word; as on **the first Altar**, Thy lap; as in **the first Monstrance**, Thy arms, before which the Angels, shepherds and kings knelt to adore the Son of God made Man!"

Sr. Lucia also alluded to a mystery of the Holy Trinity, as well as a mystery of Our Lady's earthly life and her life in heaven when she wrote, "Since Thou art a Tabernacle, a Monstrance, a living Temple, permanent home of the Holy Trinity, Mother of God and Our Mother— '*pray for us poor sinners, now and at the hour of our death.*' "

Although previously mentioned in this book, it bears repeating, for what a breathtaking contemplation it is to always keep in mind, especially as we pray the Rosary—in Heaven and in eternity, **Our Lady is the Perpetual Tabernacle of the Holy Trinity!** Volumes might be written about this Mariophany but, for now, let it suffice to ask ourselves: Is it any wonder that to save us "in these last days" that the Rosary, which is an act of praise to God, is given a new efficacy? Or that Our Lady asked us to pray it every day? Or that Jesus wills Russia's consecration to His Mother's Immaculate Heart, so that one day the whole world will honor her Heart next to His own Sacred Heart?

After the Holy Sacrifice of the Mass, the Rosary is the most highly indulgenced prayer of the Church, which grants a plenary indulgence (the complete remission of temporal punishments of confessed sins) *every day of the year* to those who pray the Rosary in a church, oratory, or with members of the family at home, in a religious Community, or in a pious association.[970]

"Therefore, it is necessary to pray the Rosary in cities, in towns and in villages, in the streets, on the road, while traveling or at home, in churches and in chapels!" wrote Sr. Lucia. "It is a prayer that is accessible to all and everyone can and should pray. There are many who do not attend the liturgical prayer of the Holy Mass on a daily basis. If they do not pray the Rosary, what praying do they accomplish? And without prayer, who can be saved? *'Watch and pray that ye enter not into temptation.'*"

"It is necessary, then, to pray and pray always," Sr. Lucia concluded. "This means that all our activities and labors should be accompanied by a great spirit of prayer. It is in prayer that the soul meets God. In this meeting, grace and strength are received, even when one's prayers are accompanied by distractions. Prayer always brings an increase of Faith to souls, even if it be no more than a momentary remembrance of the Mysteries of our Redemption—recalling the Birth, Death and Resurrection of Our Savior; and God will dismiss and pardon those distractions attributed to human weakness, ignorance and littleness."

"*That Thy Kingdom come, let the reign of Mary come,*" wrote St. Louis Marie de Montfort. The reign of Mary is the reign of Christ, the same era of peace promised by Our Lady of Fatima. It was to save us "in time and for eternity" that the Mother of God came to Fatima, giving God's five-point "peaceful battle plan" to all of the Church's children, while appointing a special task to the Vicar of the Church and the bishops.

It is a sanctifying strategy we can share with others as we ourselves live it, always making our foremost intention the Collegial Consecration of Russia to the Virgin's Immaculate Heart. By these means we can follow the sound spiritual advice of Sr. Lucia, confidante of Heaven: "It is necessary for each one of us to begin to reform himself spiritually. Each person must not only save his own soul but also help to save all the souls that God has placed on our path."

---

[970] *Norms for Indulgences*, 3rd Edition (May 18, 1986): The Other Types of Indulgences Grants, #5.

CHAPTER 39

Why Daily Duty Sanctifies Us

"Our Lord does not care so much for the importance of our works,
as for the love with which they are done."
—St. Teresa of Avila

Daily duty, prayer and sacrifice, and the interior life—what do these things really mean? God, Who knows all things, knew that the Modern Age would be one of increased sin and danger. Having already given us the means to sanctity, He gave a new efficacy to "simple things," like the Rosary. Through the Fatima revelations, which are in perfect accord with Divine Revelation, Our Lord also made it known that the "true penance" He now requires of each one of us is the faithful accomplishment of daily duty. The means are prayer and sacrifice, by which the interior life may become perfect in God, because "in divine things the most simple...are also the loftiest and the most profound."[971]

Like Tradition and Scripture, prayer and sacrifice are inseparable to the spiritual life of the soul. The Rosary is the prayer Our Lady asked us to offer every day. It is a great spiritual help to know a few more reasons why we should pray the daily Rosary.

At Fatima, Our Lady often responded to the people's supplications, saying it was necessary for them to pray the daily Rosary in order to obtain these graces throughout the year.[972] At other times, she said the request would be granted within the year if the Rosary was prayed every day. As in all things, the Virgin's response is for God's glory and the salvation of souls.

To pray the Rosary, every day for a year, is to practice perseverance in prayer. Our Lord said, "All things whatsoever you ask in prayer, believing, you shall receive."[973] The daily Rosary gives us greater faith, hope and charity. It increases our belief, our adoration, our trust, our confidence and our love for God and His Virgin Mother. It multiplies sanctifying grace and helps us avoid mortal sin—even venial sin. The 15 Rosary Promises, given centuries ago to Blessed Alan de la Roche, are intended to lead us to her Divine Son. And so we begin to understand why, at every Fatima apparition, Our Lady asked for the daily Rosary.

---

[971] Garrigou-Lagrange, *The Three Stages of the Interior Life*, Vol. II, p. 165.
[972] Frère Michel, *TWTF*, Vol. I, p. 181.
[973] Matt. 21: 22.

With the daily Rosary there is always our daily duty, which Our Lord called "the true penance" He now requires. Daily duty has ever been the obligation of the faithful Catholic; it is the normal path to sanctification. As Sr. Lucia wrote concerning what Jesus said in this regard, "He wishes that it be made clear to souls that the true penance He wants and requires consists first of all in the sacrifice that each one must make to fulfill his own religious and temporal duties."[974]

What is Daily Duty?

It means faithfully fulfilling our obligations to God and in our states in life with supernatural charity, the virtue summed up by Christ Himself: "Thou shalt love the Lord thy God with thy whole heart, and with thy whole soul, and with thy whole mind. This is the greatest and the first commandment. And the second is like to this: Thou shalt love thy neighbor as thyself. On these two commandments dependeth the whole law and the prophets."[975]

How we accomplish daily duty is the secret of the interior life, which is also called "the life of the elect" or "the spiritual life." The interior life is defined as "the state of activity of a soul which strives against its natural inclinations in order to regulate them, and endeavors to acquire the habit of judging and directing in movements in all things according to the light of the *Gospel* and the example of Our Lord."[976]

When we offer our every thought, word and action of the day to Jesus through Mary, our souls gain spiritual merit. "The chief fruit of sanctifying grace is merit—a claim or right to receive an increase of sanctifying grace, together with a claim to a corresponding measure of glory and happiness in heaven," the *Baltimore Catechism* explains. "We can increase in heavenly merit indefinitely. Not only works which are by their nature good, such as prayer and the reception of the sacraments and attendance at Mass, but even the ordinary works of our day, such as the taking of our meals, study, our games and amusements, can become meritorious if we perform them under the proper conditions. These conditions are very easy—we must be in the state of grace and offer our works to God out of love for Him. We do not have to make this offering with each work we perform. It is sufficient to make it from time to time, particularly every morning..."[977]

---

[974] Frère Michel, *TWTF,* Vol. III, pp. 20-21.
[975] Mt 22: 36-40.
[976] Walsh, *Meditation on the Passion,* p. 17.
[977] *Baltimore Catechism and Mass #3,* The New Confraternity Edition, Revised [Washington, D.C: The Catholic University of America, 1949], Important Truths about the Holy Ghost and Grace: p. 65.

It was for this reason that Sr. Lucia, the last Fatima visionary (whose cause for canonization has been opened), assisted in composing what is known as the Fatima Morning Offering. As soon as we awaken, we may give our thoughts to God and consecrate the day to Him by praying the Morning Offering:

O my God, in union with the Immaculate Heart of Mary (here kiss the Brown Scapular[978]), I offer Thee the Most Precious Body, Blood, Soul and Divinity of Our Lord, Jesus Christ, joining with it my every thought, word and action of this day.

O my Jesus, I desire today to gain every indulgence and merit I can, and I offer them, together with myself, to Mary Immaculate, that she may best apply them to the interests of Thy Most Sacred Heart. Precious Blood of Jesus, save us! Immaculate Heart of Mary, pray for us! Most Sacred Heart of Jesus, have mercy on us. Amen.

This particular offering means we give everything to God, "to Jesus through Mary." It is the shorter way of spiritual perfection, as taught by St. Louis de Montfort, an interior life of simplicity. "In divine things," wrote the eminent theologian, Fr. Garrigou-Lagrange, O.P., "simplicity is united to depth and elevation, for divine things that are highest in God and deepest in our hearts are simplicity itself."[979]

"Do your duty and all will go well" was a favorite saying of Pope St. Pius X, by which he meant all will go well with the life of the soul. Daily duty, justly accomplished when we cooperate with grace, leads to infused contemplation, but only if there is "progress in the acquired virtues, the infused virtues, and the seven gifts of the Holy Ghost in interior souls truly detached from themselves and almost continually united to God."[980] To accomplish daily duty means practice of all the virtues to a heroic degree. Such is the path to sanctity.

Pitfalls on the Path

Daily duty accomplished with love, but "dying to self," is not an easy process. Although "the charity of God presseth us"[981] to return His love, there is good reason that the Scriptures warn we must work out our salvation in fear

---

[978] A partial indulgence of 500 days is granted each time the Brown Scapular of Mt. Carmel is piously kissed. An individual who wears this sacramental should be either enrolled in the Confraternity of the Brown Scapular (which imparts a perpetual blessing on the wearer, so that new Scapulars need not be blessed) or otherwise ensure that each new Brown Scapular is properly blessed by a priest.

[979] Garrigou-Lagrange, loc. cit.

[980] Ibid.

[981] 2 Cor. 5: 14.

and trembling.[982] A holy fear of the Lord means we love Him and do not want to offend Him, just because we love Him. We should always fear ourselves because, due to the effects of Original Sin, we bear four wounds—ignorance, weakness, malice and disordered desire. These four wounds are the causes of our faults, which we so carefully hide from ourselves, but they are overcome when we use God's graces well. That is why Our Lord made it clear that our daily duty should be offered up in true penance.

Due to our spiritual weaknesses, we are easily swayed into thinking we have pleased God, especially when we fulfill our religious obligations. We must guard against outward shows of piety (to garner attention for ourselves) while simultaneously fearing to do as we ought (because we are afraid of what others may think of us). Nor should we revel in spiritual consolations, for two reasons: They do not signify sanctity and they are fleeting. In fact, God eventually withdraws such consolations to help us overcome pride and whatever else may be our predominant fault.

Pride, the root of all sin, is very cunning, because it hides itself under the guise of virtue. Although we are in a state of grace, we are not "safe" from the seven deadly sins; indeed, the devil works against us even more so. His ultimate aim is to find our weak spots, blind us to our faults, retard our progress, or cause us to fall so many times that we are tempted to despair. Interior troubles often begin with temptations to pride.

Both the Old and New Testaments provide copious examples of pride, the particular danger to the faithful. For example, we recall St. Peter's over-confidence that he would never abandon Christ. Yet only hours after receiving the very first Holy Communion, he and all of the Apostles fled from Christ's persecutors. Then the first Vicar of Christ publicly denied the Lord three times. For this great fault, St. Peter wept and sincerely repented for the rest of his life. This one, painful failure was a great lesson to him and to all the Church's members throughout time: We can never be sure of ourselves, only of God and those with Him in Heaven.

Even after the Resurrection and Ascension, the Apostles' faith remained weak until the Descent of the Holy Ghost. Pentecost brought to them the second interior conversion, with the result that St. Peter fearlessly and publicly proclaimed Christ. Although greatly persecuted, they never again denied Our Lord. Despite this fidelity, human respect was the cause of St. Peter's second great public sin.

His first public offense was against God; his second was against his neighbor. The second wrong-doing seemed a very small matter at the time, but

---

[982] Phil. 2: 12.

it displayed a serious hidden fault. St. Peter caused a great scandal to the faithful when he would not sit with the Gentile converts (who were not circumcised) for fear of the Jewish converts (who were circumcised).[983] St. Peter, who thought it prudent to momentarily avoid the Gentiles, committed an act of cowardice, which artfully disguises itself as the virtue of prudence.

On the path of sanctity, our predominant fault is overcome if and when we truly love God above everything else. As trustworthy spiritual advisors like Fr. Garrigou-Lagrange point out, we (like St. Peter) usually learn of our hidden faults by trials, sufferings and humiliations. On the other hand, not all trials are due to our sins, for some are meant to perfect us while others allow us to practice greater charity in reparation for the sins of others.

Charity, the queen of virtues, is the reason why daily duty can be offered to God as "true penance." When we submit to all that God allows or wills in our lives, thinking only of Him in our joys and sufferings, we imitate Christ, Who loved us enough to live—and die—for us.

"Pick Up Your Cross Daily and Follow Me"

The sacrifice of daily duty, then, is our cross. The Cross is "all that goes against self. All that it costs to subdue self—to act on principle, submit to authority, to follow common life, to accommodate ourselves to others, to bear correction, to be faithful to irksome duties, to be submissive and humble during sickness, to struggle against self-indulgence and the softness of our times, preserving attention to the rules of modesty, to be energetic in attention to our weak point, to bear up against failure and monotony of daily routine, to be resigned when all seems to go wrong, whatever is contrary to our liking in circumstances, our health, the way things are done, the way things turn out—all that is our cross." The truth is that "true holiness does not consist in not feeling the Cross, but in bearing the pain with true conformity to God's will."[984]

As St. Vincent Ferrer said, "Whatever you do, think not of yourself, but of God."

---

[983] Gal. 2: 11-14.
[984] Walsh, op. cit., p. 222.

CHAPTER 40

Why Saturday is Our Lady's Day

"In danger, in anguish, in uncertainty, think of Mary, call on Mary. May she never be far from your lips, from your heart; and thus you will be able to obtain the help of her prayer, never forget the example of her life. If you follow her, you cannot go astray; if you pray to her, you cannot despair; if you think of her, you cannot be mistaken. If she sustains you, you cannot fall; if she protects you, you have nothing to fear; if she guides you, do not tire; if she is propitious to you, you will reach the goal ..."

−St. Bernard of Clairvaux,
Hom. II super "Missus est," 17: PL 183, 70-71

Some may wonder why the Virgin Mary specifically chose Saturday as a day of reparation. Why Saturday and not another day, other than the Lord's Day?

"To you it is given to know the mystery of the Kingdom of God,"[985] Our Lord revealed to His Apostles, but how much more do His words apply to Our Lady, whose singular office surpasses that of the disciples. Theologians are accustomed to point out that when God calls a human being to any office, He gives that person all the graces needed to fulfill its obligations.[986] Naturally, that teaching applies to Our Lady and never was it truer than on the first Holy Saturday, when the grieving Blessed Mother alone remained constant in faith.[987] It is for this reason that **Saturday**, especially Holy Saturday, **is considered by the Church as** *Our Lady's Day.*

When the Jewish Sabbath began at sunset on Good Friday and all through Saturday, Our Lady and Jesus' disciples, including the Holy Women, were prostrate with sorrow. Amongst all of them, only the Virgin Mary fully understood her Son's promise of His Resurrection, keeping its unwavering hope in her Sorrowful and Immaculate Heart.

Think of all that must have transpired in the Heart and Soul of the Virgin Mother as she remembered those most dreadful hours of her Son's Passion.

---

[985] Mk. 4:11.
[986] Smith, *The Teaching of the Catholic Church,* p. 538.
[987] de Liguori, St. Alphonsus. *The Glories of Mary,* p. 602.

The mere thought of a beloved child, enduring such suffering and abuse, would bring to the heart of any other human mother deep pangs of grief. Imagine the sorrow of the Immaculate Heart of the Mother of God! How much Our Lady endured–*for us!*

Throughout the Sabbath, the Blessed Mother recalled the betrayal, saw again the most grievous Passion, and once more heard the contemptuous words that insulted and blasphemed Our Lord. Tortured and ridiculed from all sides, Jesus was never given a moment's peace from the second that His Passion began. *God is not mocked,*[988] but He allowed Himself to be mocked as a prophet who said that He could raise the destroyed temple in three days, mocked in His quality of Son of God, mocked as a miracle-worker who healed others but could not help Himself, mocked for His sanctity and confidence in God, mocked as the Messiah and mocked as the King of the Jews.[989]

Loving and grieving witnesses of the Passion, Our Lady and the few who had been with her at the Foot of the Cross must have later told the other Apostles of Our Lord's last words:

His First Plea to God the Father: "Father, forgive them, for they know not what they do."[990]

To the Good Thief: "Amen, I say to thee: This day thou shalt be with me in Paradise."[991]

To His Virgin Mother and St. John: "Woman, behold thy son... son, behold thy Mother."[992]

A Second Cry to God the Father: *"Eli, Eli, lamma sabacthani?* That is, My God, my God, why hast thou forsaken me?"[993]

Through parched lips: "I thirst."[994]

For all to hear: "It is consummated."[995]

A Third Prayer to God the Father: *"Father, into thy hands I commend my spirit.* And saying this, he gave up the ghost."[996]

---

[988] Gal 6:7.
[989] Walsh, *Meditation on the Passion*, p. 249.
[990] Lk. 23: 34
[991] Lk. 23: 43.
[992] Jn. 19: 26–27.
[993] Matt. 27: 46.
[994] Jn. 19: 28.
[995] Jn. 19: 30.

As if it was not enough to remember Jesus' cruel sufferings during His Passion and at His Death, they saw again Our Lord's side not only pierced but opened wide by a lance, His Sacred Heart laid bare and gushing forth blood and water. For Our Lady, witnessing this last and vicious sacrilege of her beloved Son's Body, Simeon's prophecy came to pass: "*And thy own soul a sword shall pierce that, out of many hearts, thoughts shall be revealed.*"[997]

Ancilla Domini (Handmaiden of the Lord)

In those after-hours, the Virgin Mary would repeatedly behold in her memory Jesus' Sacred Body removed from the Cross and the withdrawing of the cruel nails and the Crown of Thorns, feeling again His Holy Form, torn to shreds, and lying limp in her arms. Transfixed by the uttermost sorrow, Our Lady was silent in her anguish, but how the others must have wept at the sight of His beautiful and Holy Face, now so pale and disfigured. Relived once more was the rushed, distressing burial in a freshly-hewn and donated tomb.

Above the deep heartache of the faithful St. John and St. Mary Magdalene, the Apostles and the Holy Women, Our Lady's immaculate soul was crucified when her Son was crucified, which is why the Immaculate Heart is also the Sorrowful Heart of the Virgin Mother.

It was during the Passion that the Lady, full of grace, rose to the supreme and most terrible Sacrifice. Her prayer then consisted of the same words she spoke to the Angel Gabriel thirty-four years before: *Ecce Ancilla Domini*—that is, "*Behold the handmaid of the Lord;* be it done to me according to Thy word.*"[998] During the terrible Passion and Death of her Divine Son, the overflowing graces and virtues of this humble Maiden never allowed her to even once doubt what the Angel said to her long ago: "*The Lord will give Him the throne of David His father, and He shall be King over the house of Jacob forever, and of His kingdom there shall be no end.*"[999]

City of God: The Joys, Sorrows, and Glories of Mary

"I am the mother of fair love, and of fear, and of knowledge, and of holy hope. In me is all grace of the way and of the truth, in me is all hope of life and virtue."[1000] In explaining these words from the Old Testament, St. Alphonsus taught, "As the Blessed Virgin is the mother of holy love and hope, so also is she the mother of faith."[1001]

---

[996] Lk. 23: 46.
[997] Lk. 2:35.
[998] Lk. 1: 38.
[999] Lk. 1:32.
[1000] Eccles. 24:24-25.
[1001] de Liguori, op. cit., p. 564.

"Hope takes its rise in faith," the saint continued, "for God enlightens by faith to know His goodness and the promises He had made, that by this knowledge we may rise by hope to the desire of possessing Him. Mary, then, having had the virtue of faith in its highest degree, had also hope in the same degree of excellence, and this made her say with David, *But it is good for me to adhere to my God, to put my hope in the Lord God.*"[1002]

In all of the joyful, sorrowful, and glorious events of her life, Our Lady "stood alone, in a position apart, in her relation to the Redeemer and to His work of Redemption."[1003] As St. Alphonsus also taught, "the most holy Virgin had more faith than all men and angels. She saw her Son in the crib of Bethlehem, and believed Him the Creator of the world. She saw him fly from Herod, and yet believed Him the King of Kings. She saw him born and believed Him eternal. She saw Him poor and in need of food, and believed Him the Lord of the universe. She saw Him lying on straw, and believed Him omnipotent. She observed that He did not speak, and She believed Him infinite Wisdom. She heard Him weep, and believed Him the joy of Paradise. In fine, she saw Him in death, despised and crucified and, although faith wavered in others, Mary remained firm in the belief that He was God."[1004]

It may seem that such things were effortless for the Blessed Mother because she is the Immaculate One. It is true that she was full of grace from the very first moment of her existence, but it was through her continual efforts and merits that grace overflowed in her soul—making her the aqueduct of grace for all souls. *In me is all grace...*

"Among the many beautiful qualities attributed by the Holy Ghost to the Blessed Virgin Mary, one stands out preeminently," wrote St. John Eudes. "It is contained in these words of the eighty-sixth Psalm, which Holy Church and her Doctors apply to the Mother of God, *'Glorious things are said of thee, O city of God.'*"[1005]

"**Mary is indeed the great and glorious city of God**, the holy city, the city of Jerusalem, the city of peace, the royal city, 'the city of the Great King.'[1006] The King of Kings built this city with His own hands; He exempted her entirely from the infamous tribute of sin; He honored her with countless great and extraordinary privileges; He enriched her with inestimable gifts and treasures and He established His first and most glorious abode within her heart...Thou are not only the city of the great King, O Incomparable Virgin,

---

[1002] Ibid., p. 568.
[1003] Smith, op. cit., p. 528.
[1004] Loc. cit., p. 565.
[1005] Ps. 86: 3.
[1006] Ps. 47.

thou art also His royal and eternal palace…Now if Mary is the palace of the King of Kings, her Heart must be the King's imperial throne."[1007]

The Virgin always cooperated with her Spouse for "in Mary is the fullness of the gifts of the Holy Ghost; plenitude of all the interior gifts; plenitude of the gifts of Wisdom and Understanding, plenitude of the gifts of Counsel and Knowledge, plenitude of the gifts of Piety and Fortitude, and of the Fear of the Lord; plenitude of all the exterior gifts, the gifts of miracles, healing, prophecy, and of tongues."[1008]

St. John Eudes also testified, "St. Bernadine of Siena expressly stated that Our Lady…knew all these things in God, as in their first and universal cause…*She saw God in all things, and all things in God.*"[1009] This is the great gift of grace that, when cooperated with, creates great saints; and it was this great grace which mainly sustained the Virgin Mary in all the mystical and mysterious events of her life, especially during the Lord's Way of the Cross and His Crucifixion.

Five Means and Mysteries of the City of God
In the Good Friday Passion and during the desolate hours in which Our Lord laid in the tomb, the faithful Virgin Mother–like her Divine Son, Our Model, throughout His Life and Death–did not abandon even one of **the five means of salvation and sanctification,** in order to be the holiest example for us to imitate. St. Louis Marie de Montfort reminds us that these five means are known to all and that "they are laid down in the *Gospel*, explained by the masters of the spiritual life, practiced by the saints, and necessary to all who wish to be saved and to attain perfection. They are: **humility of heart, continual prayer, mortification in all things, abandonment to Divine Providence, and conformity to the Will of God**."[1010]

Conceived Immaculate and always full of grace, still Our Lady carefully guarded the gifts bestowed on her by the Holy Trinity. St. John Eudes affirmed that "the Holy Virgin's heart exercised perpetual vigilance over her own thoughts, words, and actions, over her passions and inclinations, over all her interior and exterior senses, and over all the powers of her soul, that she might drive far away from herself anything that could possibly displease God and to use her faculties as perfectly and as virtuously as possible."[1011] In her

---

[1007] Eudes, St. John. *The Admirable Heart of Mary*, p. 77.

[1008] *Rosary Crusade Clarion*, June 2001 (Issue 6).

[1009] Bernardine, St. *Serm. 13 de Exalt. BV in Gloria*. Cited in St. John Eudes, op. cit., p. 116. [Emphasis added.]

[1010] de Montfort, .*The Secret of Mary*, p. 11.

[1011] Eudes, op. cit., pp. 164-165.

Immaculate Heart, she pondered many things, and it was her Immaculate Heart, the highest faculty of her soul, that was pierced by a mystical sword of sorrow.

Since all the glories of Mary are for the sake of her Divine Son, as John Cardinal Newman once said in a sermon,[1012] the same can be said of her sorrows. "She had lived of her Son's life, and when He died on the Cross, she died with Him," a holy abbot once said.[1013] "Both Mother and Son were nailed to the Cross, the Son in the Body, the Mother in her Heart," exclaims St. Lawrence Justinian.[1014] "Could not Mary die in her Heart, as Jesus died in His Body?" St Bernard asked.[1015]

Nevertheless, the Virgin did not perish with her beloved Son, but it was "only by a miraculous interposition on the part of God that she did not die." [1016] Her mission on earth was not yet fully accomplished, for the Passion and Death of Our Lord was the means by which Christ offered us Redemption and by which, in the order of grace, Our Lady became Our Mother.

Virgin Most Faithful

When Our Lady retired on Good Friday night, the evening of the Jewish Sabbath, she did so to occupy herself solely with the thought of her Divine Son. "Having cooperated in the Incarnation of the Son of God by the ardor of her love, the fervor of her desires, and the power of her prayers, **Mary's Heart also contributed to His Resurrection...**" [1017]

As the Queen of Martyrs, Our Lady followed her Son and stood at the Cross, her love and humility far overshadowing the public shame of being Mother to the One crucified as the lowest of criminals. As Queen of Prophets, the Blessed Mother stood apart from all others for only she foresaw and kept hope in the Resurrection throughout the Sabbath. It was to the gracious Virgin Mary that the Apostles and the Holy Women turned to on the Sabbath, flying to the Mother of Mercy, Mother of God and Mother of the Church.

Holy Tradition relates that Christ, having risen from dead about 3 a.m. on Easter Sunday morning, first appeared to His Virgin Mother. Scripture supports that tradition, for Our Lady was not with the Holy Women who went to Christ's tomb later on the same morning. **Why was it that the faithful Mother**—who stood at the Foot of the Cross, held her deceased Son in her arms, and hurriedly prepared Him for burial before the Sabbath began—**did**

[1012] Smith, op. cit., p. 513.
[1013] Eudes, op. cit., p. 97.
[1014] Ibid.
[1015] Ibid.
[1016] de Liguori, op. cit., pp. 527-528.
[1017] Eudes, loc. cit.

not return to Jesus' sepulcher to properly anoint His Body, according to the Jewish custom? It was because not only had she anticipated His Resurrection, but she *knew* He had risen.

Just as the Virgin preceded her Divine Son in historical time, so does **"Lady's Day"** (Saturday) precede **the Lord's Day** (Sunday). St. Thomas Aquinas explains: "Since the Resurrection took place on a Sunday, we keep holy this day instead of the Sabbath as did the Jews of old. However, we also sanctify Saturday in honor of the glorious Virgin Mary who remained unshaken in faith all day Saturday after the death of her Divine Son."[1018]

Not only on Holy Saturday but on each Saturday of the year, faithful Catholics might also recall these words of St. Bernard's: "In Mary alone did the faith of the Church remain steadfast during the three days that Jesus lay in the tomb. And although everyone else wavered, she who conceived Christ in faith, kept the faith that she had once for all received from God and never lost. Thus could she wait with assured hope for the glory of the Risen Lord."[1019]

Our Lady's Sorrowful and Immaculate Heart teaches us how to commemorate the death of Our Lord, Jesus Christ. At His Incarnation, Our Lady was the Lord's first Tabernacle. During His Passion and Crucifixion, the Sorrowful and Immaculate Heart of Mary became the living Altar on which the Lamb offered Himself for the sins of the world. But **it was on Holy Saturday that the *Sorrowful* and Immaculate Heart first reigned**, because the Virgin Mother solitarily trusted in the Resurrection of her most beloved Son, Our Lord and Savior Jesus Christ.

"**Teach souls to love the Heart of My Mother**, pierced by the very sorrow which pierced Mine...**The Heart of My Mother has the right to be called Sorrowful**, and **I wish this title to be placed before that of Immaculate, for she won it herself.**" (Our Lord to Berthe Petit)

~

[1018] Hardon, S.J., Fr. John. "Fatima in the Light of History." *The Real Presence.* [http://www.therealpresence.org/archives/Mariology/Mariology_030.htm]
[1019] Ibid.

PRAYERS AND PROMISES
~The Five First Saturdays of Reparation~

I. THE HISTORY AND TEXT OF THE PROMISE

As explained by Sr. Lucia and documented by Frère Michel de la Sainte Trinité: "On December 10, 1925, the Most Holy Virgin appeared to Sister Lucia (then a postulant of the Institute of the Dorothean Sisters at Pontevedra, Spain) and by her side, elevated on a luminous cloud, was the Child Jesus. The Most Holy Virgin rested her hand on her shoulder and as she did so, she showed her Heart encircled by thorns, which she was holding in her other hand.

"At the same time, the Child said: 'Have compassion on the Heart of your Most Holy Mother, covered with thorns, with which ungrateful men pierce it at every moment and there is none to make an act of reparation to remove them.'

"Then the Most Holy Virgin said: 'Look, my daughter, at my Heart, surrounded with thorns with which ungrateful men pierce me at every moment by their blasphemies and ingratitude. You at least try to console me and announce in my name that I promise to assist, at the moment of death, with all the graces necessary for salvation, all those who:

(1) on the first Saturday of five consecutive months,

(2) shall confess,

(3) receive Holy Communion,

(4) recite five decades of the Rosary and

(5) keep me company for fifteen minutes while meditating on the fifteen mysteries of the Rosary,

(6) with the intention of making reparation to me.'"

II. WHY FIVE FIRST SATURDAYS?

Our Lord Himself gave the answer to Sister Lucia:

"My daughter, the reason is simple. There are five types of offences and blasphemies committed against the Immaculate Heart of Mary:

1–Blasphemies against the Immaculate Conception;

2–Blasphemies against Her Virginity;

3–Blasphemies against Her Divine Maternity, in refusing at the same time to recognize her as the Mother of men;

4–The blasphemies of those who publicly seek to sow in the hearts of children, indifference or scorn or even hatred of this Immaculate Mother;

5–The offenses of those who outrage Her directly in Her holy images. Here, my daughter, is the reason why the Immaculate Heart of Mary inspired Me to ask for this little act of reparation. (May 29, 1930)

(2) THE CONFESSION

Sister Lucia asked Our Blessed Lord: "My Jesus! Many souls find it difficult to confess on Saturday. Will Thou allow a confession within eight days to be valid? He replied: "Yes. It can even be made later on, provided that the souls are in the state of grace when they receive Me on the First Saturday and that they had the intention of making reparation to the Sacred Heart of Mary."

Lucia then asked, "My Jesus! And those who forget to form this intention?"

"They can form it at the next confession, taking advantage of their first opportunity to go to confession." (February 15, 1927)

In brief, therefore (a) the Confession should be made as close as possible to the First Saturday; (b) we must be sorry for our sins, not only because we have offended God but also with the intention of making reparation to the Sacred Heart of Mary.

(3) THE HOLY COMMUNION

Father Goncalves, Lucia's confessor, asked her in a letter of May 29, 1930 if one cannot fulfil all the conditions on a Saturday, can it be done on Sunday? People in the country, for example, will not be able very often because they live quite far away. Our Lord gave the answer to Sister Lucia during the night of May 29–30:

"The practice of this devotion will be equally acceptable on the Sunday following the First Saturday when My priests, for a just cause, allow it to souls." Let us note that it is to His priests, and not to the individual conscience, that Jesus gives the responsibility of granting this additional concession.

(4) THE ROSARY

Since it is a question of repairing for offences committed against the Immaculate Heart of Mary, what other vocal prayer could be more pleasing to her than that which she requested the people to recite every day?

(5) THE 15 MINUTE MEDITATION

This is in **addition** to the recitation of the Rosary. It requires, in Lucia's own words, to keep Our Lady company for fifteen minutes while meditating on the mysteries of the Rosary. It is not required to meditate on all fifteen mysteries. To meditate on one or two is sufficient.

(6) THE INTENTION OF MAKING REPARATION

"You, at least, try to console me." Without this general intention, without this will of love which desires to make reparation to Our Lady, to console her, all these external practices are worth nothing for the Promise. This is clear.

III. THE PROMISES ATTACHED TO THIS DEVOTION
(I) THE SALVATION OF OUR OWN SOUL

"To all those who, on the First Saturday of five consecutive months...fulfil all the conditions requested, I promise to assist them at the hour of death with all the graces necessary for the salvation of their soul." This little devotion practiced with a good heart, is then enough to procure infallibly for us...*ex opere operato,* so to speak–as with the sacraments–the grace of final perseverance, of eternal salvation! And this promise is without any exclusion, limitation, restriction. "To all those... I promise" Heaven for eternity for five Holy Communions!

(2) THE SALVATION OF SINNERS

"So numerous are the souls which the justice of God condemns for sins committed against me that I come to ask for reparation. Sacrifice yourself for this intention and pray." (Our Lady to Sister Lucia at Tuy, June 13, 1929)
"In consideration of this little devotion, They (Jesus and Mary) wish to give the grace of pardon to souls who have had the misfortune of offending the Immaculate Heart of Mary," wrote Sister Lucia in a letter of May, 1930.

(3) PEACE IN THE WORLD

"Whether the world has war or peace depends on the practice of this devotion, along with the consecration of Russia to the Immaculate Heart of Mary. This is why I desire its propagation so ardently, especially because this is also the will of our dear Mother in Heaven." (Sister Lucia, March 19,1939.)
    (Source: Frere Michel de la Sainte Trinite, *The Whole Truth about Fatima: The Secret and the Church,* Vol. II, pp. 245-277.)

~Fatima Prayers~

I. PRAYERS TAUGHT BY ST. MICHAEL

Prayer of Adoration
"My God, I believe, I adore, I trust, and I love Thee. I beg pardon for those who do not believe, do not adore, do not trust, and do not love Thee."

Prayer to the Holy Trinity in Reparation and for the Conversion of Sinners
"O Most Holy Trinity, Father, Son and Holy Spirit, I adore Thee profoundly, and I offer Thee the most precious Body, Blood, Soul and Divinity of Jesus Christ, present in all the tabernacles of the world, in reparation for the outrages, sacrileges and indifference by which He Himself is offended. And through the infinite merits of His most Sacred Heart, and the Immaculate Heart of Mary, I beg of Thee the conversion of all poor sinners."

Prayer to the Most Blessed Sacrament
"O most Holy Trinity, I adore Thee! My God, my God, I love Thee in the Most Blessed Sacrament."

II. PRAYERS TAUGHT BY THE VIRGIN MARY

Rosary Decade Prayer
"O my Jesus, forgive us our sins, save us from the fires of hell. Lead all souls to Heaven, especially those with the greatest need of Thy Mercy."

Fatima Sacrifice Prayer
"O my Jesus, it is for love of Thee, for the conversion of sinners, and in reparation for the sins committed against the Immaculate Heart of Mary."

III. FATIMA MORNING OFFERING
COMPOSED BY SR. LUCIA, SERVANT OF GOD

"O my God, in union with the Immaculate Heart of Mary (here kiss the Brown Scapular), I offer Thee the Most Precious Body, Blood, Soul and Divinity of Our Lord, Jesus Christ, joining with it my every thought, word and action of this day.

O my Jesus, I desire today to gain every indulgence and merit I can, and I offer them, together with myself, to Mary Immaculate, that she may best apply them to the interests of Thy Most Sacred Heart. Precious Blood of Jesus, save us! Immaculate Heart of Mary, pray for us! Most Sacred Heart of Jesus, have mercy on us. Amen."

~The Little Crown of Twelve Stars~

I. CROWN OF EXCELLENCE
(To honor the Divine Maternity of the Blessed Virgin, her ineffable Virginity, her purity without stain and her innumerable virtues.)

1.) *Our Father, Hail Mary.*
  Blessed art thou, O Virgin Mary, who didst bear the Lord, the Creator of the world; thou didst give birth to Him Who made thee, and remainest a Virgin forever.
  Rejoice, O Virgin Mary; Rejoice a thousand times!

2.) *Hail Mary.*
  O holy and immaculate Virgin, I know not with what praise to extol thee, since thou didst bear in thy womb the very One Whom the Heavens cannot contain.
  Rejoice, O Virgin Mary; Rejoice a thousand times!

3.) *Hail Mary.*
  Thou are all fair, O Virgin Mary, and there is no stain in thee.
  Rejoice, O Virgin Mary; Rejoice a thousand times!

4.) *Hail Mary.*
Thy virtues, O Virgin, surpass the stars in number.
  Rejoice, O Virgin Mary; Rejoice a thousand times!
  Glory be to the Father, etc.

II. CROWN OF POWER
(To honor the royalty of the Blessed Virgin, her magnificence, her universal mediation and the strength of her rule.)

5.) *Our Father, Hail Mary.*
  Glory be to thee, O Empress of the world! Bring us with thee to the joys of Heaven.
  Rejoice, O Virgin Mary; Rejoice a thousand times!

6.) *Hail Mary.*
Glory be to thee, O treasure house of the Lord's graces! Grant us a share in thy riches.
Rejoice, O Virgin Mary; Rejoice a thousand times!

7.) *Hail Mary.*
Glory be to thee, O Mediatrix between God and man! Through thee may the Almighty be favorable to us.
  Rejoice, O Virgin Mary; Rejoice a thousand times!

8.) *Hail Mary.*
  Glory be to thee who destroyest heresies and crushest demons! Be thou our loving guide.
  Rejoice, O Virgin Mary; Rejoice a thousand times!
  Glory be to the Father, etc.

III. CROWN OF GOODNESS

(To honor the mercy of the Blessed Virgin toward sinners, the poor, the just and the dying.)

9.) *Our Father, Hail Mary.*

Glory be to thee, O refuge of sinners! Intercede for us with God.
Rejoice, O Virgin Mary; Rejoice a thousand times!

10.) *Hail Mary.*

Glory be to thee, O Mother of orphans! Render the Almighty favorable to us.
Rejoice, O Virgin Mary; Rejoice a thousand times!

11.) *Hail Mary.*

Glory be to thee, O joy of the just! Lead us with thee to the joys of Heaven.
Rejoice, O Virgin Mary; Rejoice a thousand times!

12.) *Hail Mary.*

Glory be to thee who are ever ready to assist us in life and death! Lead us with thee to the kingdom of Heaven!
Rejoice, O Virgin Mary; Rejoice a thousand times!
Glory be to the Father, etc.

Let Us Pray:

-Hail, Mary, Daughter of God the Father;
-Hail, Mary, Mother of God the Son;
-Hail, Mary, Spouse of the Holy Ghost;
-Hail, Mary, Temple of the most Holy Trinity;
-Hail, Mary, my Mistress, my treasure, my joy, Queen of my heart; my Mother, my life, my sweetness, my dearest hope—yea, my heart and my soul!

I am all thine and all that I have is thine, O Virgin blessed above all things! Let thy soul be in me to magnify the Lord; let thy spirit be in me to rejoice in God.
Set thyself, O faithful Virgin, as a seal upon my heart, that in thee and through thee I may be found faithful to God.

Receive me, O gracious Virgin, among those whom thou lovest and teachest, whom thou leadest, nourishest and protectest as thy children.

Grant that for love of thee, I may despise all earthly consolations and ever cling to those of Heaven until, through the Holy Ghost, thy faithful Spouse, and through thee, His faithful spouse, Jesus Christ thy Son be formed in me for the glory of the Father.
Amen.

~The 15 Rosary Promises~
(Given by Our Lady to Blessed Alan de la Roche)

1. Whoever shall faithfully serve me by the recitation of the Rosary shall receive signal graces.

2. I promise my special protection and the greatest graces to all who shall recite the Rosary.

3. The Rosary shall be a powerful armor against hell. It will destroy vice, decrease sin, and defeat heresies.

4. It will cause virtue and good works to flourish; it will obtain for souls the abundant mercy of God; it will withdraw the hearts of men from the love of the world and its vanities, and it will lift them to the desire of eternal things. Oh, that souls would sanctify themselves by this means!

5. The soul which recommends itself to me by the recitation of the Rosary shall not perish.

6. Whoever shall recite the Rosary devoutly, applying himself to the consideration of its sacred mysteries, shall never be conquered by misfortune. God will not chastise Him in His justice; he shall not perish by an unprovided death; if he be just, he shall remain in the grace of God and become worthy of eternal life.

7. Whoever shall have a true devotion for the Rosary shall not die without the Sacraments of the Church.

8. Those who are faithful in reciting the Rosary shall have during their life and at their death the light of God and the plenitude of His graces; at the moment of death, they shall participate in the merits of the saints in Paradise.

9. I shall deliver from Purgatory those who have been devoted to the Rosary.

10. The faithful children of the Rosary shall merit a high degree of glory in Heaven.

11. You shall obtain all you ask of me by the recitation of the Rosary.

12. All those who propagate the Holy Rosary shall be aided by me in their necessities.

13. I have obtained from my Divine Son that all the advocates of the Rosary shall have for intercessors the entire celestial court during their life and at the hour of death.

14. All we who recite the Rosary are my sons, and brothers of my only Son, Jesus Christ.

15. Devotion to my Rosary is a great sign of predestination.

~The Rosary of St. Louis de Montfort~

I unite with all the saints in Heaven, with all the just on earth, and with all the faithful here present. I unite with Thee, O my Jesus, in order to praise worthily Thy holy Mother and to praise Thee in her and through her. I renounce all the distractions I may have during this Rosary, which I wish to say with modesty, attention, and devotion, just as if it were to be the last of my life.

We offer Thee, O most Holy Trinity, this *Creed* in honor of all the mysteries of our Faith; this *Our Father* and these three *Hail Mary's* in honor of the unity of Thy Essence and the Trinity of Thy Persons. We ask of Thee a lively faith, a firm hope, and an ardent charity. Amen.

Apostle's Creed, Our Father, 3 Hail Mary's, Glory Be.

~THE FIVE JOYFUL MYSTERIES~

First Joyful Mystery: *The Annunciation*

We offer Thee, O Lord Jesus, this decade in honor of Thy Incarnation in Mary's womb, and we ask of Thee, through this Mystery and through her intercession, a profound humility. Amen.

One *Our Father,* 10 *Hail Mary's,* one *Glory Be.* At the end of the *Glory Be,* pray the "Fatima Decade prayer, as requested by Our Lady of the Rosary at Fatima:

O my Jesus, forgive us our sins. Save us from the fires of hell. Lead all souls to Heaven, especially those with the greatest need of Thy mercy.

Conclude the mystery: **May the grace of the Mystery of the Annunciation come down into our souls. Amen.**

Second Joyful Mystery: *The Visitation of the Virgin*

We offer Thee, O Lord Jesus, this decade in honor of the Visitation of Thy holy Mother to her cousin St. Elizabeth and the sanctification of St. John the Baptist in the womb, and we ask of Thee, through this Mystery and through the intercession of Thy holy Mother, charity toward our neighbor. Amen.

One *Our Father*, 10 *Hail Mary's*, one *Glory Be*, and *O my Jesus*.

Conclude the mystery: **May the grace of the Mystery of the Visitation come down into our souls. Amen.**

Third Joyful Mystery: *The Nativity of Our Lord*

We offer Thee, O Lord Jesus, this decade in honor of Thy Nativity in the stable of Bethlehem, and we ask of Thee, through this Mystery and through the intercession of Thy holy Mother, detachment from the things of the world, contempt of riches, and love of holy poverty. Amen.

One *Our Father*, 10 *Hail Mary's*, one *Glory Be*, and *O my Jesus*.

Conclude the mystery: **May the grace of the Mystery of the Nativity come down into our souls. Amen.**

Fourth Joyful Mystery: *The Presentation in the Temple*

We offer Thee, O Lord Jesus, this decade in honor of Thy Presentation in the Temple and the Purification of Mary, and we ask of Thee, through this Mystery and through the intercession of Thy holy Mother, purity of body and soul. Amen.

One *Our Father*, 10 *Hail Mary's*, one *Glory Be*, and *O my Jesus*.

Conclude the mystery: **May the grace of the Mystery of the Presentation in the Temple come down into our souls. Amen.**

Fifth Joyful Mystery: *The Finding of the Christ Child in the Temple*

We offer Thee, O Lord Jesus, this decade in honor of Mary's finding Thee in the Temple, and we ask of Thee, through this Mystery and through her intercession, the gift of true wisdom. Amen.

One *Our Father*, 10 *Hail Mary's*, one *Glory Be*, and *O my Jesus*.

Conclude the mystery: **May the grace of the Finding of Our Lord in the Temple come down into our souls. Amen.**

~THE FIVE SORROWFUL MYSTERIES~

First Sorrowful Mystery: *The Agony in the Garden*

We offer Thee, O Lord Jesus, this decade in honor of Thy Agony in the Garden of Olives, and we ask of Thee, through this Mystery and through the intercession of Thy holy Mother, contrition for our sins. Amen.

One *Our Father*, 10 *Hail Mary's*, one *Glory Be*, and *O my Jesus*.

Conclude the mystery: **May the grace of the Mystery of the Agony in the Garden come down into our souls. Amen.**

Second Sorrowful Mystery: *The Scourging at the Pillar*

We offer Thee, O Lord Jesus, this decade in honor of Thy bloody Scourging, and we ask of Thee, through this Mystery and through the intercession of Thy Holy Mother, the grace of mortifying our senses. Amen.

One *Our Father*, 10 *Hail Mary's*, one *Glory Be*, and *O my Jesus*.

Conclude the mystery: **May the grace of the Mystery of the Scourging come down into our souls. Amen.**

Third Sorrowful Mystery: *The Crowning of Thorns*

We offer Thee, O Lord Jesus, this decade in honor of Thy being crowned with thorns, and we ask of Thee, through this Mystery and through the intercession of Thy holy Mother, contempt of the world. Amen.

One *Our Father*, 10 *Hail Mary's*, one *Glory Be*, and *O my Jesus*.

Conclude the mystery: **May the grace of the Mystery of the Crowning with Thorns come down into our souls. Amen.**

Fourth Sorrowful Mystery: *The Carrying of the Cross*
We offer Thee, O Lord Jesus, this decade in honor of Thy carrying of the Cross, and we ask of Thee, through this Mystery and through the intercession of Thy holy Mother, patience in bearing our crosses. Amen.
One *Our Father*, 10 *Hail Mary's*, one *Glory Be*, and *O my Jesus*.
Conclude the mystery: **May the grace of the Mystery of the Carrying of the Cross come down into our souls. Amen.**

Fifth Sorrowful Mystery: *The Crucifixion of Our Lord*
We offer Thee, O Lord Jesus, this decade in honor of Thy Crucifixion and ignominious death on Calvary, and we ask of Thee, through this Mystery and through the intercession of Thy holy Mother, the conversion of sinners, the perseverance of the just, and the relief of the souls in Purgatory. Amen.
One *Our Father*, 10 *Hail Mary's*, one *Glory Be*, and *O my Jesus*.
Conclude the mystery: **May the grace of the Mystery of the Crucifixion come down into our souls. Amen.**

~THE FIVE GLORIOUS MYSTERIES~

First Glorious Mystery: *The Resurrection of Our Lord*
We offer thee, O Lord Jesus, this decade in honor of Thy glorious Resurrection, and we ask of Thee, through this Mystery and through the intercession of Thy holy Mother, love of God and fervor in Thy service. Amen.
One *Our Father*, 10 *Hail Mary's*, one *Glory Be*, and *O my Jesus*.
Conclude the mystery: **May the grace of the Resurrection come down into our souls. Amen.**

Second Glorious Mystery: *The Ascension of Our Lord into Heaven*
We offer Thee, O Lord Jesus, this decade in honor of Thy triumphant Ascension, and we ask of Thee, through this Mystery and through the intercession of Thy holy Mother, an ardent desire for Heaven, our true home. Amen.
One *Our Father*, 10 *Hail Mary's*, one *Glory Be*, and *O my Jesus*.
Conclude the mystery: **May the grace of the Resurrection come down into our souls. Amen.**

Third Glorious Mystery: *The Descent of the Holy Ghost on*
Mary and the Apostles
We offer Thee, O Lord Jesus, this decade in honor of the Mystery of Pentecost, and we ask of Thee, through this Mystery and through the intercession of Thy holy Mother, the coming of the Holy Ghost into our souls. Amen.
One *Our Father*, 10 *Hail Mary's*, one *Glory Be*, and *O my Jesus*.
Conclude the mystery: **May the grace of the mystery of Pentecost come down into our souls. Amen.**

Fourth Glorious Mystery: *The Assumption of the Virgin Mary*

We offer Thee, O Lord Jesus, this decade in honor of the resurrection and triumphant Assumption of Thy Holy Mother into Heaven, and we ask of Thee, through this Mystery and through her intercession, a tender devotion for so good a Mother. Amen.

One *Our Father*, 10 *Hail Mary's*, one *Glory Be*, and *O my Jesus*.

Conclude the mystery: **May the grace of the mystery of the Assumption come down into our souls. Amen.**

Fifth Glorious Mystery:
The Coronation of the Blessed Virgin

We offer Thee, O Lord Jesus, this decade in honor of the Coronation of Thy Holy Mother, and we ask of Thee, through this Mystery and through her intercession, perseverance in grace and a crown of glory thereafter. Amen.

One *Our Father*, 10 *Hail Mary's*, one *Glory Be*, and *O my Jesus*.

Conclude the mystery: **May the grace of the mystery of the Coronation of the Blessed Virgin come down into our souls. Amen.**

Concluding Prayer

Hail Mary, beloved Daughter of the Eternal Father, admirable Mother of the Son, faithful Spouse of the Holy Ghost, august Temple of the Most Holy Trinity! Hail, Sovereign Princess, to whom all owe subjection in Heaven and on earth! Hail, sure Refuge of Sinners, Our Lady of Mercy, who hast never refused any request. All sinful though I am, I cast myself at thy feet and beseech thee to obtain from Jesus, thy beloved Son, contrition and pardon for all my sins, as well as the gift of divine wisdom. I consecrate myself entirely to thee with all that I have. I choose thee today for my Mother and Mistress. Treat me, then, as the least of thy children and the most obedient of thy servants.

Listen, my princess, listen to the sighs of a heart that desires to love and serve thee faithfully. Let is never be said that of all who have had recourse to thee, I was the first to be abandoned. O my hope, O my life, O my faithful and Immaculate Virgin Mary, defend me, nourish me, hear me, teach me, and save me. Amen.

~The Rosary Mysteries for Beginners~

A Rosary is one-third of Our Lady's Psalter. The **Psalter** is comprised of all 15 "decades" (meaning ten *Hail Mary's*, which are preceded by an *Our Father* and followed by the *Gloria*, otherwise known as the *Glory Be*) while meditating on the Joyful, Sorrowful, and Glorious Mysteries in succession. A **Rosary**, however, includes only **one set of Mysteries** while praying five decades.

Traditionally, each day of the week is set apart for a particular Rosary Mystery, as follows:

THE JOYFUL MYSTERIES (Monday and Thursday)

1–**The Annunciation of Gabriel to the Virgin Mary**
2–**The Visitation of Mary to Elizabeth**
3–**The Nativity of Our Lord**
4–**The Presentation of the Infant Jesus**
5–**The Finding of the Child Jesus**

THE SORROWFUL MYSTERIES (Tuesday and Friday; also on all Sundays of Advent and Lent)

1–**Agony of Jesus in the Garden**
2–**Jesus is Scourged at the Pillar**
3–**Jesus is Crowned with Thorns**
4–**Jesus Carries His Cross**
5–**The Crucifixion of Jesus**

THE GLORIOUS MYSTERIES (Wednesday and Saturday; also on all Sundays after Easter, inclusive–but not on Sundays during Advent and Lent because they are penitential seasons of the Church)

1–**The Resurrection of Jesus**
2–**The Ascension of Jesus**
3–**The Descent of the Holy Ghost**
4–**The Assumption of the Virgin**
5–**The Coronation of Mary**

~The Rosary for Beginners~

1. While holding the Crucifix, make the Sign of the Cross and pray:
In the name of the Father, and of the Son, and of the Holy Spirit. Amen.

2. While still holding the Crucifix, next pray the **Apostles Creed:**
I believe in God, the Father Almighty, Creator of heaven and earth; and in Jesus Christ, His only Son, Our Lord; Who was conceived by the Holy Spirit, born of the Virgin Mary, suffered under Pontius Pilate, was crucified, died, and was buried. He descended into hell; the third day He arose again from the dead. He ascended into heaven, and sits at the right hand of God, the Father Almighty; from thence He shall come to judge the living and the dead. I believe in the Holy Spirit, the Holy Catholic Church, the communion of Saints, the forgiveness of sins, the resurrection of the body and life everlasting. Amen.

3. Pray the **Our Father** on the first large bead.
Our Father, who art in heaven, hallowed by Thy name. Thy kingdom come, Thy will be done on earth as it is in heaven. Give us this day our daily bread, and forgive us our trespasses as we forgive those who trespass against us, and lead us not into temptation, but deliver us from evil. Amen.

4. Pray the **Hail Mary** on each of the next three beads, asking for an increase in the virtues of faith, hope and charity.
Hail Mary, full of grace, the Lord is with thee; blessed art thou among women, and blessed is the fruit of thy womb, Jesus. Holy Mary, Mother of God, pray for us sinners, now and at the hour of our death. Amen.

5. Pray the **Gloria** (the Glory Be) on the large, middle bead between each 10 beads.
Glory be to the Father, and to the Son, and to the Holy Spirit. As it was in the beginning, is now, and ever shall be, world without end. Amen.

6. Announce the first **Rosary Mystery** and pray the **Our Father** on the same middle bead.

7. On each of the ten following small beads (also referred to as a decade) recite a **Hail Mary** while reflecting on the mystery.

8. On the next large bead between the decades pray the **Gloria:**
Glory be to the Father, and to the Son, and to the Holy Ghost. As it was in the beginning, is now and ever shall be, world without end. Amen.

9. At the end of each mystery, pray the **Fatima Prayer** requested by the Virgin of Fatima.

O my Jesus, forgive us our sins, save us from the fires of hell. Lead all souls to Heaven, especially those with the greatest need of Thy mercy.

10. Repeat all the steps above for each mystery.

11. When the fifth mystery is completed, again pray the Fatima **Prayer** and the **Gloria**. The Rosary is then customarily concluded with the **Hail, Holy Queen**, followed by the prayer to God and then three prayers for the intentions of the Holy Father. This last part is just as important, since the prayers for the Pope complete the requirements to gain a **plenary indulgence**. Customarily, the three prayers are one *Our Father*, one *Hail Mary*, and one *Gloria*, as follows in Step 12.

12. HAIL, HOLY QUEEN

Hail, holy Queen, mother of mercy, our life, our sweetness and our hope. To thee do we cry, poor banished children of Eve. To thee do we send up our sighs, mourning and weeping in this valley of tears. Turn then, most gracious Advocate, thine eyes of mercy towards us, and after this our exile, show unto us the blessed fruit of thy womb, Jesus.

O clement, o loving, o sweet Virgin Mary!

Pray for us, o holy Mother of God, that we may be made worthy of the promises of Christ.

O God, whose only begotten Son, by His life, death, and Resurrection, has purchased for us the rewards of eternal life, grant we beseech Thee that by meditating upon these mysteries of the Most Holy Rosary of the Blessed Virgin Mary, we may imitate what they contain, and obtain what they promise. Through the same Christ, Our Lord. Amen.

Then make the following request: **"For the intentions of the Holy Father and to ask for the plenary indulgence"** (acquired when praying a Rosary with the family, in a church group, etc., each person who prays the Rosary may also offer the plenary indulgence to the Poor Souls in Purgatory). If praying privately, this sentence can still be said aloud. What is necessary is that the three following prayers should be offered with the explicit purpose of praying for the current Pope's intentions (that is to say, to offer prayers so that he may fulfill the duties of the papal office in accordance with God's most holy Will):

Conclude with one *Our Father*, one *Hail Mary*, one *Gloria*.

About the Author

Marianna Bartold is the author of *Guadalupe: Secrets of the Image* and *Fatima: The Signs and Secrets*. Her other works include the Keeping It Catholic *Home Education Guide* books (Volumes I and II), *The Age of Mary Catholic Study Guides,* and other titles. Mrs. Bartold served as the original homeschool editor of *Sursum Corda* (now included in *Latin Mass* Magazine) and she was the founding publisher of *The Catholic Family's Magnificat! Magazine*.

A Catholic wife and homeschooling mother, Mrs. Bartold is also a speaker and occasionally contributes to various journals. For five years, her column "Secrets of the Catholic City" was published in *Catholic Family News*. An online moderator for various Catholic discussion groups, including many on Facebook, currently Mrs. Bartold is working on several writing and publishing projects.

Made in the USA
Middletown, DE
15 March 2021